European Studies in English Literature

The fall of women in early English narrative verse

The image of the 'fallen woman' was a common one in Elizabethan literature. This study deals with an unconventional aspect of the image, the genre of 'Complaint' in which writers enabled women to put their own case, bewailing their fate, evoking pity, and stressing private rather than public virtues. The book centres on a group of Elizabethan poems in which women such as Fair Rosamund and Jane Shore, the concubines of Henry II and Edward IV, lament their unfortunate lives. It also deals with a range of other works, tracing the Complaint from classical models such as Ovid's *Heroical epistles* to Chaucer's *Legend of good women* and Shakespeare's *Lucrece*. Dr Schmitz shows that the mode is not confined to historical tales, nor to the medieval or early modern periods. In Elizabethan times it occurs in novellas and meditations and it can be seen as the inspiration for eighteenth-century Roxanas and the nineteenth-century Magdalen. The personal perspective which characterises the Complaint constitutes a basic narrative mode, the elegiac qualities of which are set against the heroism of the epic.

This important genre study will be of interest to scholars in the fields of medieval and Renaissance English literature, classical and medieval Latin literature, comparative literature, literary theory, and women's studies.
European Studies in English Literature

T0381605

European Studies in English Literature

SERIES EDITORS
Ulrich Broich, Professor of English, University of Munich
Herbert Grabes, Professor of English, University of Giessen
Dieter Mehl, Professor of English, University of Bonn

Roger Asselineau, Professor Emeritus of American Literature, University of
    Paris–Sorbonne
Paul-Gabriel Boucé, Professor of English, University of Sorbonne–Nouvelle
Robert Ellrodt, Professor of English, University of Sorbonne–Nouvelle
Sylvère Monod, Professor Emeritus of English, University of
    Sorbonne–Nouvelle

This series is devoted to publishing translations into English of the best works
written in European languages on English and American literature. These may
be first-rate books recently published in their original versions, or they may be
classic studies which have influenced the course of scholarship in their field
while never having been available in English before.

To begin with, the series has concentrated on works translated from the
German; but its range will expand to cover other languages.

TRANSLATIONS PUBLISHED
Walter Pater: The Aesthetic Moment by Wolfgang Iser
The Theory and Analysis of Drama by Manfred Pfister
*The Symbolist Tradition in English Literature: A Study of Pre-Raphaelitism and
    'fin de siècle'* by Lothar Hönnighausen
The Rise of the English Street Ballad 1550–1650 by Natascha Würzbach
Oscar Wilde: The Works of a Conformist Rebel by Norbert Kohl
The Fall of Women in Early English Narrative Verse by Götz Schmitz

TITLES UNDER CONTRACT FOR TRANSLATION
Studien zum komischen Epos by Ulrich Broich
Redeformen des englischen Mysterienspiels by Hans-Jürgen Diller
Die romantische Verserzählung in England by Hermann Fischer
*Studien zur Dramenform vor Shakespeare: Moralität, Interlude, romaneskes
    Drama* by Werner Habicht

Shakespeare et la Fête by François Laroque

The fall of women in early English narrative verse

Götz Schmitz

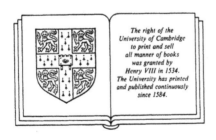

The right of the
University of Cambridge
to print and sell
all manner of books
was granted by
Henry VIII in 1534.
The University has printed
and published continuously
since 1584.

Cambridge University Press

Cambridge
New York   Port Chester   Melbourne   Sydney

CAMBRIDGE UNIVERSITY PRESS
Cambridge, New York, Melbourne, Madrid, Cape Town, Singapore,
São Paulo, Delhi, Dubai, Tokyo, Mexico City

Cambridge University Press
The Edinburgh Building, Cambridge CB2 8RU, UK

Published in the United States of America by Cambridge University Press, New York

www.cambridge.org
Information on this title: www.cambridge.org/9780521179270

Originally published as Die Frauenklage: Studien zur elegischen Verserziihlung
in der englischen Literatur des Spiitmittelalters und der Renaissance, by Giitz
Schmitz (Max Niemeyer Verlag, Tiibingen, 1984)

First paperback edition 2011

A catalogue record for this publication is available from the British Library

Library of Congress cataloguing in publication data
Schmitz, Götz, 1944-
[Frauenklage. English]
The fall of women in early English narrative verse I Götz
    Schmitz.
        p. cn. - (European studies in English literature)
Translation of: Die Frauenklage.
Includes bibliographical references.
ISBN o 521 30961 1
1. English poetry - Early modern, 1500-1700 - History and
criticism.   2. Women in literature.   3. English poetry - Classical
influences.   4. Elegiac poetry, English - History and criticism.
5. Complaint poetry, English - History and criticism.   6. Narrative
poetry - Middle English, 1100-1500 - History and criticism.
I. Title.   II. Series.
PR535.W58S3613   1990
821' .0309352042 - dc20   89 - 38033 CIP

Contents

Preface

The foundations for this study of poems on the fall of famous women were laid in the middle of the 1970s, when a scholarship from the Deutsche Forschungsgemeinschaft enabled me to spend several months reading in some of the major British libraries. In 1981 I submitted a German version of my work to the Philosophical Faculty of the University of Bonn under the title of 'Tragick plaints and passionate mischance' (the learned title referred to Samuel Daniel's poem on the fall of Fair Rosamond which was, and is, a cornerstone of the study). This 'Habilitationsschrift' was published in 1984 as *Die Frauenklage*; I have now translated and revised it for the European Studies in English Literature Series.

My study has two focal points, a minor one in the late Middle Ages, and a major one in the late Elizabethan Age. It concentrates on such poems as Chaucer's *Legend of good women* and Shakespeare's *Lucrece* – poems which treat fallen women as martyrs and as heroines. The status of these women was, at least by poetic standards, doubtful. Even Shakespeare's Lucrece is, at best, a passive heroine, and some of Chaucer's martyrs are dubious by any standards. To take them seriously as poetic subjects, Chaucer, Shakespeare and their contemporaries had to generate new strategies because the graver genres were traditionally reserved for more active or less doubtful heroines, and mainly for heroes, anyway.

What attracts me most to these poems is the tension between subject matter and poetic form. It is, in a word, the question of decorum – not, I should like to add, the 'woman question'. The *querelle des femmes* was, of course, discussed in satirical and didactic literature of the periods covered in my study, most sympathetically by Christine de Pisan in the late Middle Ages, for instance, and by Thomas Bentley under Elizabeth; the problem of decorum, however, is raised mainly in poems placed between the epic and the tragic genres. My approach, then, is primarily poetological, not sociological. Though women's studies had hardly reached Germany, or a certain small town in Germany, I was aware of the links between genre and gender when I entered on my study, and I still think there are good methodological reasons for keeping them apart while discussing poetry of a less topical nature.

My starting point was a group of Elizabethan poems in which unfortunate women such as Rosamond Clifford and Jane Shore, the popular concubines of Henry II and Edward IV, complain about their unfortunate lives. These poems are usually related to the collection of Complaints on the fall of famous men known as *A mirror for magistrates*, or to its predecessor, John Lydgate's *Fall of princes*. Indeed, the women's Complaints share certain features with their masculine counterparts: the matter is taken from legend or history and delivered in person in seven-line stanzas; in spirit, however, there are considerable differences. The women's concern is with private, rather than public issues; they look into their own mirrors, the men hold them up to their peers, the princes.

To find analogues and origins for the attitude behind these women's Complaints, I looked for possible models and found them in medieval and classical literature, and in Chaucer's *Legend of good women* and Ovid's *Heroides* in particular. The very titles of these models suggested a further extension of my study – systematical, this time, rather than chronological: at first sight, neither Chaucer's nor Ovid's love-lorn ladies have much claim to sanctity or heroism. It takes some wrenching of the evidence to turn Cleopatra into a martyr, or Phaedra into a heroine.

This seems to be mainly a question of perspectives. A heroine such as Dido can be allowed to present herself as a victim, as in Ovid's *Heroides*, from a domestic point of view, or she can be presented as a fury, as in Virgil's *Aeneid*, from an Olympian point of view; 'hic amor, haec patria' is what it looks like to Aeneas. It is more than a matter of perspective, then; I came to distinguish between two basic modes of presenting the life of a heroine in narrative poetry which I called, borrowing terms from the Latinist Richard Heinze, the elegiac and the epic mode.

Besides presenting a survey of the Elizabethan genre of women's Complaints, my study has two more aims: one is to trace this genre to its roots in medieval and classical literature, the other to establish the elegiac as a basic mode of narration, not only of Elizabethan, but of all times. The number of novels written in this mode in recent years might serve to support this last aim; but I will not extend my survey into our second Elizabethan age.

I gladly seize the opportunity to acknowledge once more my debts to all those who helped me to complete the German version of this study: in particular the librarians and staff of the British Library, London, and the Bodleian Library, Oxford, but also of the John Rylands Library, Manchester, the National Library of Scotland, Edinburgh, the libraries of Eton and of Stonyhurst College, and of the Humberside County Council in Beverley, the University Library, Bonn, and the English Departments in Münster and in Bonn; the Deutsche Forschungsgemeinschaft for their scholarship and their financial assistance in its first publication; the editors of *Anglia*, who accepted it for their 'Buchreihe', my colleagues in the English Department at Bonn University who read the typescript and gave valuable suggestions for its improvement, and above all my 'gentile maister', Arno Esch, for his encouragement and kindness.

For their help in the preparation of this revised translation I should like to give thanks to the publishers of the German version, Niemeyer, for consenting to an English edition so soon after its publication in German; to the Deutsche Forschungsgemeinschaft for a travel grant which helped me to visit the Folger Shakespeare and the Huntington Libraries; to the staff of these libraries for their friendliness; to the syndics of the Cambridge University Press and the editors of European Studies in English Literature, particularly Dieter Mehl, for including it in their series, to Klaus Bitterling of the Free University of Berlin for his review and his list of corrections; finally, to Guy Moore for touching up my English, and to Con Coroneos for bringing my typescript up to Cambridge standards.

Note on titles and quotations

Titles of early English books and poems are shortened and modernised throughout, with the time-honoured exception of Spenser's *Faerie queene*. Quotations from these early texts are given in their original spelling, except for such typographical features as black letter, ornamental initials, swash capitals and ligatures. Contractions and abbreviations such as the tittle for 'm' and 'n' and the ampersand are kept, while the superscript sign in 'per' and 'pro' has been extended. Thorn and yogh have been adjusted to modern usage; long 's' has generally been shortened, but not in 'ß'. The names of characters have been standardised, except where different spellings help to distinguish between different poems (as in the case of Chaucer's Criseyde, Henryson's Cresseid, and Shakespeare's Cressida).

1   Introduction

The sentimental tradition in English literature

In his essay on Thomas Heywood, T.S. Eliot placed Mrs Frankford, the heroine, or rather victim, of *A woman killed with kindness*, at the beginning of a sentimental tradition in English literature which he saw extended to the little Em'lys of nineteenth-century fiction and unnamed 'robuster heroines' of his own day. This has now become an international phenomenon: one might easily pick about a dozen Mrs Frankfords, with cruelty exchanged for kindness, from all kinds of literature of the past decade. To name but a few, there is Christa Wolf's complaint of ancient *Cassandra* (1983), Dan Jacobson's future scholar in search of *Her story* (1987), and several galleries of sentimental portraits including Christine Brückner's *Wenn du geredet hättest, Desdemona* (1983) and Françoise Xenakis' *Zut, on a encore oublié Madame Freud* (1985). Such galleries are very much a feature of medieval and Renaissance literature, and it is with these forerunners of what Eliot calls the sentimental tradition that this study is concerned.

For Eliot who, by the time he wrote the essay on Heywood (1931), had turned towards the classical, the royalist and the orthodox, this sentimental tradition lacks in dignity 'because it has no vital relation to morals at all' and therefore fails to be edifying. Moreover, Heywood's domestic tragedy falls short not only of the ethical but also of the tragic 'in [its] highest sense' because Heywood concentrates on the pathetic appeal of his heroine: 'he is eminent in the pathetic, rather than the tragic'. Eliot apparently uses the terms 'sentimental' and 'pathetic' in a derogatory sense.[1]

It is not my office to take issue with Eliot's ethics; nor am I primarily concerned with his poetics – though I will take up the question of the relations between the tragic and the pathetic in my last chapter. My chief aim is to trace the sentimental tradition back to some of its origins which, before the seventeenth century, lay in the field of narrative rather than

1

dramatic literature, and in particular in chorus-like commentaries chanted by women on events of a highly ethical and, at least for them, tragic nature. Their wailing is heard in the background of tragedies and epics recounting the destruction of Troy or the foundation of Rome; it replaces the supernatural music that, according to Eliot, should be heard from behind the wings of a tragedy in the highest sense. The origins of such unclassical poetry lie in classical times, well before the term 'sentimental' in any, and certainly in its modern sense, was heard of. I will therefore use the term 'elegiac' to describe the sort of poetry in which I think the so-called sentimental tradition is rooted. My chief example, a letter of complaint written by Dido to Aeneas, is taken from Ovid's *Heroides*, a collection of verse letters which slyly and pathetically challenges the high seriousness of Virgil's *Aeneid* and the various classicisms derived from it by poets from Dante to Eliot.

Elegiac poetry of this kind is based on an attitude rather than a specific form. It runs through different literary genres. In medieval England these include Old English elegies as well as Goliardic *planctus*. The elegiac tradition reaches a climax point in the works of Chaucer, and in particular 'the Seintes Legende of Cupide' as the Man of Law, himself a master of the elegiac mode of telling a story, calls the *Legend of good women* (he relates it to Ovid's *Heroides*, too; 'Man of Law's Tale', 54–5, 61). Chaucer's sense of tragedy as revealed in these legends and comparable stories from the *Canterbury tales*, has always been felt to be of a kind somewhat different from both classical and medieval models; in recent criticism it has been labelled 'pathedy', and its debt to the model of Ovid has been increasingly recognized – not only in the more obvious cases of the legendary tales, but also in his exercises in the grand style, even the epic *Troilus and Criseyde* which he studded with references to the *Heroides*.[2]

The tradition is continued by Chaucerians in the fifteenth century who often take their cue from the *Legend of good women* and place their works under its guidance. Seemingly disparate poems like the anonymous 'Letter of Dydo to Eneas', Robert Henryson's *Testament of Cresseid*, the anonymous 'Lamentation of Mary Magdalen' and Gilbert Banester's 'Legenda Sismond' are attached to the 'legende of martirs off Cupide', as Lydgate calls his master's work, by author, copyist or printer. The heroines of these works might serve as figureheads pointing in the different directions that the tradition takes in subsequent years. In the course of the sixteenth century the elegiac narrative grows into a distinct genre, the tragical Complaint. With the added influence of Senecan drama, native verse history, medieval meditations and Italian novelle the Complaint develops distinct historical, romantic, religious and novelistic branches. The genre has its heyday around the turn of the century with

poems such as Thomas Middleton's *Ghost of Lucrece* (1600), Samuel
Daniel's *Complaint of Rosamond* (1592), Gervase Markham's *Mary
Magdalen's lamentations* (1601) and Thomas Churchyard's *Dolorous
gentlewoman* (1593), to name but one flower from each of its branches.

This essentially elegiac tradition is under constant threat from the epic
against which Ovid had set it right from the start. There had been Eliot-
like calls for edification and the supernatural throughout the development, louder, in fact, in the Renaissance than in the Middle Ages, and
this led to a predominance of amazonian heroines in appropriately epic
guise in the earlier seventeenth century. The term 'heroine' was taken at
its root value and we find an increasing series of poems dealing with
women on a more or less heroic scale. This extends, again, to all of the
above-mentioned branches; examples would be David Murray's *Tragical
death of Sophonisba* (1611), Michael Drayton's *Miseries of queen Margarite* (1627), George Ballard's *History of Susanna* (1638) and Thomas
Cranley's *Amanda* (1635). This amazonian literature is perhaps 'robuster', but no less sentimental than the amorous kind it was meant to
check; it is rather more so in being 'ful of hy sentence' like the words of
Chaucer's philosophic Clerk, though not as 'short and quyk'.[3] If Ovid's
elegiac can be seen as an attack on the royal epic, the epyllion of the early
seventeenth century represents a counterattack on the elegiac queen: this
was part of a perennial game of literary chess. The next moves came by
the end of the century, with the She-tragedies of John Banks and Nicholas
Rowe versus heroic tragedy, and later on Richardson's grave novel in
letters versus epistolary romances modelled on the *Lettres portugaises*.

This study finds its focus in the tragical Complaints ascribed to famous
women which emerge in the second half of the sixteenth century. Their
standard form is derived from their masculine counterparts in the *Mirror
for magistrates*: a legendary figure, come back from the dead, recounts
her misfortunes in an extended monologue. Ovidian pathos is tempered
with Senecan gloom. With women as complainants, some of the restric-
tions of the *Mirror*-form, for example the passive situation, the narrow
perspective and the apologetic tone, are employed to more plausible
effects. Usually the women speaking in these Complaints present themselves as victims overruled by tyrannical circumstances. They nourish
what Howard Jacobson, with respect to Ovid's *Heroides*, has termed a
'reductionist tendency' to view the world from a more private angle than
is usually allowed heroic characters.[4] They often seem unable not only
to alter but also to analyse their situation and are reduced to emotional
responses. To the modern eye – not only T.S. Eliot's – a poetry which
accepts without question this severely limited point of view may look like
being 'interested not to analyse the ethics but to exploit the sentiment'[5],
but this would mean viewing the poems from the vantage point of a

higher morality, a vantage point, of course, which from an even more advanced position may look backward in its male orientation. Both these views are inadequate because they are unhistorical. The best of the Complaints question a higher morality of some kind, but this makes them neither feminist nor defeatist. It is true that usually the higher morality is that of male superiors, but there are exceptions, for example in Complaints by courtesans such as Rosamond Clifford, which are directed at a rival spouse. There is no reason why only women should feel victimised by the guardians of that morality – the exiled warrior of the Old English elegy may serve as an example to the contrary. The reductionist tendency of the Complaints need not be adopted by the critic.

My main concern in this study is with genre rather than gender. I would like to see the elegiac mode established side by side with the epic and the tragic, and I regard the women's Complaints which are at the centre of this study as prime expressions of a mode which is not constricted by genre or by gender: it can just as easily be presented in domestic dramas such as Heywood's *Woman killed with kindness* or in novels such as the ones I mentioned earlier on. What is essential is the shift in perspective that the handling of a story in the elegiac mode effects compared with traditionally higher genres such as tragedy and epic, and the emotive power this sets free. This power can have a considerable impact. On the crest of a wave of feminist literature we can see this more clearly than T.S. Eliot, who wrote in the wake of a similar wave which had helped to erode the Victorian ethic. What Eliot was reacting against was not, as we tend to assume, the rigidity but the softness of late Victorianism. The maudlin and the amazon characters of the Renaissance look even less robust, at least ethically, than the Little Em'lys of high Victorianism. Eliot's reaction was comparable to that of the Jacobeans in their quest for a new heroism. Like them Eliot was weary of the elegiac spirit, of 'love's soft lays and looser thoughts' which, according to Spenser, were the subject of poets like Samuel Daniel, the author of a *Complaint of Rosamond*. And naturally Eliot found it hard to appreciate the refreshing, if not shocking, effect an injection of this spirit can have on a less weary age.

Writers in the vanguard of an elegiac wave are in a completely different position. They react against a rigid orthodoxy, and theirs can be a dangerous task, as witness the fate of Ovid or Southwell, whose elegiac poetry threatened to undermine the Pax Augusta or the Elizabethan Settlement. The orthodox ethic of these periods was upheld in epic poetry by their respective colleagues Virgil and Spenser. In both the *Aeneid* and the *Faerie queene* emotions are ultimately controlled by reasons of state, and conflicts between public and private are to be decided in favour of the public, if needs be by fire and sword. Even pity is viewed with a jealous eye; the reader is to be kept in awe, the emotion appropriate to heroic poetry. Mercilla's treatment of Duessa is a case in point (*The faerie queene*, V, ix, 50). The overriding factor in the literary treatment of such cases is decorum, and the rules of decorum were kept more strictly in Renaissance than in ancient poetry. Only in times of political crises, when governments try to rule out certain attitudes, does a breach of literary decorum have political as well as poetical consequences, and this was, of course, much more pronounced in Augustan Rome than in Elizabethan England, where only limited areas were sensitive (recusancy and the question of succession are those relevant to this study). Otherwise, the spirit of an age (which can be domineering, too) informs its poets, particularly those of a less independent mind, to turn to poetical modes and forms appropriate to their needs. The elegiac is one of these modes, and the Complaint one of its forms.

There are many reasons why a considerable number of poets of the later sixteenth century chose to employ this mode and form. There is, probably, a connection with other signs of spiritual unrest and unorthodoxy emerging towards the end of the century. One reason, however, should be ruled out: the emergence of a poetry of pity should not be confused with a process of emancipation. It has become the custom with critics of a sociological bend to link the development of literary forms with the rise and fall of ranks or classes in a given society. This is a curious inversion of the rules of decorum which, in their most material form, demand that certain literary forms be used to deal with certain subjects: the epic with heroes and horses, for example, and the pastoral with shepherds and sheep. They do not say that heroes should produce epics and chant them only to their equals (nor do they suggest that real shepherds break into song as readily as they do in pastoral poetry). From the later Middle Ages, however, most of the genres considered 'new', and in particular those considered 'low' like the novella and the novel, have been associated with the ever-rising middle class. With respect to domestic tragedies like *A woman killed with kindness* this association has hardened into a habit. Something like this habit lurks behind T.S. Eliot's comment on the sympathy which Heywood extends to Mrs Frankford: 'it is only the kind of pity that the ordinary playgoer, of any time, can appreciate' (p. 181). The sentiment may have been prompted by the heroine's ordinary name; and since some of the heroines treated in this study carry similar names, there is the temptation to link their rise to eminence in Renaissance poetry with the prospering of trade in Elizabethan London. Figures like Mrs Shore and Mrs Frankford share, indeed, what one might call a domestic ethos (not a bourgeois background: Mrs Frankford is a gentlewoman by birth), but this ethos is not by any means restricted to the English or any other middle class. We shall find the same concern with private rather than public affairs in a palace of Carthage and in the Fleet in London. It is a matter of perspective rather than of provenance. When John Dryden in his adaptation of *Antony and Cleopatra* tries to soften the image of Cleopatra, he reduces Shakespeare's queen of infinite variety to 'A wife, a silly, harmless household dove' (*All for love*, IV, 92).

The opposition that was voiced in Elizabethan literature to the rise to prominence of lowly figures like Mrs Shore arose in part from a confusion of the erotic with the elegiac, or the epyllion with the Complaint, a confusion created by the fact that both these genres stem from Ovid: the erotic epyllion goes back to his *Metamorphoses*, the elegiac Complaint to his *Heroides*. There is a family likeness in that both treat mainly of love, but they do so in widely different ways: the epyllion usually presents a pair of lovers against a mythical background (the most outstanding examples are Shakespeare's *Venus and Adonis* (1593) and Marlowe's unfinished *Hero and Leander* (1598, entered 1593), whereas the Complaint is given to a single maiden or matron lost or left behind in the borderland between myth and history like George Whetstone's 'Piteous complaint of Medea' (in *The rock of regard*, 1576) or 'Helen's complaint' from Thomas Procter's *Triumph of truth* (1585). The epyllion appears easy-going compared with the more stately Complaint, even the sixain stanza it usually employs seems more light-footed than the rhyme royal of the Complaint which, according to George Puttenham's *Art of English poesy* (1589) is 'used by any rimer writing any thing of historical or graue poeme'.[6] The epyllion treats of love in a light-hearted, often frivolous vein; one of the partners is usually a goddess or a god, the female often takes the initiative, the myth is related by a conspiring, if not perspiring, narrator from a voyeuristic point of view. The love affair may prove futile, but it is never fatal in the direst sense; tragic endings are cushioned in a metamorphosis: there is supernatural music in the wings. Epyllia, as the term implies, are closely related to the epic where metamorphic marvels are accepted. If they seem to belittle the heroic ethos it is because they are epics on a much smaller scale and concentrate on that part of the Renaissance epic formula that was minimised in antiquity: they sing, to use Spenser's definition, of ladies rather than of knights and of loves (not always faithful) rather than fierce wars. There is an inherent tendency towards the parodic in the erotic epyllion which threatens the epic spirit in a less heroic, Alexandrian age.[7] The first fully-fledged Elizabethan epyllion of this kind, Thomas Lodge's *Scilla's metamorphosis* (1589), already exhibits this tendency.

Elizabethan epic poets tended to moralise their song, not only by praise and precept, as in the grand epic and romance like Spenser's *Faerie queene* or Sidney's *Arcadia*, but also by allegory and satire which were introduced into the epyllion to balance its bias towards frivolity. Chapman's efforts to idealise Marlowe's *Hero and Leander* are evidence of the former, as is Michael Drayton's *Endymion and Phoebe: Idea's Latmus* (1595); the latter is evidenced by John Weever's *Faunus and Melliflora: the origin of our English satires* (1600). William Keach devotes the second half of his study *Elizabethan erotic narratives* (Hassocks, 1977) to the affinity of 'The epyllion and late Elizabethan satire'.

In both allegory and satire the figures of myth are propped up by rigid ideological frameworks. In their Classical surroundings, mainly Ovid's *Metamorphoses*, they did not need this kind of support. There, such plant-like heroines as Daphne, Syrinx, Myrrha, are firmly rooted in their native, mythological soil. Historical figures lack such sustenance. It is harder to transform them into something either subhuman or superhuman. The tension between subject and form can be felt even if classical figures from the borderland between myth and history are treated in epic poetry. Ovid tries to incorporate Hecuba, the mobbled queen of Troy, in his *Metamorphoses*, but her transformation into a dog can hardly relieve the human impact of her story; Lucretia, who must have been a historical figure for Ovid, is treated in his *Fasti* – without a mythical transformation. Shakespeare, on the other hand, for whom Lucretia must have receded into pre-history, tried to introduce a mythological element, the *aition* about Lucretia's curdling blood, into his tragic epyllion, and again one feels the tension. At least, C.S. Lewis did; he found this myth 'repellent'[8].

There is, apparently, an essential difference between myth and history, and the literary genres conform to this difference. In the last resort, the epic is concerned with myth, and if it deals with historical material, an almost religious effort is necessary to lift this material onto a mythical level. Shakespeare may have had a mythic sense of English, or of Tudor, history (Spenser certainly did); with Roman history this does not work the way it does with Virgil (I am not sure about Ovid). Shakespeare's Lucrece is too much a sublunary creature for a *deus ex machina* or any other supernatural machinery to sort out her dilemma. For a patriotic historian like Livy this poses no problem: he substitutes Olympus with the Capitol, and in his republican view of history Lucretia achieves a kind of immortality by instigating the expulsion of the kings. With less patriotic writers like Ovid, a more private ethos becomes dominant, and Lucretia's stature becomes less secure, though she finds a niche in the legendary framework of the *Fasti*. In English Renaissance treatments of heroines from Roman history the public and the private point of view become dissociated. As in the field of the erotic epyllion with his *Venus and Adonis*, Shakespeare leads the way with his public-minded tragic epyllion *Lucrece*. This epyllion's tendency towards the epic shows itself not only in its etiological elements, but also in the religious (or pseudo-religious) language and imagery with which he supplies his 'earthly saint' and which C.S. Lewis wondered at: 'Even Christianity creeps in'.[9] The epic character of the poem becomes most evident in its finale; Lucrece commits the one heroic act traditionally open to a heroine: she commits suicide, and she does it in public.

The private point of view is chosen in Complaints, in the case of Lucretia by Thomas Middleton. His *Ghost of Lucrece* (1600) shows the *matrona virilis* in an almost deranged state of mind and looking downward into the hell she is sure to share with her ravisher for ever. She is denied all action, and she tries in vain to justify her fate. The need to 'justify their foul attaint', as it is phrased in Daniel's *Complaint of Rosamond*, is one of the chief aims of the historical heroines that appear in Complaints of the *Mirror for magistrates* type, and these heroines have more reason to feel condemned in the eyes of the public than Lucretia, for some of them are figures of doubtful repute like Fair Rosamond, the concubine of King Henry II. They can hardly claim to have given history a new direction, rather they have hindered its course; we usually find them stranded Ariadne-like on some island in its course, straining their eyes for a glimpse of their hero's sails. Complaints usually ring with an apologetic note, the speakers have to create their own legends in the face of an unheeding public.

It takes a certain amount of special pleading to set up a calendar with Cupid's saints like Rosamond and Mrs Shore. George Ferrers and William Baldwin must have known why they left Churchyard's Complaint of 'Shore's wife' (1563) out of the first edition of their *Mirror for magistrates* (1559), and Samuel Daniel makes his Rosamond voice a spite against their eventual success which thinly disguises similar doubts:

> Shores wife is grac'd, and passes for a Saint;
> Her Legend iustifies her foule attaint.
> > (*The complaint of Rosamond*, 25–6)[10]

Like Mrs Shore, she will have to base her claim to sanctity on other than patriotic virtues.

Definitions old and new

This short look at the various offspring of the Ovidian tradition should suffice to give a preliminary idea of the distinction between the Complaint and its closest relatives, the erotic or the heroic epyllion. Further distinctions will, I hope, become evident in the main chapters of this study, when the influences of neighbouring genres such as the heroical epistle, the death lament, *de casibus* tragedy, the saint's legend and the novella will be discussed in detail. Elizabethan and Jacobean authors appear to be rather cavalier about such distinctions. Even if an author couples an elegiac narrative with poems in the erotic vein, this serves to emphasise rather than obscure the differences. Samuel Daniel set a kind of fashion by publishing a Complaint with a sonnet sequence in his *Complaint of Rosamond with Delia* (1592), and he tried to link them by making Rosamond in her Complaint plead for compassion with the Delia of the sonnets. But the differences between the dainty Petrarchan and the dire Complaint traditions persist. Spenser had these differences in mind when he spoke of 'loues soft laies and looser thoughts' on the one hand, and 'Tragick plaints and passionate mischance' on the other in young Daniel's poetry.[11] The fashion set by Daniel was soon followed by Thomas Lodge in his *Phillis . . . with the tragical complaint of Elstred* (1593) and Richard Barnfield, who published a 'Legend of Cassandra' in his *Cynthia* (1595), and later on by Sir David Murray, who joined the *Tragical death of Sophonisba* with *Caelia: containing certain sonnets* (1611), though Murray's Sophonisba is modelled on Shakespeare's Lucrece, not on Daniel's Rosamond.

A similar difference is tacitly observed between poems on mythological or pseudo-mythological and on historical subjects – the difference which Shakespeare had stressed when, in the dedication of his *Venus and Adonis* to the Earl of Southampton, he promised to atone for this 'first heir of [his] invention', with 'some graver labour' which, of course, turned out to be *Lucrece*. These different veins were also worked by a number of followers, by Thomas Lodge again, who set the grave German princess Elstred side by side with Scilla, his lively Italian nymph (the only thing they have in common being their etiological relation to local waters), and by Patrick Hannay, who published a volume containing his operatic version of the Philomela-myth together with a long Complaint set in Vienna during the Turkish wars and threw in a couple of sonnets for good measure (*The nightingale. Sheretine and Mariana . . . songs and sonnets*, 1622). The older collectors seem to have appreciated the traditions in which these poems stood; with their younger followers, such appreciation seems to have diminished: in his edition of Hannay's poems George Saintsbury notices that *Sheretine and Mariana* is told throughout by the heroine and wonders about the 'peculiarity, unusual in a piece of such length, of being written in the first person'.[12] This would be peculiar, indeed, if the piece were, as Saintsbury supposes, an anticipation of the Caroline heroic poem; it is, however, a late example of the Elizabethan Complaint, modernised only to the extent that it takes up recent historical events. Not even the fact that its heroine Mariana is descended from a middle class background ('My parents had not base, nor noble blood/

But betwixt both in a mean order stood', 65–6) is indicative of 'the strange difficulty with which straightforward prose fiction got itself born' (presumably Saintsbury is thinking of the eighteenth-century novel), for most of the English heroines of Complaints come from a similar background.

The first person female narrator is in fact the specific difference that separates Complaints in the tradition of Churchyard and Daniel from their epyllic relatives. Otherwise, this tradition is hard to segregate. There is, to start with, no single English term for this tradition. The term I offered in the German version of this study, *Die Frauenklage*, is hard to translate; several terms used in unpublished American dissertations such as 'Female-Complaint' or 'feminine complaint' raise doubts as to their grammar or their subjects. Willard Farnham called the tragical Complaints in the wake of Churchyard's 'Shore's wife' 'feminine tragedies'.[13] Medieval and Renaissance authors most often use the term 'complaint' to designate poems in the *Mirror for magistrates* tradition, regardless of the gender of the complainant; besides, terms such as 'legend', 'lament', 'lamentation', 'elegy', 'history' and 'ballad' are employed. This is not surprising in the late Middle Ages when a poet such as Chaucer uses the term 'compleynte' for both the love-complaint of the Black Knight and Oenone's *Heroides*-style letter to Paris (*Book of the duchess*, 464; *Troilus and Criseyde*, I, 655). Nor is it later on when an admirer calls Gervase Markham's poem on the Magdalen a 'lamentation', an 'elegy' and a 'complaint' all in a single breath, and Markham himself adds the terms 'pensive passion' and 'lugubre carmen' to the list.[14] Even as learned and genre-conscious a writer as Michael Drayton, who tries to define not only the heroic quality of the letter-writing heroines in his *Heroical epistles* ('To the reader', 1598 edition, A2r–v), but also the relationship between historical legend and epic poetry (Dedication of the 1619 edition of his *Poems*), even he calls his *Matilda* (1594) a 'legend' in its title, a 'tragicall complaynt' in the first, and a 'tragicall historie' in the second edition (1596).

In spite of their rigorous divisions and sub-divisions, contemporary treatises on poetry and rhetoric use a terminology which is just as loose; it makes little sense to regularise them with the wisdom of hindsight. I am not primarily concerned with terminology, nor with the definition of a genre. In the course of this study I will use the term Complaint (with a capital C) with respect to the kind of first person narrative that stems from the *Mirror for magistrates*, not in its earlier meanings of the predominantly formal French 'complainte' or the medieval Latin 'planctus'.[15] The 'complainte' as well as the 'planctus' are predominantly lyrical forms; the Complaint tells, or implies, a story which is usually set in a legendary background.

The epithet most commonly applied to the Complaints by famous women which are at the centre of my interest is 'tragical'. Since we are dealing with narratives, this can only refer to a medieval concept of tragedy, sad tales of the 'harm of hem that stoode in heigh degree' like those of Chaucer's monk; the questions of tragic weight that arise from the assumption that such tales should deal with 'popes, emperours, or kynges' rather than with women of low degree will be discussed in the last chapter of this study. There have been, however, links between the elegiac narrative and the tragedy proper (i.e. the dramatic form) from its origins in classical literature. Ovid's *Heroides* have already been influenced by the lamentations of women in tragedies, particularly the women tragedies of Euripides. Ovid wrote his own version of Euripides' *Medea* (which is lost); parallels between his *Heroides* and the Greek tragedy have been listed by Helmut Hross in his thesis on the plaints of forsaken women in Latin poetry.[16] Some of the English Renaissance heroical epistles – except those of Drayton – are similarly close to tragedies in the Senecan style, for example Samuel Brandon's 'Octavia to Antonius, Antonius to Octavia' (1598) and Samuel Daniel's 'A letter sent from Octavia to her husband Marcus Antonius into Egypt' (1599), both published as postscripts to classicist tragedies.

There are, however, differences between the monody, a lament enfolded in a dramatic action of the kind Wolfgang Clemen treated in his *English tragedy before Shakespeare* (London, 1961, chapters 14 and 15), and the independent verse letter. It is, to put it simply, the difference between a fragment and a whole, the same difference that exists between a Complaint and an epic; a great part of the effect of an isolated verse-letter or Complaint depends on its being broken out of a supporting context which the tragedy or the epic provides. Even if the support given is as fragile as in the various collections of *De casibus* tragedies, the comments by Boccaccio or the editors of the *Mirror for magistrates* make all the difference. The praise and the apologies which accompany the tales in these collections show how embarrassing they might prove if left alone. Dido is thus cleared of the blame of having been the mistress of Aeneas by Boccaccio before she is allowed access to his *De claris mulieribus*, and 'Shore's wife' (she has no Christian name yet) is allowed to add her Complaint to the second edition of the *Mirror for magistrates* only after a welter of apologies from the editors. Why they were admitted at all is a question largely neglected in the studies which have dealt with the *De casibus* tradition, for example the pioneering studies of W.F. French and Willard Farnham.[17] This has been redressed, at least in parts, with the advent of feminist criticism, and the influx of Ovidian heterodoxy that contributed to a gradual change from the patriotic to the pathetic in this tradition has been recognised. Esther Beith-Halahmi speaks of the creation of 'a new genre of poetry – the pathetic complaint'.[18] The extent of this influence is far greater than has so far been realised. We still lack an exhaustive study of the reception of Ovid's *Heroides* in England; Heinrich Dörrie's magisterial survey, *Der heroische Brief: Bestandsaufnahme, Geschichte, Kritik einer humanistisch-barocken Literaturgattung* (Berlin, 1970) is almost too comprehensive and has its centre in the Romance literatures.[19]

Modern criticism thus echoes the somewhat belated and slightly biassed reaction to the Ovidian Complaint. Some of this is probably due to the closeness of medieval and Renaissance elegiac literature to the main epic and dramatic works of Chaucer and of Shakespeare. Even Chaucer's *Legend of good women*, if studied seriously at all, is usually seen as a kind of five-finger exercise for his *Canterbury tales*. This applies even to Robert W. Frank's *Chaucer and 'The legend of good women'* (Cambridge, Mass., 1972), the first book-length study of the subject, though Frank acknowledges, too, 'the birth of a genre in English narrative' in the tales of the *Legend*. He relates the emergence of this genre to Northrop Frye's concept of low mimetic or domestic tragedy, and its heroines to figures such as Clarissa Harlowe, Tess of the d'Urbervilles or Daisy Miller. Lisa Kiser has recently looked in the opposite direction, towards the classical background of the *Legend of good women*, and interpreted it as a faithful, but not always serious act of *translatio studii* intended to be set against the more creative *Troilus*.[20] The new genre, it seems, is stretched between widely distant poles, and is still liable to suffer from its relation to other, and not always apposite, works.

Something similar has happened to the Complaints of Shakespeare's time. In his volume of the Oxford History of English Literature C.S. Lewis, for example, has stamped everything 'drab' that looks like a Complaint. It appears to be his lively sense of contradiction only which makes him value Shakespeare's *Lucrece* higher than his *Venus and Adonis*, for most other critics have opted for the erotic epyllion. There have been several book-length studies of such epyllia in recent years, for instance William Keach's *Elizabethan erotic narratives* (Hassocks, 1977) and Clark Hulse's *Metamorphic verse: the Elizabethan minor epic* (Guildford, 1982).[21] Both authors quite rightly stress the influence of Ovid's *Metamorphoses* on the epyllion tradition, and they both relate it to the great epic of the period, Spenser's *Faerie queene*. There is the danger, however, that the stress on the epic quality of Ovidian poetry obscures the fact that Ovid and his followers excelled equally, if not more, in verse of the opposite elegiac quality. This applies not only to amatory verse, where it is obvious (William Keach acknowledges the comic spirit of the *Amores*, pp. 14–15), but also to the pathos displayed in heroical epistles and legends of the *Fasti* kind.

The distinction between Ovid's epic and his elegiac mode of telling a story was first drawn some seventy years ago by the classical scholar Richard Heinze. Taking his cues mainly from tales about women in the *Fasti* (for instance the legend of Lucretia) and in the *Metamorphoses* (for example the apotheosis of Ariadne) Heinze developed at length the characteristics of the epic and the elegiac 'types of poetic narration', as he called them.[22] For him, this is more than a stylistic distinction: the epic narrative shows strong and active passions, the elegiac the softer emotions; in the epic humans are given superhuman stature, in the elegiac gods are reduced to human proportions; surroundings in the epic are grand, in the elegiac they are homely, and so on. It is a generic difference which affects all the ingredients of a poem and which is not (this is my extension now of the lines drawn out by Heinze) confined to certain times or forms. It results from a basic attitude to be set alongside other poetic modes like, for instance, the pastoral mode which can also colour widely different genres. The Elizabethan Complaints which occupy the centre of this study are a sample of this basic mode, pure enough, I hope, to bring out some of its strengths and weaknesses, but no absolutes. There have been, and there will be, others.

The scope and contents of this study

The first main chapter of my study is devoted to Dido, the legendary queen of Carthage. It tries to give a detailed distinction, along the lines of Heinze's paper, between epic and elegiac treatments of this classical heroine. My points of departure are Virgil's Dido-episode in the *Aeneid* and Ovid's 'Letter of Dido' from the *Heroides*. Ovid's letter-writer is no longer the foundress and the fury she was in the *Aeneid*, but already shows traits of the forlorn paramour of later romances. The hero's imperial mission, seen through the eyes of the lady, shrinks to the domestic proportions of a stealthy deceit. Ovid's elegiac attitude dominates in late medieval retellings of the story, most notably in the anonymous 'Letter of Dydo to Eneas' of the fifteenth century. In Tudor literature there was a tendency to redress the balance and to fill the heroical epistle with a truly heroic spirit (by, for example, allowing the hero to have the last word); the elegiac mode found a new outlet in Complaints spoken by women which developed alongside erotic epyllia modelled on Ovid's *Metamorphoses*. Chapter 2 will follow this development of the Ovidian sister forms, concentrating on Philomela-poems like George Gascoigne's *The complaint of Philomene* (1576), Patrick Hannay's *The nightingale* (1622) and Martin Parker's *The nightingale warbling forth her own disaster* (1632) and epyllia involving mythical figures such as Oenone in Thomas Heywood's *Oenone and Paris* (1594), Cassandra in Richard

Barnfield's *Legend of Cassandra* (1595) and Helena in John Trussell's *Raptus I. Helenae* (1595).

These two chapters contain preliminary surveys. The central parts of my study will chart the various directions Complaints ascribed to famous women took under the impact of different influences on Elizabethan and Jacobean literature. In chapter 3 the classical tradition will be followed. There are numerous classical heroines in Complaint literature, mainly victims of the fall of Troy or the dawn of Rome; I have chosen Hecuba of Troy (in Thomas Fenne's 'Hecuba's mishaps', 1590) and Lucretia (with Shakespeare's epic *Lucrece*, 1594, and Thomas Middleton's elegiac *Ghost of Lucrece*, 1600) to represent subjects taken from what was taken to be ancient history. The longest chapter is devoted to poems written about heroines from English history, usually heroines of a dubious character such as Rosamond Clifford (Daniel's *Complaint of Rosamond*, 1592) and Mrs Shore (Anthony Chute, *Beauty dishonoured: written under the title of Shore's wife*, 1593). The emergence of a female variety of Complaints from the predominantly male *Mirror for magistrates* is described (Churchyard's 'Shore's wife', 1563, 1593). The peculiar apologetic tendency of these Complaints leads to a concentration on emotional means of expression: broken language is used, and pity rather than justice is evoked. The softness of this approach called forth rigorous replies from steadfast saints and martyrs such as the nun Matilda in Michael Drayton's *Matilda* (1594) or Queen Elizabeth in Christopher Lever's *Queen Elizabeth's tears* (1607) and from hardened sinners such as the Queen of Scots in an anonymous 'Legend of Mary, queen of Scots' (*c* 1601).

The earthly saints of this secular tradition provoked in turn religious counterparts, again in both the epic and the elegiac mode. There were Protestant epyllia praising Old Testament heroines such as Susanna, for instance Robert Roche's *Eustathia: or the constancy of Susanna* (1599) or Robert Aylett's *Susanna* (1622), and Catholic Complaints presenting the holy sinner Mary Magdalen weeping at Gethsemane as in Gervase Markham's *Mary Magdalen's lamentations* (1601). The Magdalen poems are shown to go back – via a meditation by Robert Southwell, *Mary Magdalen's funeral tears* (1591) – to a medieval sermon, the so-called *Omelia Origenis*, not the Italian tradition of *Lagrime* poems, as has been supposed. Magdalen Complaints were adapted to Protestant purposes by poets such as Nicholas Breton and the Earl of Essex, who substituted scrupulously pious souls for the unorthodox Magdalen, as in *The longing of a blessed heart* (1601) or *The passion of a discontented mind* (1601).

Of truly Italian origin is a last variant of the tradition, Complaints spoken by courtesans of a lower order than the English concubines. The matter for these poems (for example, George Whetstone's 'The disordered life of Bianca Maria', 1576) is taken from novelle of the second, rather lurid generation. It came to England in moralised French redactions and was developed into the sort of contrite confessions of fallen women which became dear to later, more sentimental or melo-dramatic times. Complaints like Gervase Markham's *Lamentable complaint of Paulina* (1609) and Thomas Cranley's *Amanda: or the reformed whore* (1635) were collectors' items in the late nineteenth century, and not only because of their rarity.

There are no clear lines of demarcation between these different kinds of Complaints; taken as a whole, they constitute a distinct body of litera-ture that was recognised by authors and readers (or collectors) alike. This is evident from internal as well as external evidence. Poets composed works in several of the strains delineated: George Whetstone, for instance, wrote Complaints for mythological and novellistic figures; Thomas Lodge, a *Tragical complaint of Elstred* (1593) and (probably) a *Prosopopeia containing the tears of the lady Mary* (1596); Gervase Mark-ham, a *Lamentable complaint of Paulina* (1609) after his *Mary Magda-len's lamentations* (1609), and so on. There are cross references in prefaces, dedications and the poems themselves. Drayton's *Legend of Matilda* (1594), for example, expressly sets out to eclipse Churchyard's 'Shore's wife' (1563), Daniel's *Rosamond* (1592), Lodge's *Elstred* (1593), and Shakespeare's *Lucrece* (1594), and there are numerous allusions in imagery, motif, theme and manner of presentation; my last chapter tries to assess these common features and to evaluate the generic potential in the elegiac mode of telling a tragic story.

As to external correspondences, there is the bibliographical evidence of early collections of Complaints and similar pieces: late medieval com-pilers and early Renaissance printers of Chaucer's works, for instance, sought to increase his output (and their income) by adding to the canon of his *Legend of good women* poems such as the anonymous 'Letter of Dydo to Eneas' and 'The complaint of Saint Mary Magdaleyn' or Gilbert Banester's 'Legenda Sismond'. There are later collections like the Calde-cott volume, which contains a number of poems about women of Greek legend (Thomas Heywood's *Oenone and Paris*, 1594; John Trussell's *Raptus I. Helenae*, 1595; Peter Colse's *Penelope's complaint*, 1596), or volume 393 from the Malone collection with its more varied congregation of heroines (for example William Barksted's *Tragical narration of Virgi-nia's death*, 1617, Robert Aylett's *Susanna*, 1622, and Robert Stapleton's *Dido and Aeneas* [1634?]).

Some of the poems discussed in this study have not been reprinted since their original publication in manuscripts or early printed books and are therefore hard to come by. There is a descriptive bibliography of the rarer volumes in the German version of this study (*Die Frauenklage*, chapter J). The titles of early printed books are modernised; their place of publication is London, unless stated otherwise.

2

Dido and Elissa: heroic and elegiac treatment of a legendary queen

'It is but a *Dido*,' quod this doctour, 'a dysoures tale'.
William Langland, *Piers Plowman*, B, XIII, 172

Dido in classical literature

The legend of Dido has been a thrice-told tale from classical times, and the Latin line preceding the doctor's verdict in *Piers Plowman*, 'Pacientes vincunt, &c.', might have served as a password on its way from the Greek and Roman chroniclers to the Renaissance ballad mongers.

The story of the princess Elissa of Tyros, who, according to Servius, was titled 'Dido', i.e. 'the valiant', only after her death as queen of Carthage, has been passed down to us from ancient sources in two versions: the legend, preserved in Justin's *Epitoma historiarum Philippicarum*, which record that she gave her life to escape the suit of Iarbas, the king of Gaetulia; the episode in Book IV of Virgil's *Aeneid*, in which she royally receives the Trojan Aeneas, who is cast on her shore – 'animoque domoque', as Ovid puts it, or, in Boccaccio's less courteous phrase, 'amicitia et lecto' – and kills herself in despair when the hero leaves her to follow his destiny.[1] Ovid's 'Letter of Dido' (*Heroides*, VII) follows Virgil's account; the heroine's point of view, however, makes Aeneas look less like a fated hero than a faithless lover.

This last view was the one to dominate in the Middle Ages. It was strengthened by the 'eyewitness' reports of the fall of Troy and its aftermath by Dares Phrygius and Dictys Cretensis which branded Aeneas as a traitor to his town.[2] With respect to the tradition of Complaint literature, the Ovidian version is of prime importance. It is my aim in this chapter to distinguish the elegiac mode which informs this letter from the historical behind Justin's legend and the heroic behind Virgil's episode.

Justin's legend of Elissa

The legend of the founder queen Elissa has had little impact on medieval treatments of her fall, although one would have thought her eminently suited to serve as an example of a chaste and steadfast widow. Jerome, the Church Father who collected such examples in his polemic letter *Adversus Jovinianum* had, in fact, praised her as a kind of proto-martyr of chastity (I, xli–xlvi),[3] but the tearful remembrance of Augustine in his *Confessiones* (I, xiii)[4] proved more influential: in dozens of catalogues and processions she appears as an example of unhappy love.[5] This reputation of a lost lady is probably the reason why Chaucer leaves her out of the long list of virtuous matrons in Dorigen's complaint although this is based on Jerome's pamphlet ('Franklin's tale', 1,367–456). It was in early humanist literature that Justin's version of the Dido-story was revived. Boccaccio made use of it in both his treatises of tragic falls, *De casibus virorum illustrium* (II, xvi–xvii) and *De claris mulieribus* (XL) and he accompanied his tales with moralising comments. Petrarch, in his epic *Africa*, turned it against Virgil and Ovid by pointing out the obvious anachronism that lies in linking a Trojan myth with Roman history.[6] Both Petrarch and Boccaccio accuse the classical poets, more or less explicitly, of detracting from Elissa's valiant name. There is some irony in the fact that enlightened humanists, not dark-age Church Fathers, cast a critical eye on poetic accounts of the pagan queen.[7]

In England, too, it is the humanists who introduce the legend into historical and exemplary literature, half-hearted humanists like Lydgate and Caxton, whose all-embracing sense of history lets them render different versions of the Dido-story side by side without much effort at a reconciliation. Caxton, who in his *Book of Eneydos* claims to be translating 'a little book in French', prints first Boccaccio's *De casibus* example (vi–ix), then, for the sake of completeness, Virgil's episode, which fills the bulk of the volume (x–xix). This garbled version so vexed Gavin Douglas, the Scottish humanist, that he produced his superb translation of the *Aeneid*.

Lydgate had commemorated Dido as love's victim in several of his shorter poems before he treated her extensively in his *Fall of princes* (II, 1,898–2,233). He faithfully follows two steps behind Boccaccio, not only pursuing the moralistic tendencies of his *De casibus* collections, which his immediate predecessor Laurent de Premierfait had already extended with plenty of serious comments, but also adding a number of satirical sniggers of his own. The inconsistencies of his version are even more significant than those of Caxton's, resulting, as they do, not so much from comprehensive (and possibly commercial) motives as with Caxton, but from a wish to draw as many lessons from a case like Dido's as possible – be they controversial or even contradictory. Aeneas is not mentioned in Lydgate's story, and Dido is allowed to live up to her name of being a virago. To keep her portrait spotless Lydgate passes over the small ruses Dido employs to escape Phoenicians, Cypriots and Africans in Justin's legend: she does not trick her companions into the flight from

Tyre by pretending first to go on a family visit only and then to throw the treasures of her murdered husband into the sea; the girls she rather ruthlessly requisitions on the coast of Cyprus are not prostitutes but virgins who volunteer to join her expedition; and the bull's hide strat- agem is suppressed (which destroys the etiological basis of the Byrsa legend). On the other hand Lydgate takes the utmost care with details which indicate the female virtues or the heavenly connections of his her- oine: he turns the priest of Jupiter who casts a propitious lot over her enterprise into a prophet of Juno, and he makes the most of Dido's apotheosis after her sacrificial death: she is worshipped not only as the patron saint of Carthage but as a goddess of chastity as well.

Dido's constancy is one point of Lydgate's interest: she is given two long speeches to bring it home. Another point is her role as a ruler: the care of Carthage is foremost in her mind right to the end. Dido does not hesitate to choose death before dishonour; there is not even the usual soliloquy of deliberation. After Iarbas has set his ultimatum she asks for respite merely to fortify her city. Lydgate fully corroborates Boccaccio's commendation: 'O mulieris virile robur. O foeminei pudoris decus laude perpetua celebrandum'.[8] This heightening of Dido's character is brought to culmination in her death: the funeral pyre is lighted on the highest tower of her fortress, as a beacon of strength and virtue. A tale which otherwise might have profited from a touch of Virgilian epic is thus brought to a grand conclusion.

By placing Dido firmly in the exemplary tradition Lydgate does little to make her an amiable heroine; an Ovidian streak here or there would have become her better and might have brought out in Lydgate some of the tenderness he had extended to less virtuous figures earlier in his compilation. In the first book of the *Fall of princes* he had told the story of incestuous Canace and added not only an extensive complaint which ends as an Ovidian letter (I, 6,882–7,035),[9] but also a chapter inscribed 'Bochas on the malice of women' (I, 6,511–734) in which he defends women in general from Boccaccio's calumnies against the sex.

After this vindication of scandalous Canace and the efforts at white- washing Dido it comes as even more of a surprise when the legend of Dido in the *Fall of princes* is followed by two epilogues of a very mixed appearance. The first is a praise of her loyalty to Sychaeus, her husband, with stanza-endings looking back, refrain-like, to the beacon of virtue: 'With liht off trouthe alle widwes tenlumyne' (II, 2,177, 2,184, etc.). The second is a warning to all widows not to follow Dido's example, and always to keep a lover in reserve to make up for losses; the refrain changes to: 'Contraire to Dido, that was queen off Cartage' (II, 2,226, 2,233). This touch of facetiousness in the second epilogue is Lydgate's own; its burden does not, like the rest of the story (including the eulogy) go back to Boccaccio's *De claris mulieribus*. Boccaccio has a dispute with some imaginary women who question the wisdom of Dido's decision: one of them asks, with reference to St Paul, the macabre question whether it would not have been better to get married than to get burnt. Boccaccio conducts this dispute in the manner of a church-father and expounds the lesson to be learned from Dido's example: if a pagan woman prefers death to dishonour, how much more reason has a Christian widow to withstand her carnal desires. Lydgate turns Boccaccio's diatribe into derision, playing the role of a beldame rather than a preacher and arguing like the Old Woman in Jean de Meun's part of the *Roman de la rose*: she tells Dido's story (Virgil's version) as an example for male fickleness which should be warded off by spreading the risk and keeping several lovers at a time (*Roman de la rose*, 13,173–210). It appears that the high moral seriousness of an overly didactic treatment of a story like Dido's required some sort of low-style satirical complement.

This seems to be one of the rules that govern the literature of debate: no matter how lofty its aims, it tends to stylise its exemplary figures out of human likeness and asks for similarly distorted likenesses from below. This tendency works in either direction: Jean de Meun's *Roman* is known to have provoked Christine de Pisan into writing her *Cité des dames* (1405, tr. Bryan Anslay, 1521) as an allegorical fortress against detractors of the female sex. The foundation-stone of her fortress is laid by Lady Reason, and Dido's double sorrow is used for two of its pinnacles of probity: she serves as an embodiment of prudence in a very long chapter that goes back to Justin or one of his followers (xlvi), and she is mentioned as a warning against love's folly in a small chapter based on Ovid or one of his successors (liv).

Legend and satire, then, are able to throw light and shade on one and the same story, and sometimes in rapid succession. Both tend to allegorise their exemplary figures out of proportion, the one by whitewashing, the other by blackening them. In exemplary and controversial literature Justin's and Boccaccio's black and white version of the story survived even the most successful attempts of Renaissance poets to give it a more human aspect, be it in the light of Virgil's passionate or in Ovid's pitiful rendering. When the first translations and imitations of Virgil's and Ovid's works appeared in England, Thomas Salter, a schoolmaster with Puritan leanings, was alarmed and gave warning in his *Mirror of modesty* (1579) about the damage that reading in general, and in particular reading in elegiac poetry (with which he associated Book IV of the *Aeneid*) might cause, especially in girls. Better keep them illiterate, he suggests, for once they have mastered the art of reading, who is to make sure they do not turn to 'Lasciuious bookes, of *Ouide*, *Catullus*, *Propercius*, *Tibullus*, and in *Virgill* of *Eneas*, and *Dido*' (B7v)? Instead, Salter recommends, girls should read the Bible or the works of Plutarch, 'made of such renowmed and vertuous women as liued in tyme paste, and those of *Boccas* tendyng to the same sence' (C3v). In 1579 this concern may seem exaggerated, for the tide of elegiac poetry had only just set in. But others were equally worried, and began to construct citadels as Christine de Pisan did in her *Cité des dames* (1404–5; tr. Brian Ansley, 1521). Thomas Bentley, for example, published his *Monument of matrons . . . compiled out of the sacred Scriptures, and other approved authors* in 1582, and when the tide of Ovidian literature had gone out, Justin's legend and Petrarch's spirit were once more revived with the emergence of a sober heroism, for instance by George Rivers in his collection of biographical sketches, *The heroinae* (1639). Rivers dismisses Virgil's Dido with an almost contemptuous hint at historical facts:

The meeting of *Dido* and Aeneas (in which *Virgils* Muse hath sweat to the dishonour of them both; her for love, him for ingratitude) is so meerly fabulous, that it is scarce worth the expence of paper to disprove it, onely I am bound to vindicate her honour.   (p. 83)

I need not follow up this strain of didactic and contentious literature any further; the pros and cons of educational and recreational reading for women have recently been investigated in detail by Suzanne W. Hull in her *Chaste, silent and obedient: English books for women 1475–1640* (1982). My study will concentrate on poetic treatments of stories such as Dido's and on such poets as prefer the disgraced Dido to the immaculate Elissa. As stated above, poets of the Middle Ages show this preference to a marked degree. This is the more surprising because these are the poets reputed for their didactic leanings. Their chivalrous attitude is to be found all over Europe. In England, where Dido had her staunchest supporters in Gower and Chaucer, there is, in addition, an equally marked preference for Ovid's over Virgil's heroine. It is a surprising choice for the authors of a *Mirour de l'omme* and a *Legend of good women* – if it was a choice. This we can safely assume with Chaucer who must have known, however superficially, both Virgil's and Ovid's versions of the story from his days at school, and probably came to know Boccaccio's version later on. With him (Gower's case is different, as we shall see) this preference must have been a deliberate choice, and he may have seen the essential difference that lies in Ovid's elegiac as opposed to Virgil's epic treatment of the fate of Dido. I will now turn to the *Aeneid* and the *Heroides* to point out a few features of this difference.

The Dido episode in Virgil's *Aeneid*

Thomas Salter, being opposed to fathers who indulge the whims of their daughters (he calls such fathers 'effeminate' at the beginning of his *Mirror of modesty*, B2v), is suspicious only of Dido's detracting role in the *Aeneid*, not of Aeneas in his role of *translator imperii*, the hero who has to shake off the African dust to fulfil his destiny as founder of a Roman empire. Not even Virgil, the creator of 'pius' Aeneas, has taken quite as one-sided a view of the African episode as Salter. In the *Aeneid*, Dido presents a very real challenge for the hero, and Aeneas does not escape the adventure unscarred. The scars may be hidden deep inside, but they are there nevertheless; this shows nowhere more clearly than later on, in the underworld encounter of the lovers in Book VI. In Book IV, Dido attains at least equal status with Aeneas, and a tragic stature that is (by definition, one might say) denied to the epic hero. Friedrich Leo, looking back from the Hades episode, has called Book IV of the *Aeneid* the only real Roman tragedy, and it is, of course, mainly Dido's tragedy.[10] The tragic impact is partly due to a reversal of roles which diminishes the heroic effect of the African episode: the hero's escape looks rather infamous if looked at not only from an amatory, but also from a purely martial point of view, the point of view critics like Salter tend to take. Aeneas himself shows signs of effeminacy in his character if looked at from that angle: he is allowed to weep (which is not unusual in a classical hero), Mercury upbraids him as 'uxorius' (266), and Dido, after the first of her invectives, leaves him trembling with fear, 'multa metu cunctantem' (390).[11]

The confrontation with Dido is apt to produce real doubts about the stature of Aeneas and the nature of his vocation, partly because of the passive role he is reduced to in the Carthaginian episode (he is cast ashore in the beginning, and loath to leave in the end, 'Italiam non sponte sequor', 361), partly because of the activities and questionings of Dido. The whole of the epic structure which demands that the hero's values be upheld might become unhinged were it not supported by the Olympian gods and an Olympian narrator. The interventions of Venus and of Mercury direct the action according to an ultimately beneficial plan, and the narrator, for all his compassion with the heroine, directs the sympathies of his audience away from her ultimately pernicious acts.

This last effect is achieved with great subtlety. Almost imperceptibly Virgil moves his heroine away from the image Justin had created, the image of a queen who keeps loyal to her husband and her people. From the beginning the narrator throws in remarks which undermine that dual image. Dido is said to cast aside all thoughts of her husband Sychaeus and thus to cast off her modesty, 'solvit pudorem' (55, cf. 24–7; 'pudor' is the womanly equivalent to the manly virtue of 'pietas' associated with Aeneas). Later on we are told that works on the fortification of the city came to a standstill the day after Aeneas arrived ('non coeptae adsurgunt turres', 86; cf. III, 503–4). In the legend, we remember, Dido manages to save both her virtue and her city with her last stratagem of pretending to accept the suit of Iarbas.

By dropping such hints and comments throughout his narrative the epic voice keeps the audience alerted to the selfishness of Dido's actions and the providential background which Aeneas has to keep in mind. It is easy to overlook these hints (medieval redactions of the love story at the heart of the book apparently eliminated them), for on the whole Virgil has given Dido more than her due to vent her passions and express her point of view. Aeneas looks rather pale in comparison with her full-blooded performance. He is driven into a defensive position in the end, and we are almost on Dido's side when she eventually challenges the whole idea of his divine mission. Should not the gods know better, indeed, than trust someone like him with the founding of empires:

> scilicet is superis labor est, ea cura quietos
> sollicitat. neque te teneo neque dicta refello:
> i, sequere Italiam ventis, pete regna per undas. (379–81)

When even Aeneas begins to doubt his destiny and Fama has started rumours about his neglect of duty Jupiter interferes and Mercury calls him to order: in serving Dido he has become oblivious of his proper duties ('regni rerumque oblite tuarum', 267). Fama had put it even more bluntly by saying that the lovers spent a whole winter in vile, neglectful ease, 'regnorum inmemores turpique cupidine captos' (194).

Virgil leaves little doubt that this love-affair is dishonourable, and he places most of the blame on Dido. Not only has she broken her vow to Sychaeus, her claim to be married to Aeneas is a pretext that the narrator is quick to expose: 'coniugium vocat, hoc praetexit nomine culpam' (172). Aeneas, on the whole rather taciturn in Book IV, is given opportunity to deny the very thought of such a union (338–9). Moreover, Dido's love is clearly not of the conjugal kind. It is presented as a violent passion that develops an almost infernal force and eventually turns the heroine into a fury – a climactic development which enables the poet to save Dido some dignity and which makes the flight of Aeneas less ignoble: both lovers act under pressure, he from above and she from below, and, of course, Aeneas must avoid being drawn into the gulf in the end. There is a sinister greatness in Dido's passion as she becomes increasingly entangled in the snares of a superhuman destiny. In the preparations for her death and in the imprecations she sends after her lover she combines the features of sorceress and prophetess, Medea and

Cassandra. In lighter moments her vision comprises the past as well as the future. She is allowed to look back on her achievements as foundress of Carthage and feels confident of her greatness: 'vixi et quem dederat cursum Fortuna peregi, / et nunc magna mei sub terras ibit imago' (653–4). This is confirmed in Book VI when she meets Aeneas in the Underworld.

Eventually Dido becomes reconciled with her fate; her suicide is less an act of despair than of spite, the one heroic deed traditionally left to a heroine in her situation. She appears the mistress of her fate, not the victim of her lover: she is, in a word, exalted, as far as decorum allows, to epic heights. Her magnificent death casts a lasting shadow over the true hero of the epic, but deeds of arms and a purer love will, of course, polish his repute in due time. With respect to the whole of the epic, the African adventure was no more than an episode – an episode, however, which throughout the centuries has threatened to eclipse the splendour of the rest. This is no doubt due to the empathy with which Virgil depicted his passion-rent Dido; up to the present there is disagreement even among Latinists on how far he allowed himself to be carried away by his compassion for the queen. I would agree with Erich Segal who, in a review of Richard C. Monti's book-length study of the episode, stresses its pathetic rather than political weight, although I would ascribe its permanent appeal at least as much to Ovid's reworking of the Carthaginian encounter. Segal points out that this appeal is witnessed by – among other proofs – nearly a hundred operas of the *Didone abbandonata* type, but it was Ovid who created the model for this type.[12]

The 'Letter of Dido' in Ovid's *Heroides*

Ovid's elegiac treatment of the abandoned Dido in the seventh of his *Epistulae heroides* is so clearly based on Virgil's epic, but reworks the Dido episode so freely, as to amount almost to a parody. An anti-heroic tendency, however, is inherent in the genre of the not very aptly named heroical epistle. As shaped by Ovid, an heroical epistle presents the letter of a heroine, that is a woman related to an ancient hero, in which she calls or claims him back as husband or as lover, usually with little hope of ever being answered. Ovid's first set of *Heroides* were single letters, and I leave aside for the moment the three pairs which were later added to the fifteen singles. The typical situation of the heroine is private in a double sense: she is deprived of the hero's (and often all other) company, and she is concerned with personal affairs. The heroes addressed are those of ancient myth and history, the warriors and adventurers whose deeds are traditionally dealt with in epic poetry, like Theseus, Ulysses and, of course, Aeneas. But what is Troy to Penelope, years after its fall, or Rome to Dido, years before its foundation? From the point of view of Ovid's heroines, whose only claim to heroism is their involvement with a hero, these are phantom fields, subterfuges of sluggish or of faithless men. It is on this point of view that most of the effects of the *Heroides* depend.

Letter-writing is by necessity a quiet activity. What action there is in the background of the heroical epistles is taken out of the great epic cycles and is only alluded to by bits and pieces. This gives the *Heroides* a fragmentary aspect; the letters lack the overarching structure that the rounded action of an epic provides for each of its episodes. The letter form also brings about that the epic world is narrowed to domestic proportions. Furthermore, the constant flow of time that gives the epic a sense of purpose is arrested in the letter to a short and indecisive span. And lastly, there is no narrator in a letter who comments on the proceedings from a superior point of view; instead we share the limited outlook of a victim of the action around her who is only affected by the past and blind to the future.

All these factors add to the almost parodistic effects Ovid's 'Letter of Dido' has if compared to its epic model. Like any parodist Ovid remains to a certain extent tied to this model; his possibilities lie in light and sleight-of-hand deviations from its designs. It is a proof of his art that the subtlety of his alterations has until recently hardly been noticed. On the face of it Ovid in his portrait of Dido does no more than sketch out certain features he found in Virgil's epic. Howard Jacobson has collected a number of parallels in his book on the *Heroides*: he thinks they show an artisan tampering with the work of an artist. The overall effect is one of debasement, but this seems to develop in a hardly perceptible, underhand way, and one cannot be sure whether it was intended or not. Even recent critics like W.S. Anderson think it was not.[13]

One of the main effects of Ovid's deviations is a softening of Dido's character: she is a gentler figure than with Virgil. Her violent wish in the *Aeneid* to visit her lover as a spectre in his last hour is mellowed to a hortatory vision in her letter (*Aeneid*, IV, 382–7; *Heroides*, VII, 53–60); threats and imprecations are generally toned down to anxious plaints; 'queri' and its derivatives is one of Dido's (and Ovid's) favourite words: 'sed queror infidum quaestaque peius amo' (30) is a significant line.[14] When in her letter Dido asks Aeneas to delay his voyage, it is to cope with her sorrows; in the epic it is to calm her raging anger (*Aeneid*, IV, 433–6; *Heroides*, VII, 179–80). Ovid's letter-writer is willing to humble herself by waiving all claims to the title of a wife ('uxor') and to be content with the role of a hostess ('hospita'), whereas Virgil's heroine has nothing but harsh words about a husband ('coniux') turned guest ('hospes'; *Aeneid*, IV, 323–4; *Heroides*, VII, 167–8). There is a similar shift of emphasis towards the piteous in the handling of the child motif. Virgil uses it to show Dido's lapse from passion to fury: she first rocks Ascanius on her lap, thinking of his father (84–5), then threatens to slaughter him like Medea or Progne (601–2); a child of her own by Aeneas is nothing but a wish (327–30). With Ovid, this motif is developed in a different direction. Dido, who has shown concern that Ascanius might be drowned with Aeneas (75–7), threatens to kill herself and more than hints at the possibility that an unborn child – whom she calls a brother of Ascanius – might have to die with her (133–8).

Most of the humility and altruism in Dido's letter is calculated for effect, of course, and the echoes from the *Aeneid* give them an edge that sometimes threatens to undercut the sympathy they are, if taken at face value, apt to arouse. Dido's softness has a cattish side to it, and sometimes the claws beneath can be felt, for example when she intimates that Aeneas may have forsaken his first wife Creusa like herself and when she warns him that it may prove difficult for him to find a third as credulous as them (81–5; 17–22).

Insinuations like these, besides their parodistic effect, serve the double purpose of making both Dido and Aeneas look more human and less heroic. This is enhanced by the limited perspective. The narrative situation, freezing the epic movement at an emotive moment, radically alters the outlook on past and future events. Not only does Dido question the fidelity of Aeneas towards his wife, but also his loyalty towards his father and his household gods (77–82). The whole of his past achievements and future tasks, the Matter of Troy, is called into question. There was no numinous guidance for Aeneas; on the contrary, Dido has no doubt that he lives under an evil spell: 'Nec mihi mens dubia est, quin te tua numina damnent.' (87) The same applies to future events. Here, too, Ovid makes use of the restricted view of the letter writer: Dido stresses several times the doubtfulness of the future; Aeneas does not even know where exactly his promised lands lie ('quaeque ubi sint nescis, Itala regna', 10); he is chasing the end of a rainbow and losing sight of reality (an incisive blow at the errant knight's, or merchant venturer's ethos): 'facta fugis, facienda petis; quaerenda per orbem / altera, quaesita est altera terra tibi' (13–14).

These doubts and questions, though put into softer words, are much more radical than anything raised in the epic, and being expressed in a single letter, they are, of course, allowed to stand. The hero has no chance to answer, nor is there a narrator to set the perspective right, or a Mercury to intervene. What prevails is the point of view of the woman who is left at home to worry. It is an unheroic point of view. Dido herself makes this quite plain when she says that she is not sprung from a place where heroes like Achilles were born: 'non ego sum Phthias magnisque oriunda Mycenis' (165). This echoes *Aeneid*, IV, 425–6, ('non ego cum

Danais . . .'), but with Dido's record in the *Aeneid* she might well have been able to send a few ships to Troy. In Ovid's letter the 'quid feci' topos is seen from the amorous side: 'quod crimen dicis praeter amasse meum' (164). It is a matter of choice, and Ovid's Dido takes as naturally to the one as Virgil's Aeneas to the other possibility: 'hic amor, haec patria' (*Aeneid*, IV, 347).

From the limited point of view of the letter-writer, past, present and future all merge into the resentment of a passive and impassioned victim. When Ovid's Dido looks back on her own past she does not remember her great achievements like Virgil's but her narrow escapes (*Heroides* VII, 111–24; cf. *Aeneid*, IV, 655–6); she counts as praiseworthy only the gifts she showered on Aeneas and his fellow Trojans (89–92; cf. *Aeneid*, IV, 373–6, where the motif is used to incite wrath, not pity).[15] Her present situation is as miserable as it can be, and as to the future, she apprehends what is in store for her once she is at the mercy of either her barbarous suitor or her murderous brother. She spikes this prospect with one of her most stinging insinuations: the pious Aeneas might as well throw her manacled to Iarbas, with an impious hand, 'inpia dextra' (130); a few lines earlier the same epitheton had been used with reference to her brother, 'manus inpia' (127). Looking back, Ovid's Dido presents her life as an endless prosecution; it is a purely personal history, with herself as victim at the centre. She is not the heroine who picks herself up in the end, like Virgil's Dido, to become the mistress of her fate at least in death: her suicide is, of course, a matter of conjecture only. She does, like the other Dido, look beyond her grave, and it is interesting to compare the visions they have of their afterlife appearances: whereas Virgil's Dido expects to go down to the nether world in grand style (and that is how she meets Aeneas in Book VI of the *Aeneid*), Ovid's expects to meet her lover like a weeping statue. Virgil's 'magna mei sub terras ibit imago' (*Aeneid*, IV, 654) is recalled in Ovid's 'stabit imago / tristis et effusis sanguinolenta comis' (*Heroides*, 69–70). Even the difference between the active 'ibit' and the passive 'stabit' is significant.

The overall effect of Ovid's elegiac treatment of the fall of Dido as compared with the epic version in the *Aeneid* is one of cutting down the heroic to domestic proportions and, in terms of the underlying ethos, shifting significance from the public to the personal. Under Ovid's hand the legend assumes the shape of an almost ordinary, certainly no more than human, love story. Owing to the private perspective, the public importance of the story is not even envisaged; in fact, given the epistolary fiction, it is hard to see how it could come into view without straining the probability of character and situation. For the forsaken Dido, what should be wrong with her love or right with the flight of her lover is unintelligible. She is sure that she can justify her love even to her former husband. Only

Aeneas, who deceived her and did not keep his word (105–10; 164), is to blame.

This takes sympathy with Dido's plight to the limit, particularly for a public aroused to the old Roman ideals of piety and probity. And sometimes Ovid takes his heroine clearly beyond the understanding of even the most sympathetic of his readers: there are a number of contradictions in Dido's letter, and it is hard to accept them all as signs of a state of mind which makes her prone to confuse private vice and public virtue.[16] Ovid leaves open whether these inconsistencies are due to the desperate wish of a woman to retain her love with all her might and, if needs be, by crooked means, or whether we are to assume her to be writing under such emotional strain that her mind is on the verge of giving way. There is also a considerable amount of irony in her letter which can only in part be ascribed to the letter-writer herself. Some of it is of the kind that can be shared by author and reader only – a reader familiar with Virgil's version of the story. The 'knowing Ovidian innuendo' of which Charles Martindale has aptly spoken is directed as much against the heroine as against the hero.[17]

The fact that Ovid leaves his readers room for play does not, however, completely puncture the moving effects of the letter. The elegiac, being like the comic or mock-epic based on a lower ethical and stylistic plane, is capable of undermining the higher values that sustain the epic even without devaluing its agents.

In the last resort, therefore, it is hard to determine the extent to which Ovid intended to deflate the Augustan ethic or to depreciate his rival Virgil. Part of the debunking effect of his *Heroides* is due to his choice of the elegiac letter-form. It was an error of judgment on Ovid's behalf that he undervalued the erosive power of this form: there are scholars who think it was the Letter of Dido rather than the *Ars amatoria* or some personal misconduct that led to the displeasure of Augustus and his banishment from Rome.[18] However that may be, it is the technical rather than the ironical twist which gave the well-known story its devious direction in Ovid's redaction. And it is this almost underhand effect which matters in this study. By foreshortening time and space and perspective Ovid dismantled the story of its epic and ideological dimension; he removed the greatcoat, as it were, and revealed the simpler dress, if not the petticoat, underneath. In its new guise it was no longer fit to be worn on state occasions; the laws of decorum demand that it be restricted to more intimate surroundings and more private conversations where family affairs are discussed and potent heroes prove deficient lovers. It is this shift of emphasis that, in various degrees, left its mark on his followers even if they missed some of his subtlety.

Dido in late medieval English poetry

Doubts similar to those about Ovid's *Heroides* have arisen about a later string of tales concerned with love's victims, Chaucer's *Legend of good women*. If there is a certain amount of irony in these tales, and this irony directed at orthodoxy, it has not met with the same sort of reprisal; but then there were, for Chaucer, neither Virgil nor Augustus to contend with – unless, that is, we accept John Gower and King Richard as equivalents. Ovid's ironies apparently escaped his readers up to the late Middle Ages, and possibly longer, at least in England, and so did Chaucer's up to the late nineteenth century. J.A.K. Thomson thinks only Chaucer capable of grasping the ironies in the *Heroides*, but finds no indication of this in his writings.[19] His is a conservative opinion, based on a cautious estimate of Chaucer's classical learning. There are other, less guarded, critics who rate Chaucer's acquaintance with the Latin classics much higher and, in proportion, suppose him to have understood and used as much irony as his forbear.

The case for a completely ironic reading of the *Legend of good women* in the light of Ovid's *Heroides* has only recently been stated in the most spirited manner by Lisa J. Kiser.[20] Like many of its predecessors, her interpretation presupposes an erudition not only in Chaucer but also in his readers which has rarely been questioned in recent criticism.[21] Neither Richard L. Hoffman nor John M. Fyler in their book-length studies of Chaucer's relationship to Ovid, nor Robert W. Frank and Lisa J. Kiser in their books on the *Legend of good women* have thought it worth their while to touch on the question of the material basis of Chaucer's supposed intimacy with Ovidian texts.[22] I shall come back to this question in my chapter on John Gower; let me anticipate here that I think it necessary to keep the once well-established notion in mind that Chaucer is essentially a medieval poet.[23] He may have questioned his classical authorities, but he did not do this in the Renaissance spirit of a Petrarch or a Gavin Douglas. It was, in fact, his medievalism which gave him the greater freedom to question not only the letter, but also the spirit of these authorities. The quest for literal truth that drove Petrarch to turn against his admired master Virgil was not one of Chaucer's prime motives. He was also less impressed with the elegance of the *Heroides* or the heroism of the *Aeneid* which Gavin Douglas commended in his *Palice of honour* and his *Eneados*. Most of the 'subtell fair maneir' of Ovid's 'Ladyis seir' (*Palice*, II, 820, 817), and much of the 'wirschip, manhed and nobilite' (*Eneados*, Prologue I, 330) of Virgil's hero may simply have eluded English poets before the time of this first Latinist on British soil. When, therefore, poets like Chaucer and Gower chose to follow either of these classical examples it was for their matter and perhaps their moral, not their manner. And if, in the following chapters, I interpret some of their poems in close comparison with their classical masters, it is not to suggest that they competed with their models as Ovid did against Virgil, but that they followed their authorities and, in addition, observed the rules of their chosen modes.

John Gower, 'The tale of Eneas and Dido'

The erudition of the Ricardians and their knowledge of the classics may have been defective, but this certainly did not hinder them from picking up classical stories and retelling them in the most imaginative manner. The story of Dido was one of their favourites, and Ovid was their chief authority. Dido's story was a love story, and Ovid was the acknowledged master in matters of love, 'Venus clerk, Ovide', 'the grete clerc Ovide' as Chaucer and Gower respectfully call him.[24] In Gower's *Confessio amantis* the aged lover Amans is shriven of his sins against love by Genius, a priest of Venus, who conducts the shrift, somewhat incongruously, according to a classified system of the Seven Deadly Sins. In the end Genius purges the *senex* Amans of his love-sickness, but not before Amans has listened to well over a hundred stories exemplifying the ways of love in all their diversity, and several dozen of these (38 out of a total of 138, according to a count by Derek Pearsall)[25] go back to Ovid. The mere fact that Gower places his encyclopaedic poem under the aegis of the Latin elegist speaks for the estimation Ovid enjoyed and the unsuspicious way his works were read in the late Middle Ages.

Still, with a story like Dido's one might have expected Gower to have in some way responded to the critical undertones Virgil worked into his treatment of the subject: one of Gower's favourite themes is the responsibility of a king, and Virgil makes quite clear that Dido neglected her duties as a queen when she fell in love with Aeneas. Virgil, however, is mentioned in the *Confessio amantis* only as a sorcerer and a *senex amans*: the legends of the magus were better known to Gower than the works of the poet.[26]

The story of Eneas and Dido is told in Book IV of the *Confessio amantis* as an example of 'Lachesce' (i.e. laziness in matters of love), and all the blame is laid on the shoulders of Eneas (*Confessio amantis*, IV, 77–137). Although the example is told by the Confessor, and the story therefore narrated from a detached point of view, the incidents and their sequence are based on Ovid's rather biassed 'Letter of Dido'. Gower seems puzzled mainly by the technical problems posed by Ovid's unanswered letter. He tries to rationalise the epistolary fiction which in Ovid's *Heroides* is plausible only if the letter is thought of as a kind of testament. His Eneas sets sail for Italy in the orderly manner of a knight entering on a crusade ('in partes Ytalie a Cartagine bellaturum se transtulit', as he puts it in a sidenote), not as a thief stealing away by night,[27] and Dido writes her letter to call him back; she kills herself only when he fails to reply:

> Thus whan sche sih non other bote,
> Riht evene unto hire herte rote
> A naked swerd anon sche threste,
> And thus sche gat hireselve reste
> In remembrance of alle slowe.   (IV, 133-7)

Ovid's fleeting letter is thus enveloped, as it were, in a consecutive and rational sequence, and it is tied up with the framework of the lover's confession.

The imperial theme so prominent in both Virgil and Ovid is kept in a marginal position. Eneas is berated not for being slow to follow his destiny, but for neglecting his amorous duties – this looks like the Aeneas of the medieval and the courtly rather than the classical tradition, and seems appropriate to the framework of a love-shrift. But in courtly literature the service due to a lady is coupled with martial duties, and 'laches' is the reproof directed at a knight who neglects these duties. In traditional romance literature the duties of a knight were often linked with fighting the infidels, and interest in these kinds of military exploits was being revived in a new wave of crusades into eastern Europe and the Mediterranean during the fourteenth century; the traditional view of this linkage is expressed by Guillaume de Machaut in *Le dit dou Lyon* (1,368 ff.): true lovers, he says there, 'fight abroad for their lady's honour from Cyprus to Alexandria . . . to the Dry Tree . . . to Prussia . . . to Tartary, among very many other places'.[28] Gower is sceptical of the courtly ethos, and in particular of crusades; not long before telling the example of Eneas and Dido the Confessor warns his penitent that the slaying of Saracens runs counter to the commandment of charity (III, 2,485-546); shortly after his tale of Dido he pours scorn on 'men of armes' who are bent on harrying poor heathens,

> And make manye hastyf rodes,
> Somtime in Prus, somtime in Rodes,
> And somtime into Tartarie   (1,629-31; cf. III, 2,488-9).

Lines like these may be indicative of the altogether unheroic attitude that informs literature of the Ricardian age in general, as J.A. Burrow has worked out;[29] Chaucer expresses similar doubts when his Black Knight praises the lady Blanche for not sending her suitors 'into Walakye, / To Pruyse, and into Tartarye, / To Alysaundre, ne into Turkye'.[30] It seems probable that this attitude is connected with Chaucer and Gower's preference for the Ovidian, as opposed to the Virgilian, point of view, though it is hard to say which caused which. In the case of Gower, the influence of Ovid's poetry is palpable in all of his writings. He may never have read Virgil's *Aeneid* in the original, but he knew his Ovid almost by heart. In his Latin poems he borrows line after line from the works of Ovid, but few, if any, from Virgil; John H. Fisher gives an interesting list of eighteen borrowings from the *Heroides* in Book I of Gower's *Vox clamantis* alone, but none from Virgil.[31] In the Latin works such borrowings are usually made regardless of sense; Gower uses Ovid's works as a quarry for phrases and figures of speech; but he will not have escaped their mellowing influence altogether, and this influence makes itself felt in his English work where, of course, his reasons for borrowing were less nugatory.

The John Gower of the *Confessio amantis* is a much less stern mentor than the author of the *Vox clamantis*, and he is at his best when dealing with figures and situations similar to those he found in the *Heroides*; it is, as Pearsall has noticed, 'women who draw forth Gower's largest humanity'.[32] Gower does not, as might be expected from his previous works, treat these women in an allegorical manner (there is surprisingly little influence from the *Ovide moralisé*). Rather, he brings out their ethical potential, and sometimes he strikes a hidden poetical vein – inadvertently, perhaps, as in the case of Dido's story. A quaint instance of this poetical instinct is his reworking of the simile of the dying swan from the beginning of Ovid's 'Letter of Dido'. If Eneas does tarry much longer, Gower's Dido writes, she will be in a situation like the swan of old:

> Sche scholde stonde in such degre
> As whilom stod a Swan tofore,
> Of that sche hadde hire make lore;
> For sorwe a fethere into hire brain
> She schof and hath hirselve slain;
> As king Menander in a lay
> The sothe hath founde, wher sche lay
> Sprantlende with hire wynges tweie,
> As sche which scholde thanne deie
> For love of him which was hir make. (*Confessio amantis*, IV, 104–13)

The love-sick swan killing herself with a quill might serve as an emblematic frontispiece to Ovid's *Heroides* and similar epistolary fiction. Gower probably found his additions to Ovid's simile in the margin of his manuscript edition of the *Heroides* where the difficult opening lines of the 'Letter of Dido' are often glossed with a reference to animal lore about how the swan prepares for death.[33] Gower turns this into a premonition of Dido's suicide (she thrusts a sword into her heart like a swan who shoves a quill into her brain): it is a creative misunderstanding which seems natural to his sense of order and his sense of pathos.

Geoffrey Chaucer, *The house of fame* and *The legend of good women*

Little is natural in Chaucer. He is more of an artist than his artisan friend, and he seems to be more of a scholar, too. At least he knows Virgil to be a poet, and in both his versions of the tale of Dido he bows to his authority: he quotes the opening lines of the *Aeneid* in his *House of fame* (143–8), and he opens his 'Legend of Dido' with a eulogy on the Mantuan master:

> Glorye and honour, Virgil Mantoan,
> Be to thy name! and I shal, as I can,
> Folwe thy lanterne, as thow gost byforn,
> How Eneas to Dido was forsworn.   (*Legend of good women*, 924–7)

The lines following those just quoted, however, if not the last line of the quotation, already cast a doubt on Chaucer's loyalty by acknowledging a double allegiance to Virgil and to Ovid:

> In Naso and Eneydos wol I take
> The tenor, and the grete effectes make.   (928–9)

The way Chaucer stresses Aeneas' breach of faith has led the well-read listener to expect that the effects he is going to make will be of the Ovidian, not the Virgilian kind, and this applies, as we shall see, not only to his portrait of Dido in the *Legend of good women*, but also to his sketch of her in the *House of fame*.

In both tales Chaucer cuts the Virgilian story down to Ovidian size and assigns by far the better part to Dido; his rendering in Book I of the *House of fame* gives her almost half the story; in the 'Legend of Dido' she is, of course, at the centre of interest, and the events leading up to her meeting with Aeneas are given in a few lines. Such cutting down of an epic story to less than episodic length poses narrative problems that Chaucer may have sought and savoured; if we are to believe Robert Frank, who has made these problems the main subject of his detailed study of the *Legend of good women*, the whole collection was an experiment which Chaucer abandoned as soon as he had learned how to cut a long story short, and how to tell a short story well. For Lisa Kiser, too, the *Legend of good women* is primarily concerned with 'attacking narrative strategies, not saints or classical lovers'.[34]

These conclusions seem to me more appropriate to the unsettled Dido story in the *House of fame*, a poem that serves as an example in a complex argument about the value of literary tradition, than it is to the more confident 'Legend of Dido'. With respect to narrative techniques, the Dido story fits less well in the first book of the *House of fame* than it does in the *Legend of good women*. In the *House of fame* the problems of shortening the story are complicated by an elaborate framework which forces together two highly artificial conventions, the dream vision and the epic *descriptio*: the dreamer–narrator pretends to have found the story of Dido and Aeneas engraved on brass in a temple of glass consecrated to Venus. The reader or listener is constantly kept aware of these conventions by formulae like 'Ther saugh I' at the beginning of verse paragraphs (151, 162, 174, 193, etc.). On the one hand, this is a means of slackening the hold an epic narrator has on his material by making the report sound more personal; Chaucer probably took it over from Book I of the *Aeneid*, where Aeneas finds episodes from the Trojan war (with himself as one of the heroes) depicted in Juno's Carthaginian temple; Virgil refers to what he saw there in similar, but less personal terms ('videt', 456; 'videbat', 466, 'videntur', 494).[35] On the other hand, the device tends to stress the artificiality of the situation and to create a certain distance between the author and his subject.

It is significant, therefore, that Chaucer drops the device as soon as he comes to the Dido part of the story. He inflates this part by adding lyrical and hortatory elements until it breaks up not only the episodic size it had in the *Aeneid*, but also his own visionary frame. Instead of an impersonal narrator we find an avuncular figure handing on Dido's complaints, meting out advice, and matching her fate with that of similar cases. The dreamer stands firmly on Dido's side; he leaves no doubt about the treachery of Aeneas, whose vocation is mentioned only at the end of a catalogue of faithless lovers. Cut off from the main story, this reminder comes as a lame excuse and fails to justify the hero's dealings with the faithful Dido. The catalogue names heroes and heroines from the *Heroides*, and this is not the only hint at the Ovidian shape the African episode has taken in Chaucer's hands. Dido is given ample room to voice her complaints against Aeneas and men in general, and Aeneas, as in Ovid's letter, has no chance to reply. In one of her complaints Dido seems to change the Virgilian (or Mercurian) 'varium et mutabile semper / femina' (*Aeneid*, IV, 569–70) into the sorrowful 'Allas! is every man thus trewe, / that every yer wolde have a newe' (*House of fame*, 301–2), and this looks like one of the sly reverberations of the *Aeneid* that we found in Ovid's 'Letter of Dido'; on the whole, however, there are few Virgilian echoes in the episode, and there is none of the Ovidian innuendo. Chaucer's Dido is a guileless girl, with nothing left of Virgil's fury or of Ovid's vixen. 'We wrechched wymmen konne noon art' (335), is the burden of her swan song, and the dreamer supports it with equally artless comments, criticising, or rather deploring, her blind trust and reducing the significance of Dido's fate to a homely proverb:

Al this seye I be Eneas
And Dido, and hir nyce lest,
That loved al to sone a gest;
Therefore I wol seye a proverbe,
That 'he that fully knoweth th'erbe
May saufly leye hyt to his yë';
Withoute drede, this ys no lye.   (286–92)

The abuse of a woman's hospitality is an elegiac motif – Ovid uses it in
Helen's letter (where it is phrased almost proverbially, 'certus in hospi-
tibus non est amor', *Heroides*, XVII, 191) and in his version of the
Lucrece legend (more tersely phrased 'hostis, ut hospes', *Fasti*, II, 787);[36]
with Chaucer it becomes an important theme not only in the simple tale
of Dido in the *House of fame* but in the whole of his early work, where
trouthe, as Wolfgang Clemen has pointed out, serves as a kind of *leit-
motiv*.[37]

It is the importance of this theme that precludes, I think, an ironic
reading of Dido's simplicity and the homespun wisdom of the dreamer.
Most critics find it hard to believe that the same author who created a
Wife of Bath should be able to share the naivety of such a Dido, and this
has led to ever more sophisticated attempts to unwrap the various layers
of irony underneath the simple surface. But apart from the fact that the
Wife of Bath is a much later creation (there is, however, a later Dido,
too, in the *Legend of good women*) and a completely different, dramatic
character (she is one of the pilgrims, not the heroine of a story), this
view of Chaucer as an essentially ironic artist, which is meant to be
complimentary, in a way curbs in retrospect his artistic freedom and
sincerity: it presupposes that Chaucer, in whatever he writes, will be
Chaucer, that he is unable to set aside his superior knowledge and unable
to use a literary form in its own way. It is a modern, or rather a modernist,
Chaucer, who takes up literary forms only to attack them or to play with
them, and then leaves us with a heap of broken vessels. I would agree
that Chaucer takes up different literary forms and that he tests them; but
he tests them only to breaking point to find out how suitable they are to
carry certain contents to certain destinations, not in order to break them.
No legend could hold a Wife of Bath; if Chaucer had wanted to put such
a wife into one of his stories, it would have been a fabliau; so there is
little point in playing off Dido against the Wife of Bath, or May against
Griseldis. It is of primary importance to respect the laws that govern a
genre, and to assume – at least in early literature – that the author knew
and respected them, too. This is not a matter of form only; the whole
system of literary decorum rests on the assumption that matter, form and
the underlying ethos are related. And the fundamental attitude informing
a legend is simple faith. Chaucer tests this form indeed to breaking point:

he is one of the first to use both the term and the form of the legend for entirely secular purposes[38] – respecting the laws of a genre does not imply the orthodox or wholly traditional use of this genre. And he tests human faith outside the realm of religion; this is one reason why, I think, he chose classical heroines for his *Legend* – most of his serious fiction, like most of Shakespeare's serious drama, is placed outside or on the outskirts of Christianity.

If these rather sweeping general considerations hold, Chaucer is, even in his sketch of Virgil's epic in the *House of fame*, up to more than just cutting down to size the heroic or romantic proportions of a well-known story. This is true of the hero Aeneas whom Chaucer reduces to a womaniser like Paris, Jason and the rest of mankind, and of course there is an ironic contrast to the pretensions connected with these heroes in epic poetry.[39] But the irony is not all-pervasive; in particular, it does not damage his heroine. Dido is also reduced in stature to something like domestic measure, but this does not necessarily make her a hussy. Her child-like trust is not just silly, either, or it is silly in the original sense of pious and pitiable, or even holy.[40] Her trust may be foolish (as it appears to be in the eyes of a worldly-wise narrator), but it does not call for deeper moral considerations, the main response it calls for is that of pity. If trust is one key term in Chaucer's short sketch, pity is another: 'trouthe' or its antonym is three times linked with 'routhe' (331–2; 383–4; 395–6). These terms replace the piety ascribed to Aeneas by Virgil, and the admiration it is supposed to evoke in the *Aeneid*.

Chaucer's is a low-keyed version of the Dido and Aeneas story. 'Trouthe' is a value of the elementary, not of the elevated sort, and lends itself less readily to ironic treatment. That is one reason why Chaucer's tale contrasts sharply with not only the sophistication of the ancient models, but also with the rest of the *House of fame* and its intellectual irony. Dido's complaints, which are Chaucer's additions (he claims the longest of them expressly as his own, 'Non other auctour alegge I', 314) are held in an artless and timeless plain style, replete with well-worn phrases of the simplest kind ('Allas!' quod she, 'what me ys woo!', 300; 'O wel-away that I was born!', 345) and accompanied with appropriate gestures ('She gan to wringe hir hondes two', 299): these have been the conventional constituents of Complaints by forsaken women since antiquity; in such Complaints verbal dexterity is linked with masculine treason. The language of Complaint has traditionally little use for poetic flights. It tends to be repetitive or to founder altogether when poetry touches the bottom of grief. Decorum demands that the style of Complaints be 'plaine and passionate, much like a mourning garment, fitting both the time and the matter', as it is put in a later poem on the Magdalen,[41] and the plainer the style is, the more conventional it appears:

this may account for the drabness of some of the stylistic features in women's complaints. Chaucer's second rendering of the Dido story in his *Legend of good women* shows a gradual divestment towards this final state of plain and passionate speech. In the end we hear the same conventional outcry from 'sely Dido' in the *Legend of good women* that we have heard in the *House of fame*; it comes shortly before Chaucer closes his 'Legenda Didonis martiris' with a quotation from Ovid's 'Letter of Dido'.

The *Legend* begins, we remember, with a praise of Virgil in the grand style, and Dido, too, is introduced as a 'noble queen' (1,004), a shining beauty and foundress of the 'noble toun of Cartage' (1,007). In part this opening in the epic and romantic style may reflect the framework of the *Legend of good women*: the tales are, after all, ordered by a mythic, if not a real, queen, and it would be bad style to introduce the queen of Carthage to Alcestis or the queen of England in a state of destitution. For some while after the stately introduction, the narrator goes on in medieval epic style, describing feasting and hunting in some detail and adding in courtly pageantry for what he saves on Olympian pomp: the heavenly agents behind the scenes are only dimly lit, and Dido's star is made to shine the brighter, for instance, in the added list of gifts which she heaps on her guests (1,114–25; liberality is one of the chief princely virtues). This opening comes as close to a medievalised *Aeneid* as Chaucer can get, except that he elevates Dido where Virgil worshipped Aeneas (cf. *Legend of good women*, 1,039–42, and *Aeneid*, IV, 12 – this shift of emphasis again was called for by the princely order to praise women).[42]

The air of 'glamour and sentiment', as Janet Cowen has called it,[43] does not persist, however; it is only in the beginning of the tale that Chaucer follows Virgil's lantern; in the second half he gradually falls back into Ovidian twilight and casts ever deeper shadows on his heroine. The changes of tone are brought about by the narrator. Throughout the poem he has a voice of his own and interferes more and more freely as he progresses with his tale. He questions the manipulations of the gods (1,020–2; 1,139–45), he gives the lie to Venus (indirectly, 989, 998–9) and to Aeneas (directly, 1,295–302 – lying appears to run in the family).[44] Dido is granted a veritable marriage vow (1,232–9) and the promise given to Sychaeus not to remarry is passed over in silence. She can also claim to be with child (1,323); in the *Aeneid*, we remember, this is a wish (IV, 327–30), in the *Heroides* a possibility (VII, 133). Chaucer's Dido is willing to humble herself even further than Ovid's 'hospita' and offers to become the slave of Aeneas;[45] this submission is cleansed of sexual connotations immediately afterwards when Dido begs to be killed, but to be made an honest wife before, 'For thanne yit shal I deyen as youre wif' (1,322).

The gradual transformation of Dido from noble queen to humble servant, from magnanimous hostess to begging maid finds its turning point in the grotto incident. Dido falls in love before that decisive moment and shows symptoms of the *amor hereos* kind, which the narrator watches with Chaucerian listlessness: 'She waketh, walweth, maketh many a breyd, / As don these lovers, as I have herd seyd.' (1,166–7). She is then shown to have the strength to uphold her love against the opposition of her sister Anna (in the *Aeneid* Anna disperses her scruples). Again it is the narrator who in the cave scene, after Aeneas has elaborately pledged his faith, discloses that Dido has fallen for a cheat. He calls her 'sely Dido' for the first time (1,237), a label that sticks to her to the end (1,336). Dido tries to regain some of her stature in a final dispute with Aeneas, 'I am a gentil woman and a queen' (1,306), but soon afterwards she collapses into the servile state mentioned above and offers to become 'His thral, his servant in the leste degre' (1,313).

Similarly, Aeneas develops gradually from knight to knave. Almost imperceptibly his image as a courtly lover is demolished. His courtesy is of a shallow kind. In retrospect, his heartlessness is hinted at already in the casual way the loss of his first wife in Troy is referred to: 'And by the weye his wif Creusa he les' (945); the indifference of the hero is not explained away with the care Aeneas bestows on his male retinue, his son, his father and his comrades (946–51). On the contrary, this is the 'companye' he will steal to in the night when he leaves Dido, and the verbal correspondance underlines the premonition (951, 1,327).

In Dido's court Aeneas displays all the splendour of a romantic knight, and again a second reading reveals that he shines only in the eyes of the queen: 'he was lyk a knyght' (1,066), 'lyk to been a verray gentil man' (1068), 'wel a lord he semede' (1,074). Later on, after Aeneas has been revealed to be false, the narrator points back to the superficiality of his courtly manners with obvious irony: 'Tak hede now of this grete gentil-man' (1,264). The hidden irony of the tale lies in the fact that Dido is deceived in her love, although she follows the noblest of impulses – her love is induced by pity, not by passion, as in the *Aeneid*: 'hire herte hath pite of his wo, / And with that pite love com in also' (1,078–9). When the dissembler Aeneas gives his pledge (which is not in the *Aeneid*, of course; Gavin Douglas promptly corrects Chaucer, 'Ene maid nevir aith', *Eneados*, I, Prologue, 438), this is more than the narrator can bear; he bursts into a half impatient, half compassionate apostrophe:

> O sely wemen, ful of innocence,
> Ful of pite, of trouthe, and conscience,
> What maketh yow to men to truste so?   (1,254–6)

Gavin Douglas apparently identified the narrator of the *Legend of good women* with Chaucer himself when he called him 'all womanis frend'

(*Eneados*, I, Prologue, 449), but one has to allow for the role of penitent poet that Chaucer has assigned to his narrator in the framework of the *Legend of good women*. The list of amorous activities that follows the apostrophe, headed by the ironic 'Take hede now' quoted above (1,264–76), may also be a reflex of the dissatisfaction with losengers and tattlers in the Court of Love (*Legend of good women*, Prologue, G 328–9) that is visible behind that framework, and is not restricted to the poet as persona.

Dido's fall from high romance to humble complaint is also mirrored in the carefully chosen scenery of her Legend. The epic panorama of the beginning, with burning Troy on the backcloth, and the romantic settings of the middle, the hall and the hunt, give way in the end to indoor scenes and intimate props. In part this change of scenery was prepared for in the classical sources; in Chaucer's tale, however, there appears to be a definite design behind the gradual recession from open spaces to domestic rooms, and in particular to the bedroom where the last debate is set and from which the hero steals away by night (the stealth and, by implication, pettiness of this escape is mentioned four times in shortening intervals, 1,289, 1,327, 1,333, 1,335).[46] In the last scene we see Dido wake up in an empty bed, like Ariadne groping in vain for her lover and finding nothing but the remnants which he left of his spoil like a thief on the run.[47] In Virgil's *Aeneid* Dido dies on her bed ('incubuitque toro', *Aeneid*, IV, 650), but this bed has been carried onto her funeral pyre, and her death is a public event.[48] Chaucer mentions Dido's preparations for her end by sword and fire, but prefers to leave his heroine writing her last letter – the elegiac, not the epic ending.[49]

'The letter of Dydo to Eneas'

At the time when Virgil's *Aeneid* found its first accurate translator in the Scotsman Gavin Douglas an English Anonymous produced a free paraphrase of Ovid's 'Letter of Dido' which was, for a time, closely associated with Chaucer's *Legend of good women*: Richard Pynson printed a 'Letter of Dydo to Eneas' in the second volume of his collection of Chaucer's works entitled *The book of fame* ([1526?], F3v–F5r), where it is added to the minor works, side by side with an equally anonymous 'Complaint of Mary Magdaleyn' which I will take up in chapter 5 of this study. With the inclusion of Mary Magdalen's Complaint, Pynson may have followed a hint in the framework of the *Legend of good women* where Alceste lists a translation of 'Orygenes upon the Maudeleyne' (Prologue, G 418) among the works meant to exonerate the poet in the eyes of Cupid. She does not mention a 'Letter of Dido' but left ample room for further ascriptions in speaking of 'many a lay and many a thyng' (G 420) that Chaucer made besides.

Both the 'Complaint of Mary Magdaleyn' and the 'Letter of Dydo to Eneas' in Pynson's edition are clearly not of Chaucer's age but of the late fifteenth century. This was the time when hints like that of Alceste were gladly taken up as excuses for padding a volume of works by Chaucer, and the unfinished *Legend of good women* offered itself as a convenient bolster. There is almost a vogue of poems in the *Legend of good women*-style around the turn of the fifteenth century, and some of them may well owe their survival to their canonisation as Chauceriana: the 'Letter of Dydo to Eneas' is preserved only in Pynson's edition.[50] To the apocrypha I have mentioned one might add Robert Henryson's *Testament of Cresseid*, the anonymous 'Lament of the Duchess of Gloucester' and Gilbert Banester's 'Legenda Sismond'; thus all of the branches of Complaints treated in later chapters of this study can be said to have a common root in the *Legend of good women*.

Ethel Seaton ascribes the 'Letter of Dydo to Eneas', together with large parts of the *Legend of good women*, to his ubiquitous Sir Richard Roos and explains the marked difference in style by a gap in time of composition between the early (and awkward) 'Letter of Dydo' and the accomplished later *Legend*.[51] As the main source for these poems he names Filippo Ceffi's Italian translation of Ovid's *Heroides*. Sanford Meech has produced evidence that Ceffi's translation may have been used for some of the tales in the *Legend of good women*,[52] but the 'Letter of Dydo to Eneas' is certainly based on a French translation of the *Heroides* which Octovien de Saint-Gelais completed in 1497. This is easily proved by deviations from the Latin original common to Octovien's *Epistres d'Ovide* and the 'Letter of Dydo to Eneas'.[53]

It is quite correct, then, that the English author of the 'Letter of Dydo to Eneas' calls himself translator and professes to be indebted to a French source in the prologue to his work:[54]

> To translate frenche / I am nat redyest
> No marueyle is / sithe I was neuer yet
> In those parties / where I might lāgage gete   (F3v)

The author also admits that he is unversed in rhetoric and learning ('barreyne of eloquence', 'lernyng lacketh', F3v), and this, again, is more than a *captatio benevolentiae*. There is a certain rustic charm in these disclaimers, and the translator may be making a virtue of necessity, but he can also claim that his plain style accords with the rules of decorum:

> But as for me / me thynke playnnesse is best
> After your chere / to shewe your wo
> Shewe outwarde / what ye bere within your brest   (F3v)

There is little of the playfulness and subtlety with which Chaucer or Henryson handle the age-old formula of 'tristia maestum voltum verba decent' to introduce a compassionate persona.[55] With the translator of the 'Letter of Dydo to Eneas' sincerity is all, everything else is dissembling:

> Sithe ye of force / must chuse one of the two
> Eyther among the dissemblers to go
> Or els bee playne / chose after your lust
> But playnnesse is the waye of parfyte trust   (F3v)

We recognise Chaucer's theme of 'trouthe'; its opposite affects this writer even worse than Chaucer's narrator:

> Ah false vntrouth / vnkinde delyng & double
> My hāde quaketh / whan I write thy name

With him the story in hand is cut in black and white right from the start:

> this rufull songe
> Of poore Dydo / forsaken by great wronge
> Of false Ene / who causeth my hand to shake
> For great furye / that I ayenst hym take   (F3v)

The passionate interest this author chooses to take in his subject contrasts markedly with the attitude taken by humanist translators and commentators of Virgil's episode, and this appears to be a matter of deliberation even with an unaccomplished writer like him. When he disclaims learning he adds 'For lernyng lacketh / and reason is nat clere' (F3v), and this attitude is exactly opposed to that of his near-contemporary Gavin Douglas, a man not only of learning but also a defender of reason, who in his Prologue to the Fourth Book of the *Eneados* exclaims, 'Se, quhou blynd luffis inordinate desyre / Degradis honour, and resson doith exile!' (250–1) For Douglas, Dido's case is another fall, not only from the classical virtues, 'Fra nobylnes, welth, prudens and temperance, / In britell appetite fall, and wild dotage' (224–5), but also from the Christian God: 'Then is thi lufe inordinat, say I, / Quhen ony creatur mair than God thou luffis' (128–9).

With interpretations like these, Douglas closes ranks with earlier humanist exegetes of Virgil's *Aeneid*, notably Boccaccio who in his *Genealogie* had also argued that Virgil introduced Dido into the epic to demonstrate the disastrous effects of unbridled passion:

Quod sub velamento latet poetico, intendit Virgilius per totum opus ostendere quibus passionibus humana fragilitas infestetur, et quibus viribus a constanti viro superentur. Et cum iam non nullas ostendisset, volens demonstrare, quibus ex causis ab appetitu concupiscibile in lasciviam rapiamur, introducit Dydonem.[56]

The author of the 'Letter of Dydo to Eneas' moves on an altogether different, lower plane, not only of style but also of values. There are no invocations: he looks in vain for goddesses or heroines to be invoked; Niobe, Myrrha, Byblis, Medea or Lucretia are of no use, Venus is partial and Juno was unable to safeguard the marriage she arranged, so he settles for one of the harpies, 'ye cruell Celeno' (F3v). And there is no high moralising, only pity for the human frailty Boccaccio denounces; the virtues at stake are of an ordinary sort, the moral to be drawn from Dido's fall is a simple warning directed at good women in the envoy, 'Beware of loue / sithe men be full of crafte' (F5r). This is the same homespun wisdom that Chaucer's dreamer drew from the story in his *House of fame*, and it will still be drawn from similar, originally public-spirited stories if they are seen from the good woman's point of view in Shakespeare's time. Samuel Daniel, for example, says in the Argument to his 'Letter from Octavia' about the truant Antony that he, in his 'licentious soueraignty',

could not truly descend to the priuate loue of a ciuill nurtred Matron, whose entertainment bounded with modesty, and the nature of her education, knew not to clothe her affections in any other colours, than the plaine habit of truth:[57]

The main points our translator makes in his rendering of Ovid's (or rather Octovien's) 'Letter of Dido' are set accordingly. Dido's misfortune begins when she lends her ear to the grand report Aeneas gives of his heroic exploits. Contrary to the source, where it is only alluded to, this archetypal scene (its chief example is Othello's story of his life in I, iii, which inspired one of the stock scenes in nineteenth-century melodrama) gains prime importance in the second part of the English letter. The first part follows Ovid fairly closely, up to the passage where Dido insinuates that Aeneas may have shouldered neither *pater* nor Penates (*Heroides*, VII, 79–80). Apparently this sorted ill with the guileless nature that had been ascribed to Dido earlier in the poem (terms like 'trust' and 'trouthe' ring through the letter with even greater insistence than in Chaucer's *Legend of good women*): the author swerves from his copy-book, jumps at Ovid's 'tua fallere lingua' (81), and gives Dido a chance to remember the tearful scene when Aeneas told her the story of his life:

> I am nat the fyrst / I knowe for certayne
>   Whom your langage / hath caused to cõplayne
> But ye that were / well lerned for to lye
>   Haue abused me alas / through my folly
> your pitous wordes / whã I herd with myn eres
>   My eyes were moued to stãde ful of teres
> After / my hert moche enclyned to pyte

> Was holly moued / to haue your amyte
> That redy wyll / and my defaut sodayne
> Shall nowe be cause / of my later payne   (F4v)

A similar passage of mournful memory ('I was to blame / to enclyne and reioyce / In the swete wordes of your pitous voice', F5r) supplants Dido's uneasy thoughts about the pledge she gave her first husband Sychaeus in the *Heroides* ('Exige, laese pudor, poenas! violate Sychaei', 97). Dido's guilt, so relentlessly expounded by the humanists, is reduced to the fault of having been misled by her soft heart. It is by purifications like these that even promiscuous queens like Cleopatra can be made household doves. In the end, Dido presents herself in phrases which must have reminded a medieval reader of the Lady of Sorrows: the sword Aeneas had left ('to encrease my sorowe') is not the first that will pierce her heart:

> This shall nat be the fyrst glayue or darte
> That hath peersed me to the herte
> For afore this / loue that setteth folke to scole
> Wounded me sore   (F5r)[58]

In the British Library's unique copy of Pynson's *Book of fame* the 'Letter of Dydo to Eneas' is headed by a woodcut representing Dido's death by sword in a quasi-hagiographical manner.[59] Together with the double-column, black-letter appearance of the text, this turns perusing the poem into an almost devotional exercise. Considering the scarcity of the volume, there cannot have been too many worshippers, and, from an artistic point of view, what the others missed was not an exquisite experience. Historically, however, the letter forms an important link in the tradition of classical literature in the vernacular and on a popular level, a tradition that is also evident in ballads such as 'The wandering prince of Troy', subtitled 'or Queen Dido', which bears a number of Ovidian features.[60] A more sophisticated audience had to wait for the appearance of George Turberville's literal translation of *The heroical epistles of Publius Ovidius Naso* in 1567.

3

Philomela and Lucretia: classical heroines in English Complaints

> Beauteous in a wilderness
>
> S.T. Coleridge, 'Christabel', 321

Libertinae and *matronae* in Ovid's *Metamorphoses*

The 'Letter of Dydo to Eneas' is not an exercise in the classical spirit; it shows neither Virgil's high ethos nor does it share Ovid's relativist ethics. With its insistence on the basic virtues of 'trouthe' and 'pité' it is closer to medieval than to classical thinking, particularly that of the Ricardian period. Nevertheless, some of the features of this second-hand translation are significant beyond the translator's intention. One of these features is the negative invocation in the prologue, where the author looks in vain for support from Dido's classical sisters in distress:

> What remedy / where shulde I seke socour
> Of Niobe / of Myrra / or of Byblis
> Of Medea or Lucrece / the romayne flour
> None of thē all / may graūt me helpe in this (F3v)

The ease with which this group's figures mix, figures which a more discriminate mind would have separated as *matronae* and *libertinae*, as good and bad women, has a medieval aspect, although it may go back to Ovid, who has a similarly mixed catalogue of lovers in his *Remedia amoris* (55–68). One remembers, too, the mural in the brass temple of Chaucer's *Parliament of fowls* (280–94) or the procession of lovers at the end of Gower's *Confessio amantis* (VIII, 2,550–656).[1]

Renaissance authors distinguished more sharply between wheat and chaff. They tried to develop a female heroic ideal, and they proved to be a good deal more literal and doctrinal than their medieval predecessors. This can be inferred from the way they handled the heroical epistle in the later sixteenth century. Authors of translations or adaptations of the *Heroides* took the title of this collection seriously and looked for the true heroic spirit in its letters. Since this spirit was felt to be lacking in many cases, several of them undertook to write reply letters which gave them a chance to counterbalance the deficient female with a commanding male voice. Thus John Shepery (or Shepreve) wrote a neo-Latin refutation of Phaedra's scandalous letter, *Hyppolitus Ovidianae Phaedrae respondens* (published Oxford, 1586, but composed under the reign of Henry VIII) with the Egyptian Joseph in mind (at least that is how the Elizabethan editor, George Etherege, puts it).[2] Two generations later an anonymous F.L. gave Aeneas a chance, at last, to answer Dido's letter and added a reply to his translation of Ovid's *Heroides* VII. Both letters were published, quite appropriately, as an appendix to F.L.'s translation of *Ovidius Naso his remedy of love* (1600; 'Dido to Aeneas', E4r–G2r; 'Aeneas to Dido', G2v–H3v). The reply letter has a slightly softer appeal than the hard-headed rebukes of Hippolytus, another hunter with the marble quality of Shakespeare's Adonis, but in the end Aeneas asks Dido to acknowledge the superior reasons that govern the upper regions and to find comfort in the thought that he, too, has been overruled:

> Religion, Honour, Destinies decree,
> Three by poor one, how can resisted be?   (*Remedy of love*, H3v)

Elizabethan England was proud of its history, and translations and complementations of the *Heroides* were soon countered with imitations based on the Matter of Britain. Most prominent among the imitators was Michael Drayton, who won himself the title of an English Ovid with a collection of *England's heroical epistles* (1597), which became his most popular work. Drayton wanted to improve on his model in several ways: he tried to infuse his letters with an heroic and historic air, and he tried to give more balanced views by writing pairs of letters instead of singles. In the preface to the second edition of his *Heroical epistles* (1598), he defines the epithet 'heroical' as 'nothing els but to haue a great and mighty spirit, far aboue the earthly weaknesse of men' (A2r). Though he claims Ovid's authority for the definition he can hardly have found this spirit in the *Heroides*.[3] With regard to the single letters, this will have become apparent in my analysis of the 'Letter of Dido'. And the double letters are unqualified to support the claim: the pairs of letter-writers are united in a single erotic, rather than heroic, spirit. It is a spirit of amorous complicity, open in the Paris–Helena letters, unavowed but nonetheless discernible in the case of the coy Cydippe.[4]

In contrast, most Renaissance imitators used the second letter to set the balance right between heterodox proposal and orthodox reply. Besides rectifying the asymmetric single-letter form of the *Heroides* these authors developed narrative genres which enabled them to set right Ovid's epic heritage. This was, first of all, a matter of separating what was mixed in earlier Ovidian tradition: distinct genres evolved which dealt with *libertinae* like Myrrha in light-hearted erotic and with *matronae* like Lucretia in heavy-minded tragic epyllia. The Complaint form that I am mainly concerned with in this study is related to all these genres: it is an elegiac narrative which takes both *matronae* and *libertinae* seriously, makes use of the first-person-singular voice of the heroical epistle, but takes its subject matter from the great epic cycles. One of the aims of this chapter is to define the position of the heavy-hearted Complaint between these rival genres.

Ovid shows a predilection for *libertinae*, not only in his erotic poetry, but also in his mottled epic *Metamorphoses*, and many of the erotic epyllia of the late sixteenth century took their subject matter from his epic. Drayton probably had such epyllia in mind when he made the chaste Matilda in his *Heroical epistles* cry out against 'Lascivious Poets' and their *puellae sceleratae* such as Myrrha, Scylla and Byblis.[5] There were quite a few 'lascivious poets' by the time Drayton wrote his *Heroical epistles*, and illustrious names among them; the genre of erotic epyllia had been launched by Thomas Lodge's *Scilla's metamorphosis* in 1589 and was already past the double peak it reached in 1593 with Marlowe's *Hero and Leander* and Shakespeare's *Venus and Adonis*. It reached a trough later in William Barksted's *Mirrha* (1607) and *The Scourge of Venus* (1613), another Myrrha-poem, probably by Henry Austin, which really can be called lascivious.[6] The genre followed an apparently inherent bias towards allegory or satire, which is already evident in Lodge's *Scilla*, and is made explicit in the subtitles of later poems such as Michael Drayton's *Endymion and Phoebe: Idea's Latmus* (1595) or John Weever's *Faunus and Melliflora: The origin of our English satires* (1600). It is a tendency which deflects from the personal view of the figures in these poems towards some kind of public outlook. To a certain extent this tendency is indigenous to the epic form with its detached narrator; these authors, however, use the narrator's freedom much more intrusively than, for instance, Ovid does in his *Metamorphoses*.

Naturally, an epyllion looks dwarfish if compared to epics of the grander size, even to Ovid's *Metamorphoses* which is, in a way, a collection of epyllia held together by a common theme and a chronological frame. In taking single tales out of this framework the Elizabethan authors followed a line already drawn out by Ovid himself. Like Ovid's epic, the epyllia deal with heroes and heroines of mythic origin, with immortal gods and nymphs made immortal. The *dramatis personae* are no different from those that act in tragedy and epic since Homer's time. Compared with their Homeric models, however (and with Virgil's imitations of them), the heroic appeal of these figures had already shrunk considerably in the *Metamorphoses*. There is no single hero, but at best a single theme; there are few martial deeds, but many amorous pursuits, with comic or macabre effects (gods panting after nymphs, nymphs changed into plants). Ovid retains all the epic features in his *Metamor-*

phoses, particularly the elated style and the numinous air, but the effect is rarely uplifting or purifying: rather it is amusing, and sometimes it seems morbid.[7] There is, occasionally, a glimpse of the dark forces driving gods and men in the *Metamorphoses*, but these have only recently been unearthed. The authors of erotic epyllia disregarded the darker forces behind the myths, as they had to disregard the great plan behind Ovid's epic. They took the *Metamorphoses* as a string of stories from which they picked their pearls. These they were content to polish, and they further reduced their size in the process.

I will give but a few instances. One is the way formal descriptions are handled in the epyllia: they become ever more dainty and concentrate on items of dress. An example would be Chapman's description of Hero's scarf in the Fourth Sestiad of his continuation of Marlowe's *Hero and Leander*.[8] Another is the treatment of the etiological element which constitutes many myths: it is frequently exaggerated out of all proportion. Barksted, for example, explains the reddening of the sun at dawn as his blushing at the sight of Myrrha stealing out of her father's room.[9] And lastly, the erotic element which should hold the epyllion together often undermines its significance because the sexual comedy is coarsened into farce, as it is in Shakespeare's *Venus and Adonis* when the middle-aged goddess is made to grasp after a boy.

The air of parody that surrounds the epyllion, its dwarfish personnel still acting against an epic background, evaporates and is watched from Olympian heights. A change of perspective from the epic to the personal, from distant observer to dwarfed agent, brings changes reaching far beyond mere technicalities. The difference becomes obvious if one compares, for instance, Ariadne's letter, which ends in despair (*Heroides*, X), with her story in the *Metamorphoses*, which ends in her apotheosis (VIII, 174–82), or the elegant epyllion by Catullus (*Carmen* 64), which adorns a wedding. Looked at from below and before the happy ending is in sight, the mythic incident makes no sense, and the narrator feels insecure. The dark element present in every myth, and often visible under the surface of Ovid's *Metamorphoses*, makes itself felt. The brute sexual force, for example, which drives even the most comical hunt of nymph by god, is not as easily civilised into ceremony or harmonised into cosmic nature from this point of view.

There are a number of female heroines, both of the *libertinae* and the *matronae* kind, in the *Metamorphoses* who might lend themselves, like Ariadne, to both the epic and the elegiac mode of presentation. One might even wonder why Ovid did not add a letter of Byblis or Alcyone in his *Heroides*. Byblis does, in fact, write a letter in the *Metamorphoses* (IX, 517–63; surprisingly, Drayton transfers her trepidations on settling down for the task to his nun Matilda; cf. *Metamorphoses*, IX, 523–4, and

'Matilda to John', 35–8); her situation is comparable to that of Canace in his *Heroides*, XI, and the duplication may have kept him from including her in his circle of letter-writing ladies (but then, all of the *Heroides* are variations on a single theme). The main reason probably was, however, that Byblis like other mythic heroines is too far removed from common experience; she is too depraved, and Alcyone too devoted, they both leave little room for doubt and deliberation and are best treated in a manner that allows for the wonderful and the outrageous. Most of the heroines chosen for the *Heroides* are taken from the borderland between myth and history, and this seems more appropriate for the insecurity and fragility which looks strained even in heroines like Ariadne or Medea. It is significant that in the case of Ariadne the divine rescue is left out; Chaucer must have seen the reason why: he always stops short of a metamorphosis.

Philomela in legend, ballad and epyllion

Ovid, Chaucer, Gower, Caxton

The difference in treatment between the *Metamorphoses* and the *Heroides* is rooted in different attitudes which are not necessarily bound to a definite genre or a metrical form like the epic hexameter or the elegiac distich. In German it is easier to distinguish between the epic as a definite genre (by using the noun, 'Epos') and the less definite epic attitude (by using the adjective 'episch'), and the Swiss critic Emil Staiger has taken advantage of this distinction to establish a basic difference between attitude and genre.[10] Different attitudes can be mixed in a single genre (the ballad, for example, is made up of lyric, epic and dramatic elements), and they can modify different genres (there are, for instance, epic dramas and dramatic novels); therefore, mode is perhaps the better English term to designate this modifying power. To Emil Staiger's list of basic terms (epic, lyric, dramatic) I would add the elegiac, again as a definite form (the elegiac metre and, for example, the erotic elegy written in that metre) and a poetical attitude which is not so easy to define and can influence quite different forms and genres; in the field of narrative poetry it finds, as I hope to establish by examples first, and then, in my final chapter, by precept also, its most eloquent expression in women's Complaints.

Poetic attitudes like the epic and the elegiac may be adaptable (up to a point) to different forms, but they are not independent of subject matter. Most of the uneasiness, I think, that arises from some of the tales and letters of tragic women in the *Metamorphoses* and the *Heroides* is due to the fact that these women are ill suited to the epic or the elegiac attitudes underlying these poems, and that the stylistic virtuosity needed to adapt them to their surroundings makes their tales or letters look like *tours de force*. With her fury and her magic Medea, who writes a heroical epistle, might have cut a better figure in the *Metamorphoses*, whereas the gentle, fearful Alcyone, who is made the subject of a metamorphosis, looks like an ideal letter-writer. Perhaps more can be said in favour of even the material demands of decorum than modern emancipative criticism has allowed.

There are border-cases, of course, figures whom it is possible to treat in either mode, and these are of special interest. One of these border-cases is, I think, the fall of Philomela, neither matron nor *libertina*, but surely one of Ovid's most moving creations. She might serve as a test case for the interdependence of matter, form and attitude.

A metamorphosis, and myth in general, usually presents some kind of solution to a painful or puzzling situation, be it the explanation for a name or a natural phenomenon. In the background of the tale of Philomela we find an ancient animal fable which explains the creation of a number of birds, chiefly the nightingale, but also, in different versions, the swallow and the hoopoe. The names and persons of this fable had become confused in the course of time, and Ovid, who tells Philomela's story in his *Metamorphoses* (VI, 424–674), confounded them still further. In particular, he did not settle the question of who was changed into what, which is somewhat disappointing in a book which has been called the *Who's who* of Classical mythology. Even as learned a classicist as Matthew Arnold was bewildered. His 'Philomela' poem begins with the speaker listening to a 'tawny-throated' nightingale (line 2), and apparently identifies Philomela with the bird of song. In the latter part of the poem, however, the speaker imagines the bird as reading, with 'hot cheeks and seared eyes', the 'too clear web' into which is woven her 'dumb sister's shame' ('Philomela', 20–1). According to Ovid's version of the story, this would point to Philomela's sister Procne who reads in a piece of cloth the news that her husband Tereus has raped her sister. Tereus has also cut out Philomela's tongue and shut her away in the forests of Thracia, so Philomela has only her needlework to make her shame known. Arnold must have used an earlier Greek version of the fable where the wife of Tereus (Homer calls her Aedon, 'nightingale') is eventually turned into the singing bird: Procne slaughters her son Itys and serves him as a dish to her husband in revenge for the outrage Tereus has done to her sister. After the horrible meal and to prevent further slaughters Zeus changes them all into birds: Procne into a nightingale (she laments the death of her child in her song), Philomele into a swallow (she can only twitter because of her mutilated tongue), and Tereus into a hoopoe (for no particular reason, unless it be that he wears a crest, 'in tokne he was a kniht', as John Gower supposes, who turns him into a lapwing because that is the most treacherous bird; *Confessio amantis*, V. 6044). Ovid was not, like Gower, interested in clearing up the etiological or moral significance of the metamorphoses; his interest lay in the processes of change, not its results; he did nothing to prevent the twittering Philomele changing roles, or voices, with her sister. She became a nightingale, and poets like Arnold were able to soften her pain into song.

The song of the nightingale was to become the chief motif of the myth for Renaissance and Romantic poets; medieval authors took up the etiological thread and spun it out into elaborate allegorical webs – with the exception of Chaucer who in his 'Legend of Philomela' stresses the emotional elements of the story, for instance the long and tearful leave-taking of 'sely Philomene' from her father Pandion (*Legend of good women*, 2,279–307), and omits, as he usually does, the metamorphoses altogether. Chaucer leaves his heroine in the end, together with her sister, in the Thracian wilderness, locked up in a stronghold, 'And thus I late hem in here sorwe dwelle' (2,382). Dido was thus left with Anna; we shall meet Shakespeare's Lucrece with her maid and Warner's Elizabeth Gray with her infant sons in similarly isolated surroundings (*Lucrece*, 1,212–95; *Albion's England*, VII, xxxiv); it is one of the stock situations of the elegiac narrative.[11]

By leaving his heroines in the wilderness Chaucer cuts off the whole of Progne's horrible revenge – and this is, of course, in keeping with the framework of the *Legend*; even Progne has to be a good woman, 'With al humblesse of wifhod, word and chere' (2,269).[12] Gower keeps both revenge and metamorphoses in his extensive version of the story (*Confessio amantis*, V, 5,551–6,047), but he mitigates the cruel elements and dwells on the poetical justice meted out to the protagonists (Itys is, as usual, left aside): Tereus, who robbed Pandion of a daughter, loses his son, and the slaughter of Itys is as unnatural as the rape of Philomel. The metamorphoses are drawn out accordingly; the marvellous, like the macabre, gains a tropological rather than etiological significance. This is only another kind of rationalisation of the myth, though not as lame as some of the reasons given in late antiquity (Pausanias explains the metamorphosis of Tereus by the fact that hoopoes were first watched in Megara, near the tomb of Tereus).[13] Gower's rationalisation uses the supernatural elements of the myth to show the workings of divine justice; this is stressed by a number of prayers which are answered in the end, and he curbs the natural, destructive elements at work in the myth by explaining them in terms of a conventional psychology of animal love: it enters Tereus through the eyes and puts him into a rage, but he still looks like an unreasonable, yet not completely irrational ravisher: 'he was so wod / That he no reson understod' (5,639–40).

Despite the curtailment of its supernatural and cruel elements, the story retains more of its irritation in Chaucer's legend because there are fewer rational and explanatory elements and it concentrates on the emotional states of the heroines instead. But Gower's was the more usual practice in the later Middle Ages. Caxton, for example, whose prose version of the *Metamorphoses of Ovid* (1480) is based on the *Ovide moralisé*, rationalises too, though he moves like Pausanias mainly on the first, historical plane of exegesis. In an appendix on the 'sens hystoryal of the fable' he looks for natural explanations for the etiological elements of the myth, some of which must have sounded strange to English ears. Following his source, he reads, for instance, the French 'Occy, occy, occy' into the nightingale's song.[14] He found many followers nevertheless.

Philomela ballads: George Gascoigne and Martin Parker

Poetical explanations of the nightingale's song have their own tradition in several languages, beginning with Aeschylus, whose choir in *Agamemnon* understands the nightingale (that is Procne) as crying after her son 'Ityn! Ityn!', and well established by the time George Gascoigne wrote his *Complaint of Phylomene* in 1576.[15] The poem is cast in the form of a dream vision. Instead of the usual May morning, however, there is an April night opening: the poet listens to a nightingale chiding a number of more cheerful songsters and then bursting into a solitary complaint of which he understands only the fragments 'Tereu, Tereu', 'fy, fy, fy, fy, fy', 'Jug, Jug, Jug' and finally 'Nemesis, Nemesis'. Puzzling about this he falls asleep, leaning on his walking staff.

In this opening Gascoigne combines three strains of the Philomela tradition: the nightingale as herald of spring, as partner in a debate and as love's victim. All of these were carried on into later poetry, most notably in Keats's 'Ode to a nightingale', Swinburne's 'Itylus' and T.S. Eliot's *Waste Land* (where the 'Jug, Jug' is lined with a dirty meaning, 103).[16] The spring evening framework chosen by Gascoigne, however – a later addition to the poem which was begun in 1562 – looks back to medieval models; William C. Wallace has pointed out a close parallel in Lydgate's 'A sayenge of the Nightingale' in his edition of Gascoigne's poem.[17] This framework for the *visio*, which contains Phylomene's story, is carefully chosen; the reader is anxious to have the puzzle of the scraps of song solved and, of course, he is not disappointed. Gascoigne relieves him with a detailed explication along the lines of allegorical commentaries such as the *Ovide moralisé* (not of Lydgate who reads a spiritual meaning into the nightingale's song). Gascoigne adds a touch of slapstick in the end when the dreamer is started out of his slumber because his staff has slipped.

The inlaid 'Fable of Philomela' is told by Nemesis who has appeared to the dreamer like the figure of Sorrow in Sackville's 'Induction' to the *Mirror for magistrates*. Gascoigne's tale of Philomela is not, however, a proper fable, nor a first person Complaint in the *Mirror for magistrates* style, but rather a ballad-like paraphrase of Ovid's epyllion. It is dealt out in Poulter's Measure, Gascoigne's equivalent to the classic hexameters, and this gives his version a sort of elegiac limp appropriate to the subtitle 'An Elegye'.[18] With regard to imagery and setting, too, the classic tale is transported to more familiar English ground and stripped of its more decorative trappings in the passage. Ovid's eagle, 'Iovis ales', rather a strange sight on board the ship of Tereus anyway, is turned into a homely 'catte' (*Metamorphoses*, VI, 517; *Complaint*, 182), the stately farmhouse ('stabula alta') into a 'sheepcote' which Gascoigne adapts quite naturally to the following stock-in-trade comparison of Phylomene with a lamb (*Metamorphoses*, VI, 521; *Complaint*, 190). This domestication goes hand in hand with the sort of simple concern and homely maxims which we have already noted in Chaucer's *Legend of good women*: 'The foe in friendly wise, / Is many times embraste' (73–4; about Tereus' reception at Pandion's court in Athens); 'What could the virgine doe?' 'Ahlas what should she fight? / Fewe women win by fight' (209, 213–14; Phylomene facing the advances of Tereus in Thracia).

Gascoigne's narrator, however, is less obtrusive than Chaucer's; this is probably one of the effects of the ballad form, which demands a more detached attitude of its singer and a more dramatic performance altogether. The result is a lively, but rather crude poem compared with Chaucer's legend: the crucial incidents are quickened by dialogue, but also coarsened in broadside style by gory details, particularly in the violation and the vengeance scenes. This is how the narrator lingers after Tereus has cut out Phylomene's tongue:

> I blush to tell this tale,
> But sure best books say this:
> That yet the butcher did not blush
> Hir bloudy mouth to kisse.
>
> And ofte hir bulke embrast,
> And ofter quencht the fire,
> Which kindled had the furnace first,
> Within his foule desire.   (321–8)

The bloody kisses are Gascoigne's invention; he similarly revels in the horrible details of the revenge.

Despite these crudities, Gascoigne's 'Fable of Philomela' is an interest-

ing document in several respects: it popularises a classical subject in the
same way the ballad of the 'Wandering prince of Troy' mentioned in
the previous chapter popularised the Dido story, and perhaps gives an
instance of who composed such popular ballads – not necessarily gentlemen on horseback, but not necessarily wandering minstrels, either.
Douglas Bush has said that such popularisations were a feature of the
1560s; one should add that the plain style treatment of epic material had
been prepared for by late medieval examples, particularly poems in the
wake of Chaucer's *Legend of good women*.[19] Ballads such as these went
a long way towards handling Ovidian material in a homely style; they
also moved in the direction of the *Mirror for magistrates*, though
Gascoigne does not yet take the step towards first person narrative. He
does, however, pick up some of the more disturbing points in the
Philomela story, points that are not so easily resolved in explanations à
l'*Ovide moralisé*. One of these points is what we might call, in Gascoigne's terms, the bale of beauty. He mentions this twice in his poem,
once in the beginning, with reference to Pandion's daughters, 'And
bewtie was the guileful bayte, / Which caught their lives in Snare' (27–8),
and again in the middle when Phylomene stitches her story into a piece
of cloth:

> With curious needle worke,
> A garment gan she make,
> Wherin she wrote what bale she bode,
> And al for bewties sake.   (369–72)

The paradox that beauty excites passion, and the purer it is the fiercer it is the
passion, is taken up as a central theme in later Elizabethan Complaints.
  Another, equally pregnant, point is the one on which the poem closes;
it might be called the solace of song: Nemesis, the divine narrator, introduces it somewhat complacently thus:

> Ne can she now complaine,
> (Although she lost hir tong)
> For since that time, ne yet before,
> No byrde so swetely soong.
>
> That gift we Gods hir gave,
> To countervaile hir woe,
> I sat on bench in heaven my selfe
> When it was graunted so.   (761–8)

This seems to present rather a snug solution to the problems raised by
the Philomela myth, and the fact that it is the solution preferred by
Victorian poets (for example Matthew Arnold in his 'Philomela' and
Robert Bridges in his 'Nightingales') might be taken to support this,

although they were able to see the dark side of this relation, too, by turning it inside out: there is little art but that it rise out of pain. In comparison with the late medieval *Ovide moralisé* tradition, however, it is worthy of note that Gascoigne does not moralise his, or the nightingale's, song, but gives an aesthetic answer to the question of how to cope with unwarranted woe.

Gascoigne may only have stumbled on this solution, and his narrator drops it straightaway to enter on a historical explanation of the lapwing's behaviour which is as elaborate as any moralisation before. One of his descendants, however, the most famous ballad-monger of the following century, Henry Parker, discards moralisations and explanations altogether in his poem on the myth, *The nightingale warbling forth her owne disaster: or the rape of Philomela* (1632). Parker makes use of the form the elegiac narrative had developed in the meantime, and after a spring opening similar to Gascoigne's lets his Philomela recount her own story in seventy-two rhyme royal stanzas, the metre of the *Mirror for magistrates* Complaints. Parker seems fully aware of the tragic potential of his subject, but sadly ignorant of his predecessors, when he describes his poem in the advertisement as 'a Tragedy so unparaleld, that I wonder why none of our temporary Laureats have undertaken it before' (A4r). He seems not only ignorant of Gascoigne's *Complaint*, whose predilection for stark and homely details he obviously shares (his Itys is made into 'minc'd pies, / Which at the banquet was the chiefest dish', C2v), but, more surprisingly, of a contemporary version of the story too: Patrick Hannay's *The nightingale* (1622), a poem which deserves a closer look.[20]

Patrick Hannay, *The nightingale*

There is an affiliation between the Philomela myth and plaintive music which is, to a great part, due to the association with the nightingale and its enchanting song. To a lesser degree, such an affinity exists between laments of wronged women and musical means of presentation in general, whether the myth has them changed into singing birds or not. The root underlying this affinity shows in one of the most persistent motifs of the tradition of women's Complaints: that of the speechlessness of grief. Ovid's Dido composes her letter like a swan-song, and even modern critics have voiced the opinion that all of Ovid's *Heroides* were meant to be sung.[21] Erwin Rohde has written about the affinity of elegiac poetry with balladry, and dozens of Dido or of Ariadne operas would testify to its closeness to vocal music.[22] I mentioned the hundred or so Dido operas above. Ariadne is equally well-known for her musical career: she figured in one of Monteverdi's earliest operas (*Arianna*, 1608) of which little more than the famous lament is preserved; she stands at the beginning of the melodrama in Georg Benda's *Ariadne auf Naxos* (1774), which combines a spoken monologue with musical accompaniment; and she appears in Richard Strauss's *Ariadne auf Naxos* (1912, 1916), which in its second version places her complaint in a musical framework similar to Catullus' original epyllion in *Carmen* No. 64. Closer to Patrick Hannay in time and space we find William Cartwright's 'Ariadne deserted by Theseus', published in 1651 in his *Comedies, tragi-comedies, with other poems*,[23] but written much earlier (Cartwright, Oxford dramatist and 'Son of Ben', died in 1643). Cartwright's libretto provides an interesting parallel to Hannay's *Nightingale*. It was influenced by Monteverdi's *Arianna* and set to music by Henry Lawes, who opened his first book of *Ayres and dialogues* (1653) with its text. Though much shorter than Hannay's poem (102 lines to 1,680), Cartwright's 'Ariadne' shows comparable qualities; both poems have long and undulating stanza forms, which are irregular with Cartwright, and regular, canzone-like, with Hannay, and both are easily adaptable to a singing voice. Hannay, in fact, prefixes a melody to his text and expects, apparently, the poem to be sung along its lines. George Saintsbury, who incorporated the poem in his collection of Caroline verse, finds the idea that the whole poem should be sung 'a curious one'.[24] He also finds it odd that Hannay's companion piece to *The nightingale*, a long, historical Complaint called *Sheretine and Mariana*, should be written in the first person. In both cases he may have been misled by contemporary epics, for example William Chamberlayne's *Pharonnida*, to expect another of the '"Heroic Poems" of which the collection and communication to the student is one of the main objects of [his] book'.[25] I have mentioned in my introduction that pairs of poems consisting of an epyllion and a Complaint were frequently published together at the height of the Ovidian influence around the turn of the seventeenth century. It seems likely, therefore, that Hannay's *Nightingale* and *Mariana* look back on the Elizabethan elegiac tradition, not forward to the Caroline epic.

Patrick Hannay's *Nightingale* can hardly be called a proper epyllion, though, not only because of its lyricism and unusual stanza form (the form most widely used in epyllia is the sixain stanza), but also because it is a first person narrative like the Complaint of Mariana. In addition, there is the framework we have now come to expect in Philomela poems: the poet meets a nightingale in a park and he listens to her plaintive song. It is a *de luxe* edition of the conventional spring opening. The first lines already give an impression of the melodiousness of the canzone stanza with its three staves and two wheels and the exquisiteness of the diction:

WALKING I chanc'd into a shade,
Which top-in-twining trees had made

Of many several kinds.
There grew the high aspiring elm,
With boughs bathing in gum-like balm,
    Distilling through their rinds.
The maple with a scarry skin
    Did spread broad pallid leaves:
The quaking aspen light and thin
    To th'air light passage gives:
        Resembling still
        The trembling ill
Of tongues of womankind,
        Which never rest,
        But still are prest
To wave with every wind.   (1–16)

Ringing rhymes and alliterations, symbols and emblems mix as in the mannerist 'top-in-twining trees' to produce a luscious atmosphere; Hannay obviously tries to out-Ovid Ovid and his followers with highly sensuous detail. This indulgence, however, does not result in slackness of composition. The same niceness that has gone into the first stanza marks the design of the entire poem. The first part of the story, up to the meeting between Tereus and Philomela, is stretched to about half the length of the Complaint. This creates a well-balanced construction, but considerably retards Philomela's appearance on the scene. When she does enter eventually, it is with great aplomb: the centre of the tale, a kind of bravura aria, is filled with Philomela's account of the effect her ravishing beauty has on this occasion (stanzas xlix–lix out of the total 105 stanzas).

The stanzas leading up to this centrepiece tell of courtly and domestic festivities. There are extensive reports of the wooings and later doings of Tereus, who is introduced as a proud warrior affected by *amor hereos*. Progne's beauty disarms and almost unmans him: he is hardly able to press his suit, while Progne plays the coquette. Their marriage is one of perfect happiness, though: Progne's wish to see her sister is brought forth in a bedroom scene of connubial seduction. The reversal from such scenes of bliss to the barbarity of Thracia in the second half of the Complaint is the more dramatic; only a second reading reveals how skilfully it has been prepared for. Hannay adds several hidden clues to the hints already given in Ovid's version. There is, for example, a concealed reference to Plato's team-of-horses simile in the *Phaedra* dialogue in Hannay's description of the hero's steed:

His courser proud disdains
        To be control'd
        By bit of gold,
Scorning commanding reins.   (237–40)

One is reminded of these lines later on when the 'reinless love' of Tereus is mentioned (971). There are similar point-counterpoint arrangements in scenic descriptions. The luscious park of the opening finds its counterpart in a bleak forest, 'A winter-wasted aged wood' (1,185), near the end; a triumphal procession is followed by a drunken Bacchanalian rout, the love-feast by the cannibal meal. The conduct of the protagonists is equally contrasted: the dumbfounded lover of the wooing becomes an eloquent seducer; the sweet-talking wife a fulminating fury.

These changes in personality come abruptly; there is no time for gradual developments. With secondary characters such as Tereus and Progne this is not detrimental; with Philomela it poses problems. How is one to justify her change from blushing beauty to assistant butcheress? Chaucer evaded the issue by sparing his readers the gory details, Gower tried to spare his heroine by giving most of the blame to Progne, Gascoigne and Parker relished the slaughter, but they were writing in a rather thick-skinned form and catering to a less delicate public. Hannay follows in Gower's steps, letting Philomela hide behind her sister, but in his sophisticated poem this is not quite enough to maintain on the ethical plane the same careful balance that marks the construction of the whole; the poem threatens to fall into incongruous parts.

The aesthetic equilibrium of the Complaint depends, in the end, on whether its pivotal point, Philomela's grand scene in the centre, holds. At first sight this scene looks rather decorative and static. It does little to solve problems of motivation or characterisation. We do not look into Philomela, but rather at her: she mirrors her beauty, revolving around herself like the sort of delicate dancer one finds on musical boxes. Scenes of self-blazoning are a stock feature of both the epyllion and the Mirror-for-Ladies tradition, as Gary F. Bjork has pointed out;[26] Hannay's version is less offensive than others because he creates a highly artificial scene. Philomela mirrors her beauty with self-conscious, affected modesty. Her beauty, she says, is less exciting than that of Venus, but also less forbidding than that of Diana. The alabaster of her breasts has made the goddesses so envious that they yearly punish the earth by covering it in snow just to prove they are capable of producing an equally dazzling whiteness – the kind of exaggerated *aition* that had become a hallmark of the Elizabethan epyllion, and had been developed towards the facetious in its Jacobean imitators, particularly Austin's and Barksted's Myrrha poems. There is the obligatory *descriptio* too. Hannay extends it to a detailed word-painting of Philomela's elaborately decked-out dress. Minerva herself is said to have covered it with mythological figures which are obviously meant to serve more than just decorative purposes: they are grouped to form an idyllic scene which seems miraculously filled with

inaudible music. There is Apollo with his harp, the Muses join in, birds
and beasts enjoy the concert:

> A little lower from his state,
> Where Prince *Apollo* proudly sate,
>   With brightness overblown:
> The merry Muses rang'd in ranks,
> Were seated on the sunny banks,
>   With favour sweets o'ergrown:
> While one doth tune her lute, or voice,
>   One notes, one time doth measure.
> A silent sound, an unheard noise
>   Doth take the sight with pleasure.   (817–26)[27]

The radiant apparition of the sun-god, the fusion of light and sound and
odour are depicted with the delicacy of a pastel crayon. The serenity of
the immortals is a little later contrasted with the strivings of human
singers after similar effects; for them, music is a matter of life and death:
Orpheus loses his Eurydice in spite of his lyre (stanza liii), and Arion has
to fear for his life:

> Fearful on fish *Arion* sits,
> He seeming seiz'd with quaking fits,
>   Did mournful music make.
> The *Dolphins* dance now up, now down,
>   And as much pleasure have,
> As he hath pain, for fear to drown,
>   He sings his life to save,
>   His hands scarce hold
>   (With fear and cold
> Benumb'd) his instrument:
>   The swelling wave
>   The motion gave,
> The saving sound that lent.   (852–64)

In this stanza the difference between art and life, which formal descriptions of paintings or decorations often claim to eliminate, again breaks
up. As in Ovid's *Metamorphoses* with its constant shifting between the
barbarous and the beautiful, Hannay's Complaint of Philomela is set in
a much larger framework. The well-ordered park of the beginning borders on the indifferent parts of heaven and earth, with gods and dolphins
playing and dancing to the struggles of mankind. There are many similar
scenes in Ovid's epic, and some of them are alluded to in Hannay's poem.
The story of Daphne, for instance, is invoked in one of the miniatures
that surround the Apollo-scene (stanza l; cf. *Metamorphoses*, I, 452–567).
There are also parallels with the Arachne story in the *Metamorphoses*
(VI, 1–145). Like Arachne, Philomela suffers from the envy of a goddess;

it is suggested that Minerva decorated her garment out of jealousy: its 'cunning' design catches the eye of Tereus and thus contributes to Philomela's fall (stanza xlix). But there is a difference: the exquisitely woven cloth that proves fatal to Arachne is of her own proud doing, whereas Philomela is at worst guilty of a little vanity. Arachne's story, therefore, lends itself more readily than Philomela's to the moralisations dear to patristic and Renaissance interpreters. It may be doubtful whether the motif of pride and its punishment is part of Ovid's intention in telling stories like that of Arachne. This question is linked up with the difficulties of establishing the degree of seriousness behind Ovid's handling of mythic material, and ultimately with the question of the epic quality of the *Metamorphoses*.[28] In Hannay's elegiac treatment of the Philomela story this motif is ruled out by the essential innocence with which the heroine views a beauty not of her own making.

The beauty of Philomela is, in the first place, a gift of Nature. In Hannay's Complaint it is heightened by divine decoration and thus gains an unearthly quality. The more ironical is the fact that Philomela's natural beauty excites an unnatural passion in Tereus; this increases the poignancy of her fate and adds a tragic note to her song of complaint. As with Orpheus and Arion, this female singer raises questions not easily answered. Not even the change or her song afford the customary relief. For the poet, there is only the hope that his art can give belated ease:

> So far sweet *Philomela* sung,
> But here sad sorrow staid her tongue,
> Her throbbing breast did bound,
> Whereby I well might guess her grief,
> And 'cause I could not yield relief,
> Her woe my heart did wound.
> Pity with passion so me pierc'd,
> I press'd her how to please,
> Her legend if it were rehears'd,
> I deem'd would do her ease: (1,665–74)

Patrick Hannay must have felt that it would not do to put the Philomela myth in the shape of a popular ballad with its taste for the sentimental and the sanguinary, or an epyllion with its flippancy and facile decoration. He began by treating it in a highly artificial way, but never forgot that at the core of the myth irrational forces are at work, like beauty attracting barbarity, and such forces are not easily glossed or painted over. This makes his Complaint original in a double sense: by coming close to Ovid's *Metamorphoses* and by improving on contemporary models.

The matter of Troy: Oenone, Helen, Hecuba

Philomela is very much a figure of myth and miracle. There are elements of the inhuman and the superhuman in it that later authors easily transferred to the realms of romance. Ovid assigned her to his *Metamorphoses* rather than the *Heroides*, although Philomela's confinement in the Thracian wilderness, or, indeed, Progne's anxiety over her sister in the lonely palace, might have furnished an appropriate location for another letter. Hannay softened his Complaint of Philomela with musical and mythical elements and reserved his more prosaic tone for its companion piece, the historical Complaint of Mariana, whose love is thwarted by the Turkish wars. Most of the epistles in the *Heroides*, too, are written by women involved in some way in a war, mainly the aftermaths of the War of Troy. In later years these letters were often treated as historical documents, not only in the Middle Ages, when they were incorporated in verse and prose histories, but also by early Renaissance historians who wanted to give their works a touch of authenticity. An anonymous scribe of the fourteenth century managed to incorporate thirteen of the twenty-one *Epistulae heroidum* into the second redaction of the so-called *Histoire ancienne jusqu'à César*,[29] and Thomas Heywood slipped a translation of the twin letters of Paris and Helena into his epic history *Troia Britannica* (1609).

In a way, historians and poets such as Heywood repatriated these female figures to their original surroundings. What I shall consider in this chapter, however, is the opposite procedure: the extrication of such figures from an epic and heroic context, where they usually play the minor parts, and their adaptation to forms such as the epyllion and the Complaint, where they are cast in more prominent, but completely unheroic, roles. There are plenty of heroines to choose from: Oenone, Helen, Cassandra, Hecuba, to name but a few. I will begin with Helen of Greece, later of Troy (and possibly of Egypt), certainly the most versatile figure in the borderland between myth and legend which serves as a background to the Trojan War.

For authors of the Middle Ages, as for Shakespeare's Lucrece, Helen is 'the strumpet that began this stir' (*Lucrece*, 1,471), and some of them, one suspects, would gladly have scratched the face that launched the thousand ships towards their cherished Troy. It is only in later literature that one is allowed to idolise a *femme fatale* such as Helen without being damned like Faustus.[30] Although there had been attempts to rescue her reputation in ancient times, Helen was mainly a *femina letalis* in the stricter sense, particularly to partisans of Troy, and most of the medieval authors in the Latin tradition were such partisans. Even Ovid with his talent for twisting evidence chose Helen among his *Heroides* on second thoughts only, in the additional double letters (*Heroides*, XVI, XVII), and gave precedence to her rival in the love of Paris, the nymph Oenone (*Heroides*, V). Still, her inclusion in Ovid's collection qualified her to be counted in the numerous catalogues of love's victims in courtly literature; Chaucer, for instance, pays her the compliment, dubious though that may be, of figuring her in the gallery of lovers in his temple of Venus, together with Semiramis, Byblis, Dido, Thisbe, Isolde and Cleopatra (*Parliament of fowls*, 284–94) – *libertinae*, most of them, but a less infamous society than the one she finds in Dante's 'Inferno' (V, 37–69): there is compassion in Chaucer's 'and in what plyt they dyde' (*Parliament*, 294). Gower has Helen in a procession of unhappy lovers, too (*Confessio amantis*, VIII, 2,529); his Confessor tells her story (following Benoît's *Roman de Troie*) to give an example of sacrilegious love with Paris as villain (Paris abducts Helen from a temple where she is offering prayers to Venus) and only a hint at the consequences this abduction has for Troy (*Confessio amantis*, V, 7,195–590).

Again the early-Renaissance, post-Reformation authors tend to be stricter in their judgement on the *meretrix exicialis* than their medieval forbears: Helen is singled out by them as an example of the dire consequences of adultery. Richard Robinson, for instance, who wrote a treatise with the blunt title *The reward of wickedness* (1574), descends like Dante or like Sackville of the *Mirror for magistrates* to the infernal regions and finds Helen being tormented in the most excruciating manner together with, according to the even more explicit subtitle, *Popes, harlots, proude princes, tyrants, Romish bishops, and others*. Robinson's aim is not, like Dante's, to reveal the grand scheme of things, and he shows no spark of compassion. Unlike the figures in the *Mirror for magistrates*, where the fallen are given a chance to bewail their fates and to recover some of their reputation, his damned souls do nothing but accuse themselves. His is a Protestant Hell, where religious and private misconduct are unpardonable, and Helen is rightly 'tormented for her treason to her husbande, and liuing in fornication ten yeares' (C1r).

There are similarly explicit and implacable poems on Helen of Troy in the works of Robinson's contemporary Thomas Procter. One of these poems in his *Gorgeous gallery of gallant inventions* (1578) is called 'The reward of whoredom by the Fall of Helen'. This is spoken in limbo, but Helen's situation is little better than it was in Robinson's hell:

> From Limbo Lake, where dismall feendes do lye,
> Where *Pluto* raignes, perpend *Helenas* cry:
> Where fiery flames, where pittious howlings bee,
> Where bodyes burne: from thence give eare to mee.[31]

Although the poem is obviously influenced by the *Mirror for magistrates*,

the confession that follows is not so much a Complaint but a reproach.
The language, however, is less fervent than the introduction makes one
expect; sometimes it falls completely flat, when, for instance, Helen calls
herself a 'trull' and a 'flurt'. Procter may be thinking of the same simple
souls whom Salter wanted to save when he warned of the pitfalls of
literacy, or girls in danger of putting on airs because of their good looks;
it is, above all, the 'gorgious plumes' (L1r) of Helen's beauty that are
taken to task in the *Gorgeous gallery*.

Procter returned to the subject of Helen of Troy in his later volume
The triumph of truth (1595?, entered 1582) with a poem called 'Helen's
complaint'. The subtitle of this volume promises, among other things,
that in *The triumph of truth* 'Youth is admonished to withdrawe his affection from the vain seducements of Fancie'. It has the same conduct-book
look as the *Gorgeous gallery* and, like the earlier volume, is aimed at the
improvement of personal morality. Helen's Complaint is set in a short
argument sketching the destruction of Troy, and the poet is anxious to
point out how appropriate it is that Helen should find her doom in the
town which she brought to ruin (he lets her perish in these ruins):

> Great was the slaughter then in Troy,
>   ere ended was the strife,
> Wherin that Helen false of faith
>   vnto her wedded mate:
> Did lose her life as one deseru'de,
>   for causing of the hate.[32]

The historical background is here used as a means of punishing a private
fault, and this points towards a strategy that is followed by other poets
who concentrate on Helen's private fate, though for different reasons.
The burning Troy casts so deep a shadow on Helen that whoever wants
to treat her fate with more sympathy will have to keep her away from it
altogether as John Gower did, who stopped short of carrying her out of
Sparta, or the ancient Stesichorus, who transported her into Egypt. He
will also try to concentrate not on the historical aspects of her story, but
her mythic qualities, and in particular her beauty. This is exactly what
happens in the poem by an impressionable young poet, John Trussell,
written in the mad-with-beauty 1590s.

John Trussell, *Raptus I. Helenae*

The model John Trussell was most impressed with when in 1595 he wrote
his *First rape of fair Hellen* was Shakespeare's *Venus and Adonis* (1593),
the poem which had firmly established the genre of the erotic epyllion
created by Thomas Lodge's *Scilla's metamorphosis* in 1589 and had

stimulated a demand for more. Trussell imitates even Shakespeare's dedication to the Earl of Southampton by speaking of his poem as '*Primitiae*' and asking his readers to bear with 'this ouersleight first fruites of my ouer barren Muse'.[33] There have been speculations that Trussell was a close friend or even a kinsman of Shakespeare's, but these were largely dispersed by M.A. Shaaber in the introduction to his edition of the poem.[34] We know very little about John Trussell; not even his date of birth is known for sure. One is tempted to think that he was a very young man when he wrote his poem, though not quite as precocious as his Hellen, whom he has abducted by the elderly Theseus at the tender age of eight.

Trussell may have lighted on this little-known incident in Helen's life 'casting about for a wronged heroine not already treated in a complaint poem', as Shaaber imagines (p. 420), but one wonders why he did not choose her more celebrated encounter with Paris instead – Procter's poem, which is not a full-blown Complaint, need not have deterred him. As it turns out, his choice was right, for his poem proves him to possess little of Procter's gravity, and instinct as well as a sense of the erotic potential will have led him to the first rape of young Helen. The subject promises, moreover, an amusing variation on the constellation in Shakespeare's *Venus and Adonis*, where a reluctant youth is pursued by an elderly suitor, with sexes inverted to swell the farcical potential.

There is, indeed, no precedent for a poetical treatment of the delicate subject. Helen's rape by Theseus is mentioned by ancient authors in various versions; usually she is rescued by her brothers Castor and Pollux before Theseus, who abducts her as a child and stows her away to grow to nubility, has done her any harm. In Ovid's Epistle Helen maintains that she has struggled successfully against the advances of Theseus (*Heroides*, XVII, 21–8); Boccaccio, another likely source, while linking her wantonness with the fall of Troy in the first line of his Life of Helen, supports her view that Theseus could only rob her of a few kisses and vainly prided himself on having reaped her virginity (*De claris mulieribus*, XXXV). Trussell chooses a more violent variant of the story in which Helen is actually raped, and he heightens its brutality by stressing her youth and innocence at the time: before the rape, at least, Helen is unaware of the attractions of her beauty. This choice complicates matters for the poet because it paves the way for the tragic interpretation of a story which, in its harmless variants, seems eminently suited for a comedy, if not a farce. Most of the unease that Trussell's tale leaves on reading is due to the fact that he wavers between these possibilities.

The poem begins in a mixture of May morning and *Mirror for magistrates* openings. In the twilight of an evening in May (ominously filled with a nightingale's song) the poet meets the apparition of 'a Maid (a

Maiden in attire) / With haires disheueld, eyes with tears besprent'
(20–1) which turns out to be the ghost of once beautiful Hellen, and
overhears her complaint. Barring the title of the poem, one would expect
her to relate the whole of her life-story, for the complainants in the
Mirror for magistrates usually come from beyond, if not right out of, their
graves. By concentrating on the early episode with Theseus, Trussell foils
this expectation and unbalances the structure of the stately form of the
Complaint, which normally takes account of the experiences of a lifetime.
Moreover, the grief-stricken appearance of this Hellen is not easily reconciled with the fact that she is only a girl of eight and will have to excite
the passions of a Paris (not to mention Menelaus) later in life. The uneasy
balance of the poem also shows in its metre: Trussell once more takes
Shakespeare's *Venus and Adonis* for his model and writes in sixains, not
the rhyme royal stanzas used in Complaints and thought proper for grave
poems such as Shakespeare's *Lucrece*. It is not surprising, then, that we
find all the other paraphernalia of the erotic epyllion, too, in the poem:
there are elaborate conceits, there is the mythological machinery, and
there are the hydra-headed epithets which had become associated with
that form. In the end Trussell bows to the burlesque tendencies indigenous to the genre; his description of Hellen's abduction, with a short-
winded Theseus gasping for breath and taking a rest before laying hands
on his victim surpasses anything of the kind in *Venus and Adonis*. The
chance of viewing this incident from the unsuspecting girl's perspective
is not taken; Trussell is not interested in taking an inside view of the
story. Instead of developing the inner drama he strives for theatrical
effects: he reports the expressive body language of his heroine, and he
exchanges the domestic scenery of the opening for the bleak backdrop
of 'hollow woods' (190), 'Sandy desert' (239) and 'senceles rockes' (276)
in the violation scene.

After the rape the scenery changes to the more intimate interior of a
palace, and this is where Trussell's talent finally comes to life. The over-
anxious parents who, in the middle of the night, let Hellen in only after
prolonged rapping and shouting, the inquisitive maid, the embarrassed
father (comic variations on similar characters in Shakespeare's *Lucrece*),
and above all the sagacious nurse – they all seem to have sprung straight
out of a Latin comedy.[35] The nurse climbs to a commanding position in
the last parts of the poem. She offers the worldly-wise device to cover up
the whole affair, and she does it with the same arguments employed by
the beldame in Samuel Daniel's *Complaint of Rosamond*. There these
arguments help to bring about the maiden's fall; here they serve to dupe
the suitor and to procure a happy ending. The nurse has the longest
speech of all the persons in the poem; together with Hellen's mother
Leda (who also has her secret – Hellen is, after all, the fruit of another

rape) she saves her nursling's reputation, mends Hellen's somewhat ruffled beauty and arranges the marriage with an unsuspecting, even pleasantly surprised Menelaus. It is a female plot which runs counter to all the expectations raised in the beginning of the poem: the victim in this curious Complaint turns out to be not the ravished maiden but a husband henpecked well before his marriage.

It is hard to say what Trussell really had in mind when he devised this turn of events. He may have planned to show in Hellen's early development the corruption of female beauty in an unfeeling male world. Indeed, Hellen is initiated into this world where 'womanly wiles' are the weapons necessary for survival. After her first encounter with the opposite sex, she flees to the nurse and learns some of the craft at first hand, including how to lay on the rouge that will eventually stamp her as a strumpet:

> Looke what by Arte, or nature could be thought,
>   powerfull to pollish my late perish'd plumes.
> Was neither left vnvalued, nor vnbought.
>   till what by diets, paintings, and perfumes,
> My beautie of her blemish was depriued,
> And my so late-collour was reuiued.
>
> Then as the wearer of poore *Argus* eies,
>   doth vaunt his proud plumes in his maiestie:
> Yet when his Prides ill-pleasing legges he spies,
>   he falles his plumes, and vailes his royaltie.
> Shaming as seemes, his plumes with collours graced,
> Should be with such disgracing legges defaced.
>
> So did I flaunt in new-found fond disguise,
>   (such as at this day court attenders weare:
> When with newfangles they Idolatrize
>   the banckrout beautie of their borrowed haire.)
> Such did I weare, although I needed none,
> My beauty lackt no blazon but her owne.   (769–86)

The triumph of beauty appears to be a triumph of cosmetics; what looks like a passage from Thomas Procter's *Triumph of truth*, however, with its moralising about gorgeous plumes, is but an instance of the tendency towards satire that is inherent in the epyllion.

On the whole, Trussell keeps the moralising to a minimum, the minimum necessary to gloss over the more salacious part of an erotic poem. This art of glossing goes even further back than Tudor conduct books such as Procter's *Triumph of truth*. Ovid already veiled some of his more dubious tales with protective moralising of the 'parents beware' variety in his *Metamorphoses*, and he, too, showed a predilection for scarcely nubile maidens such as Myrrha or Byblis. These two, in fact, whom Ovid introduces with warnings like 'procul hinc natae, procul este parentes' (*Metamorphoses*, X, 300), provided models for wrapping up equally prurient epyllia in cheap advice. English examples are the two Myrrha poems I have mentioned already, William Barksted's *Mirrha, the mother of Adonis* (1607) and *The scourge of Venus* (1613), attributed, with doubts, to Henry Austin. The cosmetic practices of the nurse, moreover, link Trussell's poem with prostitutes' Complaints and their detailed boudoir scenes which I will discuss in chapter 6; in Gervase Markham's *Paulina* (1609), for instance, the girl is taught the secrets of the trade by her own mother who restores her to a state of virginity, as the nurse does young Hellen, several times. Despite the magisterial trimmings, then, Trussell's Complaint points forward to 'trulls' and 'flurts' such as Fanny Hill.

Thomas Heywood, *Oenone and Paris*

Whereas Trussell set out to write a tragic Complaint and ended up with an erotic verse novella, several of his contemporaries, like him under the influence of Shakespeare's *Venus and Adonis*, went straight for the epyllion form. One of them is Thomas Heywood, who had, as I mentioned before, translated the letters of Paris and Helen from Ovid's *Heroides* as a young man and had incorporated them later on in his universal history *Troia Britannica* (1609). Despite its eventual place in a historical context, this translation shows an almost Marlovian empathy in the wittily erotic interplay of the letter pair. The flirtatiousness of their language already sets these double letters apart from the singles in Ovid's series and shows elements of the erotic elegy. In Renaissance literature a similar liking for double-talk distinguishes the epyllion from its graver sister, the Complaint. The epyllion has a pair of lovers as protagonists, the Complaint is spoken by a single forsaken lover. Another element of distinction is the idyllic scenery in which the love-talk of the epyllion is often set; this can be contrasted with the historic or waste-land settings of the Complaint. English authors of the later Renaissance had Shakespeare's *Venus and Adonis* and his *Lucrece* as models for these differences, but the patterns had their origins in Ovid's poems, the epyllion in his *Metamorphoses* and erotic elegies, the Complaint in his *Heroides*.

The story of Helen and Paris somehow falls between these patterns. It is mythic and even comic in its beginnings and might well qualify for treatment in epyllic form, but it reaches out into history with its tragic consequences, and it is easy to imagine Helen complaining her fate with the ruins of Troy in the background. When, therefore, young Heywood cast about for a suitable epyllic subject, he like Trussell hit upon an earlier incident of her story which revolves around the rival nymph Oenone.

After Shakespeare's *Venus and Adonis*, the writing of an epyllion had become something of an obligatory apprentice work for aspiring poets. Heywood was about twenty when he wrote his *Oenone and Paris* (1594) and he, too, made his bow to the master by speaking of 'the first fruit of my endeavours', adding somewhat coyly 'and the maidenhead of my pen'. It was printed by Richard Jones who also took on Trussell's *Raptus I. Helenae*.[36] Heywood's main source is Ovid's 'Letter of Oenone to Paris' (*Heroides*, V); this letter, like all the epistles in Ovid's collection, concentrates on the last stage of the love affair, and Heywood follows suit. This creates a problem of perspective: since Heywood (unlike Trussell) chooses the proper form of the epyllion, which is a third-person narrative, he has to convert a static written monologue into a consecutive story. He might have introduced more action, but he borrows some material from Lucian's *Dialogi meretricii* instead.

On the whole, however, Heywood does his apprentice work in style. He expands and heightens the familiar diction of the letter into the preciosity demanded by the epyllion form. There are numerous catalogues of plants and birds and nymphs, and there are extensive descriptions to pad out the parts spoken by the desperate maid and her callous lover. Most luxurious is the picture Oenone paints of her own beauty. Not the usual lily and rose, but Titan's purple and Cynthia's silver mix on her brow; her hands are not just white, but ivory, her lips not red but coral; her hair is of golden wire, her eyes are crystal lamps, etc. (487–504).[37] This eulogy looks extravagant, not only because it comes from the mouth of the praised herself (Paris has lost interest in her charms), but also because these 'quaint conceites' (490) ill suit the simple country nymph Oenone who tries to dissociate herself from the mundane and coquettish Helen.

There are similar contradictions in the appearance and the arguments of Paris. He looks like Shakespeare's sullen Adonis (though not quite as hard, 135) when he laughs off Oenone's amorous advances, and he dons a martial harness (721–3), as if he tried to look like an Aeneas called to duty. On the other hand he professes to be a champion of women and of love: he gave the apple to Venus and had to abduct Helen because it is in his highly impressionable nature to follow beauty at all cost. This inverts Shakespeare's 'men have marble, women waxen minds' (*Lucrece*, 1,240), but it is not a gallant argument to use against Oenone, whose beauty he has just praised beyond comparison. The weakness of the arguments discredits the faithless lover; in Ovid's letter such arguments come from Oenone, and the resulting asymmetry (there is, of course, no answer) is part of the general design. In the more balanced epyllion this asymmetry looks disproportionate because one expects the hero to make a point of his own, not to support – be it unwittingly – the heroine's point of view. The point is, however, that Paris does not represent a convincing value like Shakespeare's Adonis with his male virginity or Virgil's Aeneas with his imperial mission. He appeals to principles that are shown to be incorporated in Oenone, whom he basely rejects, and this robs his performance of the seriousness these other heroes manage to secure. The sympathies of the poem remain on the side of Oenone, and never more than in the end when Paris has left and we find her in the forlorn situation that becomes the letter-writer rather than the heroine of myth: we see her roam through her natural terrain, but the once idyllic fields have taken on the aspect of a wilderness, with 'cliffes, rocks, clowdy mountains' (767) and 'desarts, dennes, and dailes' (785). Heywood intensifies Oenone's loneliness by clearing these surroundings of their guardian gods, with even a startling hint at the death of Pan:

> When Paris went, the gods went from these fieldes;
> When hee took leaue, the aged Pan departed;   (757–8)

It is as if the author would make us feel the dividing line between the gregariousness of the epyllion and the loneliness of the Complaint, leaving Oenone, as Chaucer left his heroines, 'Of her selfe forlorne, of Paris vnregarded' (804).

The mobbled queen

There are figures from legend or history that defy attempts at mockery or irony. Hecuba is such a figure. Ovid, who is capable of wringing an ironic twist into the most gruesome story, relates her fate as a god-moving coda to the manslaughter at Troy, 'Illius fortuna deos quoque moverat omnes' (*Metamorphoses*, XIII, 573). Shakespeare is haunted by the ghost of Hecuba, but seems unable to stand its presence for more than a terrifying instant. His Lucrece singles out Hecuba's portrait from a crowded painting of the fall of Troy:

> In her the painter had anatomiz'd
> Time's ruin, beauty's wrack, and grim care's reign (*Lucrece*, 1,450–1)

Spoken of as a 'mobbled queen' she moves a seasoned actor to tears in the Danish court (*Hamlet*, II, ii, 499) – but Shakespeare never gives her a role of her own, not even in his *Troilus and Cressida*. Her story may have been too passive or too painful, and Shakespeare shied away from it like the boy in *Titus Andronicus*, who runs from his mutilated aunt Lavinia:

> And I have read that Hecuba of Troy
> Ran mad for sorrow; that made me to fear   (IV, i, 20–1)

Shakespeare's Lavinia is a second Philomela, and she tries to point this out by turning over the leaves of Ovid's *Metamorphoses*, which contains

Philomela's story as well as that of Hecuba, and which is one of the books
the boy is carrying under his arm. This horror scene is interspersed with
references to 'sad stories chanced in the times of old' (III, ii, 83). Later
on Lavinia is compared to Lucretia; she can thus be called an amalgam
of the types that are more fully treated in contemporary Complaints
about mythic and historic heroines.

The book the boy referred to in the passage quoted must be Book XIII
of the *Metamorphoses*, where Ovid picks up the story of Hecuba after
she has lost her sons and Troy is already captured. Hecuba is forced to
watch her husband Priam being killed and she laments the loss of her
youngest children Polyxena and Polydorus. Her sorrows are heightened
into fury at the sight of the drowned Polydorus, and she runs mad in the
vengeance she wreaks on Polymnestor – this is the phase in her story that
led Dante to introduce her alongside the mythical Myrrha as a historical
example of excessive fury ('Inferno', XXX, 13–21).

With such a figure as Hecuba the metamorphosis may still come as a
salvatory act, but it looks strangely inept – this is probably one reason why
Dante explains her transformation into a dog euhemeristically: Hecuba's
rage, being inhuman, sounds like the barking of a bitch, and that is how
the myth came into being. This is Boccaccio's explanation, too, though
his source is Virgil (*Aeneid*, II, 515–54), not Ovid; Boccaccio adds a
sceptical 'they say' (*De claris mulieribus*, XXXII). For Boccaccio, as for
Shakespeare's Lucrece, Hecuba is 'a true example of misery' and 'a great
illustration of how prosperity perishes'.[38] Boccaccio adds to the load of
her misery by making her a witness of her last daughter Cassandra's death
at the instigation of Clytaemnestra; this severs the etiological thread
which, in the *Metamorphoses*, connects her with a promontory on the
Thracian coast where the myth has it that she was stoned to death like a
dog on her way to Greece. This ignominious death did not fit in with
Boccaccio's framework: he makes her a heroine worthy of a medieval
tragedy, as his second definition of the exemplary character of her fall
implies.

The English medieval Troy romances, most of which are based on
Guido delle Colonne's *Historia destructionis Troiae*, take a rather masculine view of this mother of heroes. Her sorrows are placed amidst actions
revolving around the deeds of love and the wars of men. The scenes of
mourning present her as member of a choir, often comforted by other
Trojan women, and rarely have the narrators as much patience with her
as Ovid has. John Lydgate, for example, cuts the lamentations at the
death of Hector short:

> What schal I seyn of Eccuba the quene,
> Or his suster, yonge Polycene,

Or Cassandra, the prudent and the wyse,
Or of his wyf, the sorwe to devise?
Whiche rent hem silf, in torment & in wo,
As finally thei wolde hem silfe for-do
By cruel deth, so thei wepe and waille.
[. . .]
And thus I leue hem sige and sorwe make,
This cely wommen, in her clothes blake,
Shroude her facis, & wympled mourne in veyn,
While I turne to my mater ageyn   (*Troy Book*, 5,549–55; 5,575–8)[39]

His matter is heroic deeds, not the wailing of women. Caxton gives them
even shorter shrift in his *Recuyell of the histories of Troy*:

What myght men saye of the sorowe that his moder the quene made after hys
susters? O what sorowe made hys wyf! Certes there can no man expresse alle the
lamentacions that there were maad.[40]

And he goes on to relate the love-affair of Achilles and Polyxena. Hecuba's end is usually dealt with very briefly: George Peele gives a later
example of the general diffidence in his *Tale of Troy* (1589), although he
puts his *praeteritio* in exaggerated language: the sun hides his face behind
clouds to avoid watching her wretched end, and Priam is fortunate in his
earlier death in native Troy.

All these treatments of Hecuba are epic or romantic in the medieval
sense. They do not go back to Homer, who introduced scenes of great
pathos in his *Iliad*, or to Ovid, who gave Hecuba a moving lament in his
Metamorphoses, but rather, ultimately, to Dares Phrygius and Dictys
Cretensis, the 'historians' medieval authors respected as first-hand
reporters of the Trojan war. The sense of pathos displayed in these narratives is narrowed by a sense of responsibility to a restricted ideal of
martial or knightly valour. The admixture of elegiac material from the
Heroides, however, which I mentioned earlier on, helped to widen the
perspective, to take in the more tender passions felt at the border of the
battlefield. John Dryden, an expert in both the epic and the elegiac
modes (he translated both Virgil's *Aeneid* and Ovid's 'Letter of Dido'),
in his critical writings established the scale by which a writer versed in
ancient literature can descend from the violent emotions displayed by
Homer and – to a lesser extent – by Virgil to the tender passions shown
by Ovid. In the dedication to his *Examen poeticum* he observes, with
reference to Hector's death in the *Iliad*, that Homer, compared with
Virgil, 'can move rage better than he can pity'.[41] In the 'Account' prefixed
to his *Annus mirabilis* he contrasts the violence of Virgil's Dido with the
tenderness of even the most passionate heroines in Ovid's *Metamorphoses* like Myrrha, Althaea or Byblis; he ascribes the difference to a
change of perspective:

Virgil speaks not so often to us in the person of another, like Ovid, but his own; he relates almost all things as from himself.[42]

In his essay *Of dramatic poesy* Dryden compares the essentially dramatic quality of Ovid's tales to one of Seneca's tragedies and examines them with regard to their impact on an audience. Ovid's stories of Myrrha, Caunus and Byblis, he argues, are similar to Seneca's motherly Andromache in that they stir up the softer emotions, particularly what he calls 'concernment'. He goes on to contrast this effect favourably with the tragedies of the ancients which

dealt not with that soft passion but with lust, cruelty, revenge, ambition, and those bloody actions they produced; which were more capable of raising horror than compassion.[43]

Observations like these are apt to serve as points of reference for some of the classical tales which deal with the matter of Troy and of Rome and which take up elements of the ancient epic, the tragic, and the elegiac.

John Ogle, *The lamentation of Troy*

One of the prerequisites for a softer treatment of heroines like the Trojan women is a slackening of their ties with the heroic actions of which they cannot be but lookers-on or victims. This is what Ovid does in his *Heroides* and, to a lesser extent, in his *Metamorphoses*, and this is what poets in the epyllion tradition do, for instance Heywood in his *Oenone and Paris* (1594), John Trussell in his *Raptus I. Helenae* (1595) or Richard Barnfield in his 'Legend of Cassandra' (1595). It is also true of Sir John Ogle's *Lamentation of Troy* (1594), which, like these contemporaneous pieces, combines the features of a Complaint with those of an epyllion, but adds, as its title suggests, elements of a poem of place.[44] Poems of place have their own venerable tradition, with roots as deep as the Old English elegy 'The ruin' (probably on ancient Bath) and analogues in contemporary poems such as Spenser's 'The Ruin of time' (on ancient St Albans). But Ogle's *Lamentation* takes its cue from epyllia in the *Venus and Adonis* line rather than the *Ubi sunt* lament; one of the few remaining copies was bound up with Heywood's *Oenone*, Trussell's *Helena* and other short epics on classical subjects in the so-called Caldecott volume.[45] Its sixain stanzas link the poem with the epyllion tradition, whereas its dream-vision framework, with a ghost of Troy addressing the poet, comes from the *Mirror for magistrates* and ultimately Senecan drama. Seneca's *Troades* may, in fact, have been one of Ogle's sources;[46] the full title with its reference to the death of Hector, however, looks back to the grand epic, possibly Lydgate's *Troy book*.

Laments over dead heroes were an element of the epic from its very beginnings;[47] Homer's *Iliad* provides some of the best examples, most notably the double lament of the women of Troy over the mangled corpse of Hector in Books XXII and XXIV. Dryden had these laments in mind when he criticised the bard's lack of tender passions. Initially, such laments were connected with funeral rites, and women played an important role in their performance. This background is still visible in the ceremonial style and the antiphonic structure to be found in classical literature, particularly in the choric parts of tragedies. Seneca made striking use of such laments in his plays; the *Troades*, for instance, look like a procession of threnodies. Both the epic and the tragedy thus retain some of the communal sense of the funeral lament, even if some of the mourners are exalted above the choir like Hecuba and Andromache, the mother and the wife, in the laments over Hector of Troy.

In this communal aspect, Ogle's *Lamentation* differs significantly from his sources: he singles out Helen and Paris as chief mourners. This comes as a surprise, at least as far as Helen is concerned. Homer keeps her in the background in his scenes of lamentation until she finds an opportunity to thank Hector for championing her cause (there are hints that she has been snubbed by her female in-laws). Seneca assigns to her the ignoble tasks of tricking Polyxena into her role of sacrificial lamb and of coaxing Andromache into her marriage with the odious Pyrrhus. Paris is barely mentioned amongst the mourners in either version; Seneca, in fact, implies that he is dead: 'solus occulte Paris / lugendus Helenae est' (*Troades*, 908–9). In Ogle's *Lamentation* Helen has been received in the family circle, and she is very much at its centre. Her beauty is undiminished; Ogle describes it in the extravagant epyllion manner: it eclipses that of her sisters-in-law and seems, for a moment at least, potent enough to revive the corpse of the slain Hector – rather a daring inversion of Helen's traditional role as bringer of death and destruction, not least to Hector ('pestis exitium lues' Andromache calls her in Seneca's *Troades*, 892). The cult of beauty celebrated in the erotic epyllion apparently ran away with Sir John here and did not stop at a scene of mourning. His interpretation of this scene implies that such beauty as Helen's is worth a Trojan war; the heroic spirit has been overruled by the erotic.

This impression is confirmed by Paris who has an entrance as effective as that of Helen (they reduce the rest of the mourners to supernumeraries). Paris enters in a melancholy outfit and seems ready to sink under the thought of his guilt, but the narrator lays all the blame for Hector's death on heavenly agents, and in particular on Venus whose prize Paris could not refuse:

> Aloofe from these did stand in sable weedes,
> '(For mourning garments fit a mourneful mind)

A man whose hart and very soule now bleedes,
To see that *Hector* was to death assignde.
        And this was *Paris* brocher of their woe,
        But he to *Greece* by Heauens instinct did go.

Venus commanded, who could hir denie?
Had she not giuen, me thinkes a man should craue it:
For such a prize who would not Fortune trie,
And venture life, and goods, and al to haue it?
        Nor fire nor water should his passage stay,
        To gaine fruition of so sweet a pray.   (C3r)

When Paris rallies enough strength to leave for the battlefield (he is not as weak a figure as in Heywood's *Oenone*), Helen's beauty withers and she loses the will to live. She, too, is allowed a strong exit, however: she would rather die than return to 'home-spun *Menalay*' (892), and she is also allowed to blame the blundering gods who forced her into the disastrous spectacle in the first place. This clears her of all responsibility for the Trojan disaster:

> For if the gods decreed it thus before,
> It vvas their vvils, and *Helen* is no whore.   (E2v)

More than that; not only is Helen no whore, she has become a saint: 'And thus a saint did act an hellish part' (1074).

This final picture of St Helen of Troy is a remarkable feat of *contrafactura*. The reversal of values it brings about is made even more conspicuous in an anachronism: Helen compares herself favourably to an exemplary Roman widow called Julia, who followed her husband into his grave. This must be the daughter of Julius Caesar whom Boccaccio remembered in his *De claris mulieribus* and for whom Thomas Howell devised a small monument in 1581.[48] The proverbial adulteress looks down on a paragon of Roman virtue: Helena has become a good woman – not even Ovid or Chaucer, 'all womanis frend', had gone that far.

Thomas Fenne, *Hecuba's mishaps*

Helen was not the first of the Trojan women to be lifted out of the choir bewailing the death of Hector. Another bright young man of Shakespeare's generation, Thomas Fenne, had published a poem on *Hecuba's mishaps* several years before in his collection of verse and prose titled *Fenne's fruits* (1590). This 'extraordinary hodge-podge' (as Douglas Bush has called it[49]) contains, as the second of its three parts, instances of 'the lamentable ruines which attend on Warre' (subtitle, A1r), and this indicates his less glamorous view of the history of Troy. The third part of the collection, to which *Hecuba's mishaps* is annexed, sets out to prove *'that it is not requisite to deriue our pedegree from the vnfaithfull Troians, who were chiefe causes of their owne destruction'* (subtitle, A1r). Fenne's Hecuba, like Ogle's ghost of Troy, appears in the dark weeds cut to the *Mirror for magistrates* model; her Complaint is, according to its heading, 'Expressed by way of apparition, touching the manifolde miseries, wonderfull calamities, and lamentable chances that happened to her vnfortunate selfe, sometime Queene of stately Troy' (Bb3v). Unlike Ogle, however, Fenne does not exchange this guise for the lighter garments of an epyllion. He gives Hecuba a first-person Complaint, and we keep the mobbled queen constantly in view. She speaks her monologue not in the customary rhyme royal stanzas, though, but in over 1,500 fourteeners. Fenne will have chosen this metre as a substitute for the classical hexameter. He handles it with scrupulous correctness, counting every foot and stopping at every caesura, with the result of rather a mechanical tone. He relieves the monotony with startling effects in the manner of a broadside ballad, with heavy alliterations to bring them home, like the apparition of Hecuba at the beginning of the vision:

> Strange fearfull fancies frighted me, by dreadfull drowsie dreames.
> In slumber sound me thought I spied a wight both fierce and fell:
> A thing despisde, in viler sort no creature was in hell.
> A woman vext with eager lookes in frantike fierie moode:
> With clapping hands and rowling eyes vncertainly she stoode. (Bb3v)

The battles around Troy are remembered in colours as garish as those Gascoigne used in his ballad of Philomene, except that men are the victims and Hecuba is only a wide-eyed witness. Troilus is one of the worst afflicted of the heroes; both the way in which he is addressed (Sir Troylus) and the way he comes to grief (he is treacherously slain by Achilles) point towards a medieval romance, but it seems to be touched up with contemporary practices of execution:

> Sir Troylus by chance thus slaine, the Greekes from armour stript,
> Whose bowels hung about his feete, for they his body ript,
> And naked on a gibe they hang for Troyans there to see
> Their champion stout whom earst before had made the Greekes to
>   flee.   (Dd1v)

Such scenes of treason and of butchery have their origin in Trojan narratives derived from Guido delle Colonne's *Historia destructionis Troiae*, which largely consists of battle scenes.[50] In the accounts given by Lydgate in his *Troy book* or by Caxton in his *Recuyell of the histories of Troy*, the most probable sources for Fenne, however, Troilus is only decapitated and his corpse dragged over the battlefield at the tail of a horse. He is not hanged, drawn and quartered like a thief. Cruel action is very much in the foreground of Hecuba's Complaint, and this is epic material not

easily adaptable to a first-person narrative. Hecuba is less involved in the
Trojan war than most of the other women of Troy – less than Helen, for
instance, who took part in its beginning, or Cassandra, who knows about
its end. In her passivity Hecuba seems well suited to the role assigned to
the speaker of a Complaint, but Fenne rarely takes the opportunity to
give an inside view of her reactions. He uses her instead as a mirror to
reflect the horrors of the war or to voice his own opinions on its progress.
Hecuba thus fails to become the centre of her monologue, and she is not,
like Ogle's Helen, brought to focus on a singular point of view or value.

Only towards the end of her tale does the perspective come to bear on
Hecuba's Complaint. She has repeatedly asked herself why it is that she,
who has so little interest in this war, is made to suffer worse than anyone
else. These questions eventually culminate in a challenge of the justice
of the gods. At this moment Fenne touches not only one of the chief
subjects of classical tragedy but also, as we shall see, some of the best
English Complaints: Thomas Middleton's Lucrece, Thomas Churchyard's Mrs Shore and Gervase Markham's Marie Magdalen all ask this
overwhelming question, and some of them find no answer. Thomas
Fenne tries to give an answer in the light of his conviction, which he
announced in the subtitle to part three of his *Fruits*, that the Trojans dug
their own graves. This is an uncommon view; it is opposed to the medieval
Latin tradition, which made the nations of Europe descendants of the
Trojans and which persisted in England longer than elsewhere. It is not
very convincing in the case at hand: Hecuba is obviously innocent of the
Trojan war, so Fenne had to find someone else to provide an explanation
for the afflictions of the queen. Fenne hit on the idea of letting Priam
join his wife near the end of her tale and act as a consoler. This breaks
up the form of the solitary Complaint, but it helps to solve a number of
narrative problems, and it gives the otherwise harsh poem a touching
finish.

One of the consequences of the final duet which evolves is that Fenne is
able to pass over Hecuba's madness and Ovid's metamorphosis, elements
inimical to a first person lament anyway. What the gods grant to some of
Ovid's heroines, ease and a sense of fulfilment, Hecuba is given by her
husband:

> VVhat shall thy ghost that now should rest, in worldly cares still dwell:
> And thinke on things that erst were past, O plague far worse than hell.
> (Ff3v)

Priam is courteous enough to take some of the blame for the disastrous
events on himself – he condoned the whims of their son Paris ('A filthy
part the letcher plaid', Gg2r); mainly, however, he explains the fall of
his family as the outcome of a curse that hangs over their house and goes

back to a perjury committed by his father; this has happened to others before, and there is no escaping the wrath of the gods:

> It is no striuing with the gods if once they haue decreed:
> Wherefore vexe not (O Hecuba) let not thy ghost so fret
> Against the gods for this their doome, and further do not thret
> Fell destinie or fortunes frowne, for this that they haue done,
> Was for some mighty sinne of ours, which fate we could not shunne,
> Or for the sinne of periurie, a vile and hatefull deede,
> Which first my father did commit, and now vpon his seede
> The plague did fall deseruedly for such his bad abuse,
> The gods themselues wil not accept for periurie excuse.   (Gg2r)

The explanation approximates the Classical concept of fate and places the Laomedons on a par with doomed dynasties like the Tantalides. To relieve the gloom this casts on his poem Fenne employs Priam as a second ghost and has husband and wife find comfort in each other's grief – a gesture without parallel in the history of the Complaint. Fenne adds one more pathetic touch. In spite of his doubtful attitude towards the Trojans and the desirability of being derived from them, he lets Priam show concern for his English descendants: with fear in his eyes he wishes that they may be spared the doom that visited his city and is transferred thence to Carthage and to Rome.

The matron of Rome: Lucrece in medieval and Renaissance poetry

Thomas Fenne may have had his doubts about the idea of *translatio imperii*, the handing-on of the empire from Troy to Rome and on to Troynovant or London. Others, like Spenser, tried to revive it. The idea has political as well as poetical dimensions; Virgil imitates Homer and promotes the Augustan empire, Spenser imitates both and glorifies the reign of Elizabeth. In Virgil's epic the bearer of the idea is, of course, Aeneas, and his chief virtue, *pietas*, is a masculine virtue; the very word 'virtus' implies masculinity. In England poets as well as statesmen were hard put to translate this into feminine terms during the reign of Queen Elizabeth. There was, however, a growing demand, perhaps called forth by the fact that the English throne was occupied by a woman, for a feminine ideal to be set up alongside or against masculine piety, and again one looked to classical literature for precedents, and mainly to works of history. Historic figures like Virginia, Sophonisba and Octavia seemed eminently suited to serve as exemplars.

Among the Roman heroines, Lucretia has always held pride of place. Her fate is less romantic than that of Dido, and it is more complicated, though one might claim that the issues involved are similar. In both cases there is a choice to be made between private and public values; in Dido's the choice is one of 'hic amor, haec patria' (*Aeneid*, IV, 347), in Lucretia's between 'private pleasure' and 'public plague' (Shakespeare, *Lucrece*, 1,478–9). The matter is clear as long as the objects of choice are assigned to different persons (Dido and Aeneas, Tarquin and Lucrece); it becomes clouded as soon as one of the parties is torn between these objects. And the case of Lucretia is complicated because she is only allowed to make negative choices.

In his history of Rome, *Ab urbe condita* (I, lvii–lx), Livy places the rape of Lucrece firmly in a military and political context. The rape itself is barely mentioned, his emphasis lies on Lucrece's justification of her conduct shortly before she kills herself: she had to submit to the outrage in order to expose the tyrant Tarquin afterwards. Her dying speech has the character of a public address; it is meant to safeguard Lucretia's reputation and to excite a political revolution. The following uprising of the Roman people is given as much scope as the events leading up to the rape. Clearly public issues are at stake, not merely private reputations.

In Ovid's *Fasti* (II, 721–852) the loose, legendary framework with its emphasis on particular 'saints' advocates a more individual accent, and the political events surrounding the rape are kept in the background. Homely scenes and emotional processes predominate, the private tragedy of the *matrona virilis* gains central importance. Lucrece no longer incites political combustion, she unwittingly sparks it off. This has consequences also for the style of presentation; Richard Heinze has analysed the difference between Livy's elevated and Ovid's emotive treatment of the story.[51]

In Christian times Lucretia's death becomes a touchstone of moral principles. For Augustine, who was puzzled by the fate of Dido, too, Lucretia poses a dilemma: if she was innocent, why did she kill herself; if not, why is she praised, 'Si adulterata, cur laudata; si pudica, cur occisa?' (*De civitate Dei*, I, xix).[52] He tries to solve this dilemma in favour of female Christian martyrs who did not have to prove their innocence in public because they could rely on the omniscience of their God. Augustine's correspondent Jerome, on the other hand, praises Lucretia without reservations and lists her among the pagan paragons of chastity (*Adversus Jovinianum*, I, 46).

Most medieval commentators follow Jerome rather than Augustine and set Lucretia first among Roman matrons, 'et primam ponam Lucretiam, quae violatae pudicitiae nolens supervivere, macellam corporis cruore delevit'.[53] Lydgate, comprehensive as ever, treats her twice in his *Fall of princes*, and presents, as in the case of Dido, both attitudes. His first version (*Fall of princes*, II, 974–1,344) is based on a rhetorical exercise by Coluccio Salutati in the casuistical tradition;[54] it adopts Augustine's line of argument and extends the alternative 'cur occisa' – 'cur laudata' to an altercation between husband and wife in the course of which Lucrece admits what Augustine had only hinted at:

> Al-be I was ageyn my will oppressid,
> Ther was a maner constreyned lust in dede,
> Which for noun power myht nat be redressid
>
> *(Fall of princes*, II, 1,282–4)

Although Lydgate does not, like Augustine, introduce anachronistic arguments into this discussion – on the contrary, he exculpates Lucretia's suicide on the grounds of an excessive regard for honour held in Roman society – his central tenet, namely that nature, and in particular female nature, is prone to concupiscence, has its basis in Christian teaching. Again the early humanist seems closer to the church-father than earlier medieval authors.[55]

Lydgate wrote a second version, however, in which he gave Lucrece an opportunity to exculpate herself. This time Lydgate borrowed from Boccaccio's *De casibus virorum illustrium*, but turned it into an apologetic complaint (*Fall of princes*, III, 932–1,148). Lucretia serves a similar double purpose in Jean de Meun's part of the *Roman de la rose*, again for encyclopaedic rather than any other reasons. In one of its misogynic passages Lucretia is named as the exception that proves the rule of female fickleness, and her case is treated favourably (8,608–50). But then the worldly-wise Ami suggests that even Lucretia – like Penelope – would have proved seducible if only the ravisher had gone about his purpose with more patience (8,651–60) – the ascetic extreme touches the extreme of cynicism.

In a way, Jean de Meun sets Ovid against Ovid in this *exemplum*: Ami's argument is taken from the *Ars amatoria*, 'Penelopen ipsam, persta modo, tempore vinces' (I, 477). The ascetic as well as the cynical attitudes survive in tales of famous women well into the seventeenth century. The cynical is demonstrated in historical epyllia such as William Barksted's *Hiren, or: The fair Greeke* (1611), where Mahomet's seductive arts are brutally summarised:

> Shew them the axe they'l suffer martyrdome,
> But if promotion to them you propose,
> And flattery, then to the lure they come   (B4v, stanza 60)[56]

The ascetic is visible in religious epyllia such as Robert Aylett's *Susanna: or The arraignment of the two unjust elders* (1622), where the heroine puts her trust like a Christian martyr in her God:

> But she that in th'Almightie put her trust,
> *Needes* no *Stilletto*, now for to defend
> Her honour [. . .]   (B5r)

What I shall follow up now is a third option, the sympathetic and pathetic rendering of Lucretia's case.

Lucretia in the Middle Ages

In John Gower's *Confessio amantis* the rape of Lucrece is related as part of a treatise on the education of princes, a kind of *Mirror for magistrates* held up, according to the Confessor, by Aristotle to his pupil Alexander (*Confessio amantis*, VII, 4,754–5,123). The tale is coupled with the similar one of Virginia, and both serve as warnings against the dangers of *libido* in a prince. The emphasis naturally falls not on Lucrece, but her ravisher, whom Gower calls Arrons. The didactic framework suggests the perspective of Livy. The Latin headnote and sidenotes which introduce and accompany the section on the princely virtue of chastity which contains the story of Lucrece confirm this expectation and add an ascetic, if not misogynic accent by linking the vice of 'voluptas' with femininity. One line in the headnote reads: 'Omne quod est hominis effeminat illa voluptas' (VII, 4,214, xi,3). Terms like 'carnis fragilitas' (4,263, sidenote) and 'concupiscence' (5,223) ring through the whole of this section. Even the Confessor Genius, whom we have come to know as the least martial of priests, commends in King David what he condemned in Aeneas, namely that he never tarries in the arms of a lady:

> Knyhthode he kepte in such a wise,
> That for no fleisshli covoitise
> Of lust to ligge in ladi armes
> He lefte noght the lust of armes. (4,347–50)

Arrons, however, succumbs to the 'lustes of his fleissh' (4,894) and mingles carnality and tyranny, 'he, which hath his lust assised / With melled love and tirannie' (4,898–9); he degenerates into barbarity and bestiality. Gower expresses this degeneration in no uncertain terms and speaks of 'wylde man' (4,905), 'Tigre' (4,944), 'wolves mouth', (4,984), and so on.

These stern passages are part of the framework of the tale. Gower's gentle art warms only in the central scenes with Lucrece, the 'Lomb', in the wolf's mouth. He is most at home in domestic surroundings, describing Lucrece at her spinning wheel, for instance, or, most memorably, at the bedside, when Arrons seizes her in his arms and she, 'thurgh tendresce of wommanhiede' (4,975) loses her voice for dread, 'lich a Lomb whanne it is sesed / In wolves mouth' (4,983–4). Scenes like these, conventional though the animal imagery may be, show Gower at his best. Derek Pearsall is right in saying that his humanity is most obvious in his tales about women and that with Lucrece he 'achieves perhaps his most perfect realisation of womanliness'.[57]

What distinguishes Gower's handling of figures such as Lucrece is the 'tenderness' which Dryden praised in Ovid. Gower adds an element of discretion in dealing with these figures which both the Latin poet and the church-father occasionally lack. His Lucrece is never submitted to the alternative, to suffer shame or defamation, and she is spared the dilemma that called forth Augustine's and Lydgate's casuistic doubts: she is allowed to swoon in the ravishment scene. Gower mentions this tenderness again when Lucrece reports the incident with a faltering voice:

> And sche, which hath hire sorwes grene,
> Hire wo to telle thanne assaieth,
> Bot tendre schame hire word delaieth,
> That sondri times as sche minte
> To speke, upon the point sche stinte.   (5,040–4)

Gower extends in these lines Ovid's formulaic (and epic) 'ter conata loqui' (*Fasti*, II, 823) into a remarkably shy version of the *semifractis verbis* motif frequently used in women's Complaints. He also transfers the final confession (possibly following a hint from Livy, 'in cubiculo', lviii, 6; Ovid, his main source, gives no exact location) into the bedroom again, and again there is an almost mute domestic scene behind closed doors. It is a scene full of intimate details and speaking gestures which have the mimic effect that Diderot observed in domestic tragedies and opposed to the grand *tragédie classique*.[58] To see a similar difference in terms of medieval narrative verse it suffices to turn to Lucretia's stilted bearing and wording in Lydgate's *Fall of princes* (III, 932–1,148).

The tendency which Gower shows in the central scenes of his tale to cut down public pronouncements and to put in silent gestures instead distinguishes his tale from similar treatments in a *Mirror for magistrates* framework, not only Lydgate's, but also others, up to Henry Carey's translation of Virgilio Malvezzi's treatise on *Romulus and Tarquin* (1637), in which Lucrece is given comparatively short shrift in a predominantly masculine world of affairs of state. Gower does not neglect his didactic purpose altogether. On the contrary, as a complement to the homely portrait he draws of Lucrece, the picture of Arrons is heightened (or lowered) into the inhuman – by the animal imagery already mentioned, and by demonic traits (there is, for example, an allusion to the Biblical figure of Satan the fowler, 4,914–5).[59] In the end Arrons gallops away stylised into a kind of personified double vice:

> And thus this lecherouse pride
> To horse lepte and forth he rod   (4,994–5)

The contrast between 'victa' and 'victor' (Ovid, *Fasti*, II, 810–11) is thus sharpened, and the public reaction to the private outrage ('Awey, awey the tirannie / Of lecherie and covoitise!', 5,118–9) not diminished, though it is seen in terms of personal morality.

In the treatise translated by Henry Carey, the key term 'tyranny' governs the story from the very start; it helps to solve the problem of suicide which Carey discusses as meticulously (and suspiciously) as Augustine. Lucrece is said to have succumbed to Tarquin's will for fear of death, which is always worse if it comes from a stranger's hand than from one's own, and to have killed herself, like so many other 'silly women', out of 'either a weaknesse of the braine, or poorenesse of courage' (p.259). The monologue of deliberation which Lucrece is given in a later chapter does little to erase that comment; at best she can hope to 'dye an example of fortitude' (p. 265) to the men around her, who seem not quite up to Carey's standards of manliness, for he shows little patience with their more private and familiar feelings:

The Father and Husband stood shedding unprofitable tears, over the body of *Lucretia*; they compassionated that chance, which not being naturall, ought rather to have moved anger in them, and animated them to revenge, than have incited them to pittie, and bedewed them with their teares   (pp. 265–6)

Carey wants to see the manly passions aroused that Dryden saw in Homer (anger, not pity), and he takes Ovid's description of Lucretia as 'matrona virilis' (*Fasti*, II, 847) literally; we have here the spirit of heroism that found its way into English literature in the course of the seventeenth century. We shall encounter several other examples in the course of this study; let me return now to the Middle Ages and authors like Gower whom her story stirred into compassion.

The chief example of this attitude is Gower's friend Chaucer, who tells the story of Lucrece in his *Legend of good women*. Chaucer had mentioned her before in his *Book of the duchess*, in a breath with Penelope, as paragon of a good woman, and referred to Livy as his source (*Book of the duchess*, 1,080–7). In the *Legend of good women* he names Ovid as an additional authority, and this is indicative of the way he turns Lucrece into a calendar saint in the manner of the *Fasti*.

Chaucer opens his 'Legend of Lucrece' in the grand style, with an epic formula, 'Now mot I seyn', but soon swerves away from the historical to the personal, from the expulsion of the kings to the praise of a good woman:

> Now mot I seyn the exilynge of kynges
> Of Rome, for here horible doinges,
> And of the laste kyng Tarquinius,
> As seyth Ovyde and Titus Lyvius.
> But for that cause telle I nat this storye,

> But for to preyse and drawe to memorye
> The verray wif, the verray trewe Lucresse,
> That, for hyre wifhod and hire stedefastnesse,
> Nat only that these payens hire comende,
> But he that cleped is in oure legende
> The grete Austyn, hath gret compassioun
> Of this Lucresse, that starf at Rome toun   (1,680–91)

This opening is remarkable for a number of reasons, not only for its twisted epic opening and the fact that Chaucer appears to lift 'wifhod' into something worthy of praise *per se* (perhaps in analogy to 'vir-tus'). There is, in addition, the intriguing invocation of 'the grete Austyn' which would be much more apposite at the beginning of the Dido legend. Augustine wept over the fate of Dido in his *Confessiones* (I, xiii) before he discarded her; he dismissed Lucretia straightaway. Unless we assume that Chaucer is simply mistaken (he may have mixed up Augustine with Jerome, or, as R.W. Frank thinks, been subject to a double error: recalling Augustine's tears over Dido and confusing the *Gesta Romanorum*, where these tears are mentioned, with the *Legenda aurea*), we must accept that he cuts both the historic and the patristic strictures off the story with a single stroke. Frank has shown in his analysis of the 'Legend of Lucrece' that this initial assumption is born out by the plain style and the pathetic tone of what follows.[60] Frank has also described the various ways in which Chaucer differs from his classical sources, Livy and Ovid.[61] In my own discussion of the legend I will concentrate on Chaucer's subtle criticism of the third authority he mentions, Augustine, and the repercussions this has for the whole of the *Legend of good women*.

What Chaucer does to Augustine's alternative 'cur occisa' – 'cur lauda-ta' is to set the ethos of 'trouthe' against Augustine's suspicion. It is a simple ethos, and it is easy to play it down as R.W. Frank appears to do when he says: 'If the moral does not seem to do full justice to the story, let it pass. It will do as well as any sentiment, any moral.'[62] But it is also easy to underestimate it. Chaucer constantly reminds us in his 'Legend of Lucrece', as he does in his 'Legend of Dido', of the importance of this ethos, from the opening lines which I have quoted to the ending when he stresses once more that he told the story for no other reason: 'I telle hyt, for she was of love so trewe' (1,874). It is obviously central to the *Legend of good women*, but I would add that it is equally central to the elegiac tradition in which he is writing and that its opposite, the notion of the frailty of women which lies at the bottom of Augustine's alternative, is central to the heroic and ascetic traditions. In both *Genesis* and the *Aeneid* it is a fragile or a variable woman who threatens to 'effeminate' man.

In the 'Legend of Lucrece' as well as in the 'Legend of Dido' the ethos of 'trouthe' is tested in the field of courtly love. The simple trust of Lucrece is set against the villany of Tarquin, who should have done 'as a lord and as a verray knyht' (1,821), but failed to do so. This seems to be in accordance with the courtly setting of the poem and the praise of women that is requested of the poet as a penance for his literary trespasses against the code of love. As a first step in the right direction, one will remember, he is asked to search his (unusually substantial) library of 'sixty bokes olde and newe' (G 273) for examples of good women. His library is said to consist mainly of 'olde bokes', that is classical texts (which, if true, would be very unusual, too). One of the two medieval writers named, and the only doctrinal authority, is Jerome (the other one is Vincent of Beauvais). Jerome's letter *Adversus Jovinianum*, with its list of pagan good women, is honoured above all the other books by being expounded at a length comparable only to the exposition of Ovid's *Heroides* in the 'Balade' that precedes the list. This in itself should rule out the possibility that Chaucer, in his remark on Augustine's alleged compassion with Lucrece, should have committed the vulgar error of confusing him with Augustine. Rather, one is tempted to assume that Chaucer both here and there gives a sly hint at Augustine's notorious criticism of women like Lucretia which is directly opposed to Jerome's commendation.

It is significant, moreover, that the God of Love, who enumerates the authorities to be consulted, claims that all the true women in Jerome's letter are pagan, 'And yit they were hethene, al the pak' (G 299). This is not quite correct, but the ordeals these 'olde wemen' (G 301) had to undergo, 'some were brend, and some were cut the hals, / And some dreynt, but they wolden not be fals' (G 292–3), would fit any of the Christian martyrs also mentioned in Jerome's treatise. In fact, the God of Love is made to stress the pre-Christian quality of these women in a way that makes their Christian counterparts look almost sanctimonious:

> For alle keped they here maydenhede,
> Or elles wedlok, or here widewehede.
> And this thing was nat kept for holynesse,
> But al for verray vertu and clennesse   (G 294–7)

It so happens that holiness, 'sanctitas', is a key term in Augustine's investigation into the case of Lucrece in which he sets out to prove the corporeal holiness of Christian martyrs:

contradicere audebunt hi, contra quos feminarum Christianarum in captivitate oppressarum non tantum mentes, verum etiam corpore sancta defendimus.

In the end he takes issue with those who, devoid of sanctity themselves, insult these Christian martyrs by placing pagan examples such as Lucretia above them:

Nobis tamen in hoc tam nobile feminae huius [i.e. Lucretiae] exemplo ad istos refutandos, qui Christianis feminis in captivitate compressis alieni ab omni cogitatione sanctitatis insultant   (*De civitate Dei*, I, xix)[63]

To safeguard the reputation of the Christian martyrs Augustine puts a question mark behind Lucretia's probity. He does this indirectly, by reporting the statement of a certain declaimer ('quidam declamans', p. 84) which is apt to sow doubt among the believers in the goodness of Lucretia. He quotes this statement, 'Mirabile dictu, duo fuerunt, et adulterium unus admisit', which McCracken translates as 'A wonderful tale! There were two and only one committed adultery' (p. 84), and he refers to it several times, so that it becomes a sort of refrain to his treatise of the matron.

If Chaucer had this passage in mind while working on his *Legend of good women* it is hard to escape the idea that he was out to defend the reputation of 'olde wemen' such as Lucretia against a narrowly Christian view which allows nothing but a religious understanding of virtue, a standard of *sanctitas* which cannot be met by anyone outside the Christian religion. This ideological background would give extra poignancy to the as yet exceptional use of the term 'legend' for a collection of classical tales in a courtly framework. The saintliness Chaucer looks for in his collection of legends is of all times; he finds it in old books like the *Fasti*, not in Christian calendars. At one point he expressly asks his readers to give credence to the wisdom of these books in the famous passage about the key of remembrance:

> And to the doctrine of these olde wyse,
> Yeve credence, in every skyful wise,
> That tellen of these olde appreved stories
> Of holynesse   (F 19–22)

This does not mean that Chaucer revives these old stories in order to replace Christian doctrines or what he calls the 'other holynesse' with respect to philosophical and theological translations (F 424), but rather that he tries to complement an overly strict Christian view of the world. He sets an attitude of down-to-earth morality against an idealism which he may feel to be no longer of this earth. Something similar happens to the courtly religion of love in his *Legend*. In the Prologue Chaucer questions not only all too exclusive Christian standards of behaviour, but also courtly practices of the affected flower-and-leaf kind. The emblem he chooses for Alceste sets his queen apart from the fashionable courtly cult: the daisy comprises elements of both flower and leaf ('Corowned with whit, and clothed al in grene', F 242), but its service is older than the courtly love-debates ('er swych stryf was begonne', F 196), and it is a humble flower, more down-to-earth than, for instance, the marguerite of French courtly poetry, and therefore better suited to symbolise the simple faith Chaucer attributes to Alceste and other classical heroines.

The homely and secular moral basis of Chaucer's *Legend of good women* deserves another look. It is surprising how often he mentions the earthly and worldly aspects of the experiences he is about to convey in his legends. This is often done in colloquial or proverbial terms; verbal tags and idioms such as 'in this world', 'syn that the world was newe', 'in youre world' abound (F 445, 489, G 302). Occasionally, however, such expressions take an extraordinary significance, as in the unexpected invocation to the daisy: 'As to myn erthly god to yow I calle' (F 95), or when the poet twice mentions the earthly origin of the endless procession of true women he sees in a vision (F 285–90). Chaucer consciously restricts his vision to a secular world, and this may well be the reason why he chooses pre-Christian settings for most of his tales, or even transfers medieval subjects to classical surroundings as in the case of the 'Merchant's tale'.

There is a pointed instance of this attitude at the beginning of the *Legend of good women* where the poet reminds us that we are to believe in heaven and hell though no one has yet returned from the dead. This statement is followed not by a Christian argument, but by the reference to the wisdom of the ancients I have mentioned above. The hell that no true lover will enter, and the paradise that Alcestis and her train retire to are clearly classical in concept (F 553; 563–4). Chaucer may be dissociating himself from Dante in passages like this; several of the lovers he praises for their 'trouthe' are to be found in Dante's 'Inferno' (Dido, for instance, and most notably Cleopatra, the 'martyr' with whom he is asked to start his legend): they are whirled around the second circle of hell with other sinners of the flesh ('Inferno', V, 37–69). Cupidity is, of course, one aspect of worldliness in its theological sense (that is, aversion from God), and it is traditionally the aspect to which women are supposed to be particularly prone.

This leads me back to Lucrece and the doubts Augustine cast on her martyrdom: the insinuating 'duo fuerunt' suggests that Lucrece may have fallen victim to her female nature and to cupidity; in this respect Augustine seems even less sure than his unnamed disclaimer that she could have remained chaste in the embrace while Tarquin was lewd. With Chaucer, as with Gower, it is Tarquin alone who is covetous, not in a theological, but in the simple original sense of the word:

And ay the more that he was in dispayr,

> The more he coveyteth and thoughte hire fayr.
> His blynde lust was al his coveytynge.
>
> (*Legend of good women*, 1,754–6)

Like Gower again, Chaucer excludes the possibility of collusion by sending Lucrece into a swoon. He makes it clear, moreover, that not only her physical sensation but also her moral sensibility has been obliterated: 'She feleth no thyng, neyther foul ne fayr' (1,818). It is with such pointed statements – they have, of course, no equivalent in any of the possible sources – that the 'Legend of Lucrece' makes one doubt if it is not written to counterbalance the high moral seriousness with which authors such as Augustine pass judgment on classical (and all mundane) standards of behaviour, and that possibly Chaucer's opening reference to Augustine's compassion is a covert criticism of the church-father: could anyone expect the author of *The city of God against the pagans* to commend Lucrece like 'these payens'?

One more sign that points to a critical meaning behind this reference is Chaucer's handling of the question of Lucrece's fear of shame. For Augustine this constitutes the second half of the dilemma: if she did not consent, she was innocent of adultery – but why should she then have killed herself, 'si pudica, cur occisa?' Even if Lucrece was strong enough to overcome the infirmity of her sex, he seems to say, she fell prey to what he calls the infirmity of her honour, 'pudoris infirmitas' (p. 88). For him, this excessive fear of shame (or avidity of praise, 'laudis avida nimium', p. 88) is part of her Roman heritage; Christian martyrs are not subject to the necessity of demonstrating their innocence and thus saving their honour: they have the testimony of their conscience which lies open to their omniscient and omnipresent God. Again, Augustine anachronistically uses his Christian law, a 'lex divina' (p. 90), to condemn pre-Christian behaviour. Chaucer, in contrast, uses a similar argument concerning the Romans' sense of honour to exculpate his lady: it is her fear of shame as much as her fear of death which makes Lucrece fall into her swoon:

> These Romeyn wyves lovede so here name
> At thilke tyme, and dredde so the shame,
> That, what for fer of sclaunder and drede of deth,
> She loste bothe at ones wit and breth.   (1,812–15)

Lucrece kills herself in the end not to save her own reputation, but that of her husband. She thus strikes once more the keynote of the *Legend of good women*, 'trouthe', and once again Chaucer uses 'wifly' as a synonym for 'virtuous':

> Hir herte was so wyfly and so trewe,
> She sayde that, for hir gylt ne for hir blame,
> Hir husbonde shulde nat have the foule name,

That wolde she nat suffre, by no wey.   (1,843–6)

The main point, then, in which Chaucer differs from Augustine's handling of Lucretia's story, is his stronger sense of historical distance and of
its complement, human closeness: women (and of course men) in ancient
times lived under secular laws, so it is unjust to blame them for their
worldliness. The fact that they lacked a self-evident divine law put them
under a strain unknown to their Christian counterparts and called for
closer human bonds. It is precisely this lack of a *lex divina* which makes
basic virtues such as 'trouthe' indispensible. If ethics on this basic level
fail, there is nothing but bottomless despair. The forlornness and godfor-
sakenness of Chaucer's heroines thus proves much more than just a sentimental ploy; it brings out their essential humanity.

Chaucer is not content to maintain the historical distance and to make
use of it in human terms; he expressly sets it side by side with the Christian
dispensation, but not necessarily to the latter's advantage as Augustine
does. He knows that the Romans had their divine laws, too, and their
calendar saints; Lucrece is made one of them:

> and she was holden there
> A seynt, and ever hir day yhalwed dere
> As in hir lawe   (1,870–2)

This links up the narrator's commission to write 'a glorious legende'
(F 483) with Ovid's *Fasti* (rather than with Livy's work of history, to
which he refers his readers, 1,873). But Chaucer goes on to connect
Lucrece's exemplary life with Christian teaching by praising her in all but
Christian terms; he quotes, or slightly misquotes again, the gospel of
Matthew and contaminates the words Jesus bestows on the centurion
('Amen dico vobis, non inveni tantam fidem in Israel', Matthew 8.10)
with those on the woman of Canaan, whose child he cured ('Magna est
fides tua', Matthew 15.28):

> For wel I wot that Crist himselve telleth
> That in Israel, as wyd as is the lond,
> That so gret feyth in al that he ne fond
> As in a woman; and this is no lye.   (1,879–82)

Chaucer may also have had in mind the Magdalen, who was forgiven her
sins because of her great love ('quoniam dilexit multum', Luke 7.47) and
of her faith ('Fides tua te salvam fecit', Luke 7.50). Mary Magdalen's
love, like that of Lucrece, is stronger than death, but all too human, and
it has also been both condemned and commended by church-fathers. Her
love and faith are treated in a sermon with strong empathetic tendencies
which Alceste mentions in the Prologue among the works that should
exculpate Chaucer in the eyes of the God of Love, 'Orygenes upon the

Maudeleyne' (G 418). This sermon contains questions as searching as those which Augustine put to Lucrece, questions which suggest a lack of faith, or a womanly weakness in the Magdalen. There is, for example, the fact that the Magdalen does not immediately recognise the risen Christ because he is transformed beyond her worldly understanding. This may raise the question why she looks for someone she hardly knows at all: 'Si quaeris, cur non cognoscis? Si cognoscis, cur quaeris?' In the sermon, this question is answered with the kind of compassion that Chaucer shows in his 'Legend of Lucrece': 'Sic error non procedebat ab errore, sed ab amore & dolore.'[64] Other holy men were not as indulgent and interpreted the Magdalen's lack of understanding as a sign of womanly weakness. This will be my starting point in a later chapter; in the meantime it is interesting to note that Lancelot Andrewes, in his Easter Sermon of 1620, perhaps led by the similarity of the questions put to Mary and Lucrece, ascribed them to Augustine, in spite of the fact that he knows the *Omelia Origenis* very well and quotes from it in the very same sermon.[65] He also knows that Augustine was not exactly 'all womanis frend'.

William Shakespeare, *Lucrece*

Chaucer's Roman matron already deserved the title of an 'earthly saint' which Shakespeare gives her near the beginning of his tragic legend of *Lucrece* (1594). This poem is the 'graver labour' announced in the dedication to its companion piece, the erotic epyllion of *Venus and Adonis* (1593). It gathers in its 265 rhyme royal stanzas nearly all the themes and motifs employed in earlier versions of the Lucrece legend. Shakespeare weaves these given themes and motifs into a fabric of so rich and varied a texture that the basic story which he, like Chaucer, took mainly from Ovid's *Fasti*, is almost hidden in ornamental details. The various strains and the decorative material he uses have been unravelled by numerous critics; there is no need to repeat the exercise or to pass on the largely negative results.[66] I shall therefore concentrate on the poem's position between the epic and the elegiac traditions and the light that questions of genre can shed on Shakespeare's treatment of the central themes of innocence and experience, public and private virtues.[67]

First, however, a few words on the structure of the poem. Both its titles (*Lucrece* on the title page, *The rape of Lucrece* as running title of the first edition) suggest a concentration on the heroine of the story, which is the rule in the Ovidian tradition. Ovid's one-sided treatment of Lucretia in his *Fasti* resulted in an asymmetry of structure and of judgment which is typical of what Richard Heinze has called the elegiac narrative; in fact, Ovid's legend of Lucretia provides Heinze with one of the

main instances of this mode of story-telling. Shakespeare is less involved
in the fate of his heroine. His narrator, though always present and ready
to throw in comments, is not as emotional in his responses as Chaucer's;
he shows less of the subjectivity which Heinze analysed as another main
constituent of the elegiac narrative, and more of the objectivity characteristic of the epic or the drama.[68] Shakespeare's view is more balanced,
and this shows in the structure of the poem: it is almost as much about
Lucrece as it is about Tarquin, her ravisher. There should be a double
title: 'This earthly saint adored by this devil' (85).

The first part of *Lucrece*, comprising more than a third of the whole
and leading up to the rape, is given to Tarquin (1–742); there follows an
equally long part devoted to Lucrece and her lamentations; the rest of
the poem shows Lucrece surrounded by her family and brings about
the heroic ending (1,583–855). This well-balanced structure does not
completely wipe out the bias in favour of the heroine, of course; Lucrece
still holds the centre of the stage, and this is stressed by the long soliloquy
she delivers after the rape, in the middle of the poem. Her central role
is also apparent from the fact that she is on stage throughout the poem,
whereas Tarquin 'like a thievish dog creeps sadly thence' (736) halfway
through. Still, no one before had paid as much attention to the prince
as Shakespeare, and the dramatist shows remarkable empathy in the
ruminations of a proud and passionate mind; Tarquin is comparable, as
has been observed, to such equally ruthless, but more robust, characters
as Richard III, Iago, or Edmund.

At first sight, this empathy does little to shift the moral weights of the
story; they remain heavily loaded in favour of Lucrece. One might even
argue that the more balanced structure favours the establishment of a
melodramatic polarity of the poem and lifts the angelic Lucrece on the
one scale as much as it debases the demonic Tarquin on the other. In the
hands of a good artist, however, the demonic characters are apt to eclipse
their angelic counterparts, as witness Milton's *Paradise lost* or Richardson's *Clarissa*: the aesthetic effects tend to outweigh the moral results,
particularly if the moral is presented in an abstract manner. Something
like this happens in Shakespeare's *Lucrece*, too. What one keeps in mind
after having read the poem are the scenes of horror and the striking
conceits, not the moral lessons. This may in part be due to the fact that
these lessons are of dubious value in spite of the numerous discussions
of moral problems in the poem. Some of these discussions seem to lead
nowhere. Ian Donaldson has shown how they are cut short by
ungrounded decisions to act (they lead up to the rape and the suicide,
both negative acts which the discussions tried to avert). The moral
problems are stated, brought to a paradoxical head, and then dropped
unsolved. In the end the moral pattern of the poem which looked melo-

dramatically clear at the beginning ('this saint' – 'this devil') appears curiously blurred, and we are left with harsh comments from the man of action, Brutus, who condemns Lucrece's suicide as a 'childish humour' sprung from a 'weak mind' (1825). This comment does, of course, little to resolve the moral confusion left by the undecided debates between or within Tarquin and Lucrece, debates which have left the critics (Donaldson among them) baffled.

One of the crucial problems raised in the poem is the conflict of classical and Christian ethics, particularly with respect to the suicide of its heroine. The issue was brought to a head, as we have seen, by the church-fathers, in particular by Augustine. Chaucer tried to solve, or rather to evade it by leaving Christian scruples aside and presenting Lucrece as a timeless type of good woman concerned with basic domestic virtues, above all 'trouthe'. It is on such virtues, he seems to say, that higher orders are built, and this is what the ancients knew; personal trust, for example, is the basis of morality, both private and public, and in this world it is just as important as Augustine's trust in God. Chaucer gives a glimpse of the Christian perspective only in the end of his 'Legend', and then only to pass it over. Although, I think, Shakespeare shares Chaucer's basically secular vision, the religious perspective is opened up more often in his poem than in Chaucer's 'Legend of Lucrece': 'even Christianity creeps in', was C.S. Lewis's exasperated comment on one of these occasions when Lucrece ponders whether she should risk the perdition of her soul (1,156–8).[69] As Ian Donaldson has pointed out, Shakespeare wavers here as elsewhere between Christian and Roman ethics; Donaldson sees 'a basic indecisiveness' at the heart of the poem.[70]

The scruples of Lucrece come close indeed to the doctrinal position taken by Augustine for whom suicide is the irredeemable sin. But classical authors were equally opposed to it, although for less doctrinal reasons. In Livy's account, father and husband try to persuade Lucrece that there is neither sin nor guilt in an act committed without consent:

dant ordine omnes fidem; consolantur aegram animi avertendo noxam ab coacta in auctorem delicti: mentem peccare non corpus, et unde consilium afuerit, culpam abesse.   (*Ab urbe condita*, I, lviii)

Ovid has a similar assertion in his legend: 'Dant veniam genitor facto coniuxque coacto' (*Fasti*, II, 829). What then is remarkable in the demeanour of Lucrece and calls for explanation is the fact that she chooses death against the ethical rules applicable in her case, both Christian and pagan. The reason why Lucrece chooses death in spite of her innocence must lie in her private ethos. She must either feel guilty or possess an uncommonly fine sense of honour. Thus far Augustine was right in questioning her attitude, 'Si adulterata, cur laudata; si pudica, cur occisa' (*De civitate Dei*, I, xix). The question is only whether he was right in condemning her on both these heads: because she felt soiled herself and because she wanted to save her husband's honour. He insinuated a possible collusion in the rape, and he found Lucretia's sense of honour excessive, which in a way it is: it is an aristocratic idea, even by Roman standards, and binding only for those who measure themselves against the highest ethic standards, standards which are not enforcible by any law: there are similar ideals in Christianity: you can enforce neither *pietas* nor *caritas*, saintliness is a self-imposed profession.

Lucretia's ethical stand, then, is as high-principled as the most ascetic Christian ideal, but it is hard to see from one peak to the other. Augustine's view was obviously clouded, but Chaucer and Shakespeare try to test Lucretia's attitude on her own ground, the one by measuring its base, the other its height. Chaucer, as we have seen, twists the historical argument that Roman ladies loved their names exceedingly into further proof of Lucrece's modesty. The question of whether Lucretia's integrity was in any way damaged by the rape or by the suicide is simply ignored. Shakespeare takes both these questions seriously. The thoughts of his Lucrece revolve very much around the point of honour, and Shakespeare makes honour the final turning point to the heroic conclusion of his tale ('honour' or one of its derivatives is mentioned five times in one stanza to mark this point, 1,184–90). Shakespeare accepts Lucrece's rigid notions of honour without measuring them against an advanced ethos of his own. He also accepts Lucrece's feeling of guilt, or rather of pollution (the subject of a striking *aetion* in the tale), and in this, I think, lies the originality of his poem. He is the first to see that a purity of mind like that of Lucrece is fated to attract and eventually to mix with its sordid opposite in an unperfect world.

Both Chaucer and Shakespeare thus move beyond merely historical arguments about the acceptability of Lucretia's behaviour and lay bare more elementary problems underneath. Chaucer solves these problems on a basic level: his Lucrece follows her simple faith and dies a martyr of conjugal love. His narrator is able to close the gap between Christian idealism and down-to-earth humanism. Shakespeare gives his Lucrece such an exalted sense of honour that the gap between her ideals and sordid reality becomes unbridgeable; there is no narrator to propose a rational solution; there is a common-sense-commentator in the end, the man-of-the-world Brutus, but his judgment is almost as unflattering as that of the man of the church, Augustine.

The gap which Chaucer had bridged with down-to-earth humanism is evident in Shakespeare's poem both in form and in substance. It is visible in the melodramatic polarisation of the characters which drives them almost outside the field of humanity; this is attested in images of the superhuman (angel-devil) and the subhuman (predator-prey) categories. Shakespeare's point is, however, that the extremes created by this polarisation meet; they meet in the middle of the story, in the rape. There is a kind of magnetism at work: the further apart the poles, the stronger the attraction. This elemental law can only be expressed in paradox, and paradox is one of the key figures in Shakespeare's poem. Figures of paradox affect even the accidentals of seemingly decorative description: there is a telling example in a passage which looks like a mixture of elements from the *Legend of good women* and an erotic epyllion: Lucrece is lying on her bed 'like an April daisy on the grass' (395); her hair looks 'like golden threads' (400), her sweat 'pearly' (396), and so on.[71] But then her head is 'entombed' in the pillow 'like a virtuous monument' (390–1), and from the description of her hair Shakespeare jumps into an entangled syntax of antitheses and, ultimately, paradox:

> O modest wantons, wanton modesty!
> Showing life's triumph in the map of death,
> And death's dim look in life's mortality.   (401–3)

The piling up of contradictions in passages like this which has attracted so much criticism is an extension only of the 'bottomless conceit' (701) at the heart of the poem which finds its supreme expression in the rape.

The rape is an essentially irrational event, a meeting of the indomitable forces of life and death; it can therefore be caught only in paradox, not in rational discourse. The structural devices which usually serve as the means for channelling such forces in didactic poetry, the formal debate and the *bellum intestinum*, only bring them to a head. Tarquin is resolved on his deed right from the start; Shakespeare forbears even to show how he arrived at his resolution; his post-haste entrance on the scene, 'Borne by the trustless wings of false desire' (2), shows him well beyond or above the hurdles of reflection. In didactic poems (not only medieval ones, as C.S. Lewis has shown) morality is a matter of rational decisions;[72] the debates Tarquin engages in before the rape are no more than what has been called see-saw rhetoric. Something similar applies to the deliberations that occupy the mind of Lucrece after the rape. There is no definite line of argument between her first helpless reactions and the swiftness of her suicide. The exclamations and declamations in between are expressions of paralysis. They do little to prepare the decision, they follow the fluctuations of a troubled mind, not the logic of discourse, and this has led critics to call them aimlessly rhetorical like the debate between Tarquin and Lucrece.[73] This view, however, wipes out the distinction between her benumbed and his impetuous attitude. The monologues of Lucrece are static, where Tarquin's arguments are active,[74] and the rhetoric in both is comparable only in that it is ineffectual in a practical

or rational sense; that is why Brutus, the politician, sheds no tears over
Lucrece and presses for action. The protagonists are both made to realise
their temperamental differences: 'My will is strong past reason's weak
removing', says Tarquin (243); 'This helpless smoke of words doth me
no right', Lucrece (1,027). In Tarquin's determination and the pleading
of Lucrece Shakespeare has set side by side elements of the epic and the
elegiac style; these elements prove as incompatible as the natures of their
bearers, and lead only to deadlock.

Both Tarquin and Lucrece are subject to impulses beyond rational
control. Their decisions are brought about by sensual impressions rather
than rational discourse. They are both susceptible to visual impressions.
As soon as one has been alerted to this fact, it is almost disconcerting to
see how often the organs of sight and their objects are mentioned in the
poem.[75] One might sense an affinity with the erotic epyllion here, and
there is talk of the rhetoric of beauty which seems to confirm this:

> Beauty itself does of itself persuade
> The eyes of men without an orator   (29–30)

This is part of the creed of eroticism, and Tarquin confesses himself to
be, like Paris in Heywood's *Oenone*, a devotee of the religion of beauty.
It is his eye that confounds his wits (290) and lures him into the bedroom
of Lucrece (365–71). In a more serious context this being led by the eye
is, of course, a grave misconduct: the senses should be subservient to
reason and will. Tarquin knows that he is about to desert his moral
faculties in following his eyes:

> But will is deaf, and hears no heedful friends;
> Only he hath an eye to gaze on beauty,
> And dotes on what he looks, 'gainst law or duty.   (495–7)

What Shakespeare describes as a process of degradation could be defined
as uplifting in the literature of courtly love and *amor hereos*. In its initial
stages, the progress of love is the same as that of lust. Love, like lust,
enters through the eye and takes possession with elemental force. If it is
pure, this force can spur the lover on to heroic exploits. This heroic
possibility is kept alive in the background of Shakespeare's poem. The
imagery Tarquin employs in his *bellum intestinum* and in his impetuous
wooing is that of maritime and military adventure, variations on the
imperial theme which we find in epic and romance, but also in Petrarchan
poetry. Tarquin chooses desire for his pilot (279) and affection for his
captain (271); the 'maiden worlds unconquered' (408) of Lucrece's
breasts excite a commander's ambition, and the rape is reported as the
siege and sacking of a town (433–41; 463–83). The difference between
Shakespeare's and a sonneteer's treatment of such material lies in the

fact that his Tarquin, unlike the lover in Petrarchan poetry, lives in a world not of romance, but of history, and this is where beauty breeds lust rather than love. Furthermore passion, if followed, can lead into disasters as devastating as the fall of Troy. Tarquin appears to have seen these consequences from the start of his enterprise, and the way he runs open-eyed to his destruction gives his fall a certain sinister, if not Satanic, greatness. It is an extreme case of *amor hereos*.[76]

The fall of Tarquin is completed in the rape. The question now is how to disentangle Lucrece from his deadly embrace. Chaucer does this by making a virtue of her humiliation: he praises her humbleness and pass-ivity; Shakespeare at first tries to lift her into active greatness. He reverses the process of humiliation and transforms her from an elegiac into an epic heroine. This can be shown, I think, by his handling of a few key motives from the elegiac tradition. After the first 'smoke of words' in her invocations of time, night and opportunity (one should notice that these are abstract, but not metaphysical addressees) Lucrece looks for solace in the natural world, and finds some in the song of the nightingale (1,128–48). Her wish, however, to follow Philomela into 'Some dark deep desert seated from the way' (1,144) proves no more than wishful thinking: this is not the way of heroism, and she does not live in a world where 'sad tunes' (1,147) can make beasts gentle (an allusion to the Orpheus or the Arion myth: we have already found them connected with Philomela in Patrick Hannay's *The nightingale*). Lucrece, however, has to find a way into, not out of, reality. The next step Lucrece takes is to write a letter to her husband; it starts like a letter in the *Heroides* tradition: the greeting has the familiar ring of Ovidian word-play:

> Thou worthy lord
> Of that unworthy wife that greeteth thee,
> Health to thy person! (1,303–5)

But again she is cut short abruptly; the futility of the enterprise becomes evident in the negation of a number of conceits which might be taken from the *Heroides*: Lucrece will not betray her grief 'Ere she with blood had stain'd her stain'd excuse' (1,316), nor will she 'blot the letter / With words, till action might become them better' (1,322–3).[77] She is clearly on her way to a different scene, and this comes into view in the historical picture which she describes soon after.

This picture (a painting or a tapestry) which in medieval fashion shows a sequence of events around the destruction of Troy, has frequently been the subject of comment and speculation.[78] Once again, I will concentrate on the generic aspects of the piece. Formal descriptions of mythological or historical scenes are, as we have noticed, familiar elements in both epic and epyllion. Formulaic phrases, such as 'There might you see'

(1,380) and 'You might behold' (1,388), are reminiscent of the brass or glass reliefs in Virgil's temple of Juno (*Aeneid*, I, 466–93) and Chaucer's temple of Venus (*House of fame*, I, 119–467). The scenes of siege and storm which Lucrece sees in the picture remind her of the rape which was described in similar imagery. Again Shakespeare directs much of the attention towards details of gesture and physiognomy – again the eyes of the persons thronged in the Trojan scenes are mainly referred to: the eyes of the dying on the battlefield (1,378), of the defenders behind their loop-holes (1,383), and those of single heroes, the rolling eyes of Ajax, the sly glance of Ulysses (1,398–1,400), and so on. The eyes of Lucrece are arrested by Hecuba's look, 'Staring on Priam's wounds with her old eyes' (1,448); she would like to scratch out the eyes of all the Greeks, particularly those of Helen and of Paris:

> Show me the strumpet that began this stir,
> That with my nails her beauty I may tear!
> Thy heat of lust, fond Paris, did incur
> This load of wrath that burning Troy doth bear;
> Thy eye kindled the fire that burneth here,
>   And here in Troy, for trespass of thine eye,
>   The sire, the son, the dame and daughter die.   (1,471–7)

The parallel with Tarquin's 'lewd unhallowed eyes' (392) is all too obvious; there is another connection with the treacherous eyes of Sinon, whose tears contributed to the destruction of the city, 'His eye drops fire' (1,552).

The parallels which Lucrece sees between the destruction of Troy and her rape open up an epic dimension to her experience. The sight of 'despairing Hecuba' (1,447), moreover, opens her eyes for the necessity to play a more active role and to extinguish the fire that Tarquin has dropped on her body and the city of Rome. She must not suffer her fate as mutely or as passively as Hecuba, but 'tune her woes' (1,465) and find an answer to the question behind the general history of destruction:

> Why should the private pleasure of some one
> Become the public plague of many moe?   (1,478–9)

The letter-writers and complainants of the elegiac tradition are forced to acquiesce in their roles as passive victims of the masters of history. Lucrece will not acquiesce, Shakespeare wants her to be the mistress of her fate. But she cannot take this into her own hand. All she can do is publicise her shame and call for revenge. That is still only words: the action will have to be taken by men, not even the men most affected by her fate, her father and her husband, but by men of action like Brutus. She can do no more than raise the alarm; the striking comparison of her words to the smoke that rises from a cannon or a volcano (1,042–3) is entirely apt for the heroic, but essentially passive role assigned to the matron.

What remains of Lucrece's resolution to follow the course of honour, then, is the smoke of words; words and the ultimate gesture, suicide. The question mark this leaves behind the possibility of female heroism can be set behind many of the stylistic means Shakespeare employs to build up his heroine to heroic status. There is, for instance, the anachronism of the cannon in Rome (but cannons are fired in Langland's hell and will be fired in Milton's heaven). Even more striking, and, in a way, anachronistic, is the etiological myth which Shakespeare attaches to Lucrece's suicide: the blood issuing from her wound is said to separate into different streams, one pure (red) and one contaminated (black), and this was the first instance of coagulation (1,737–50). C.S. Lewis finds the *aition* repellent;[79] we have come to associate etiological myths with epyllia derived from the *Metamorphoses*. It looks out of place and time in ancient Rome, like a mythic remnant in an otherwise historical setting.[80] Shakespeare apparently uses mythic and heroic elements in order to heighten the status of his heroine; what seems incongruous in these elements is not so much the anachronism, but the breach of style they bring about. Up to the middle of the poem Lucrece is associated with meek animals such as the dove or the lamb (for instance 360, 505–11, 540–6, and so on), the emblems of innocence and helplessness we find already in Ovid's *Fasti*. This traditional emblematic imagery does not accord with the heroic or the mythic imagery applied to Lucrece later on. The epic and the elegiac, like action and passion, will not readily accord.

In his desire to give the story of Lucrece a universal appeal Shakespeare drives his characters almost beyond the confines of humanity and develops them into types of obedience and brutality. But he also sees the inevitable clash of these opposite poles, and in this, I think, lies the significance of the rape of his Lucrece. In Shakespeare's universe the brutal and the innocent are not kept apart as they would be in a melodramatic context, but are fatally attracted. The forces at work behind these positions are hard to present convincingly in dramatic form; it is harder still to describe them in an epic. They are, as Lucrece is made to feel, beyond comprehension:

> O deeper sin than bottomless conceit
> Can comprehend in still imagination!   (701–2)

They are certainly beyond the sort of description Shakespeare found in contemporary epyllia. This may be the reason why he tries to show them in images like the quasi-mythic coagulation *aition*. The deeper sense hidden behind this seemingly inappropriate myth may be the conviction that a clear-cut distinction between purity and corruption is possible only outside this world.

The inevitable attraction, if not fusion, of contraries like innocence and experience has rather dark metaphysical implications and is hard to bear for those in charge of metaphysical distinctions. Poetry of the sentimental kind, which is ultimately based on a Morality-like division of heaven and hell, usually tries to keep them apart. Shakespeare rarely hints at any religious significance in his story. Like Chaucer, he seems aware of the scandal this might cause to Christian dogmatism; and like Chaucer he lays the scenes of his most serious work outside the pales of Christianity. But there are allusions in *Lucrece* which point towards a spiritual meaning behind the story. Expressed in spiritual terms, the rape of Lucrece is an act of profanation, an 'earthly saint adored by [a] devil', and on this level the suggestion of an inextricable fusion of the saintly and the satanic must startle not only the orthodox. There are indications pointing in this direction, and once more it is the eyes staring out of every corner in the poem which are expressive of this spiritual truth. There is, for instance, the scene when Tarquin draws aside the curtains of Lucrece's bed and his eyes are blinded her beauty. What looks at first sight like Petrarchan hyperbole is soon turned into a scene of profanation which changes Lucrece's bed into a shrine on which the saint-like sleeper is forced to prostitute herself:

> And holy-thoughted Lucrece to their sight
> Must sell her joy, her life, her world's delight.   (384–5)

The notion of profanation is enforced by the fact that Tarquin enters the bedroom ('the heaven of his thought', 338) with a prayer on his lips ('as if the heavens should countenance his sin', 343). Profanation has been an element in similar stories before (we remember that Gower's Helen is abducted from a temple; Marlowe's Hero catches Leander's eye on her way to the temple, and the same happens with Barksted's Hiren); but in these cases it does not have consequences as far-reaching as in Shakespeare's poem. The brightness of beauty (490) that dazzles Tarquin's eyes and looks like daylight is compared to the sun (372–3); Tarquin, on the other hand, is a creature of the night (he is compared to a night-owl, 360). After the rape, these associations are reversed: Tarquin flees into broad daylight, and Lucrece wishes for night to cover her shame (745–6). The cosmic confusion that ensues is expressed in quasi-religious language which seems to prove Tarquin's surmise right that even the 'blackest sin is clear'd with absolution' (354): he escapes a penitent, she stays behind like a lost soul:

> He thence departs a heavy convertite,
> She there remains a hopeless castaway   (743–4)

Ian Donaldson has pointed out the Christian connotations of these comparisons;[81] it is important, however, to stress again that they do not constitute a specifically Christian framework. Still, the 'music from behind the wings' is much louder in Shakespeare than in' Chaucer, at least towards the end. It is possible that Shakespeare intended to allow his heroine a metaphysical compensation for her loss. When we are told, for example, at the beginning of the tale that Lucrece loses all 'world's delight' (385) we tend to think of heavenly treasures she will win instead, but perhaps this is only so because we are accustomed to seeing heroines in domestic melodramas rewarded that way. Perhaps Shakespeare only wants to avoid the impression that his heroine suffers an irreparable loss. She lives in an unredeemed, pre-Christian world, and her story is apt to produce this impression. Shakespeare gives us glimpses of a world void of hope occasionally. There is, for instance, a moment when even the sun appears to be of the same voyeuristic disposition as her ravisher, and Lucrece asks him to look away: 'O eye of eyes, / Why pry'st thou through my window; leave thy peeping' (1,088–9). But the cosmic confusion is only temporary, and Shakespeare does his best to lift his heroine out of it. Lucrece must not sink into despair like the Hecuba she contemplates in the picture of Troy, or the Dido in Virgil's *Aeneid* who, shortly before her suicide, expresses a world-weariness ('taedet caeli convexa tueri', *Aeneid*, IV, 451) that is not relieved. The poet to explore the feelings of a desperate soul is Thomas Middleton.

Thomas Middleton, *The ghost of Lucrece*

C.S. Lewis was grateful that Shakespeare did not clothe his *Lucrece* in the form of a Complaint as almost any other poet of the 1590s would have done.[82] One of these contemporaries was Thomas Middleton, and he did exactly what Shakespeare avoided: *The ghost of Lucrece* is a Complaint in the manner of the *Mirror for magistrates*. Middleton nevertheless professes to be a follower of Shakespeare's example: he was even younger than Trussell and Heywood when they wrote their epyllia, and like them he bows to the elder poet, changing Shakespeare's modesty formula ('unpolished lines' in *Venus and Adonis*, 'untutored lines' in *Lucrece*) to 'mine infant lines' in his dedication. Only one copy of the *The ghost of Lucrece* is preserved in the Folger Library. It was printed in 1600 and rediscovered in 1920; Joseph Q. Adams, who edited the poem from this copy, dates the composition to approximately 1596–8, when Middleton was between sixteen and eighteen, and the wave of Ovidian literature already past its height.[83]

The ghost of Lucrece is an erratic and an irritating poem; it bears all the marks of an immature but exceptionally gifted poet. There are weaknesses in structure and in style, but on the whole it is one of the most remarkable experiments in the genre of Complaints. The expectations raised by its title are only partly met. One expects a Complaint in the style of the *Mirror for magistrates*; the blend of Senecan and Ovidian elements, however, which characterises the feminine examples of the kind (the emergence of this subgenre from the predominantly masculine background of the *Mirror for magistrates* will be treated in chapter 4) disintegrates into its dramatic and elegiac components under Middleton's hands. There is the familiar Senecan opening scene, which Middleton sets apart in a prologue: the poet addresses Rhamnusia, the goddess of revenge, and conjures up the ghost of the heroine from the underworld, 'the bloody crystal of a Ghost / Wrapt in a fiery web I spin' (9–10). Middleton's Lucrece does not, however, go on to deliver the expected monologue to the poet and the public at large. In Complaints of the *Mirror for magistrates* type this usually gives ample opportunity for moralising asides. Middleton changes the direction in which the Complaint is spoken and makes it a more dramatic affair: Lucrece, with blood-stained dagger in hand, is allowed to summon the ghost of Tarquin in her turn, and addresses him in a sort of one-sided dialogue or what was later called a dramatic monologue. Tarquin is called up in a series of invocations addressed at 'Tarquin the Night-Owl', reminiscent both of the night-owl metaphor and Lucrece's exclamations in Shakespeare's poem. The six-fold invocations are set at hourly intervals leading up to midnight, when Tarquin finally appears; he remains a silent phantom in the background.

The situation is hard to visualise; apparently we are asked to imagine the scene to be laid 'on the stage of Lucrece' heart' (183). This does little to reduce the artificiality of the situation, but it is in line with a process of internalisation which accompanies the development of women's Complaints, and it adds a surreal note to the claustrophobic atmosphere characteristic of the genre. This atmosphere is brought to burning, and sometimes bursting, intensity by Middleton's heated style:

> This is the tragic scene! Bleed, hearts! Weep, eyes!
> Fly, soul, from body, spirit, from my veins;
> Follow my chastity (where'er it lies),
> Which my unhallowed body now refrains.
> Look to the lamp of chastity, it wanes!
>   The star which guided all my elements
>   Pulls in her head and leaves the firmaments.   (190–6)[84]

Lucrece re-enacts her rape on this imaginary scene, and at the end of her performance she breaks down: the post mortem event has as much impact as the live one; the effect is one of a nightmare that will repeat itself

endlessly. There is no one to wake Lucrece from it. Her husband Collatine is invoked, but proves as inefficient as in all the versions of her story.
There is no political perspective, either: the man of action, Brutus, fails to
appear; the cry for vengeance which stands at the outset of the Complaint
resounds unheard. Lucrece, who entered the scene like a Senecan fury,
'sucking at Revenge's dugs' (3), is reduced in the end to the helplessness
of an Ovidian heroine: she exchanges her blood-stained dagger for a pen
and writes down her lost dream of innocence with ink drawn from her
heart.[85] She entitles it, 'The lines of blood and flame', and sends the script
after Tarquin, who has vanished into hell. She will soon have to follow
him down there, and they will be joined by the equally damned couple
of Tereus and Philomela. A sinister epilogue speaks of the baleful concat-
enation of vices and virtues, beauty and death. Strands of the revenge
tragedy, the *Mirror* Complaint and the heroical epistle are woven into
the intricate pattern which Middleton had announced in a dedicatory
poem, 'the bloody crystal of a Ghost / Wrapt in a fiery web I spin'
(9–10).

The thematic pattern of the poem is equally complex and hard to
unravel. The question of guilt and innocence, in particular, is curiously
convoluted. After the deaths of the tyrant and his victim one would have
thought the problem to be settled and Lucrece assigned to a place at least
in limbo. But Middleton's heroine is damned like Tarquin and accuses
herself of irredeemable, though inexplicable, guilt. She has lost her chastity which is, as in Shakespeare's poem, associated with star-imagery,
and this loss is for her apparently equivalent to the fall of her soul.
Shakespear's 'bottomless conceit' (*Lucrece*) is deepened into spiritual
depths, and Lucrece has in fact become a fallen angel:

> 'Twas thou, O Chastity, m'eternal eye,
> The want of thee made my ghost reel to hell!   (449–50)

The hell of Lucrece is not just a pagan Orcus; this can be deduced *e
contrario* from her description of the Elysium she has lost, and ever longs
for; it is rendered in a strange mixture of Christian and classical elements:

> That choir of saints in virgin-ornament,
> Where angels sing like choristers of heaven;
> Where all the martyrs kneel the element;
> Where Cynthia's robe and geat Apollo's steven
> Hangs at the altar of this milken haven   (442–6)

Lucretia cannot be counted among the saints, then, not even Chaucer's
'earthly saints'; she is a castaway in almost the theological sense used
only in analogy in Shakespeare's *Lucrece*. If this seems odd in terms of
morality and theology, it is in a line with a direction the genre of the

Complaint took in its religious variants at about the same time as Middleton was writing his poem: we shall find the same contrition and the same longing for a lost paradise in Nicholas Breton's Complaints of Protestant souls. Here as well as there the reasons for the sense of guilt expressed in these Complaints are never given: it must be a weakness, if not a sin, inherent in the 'waxen minds' of women that Shakespeare mentions in his poem (*Lucrece*, 1,240). Women are forced to bear the marks of sins committed not by themselves but by some marble masculine opponent. It is, as can easily be seen, a secular version of the notion of an original sin, with the difference that these latter Eves did not consent to the sin committed, let alone seduce their partners. They are damned, nevertheless, alongside the evil-doers. This is not the fancy of a misogynic mind. Middleton makes only more poignant what Shakespeare expressed in the laments of his Lucrece: that the good and the bad have to suffer the consequences of evil, regardless of guilt and of gender. Middleton accepts this notion, which lies at the heart of the genre of Complaints, without question; he does not sound the ethical or theological implications of his story, and there is little to be gained by protesting against his indifference.

Middleton, then, expresses more openly the paradox at the core of the Lucrece story, the fact that purity invites the forces of corruption and is doomed from the start to be lost irrecoverably. He expresses it above all in his remarkable imagery. At first sight the exuberance of this imagery seems to burst the frame of the poem and to drown all his concerns with character and theme. Looked at more closely, however, a recurrent pattern becomes visible which shows the basic antagonism of temperaments and of virtues and vices in repeated variations. The title Lucrece gives her letter, 'The lines of blood and flame', offers a clue to the groundwork of the fabric: Lucrece is time and again connected with blood and tears, Tarquin with fire and ashes. The temperamental differences are set up in the prologue:

> Now weepeth Lucrece with a trine of eyes,
> Quenching the fire of lust with tears and blood   (22–3)

It is there transferred to the audience: the Complaint should appeal to women, whose souls are to be 'sod in tears' (8), as well as to men, who are 'moulded in fire and dust' (17). Physiological images like these are developed in the course of the poem with almost pathological zest. Tarquin's soul burns in 'lustful fire' (140) and melts the virginal snow of Lucrece's chastity into the blood of shame (134–40). Shakespeare's etiological myth seems to have produced plentiful offspring. The unsavoury mixture of heart and breast, blood and milk in many of the conceits shows also an affinity to the baroque sensibility so conspicuous at the time in counter-Reformation religious literature, where it is applied to the Virgin Mary and her son. It becomes the less palatable in the unholy pair of Middleton's Tarquin and Lucrece:

> Thou art my nurse-child, Tarquin, thou art he!
> Instead of milk, suck blood, and tears, and all!
> In lieu of teats, Lucrece, thy nurse, even she,
> By tragic art seen through a crystal wall
> Hath carvèd with her knife thy festival.
>> Here's blood for milk; suck till thy veins run over!
>> And such a teat which scarce thy mouth can cover!   (78–84)

The discord in humours between Tarquin and Lucrece is sometimes reduced to the elementary division of fire and water (Lucrece's 'elemental eyes', 77; Tarquin's 'spirit of fire', 57), but then again forced into paradoxical compounds such as fiery blood (19), or fiery flood (518). With his violent imagery Middleton tries to penetrate deeper than even Shakespeare into the 'bloody mysteries' (47), or the 'fiery mysteries' (150) behind the ill-fated pair. This becomes obvious where Middleton uses images similar to those employed by Shakespeare. The impure flame of lust, for example, is compared to a torch in both Shakespeare's and Middleton's poem (*Lucrece*, 178, 314–5; *Ghost of Lucrece*, 41–2). Middleton may have meant to allude, as Adams supposes, to the firebrand Paris in Hecuba's dream;[86] the point to note, however, is that Middleton does not draw extended analogies of a mythical kind like Shakespeare but condenses such analogies into metaphors which mirror states of mind rather than models of action. This is also evident in Middleton's handling of military metaphors and historical allusions: they are concentrated, internalised and subservient to a private experience (see the personal pronouns in metaphoric expressions such as 'Driving the foe from scaling of my heart', 56; 'To sack my Collatine's Collatium', 98 – this refers to the body of Lucrece – and 'the foe hath sack'd thy city', 211). These metaphors are condensations of Shakespeare's extended Troy similes; the difference is also visible if Shakespeare's own metaphors are compared to Middleton's: Shakespeare turns inside out what remains internal in Middleton. In his *Lucrece* the physiological reaches out into the public: in Shakespeare's poem the eyes of Paris and of Sinon drop fire into Troy (*Lucrece*, 1,475, 1,552); in Middleton's the fire of Tarquin's lust and treason burns hearts and souls, not cities. Middleton is less interested in giving his poem a public dimension than in exhibiting the elementary human experience, and this tendency is certainly enhanced by the form of the first person Complaint which forces the poet into the personal perspective of the complainant.

Concentration on the mental state of his heroine and the narrative situation of the *post mortem* Complaint allows Middleton, on the other hand, to follow the spiritual implications of his story into depths and heights that reach far beyond its historical significance. This again is brought out best by looking at the use he makes of imagery also used by Shakespeare. Although there is a constant interplay of day and night, earth and sky in his poem, Shakespeare, as we have seen, only occasionally touches on the metaphysical implications of the tale. His sun and his stars take on symbolic, but rarely spiritual meaning. With Middleton this is different. He crams his poem with cosmological conceits, and they usually have spiritual connotations. Next to the physiological, it is metaphysical imagery which colours the poem, and these fields of reference are related to each other. I will give but a few instances: Middleton's Tarquin is associated with various planets, with Venus, like Paris, but also with the Sun (for example in line 311), whose regenerative warmth he intensifies to destructive heat:

> Thou hast burnt out the humour of thy bones,
> And made them powders of impiety   (323–4)

Like Lucifer, he is a bearer of light who has degenerated into a 'bastard of light' (360).

In contrast, Lucrece is, of course, a follower of Diana; she is forced to watch the waning of her planet:

> The star which guided all my elements
> Pulls in her head and leaves the firmaments   (195–6)

Not only her planet, but all the stars have forsaken her: ironically, the canopy and curtains of the bed where the rape is committed are embroidered with stars and gods, and there

> Diana's stars do sport
> With Venus's planets upon Cupid's stage.   (304–5)

It is a 'sky of contrariety' (349) which holds no lodestar and does not answer desperate questions such as 'O Divinity, / Where art thou fled' (92–3) or 'O my heaven, shall I forget thy spheres' (421). The spiritual anguish of Lucrece is expressed in classical terms, but classical literature held at least one remedy for desperate creatures like Lucrece: when Dido averts her face from the skies she hopes to find relief in death. But even this small hope is denied to Middleton's Lucrece. Her last prayer remains unanswered, and when she sits down to write her letter to Tarquin she gives as his address 'Chief seignior to the Phlegetontic mess' (522); and this is where she will have to return.

No one, I think, has painted as dark a picture of Lucrece as Middleton; he pushes her to extremes of emotional and spiritual pain. There is scarcely a ray of light to relieve the sinister scenery. The visions she has of a crystalline paradise only intensify the darkness of the end. There are similarly tortured souls and similar visions in Complaints of over-anxious Christian souls. But none of them will have to face a Tarquin in the afterlife.

4   Rosamond and the Virgin Queen: heroines from British legend and history

Threescore queens and fourscore concubines

Song of Solomon 6.8

Female faces in the *Mirror for magistrates:* Elianor Cobham and Mrs Shore

An intimate history of English monarchy might be written from the point of view of its concubines; affairs of state might be mixed with love affairs, the widespread taste for a peep through palatial keyholes indulged. Official historiography tends to ignore the twilit figures in the shadow of thrones – except for those who managed to supplant their legitimate rivals, most notably in the period covered by this study, the unhappy wives of Henry VIII. In a recent publication on the subject of royalty, *Royal faces: 900 years of British monarchy*, a coffee-table book aimed at a popular market and published by Her Majesty's Stationery Office on the occasion of a centenary, the names of the best known royal concubines of the Middle Ages, Rosamond Clifford and Mrs Shore, are bashfully held back. Even Elizabeth Gray, who achieved the status of queen consort to Edward IV, is treated as a mésalliance ('a pretty young widow from a low stratum of the aristocracy'); she is mentioned mainly for the political achievement of inadvertently thwarting the plans of Warwick the king-maker; the manly qualities of her husband, on the other hand, are duly recorded: 'He was unusually tall and good-looking.'[1]

Popular poetry in the late Middle Ages does not quite ignore the concubines, though it often shares the historians' disapproval. The moral verdicts on figures such as Rosamond are often harsher in ballads than in chronicles; it was an educated public with aristocratic leanings who learned to appreciate the higher aspirations which lifted the Mrs Shores into serious history. Several factors contributed to this promotion. There was the basis of patriotism which created a general interest in British history and soon outgrew the native chronicle style. Historians such as Polydore Vergil, Sir Thomas More or George Cavendish began to adopt classical models of historiography. In the first place this was often done to further a cause, to establish the greatness or the baseness of an historical

105

figure. Justifying political claims had been a chief aim of historiography from the Middle Ages; in his *Historia regum Britanniae* Geoffrey of Monmouth supports the claims of the Plantagenets, as Thomas More those of the house of Tudor in his *History of Richard III*. When these authors make use of classical models, as Geoffrey does of Virgil and Thomas More of Livy, it is to give these claims more weight. With the popular Elizabethan historians emphasis shifted from political to poetical grounds, and it was not only works of epic or historic grandeur which determined their outlook. Ovidian perspectives were applied to modern, as they had been to ancient history, and this allowed poets to cast a more sympathetic eye on figures such as Rosamond and Mrs Shore. Their epic history is tempered with the elegiac; Rosamond is not even mentioned by Geoffrey in the *Historia regum*; Morus was the first to introduce Mrs Shore into his *History of Richard III*; William Warner, apparently yielding to popular demand, added chapters on Rosamond and Dido to the later editions of his universal history *Albion's England* (1586; additions from 1592); in Thomas May's *The reign of King Henry II* (1633), finally, the 'power of beauty, and the power of Kings' (E1v) are set side by side and an Ovidian Rosamond is given as much room as Dido was in the *Aeneid*. Between More and May, then, the by now familiar possibilities of treating historic heroines are transferred into the realm of English historiography, with Spenser's *Faerie queene* at the epic, and Drayton's *Heroical epistles* at the elegiac end. In this chapter I will analyse the treatment of such women in the genre of Complaints which vacillates between these poles. Mistresses such as Mrs Shore are paid considerable respect in this genre, but they soon have to face rebuttals, abusive ones like that from Giles Fletcher's Richard,

> Shores wife might fall, and none can justly wonder,
> To see her fall, that useth to lie vnder
> (*The rising to the crown of Richard III*, 1593, L2r)

or piqued ones like that from Drayton's *Matilda* (1594), who carps that '*Shores* wife is in her wanton humor sooth'd' (43), while her own virtue rests unpraised. In its variations the genre adds to our knowledge of the Elizabethans' and Jacobeans' sense of history and humanity.

Elianor Cobham: lamentation and Complaint

The English historical Complaint was created by the ambitious and influential *Mirror for magistrates*, a continuously expanding compilation of monologues of the mighty dead which in the end came to cover the whole of British history. Its various editions were spread all over and beyond the reign of Elizabeth. The first collection of nineteen Complaints was published in 1559, the last edition came out in 1610: it included a triumphant account of the reign of the queen by Richard Niccols, *England's Eliza*, which set an epic period to the Complaint tradition.[2] But this is only the legitimate line of descent; in between, and far spread, there are numerous illegitimate offspring, and they are my main concern. Willard Farnham, who has written on both the *Mirror for magistrates* and its 'progeny', speaks of a weakening of the original mettle in the later examples of the *Mirror* type Complaints. In his judgment, 'the heroic spirit with which De casibus tragedy began reaches its thinnest dilution' in poems such as David Murray's *The tragical death of Sophonisba* (1611) and Patrick Hannay's *Sheretine and Mariana* (1622).[3] One sign of this weakening, if not the moment of bringing it about, was the appearance of Complaints spoken by utterly unheroic women such as Mrs Shore and Rosamond.

The first *Mirror for magistrates* was free of such appearances. In this respect the *Mirror* was stricter than the models it was meant to complement, Boccaccio's *De casibus virorum illustrium* and Lydgate's redaction of this work, *The fall of princes*. These both included lives of a few famous women, chiefly from antiquity. There had been a continuous demand for Lydgate's *Fall of princes*, and around the middle of the sixteenth century a bookseller hit upon the idea of extending the coverage of this work both geographically and chronologically and of including the lives of princes from recent English history. After some difficulties (an early edition was probably suppressed in 1554 or 1555) the first collection of such recent lives, which dealt with the fall of Englishmen from Robert Tresilian, Lord Chief Justice under Richard II, to King Edward IV (no Mrs Shore yet), appeared in 1559 under its own title, *A mirror for magistrates*, and in its own form, the first person Complaint. The collection was the joint enterprise of a group of authors headed by William Baldwin, and it proved an uneven performance in every respect, not least in length and form of the individual contributions. As to form, the seven-line rhyme royal stanza taken over from Lydgate was mainly used, and to good effect, for instance in Baldwin's tragedy of the Duke of Clarence (in fifty-seven stanzas). But there are many deviations from this form which make for quite different, more lyrical than narrative effects. An example is the 'Complaint of King Edward' which follows Clarence's tragedy, a macaronic *ubi sunt* lamentation in seven twelve-line stanzas ending in the refrain 'Et ecce nunc in pulvere dormio'.[4]

In spirit all these Complaints are tragedies in the medieval sense of the word. They show the fall of the great from Fortune's wheel, and they interpret this fall in terms of retributive justice. The reason for King Edward's untimely death, for instance, is given in the words announcing his Complaint: 'How King Edward through his surfeting and vntemperate life, sodainly died in the mids of his prosperity.'[5] Heavy and rather crude moralising is one of the chief features of this type of Complaint; it leaves even less room for tragic emotions in a modern (or a classical) sense than its medieval predecessors. Another distinguishing feature is its more dramatic setting which includes the editorial process. William Baldwin functions not only as editor of the collection, but also as interlocutor. There are prose links between the tales which record the meetings of the contributors; this gives an outer framework to the whole. Within this framework each contributor gives his account of the vision he had of an unfortunate prince, often after falling asleep over a chronicle. The princes are envisaged as rising from their graves, sometimes in a ghastly state corresponding to their violent deaths. Occasionally it is hard to imagine how they manage to speak at all: Richard, Duke of York, for example, who was slain and beheaded at the Battle of Wakefield (Baldwin confuses it with Bosworth Field) enters 'a tall mans body full of fresshe wounds, but lackyng a head'. The narrator turns frightened away and reports that he 'thought there came a shriekyng voyce out of the weasande pipe of the headles bodye, saying as foloweth' (p. 181). Senecan elements darken the medieval dream-vision in these headlinks, though the actual Complaints are not so much cries for vengeance (like those opening a Senecan tragedy) as pleas of 'miseremini mei' ('Edward IV', p. 236).

Still, this world of the *Mirror for magistrates* is very much a man's world. In King Edward's Complaint 'Lady Bes', the prince consort Elizabeth, is barely mentioned, and Mrs Shore not at all; the main female part is played by Lady Fortune: it is she who smiles on the untemperate king:

> She toke me by the hand and led me a daunce,
> And with her sugred lyppes on me she smyled.   (p. 237)

It is only in keeping with this privilege that a pair of poems announced in the table of contents of the 1559 edition, the joint tragedies of 'Good duke Humfrey murdered, and Elianor Cobham his wife banished' (p. 523), was cancelled altogether.[6] Whatever the reason for this cancellation, it need not have been what was later called chauvinism of the patriotic or the paternal kind. There had been precedents for admitting women to the predominantly male society of a princes' Mirror in both Boccaccio (even in his *De casibus virorum illustrium*, and not only its feminine counterpart, *De claris mulieribus*) and in Lydgate's *Fall of princes* (where not only such manlike figures as Rosamund – the spouse of Alboin of Lombardy – or Brunhild, but also, as we have seen, such dubious characters as Dido and Canace had found access).

The popular tradition, too, had set examples treating contemporary heroines in the same spirit of patriotism mingled with moralism that spurred on the compilers of the *Mirror for magistrates*. Almost a hundred years before Baldwin and his colleagues set to work an anonymous poet had written an elegy on Elianor Cobham which shows all the self-assurance of a Tudor poet:

> Wee nede not nowe to seke the croniclez olde
> off the Romans, nor bockas tragedye,
> to rede the ruyen & fallys manyffolde
> off prynces grett putt to dethe & miserye
> in sondrye landes, for wee haue hardelye
> here in thys lande with-in the xx yere
> as wonderz changes seen before our eye
> as euer I trowe before thys any were.
>
> (MS Rawlinson, C. 813, no. 10, lines 9–16)[7]

Earlier still, we find an example that is even closer to the *Mirror for magistrates* Complaints, not only in spirit but also in form, and again the unfortunate second Duchess of Gloucester, Elianor Cobham, is its subject. It is a first person ballad (and anticipates in this respect the perspective of the *Mirror for magistrates* Complaint), preserved in a Cambridge manuscript, which must have been written shortly after the historical events it describes. In 1441 Elianor Cobham was tried for witchcraft, forced to do open penance and banished to the Isle of Man – this was the beginning of Duke Hymphrey's political fall.[8] The poem was entitled 'The lament of the Duchess of Gloucester' by Rossell H. Robbins, which seems quite appropriate because it has the air of a death lament. Its framework anticipates the in-door dream-vision employed by the authors of the *Mirror for magistrates*.[9] There is a narrator who overhears Elianor lamenting her fate in a palace:

> Thorow-owt a palys as I gan passe,
> I herd a lady make gret mone;
> And euer she syghyd and said, 'alas!
> All erthly ioy is fro me gone.' (1–4)

Time and place are carefully chosen. Elianor has just come from her penitential procession through the streets of London, and is preparing for her departure to Liverpool, where a ship is waiting to take her to the Isle of Man. A poet under the influence of Ovid might have waited for her arrival on the island to catch her in an Ariadne-like situation – that is what George Ferrers will do later on in his version of an Elianor Complaint for the 1578 edition of the *Mirror for magistrates*. The poet of the 'Lament' chooses the moment when the duchess has to take leave of her worldly possessions at Greenwich palace. He stretches this moment into

an *ubi sunt* litany which extends over several stanzas, each stanza ending
in a warning for fair women:

> ffarewell, Grenewyche, for euer and ay,
> ffarewell, fayre place upon temys syde!
> ffarewell, all welth in world so wyde,
>   I am sygned where I shall be;
> At lerpole there must I nedes byde –
>   All women may be ware by me.   (107–12)[10]

The lamentation on the loss of worldly goods is an ascetic element
which goes back to earlier *contemptus mundi* literature. In English medieval poetry such lamentations are usually set in more specific religious
contexts such as a body-and-soul debate or the visit to a tomb. The
religious background makes itself felt in the course of the poem, though
the situation is, of course, different and much of Elianor's lament is taken
up with worldly concerns in the most material sense. There are several
prayer-like formulae interlaced into the poem; it ends in distinctly Christian terms with Elianor commending her soul to her saviour:

> I wot not to whom complaynt to make.
> But to hym I wyll me take,
>   That for us was put upon a tree,
> And in prayers wyll I wache and wake –
>   All women may be ware by me.   (132–6)

In Tudor poetry, as we shall see, the last concern of women such as
Elianor takes a different, more private and profane direction. Elianor's
overruling concern is with the moral and spiritual lessons to be drawn
from her case. The love she feels, or has felt, for Duke Humphrey is of
minor importance; it figures as one item in her list of lost possessions,
wedged in between, on the one hand, 'damaske and clothys of gold' (113)
and 'mynstralcy and song' (121) on the other. Elianor's 'priuy payne'
(119) is just one more warning to beware of the transience of worldly
joys.

The 'Lament of the Duchess of Gloucester' occupies, with similar
poems, an intermediate position between late medieval and Elizabethan
forms of Complaint. It is influenced by *memento mori* poems and *De
casibus* tragedy, and introduces a more lyric note into a field soon to be
dominated by the harsher voices in *Mirror for magistrates* Complaints.
Another example would be young Thomas More's 'Rueful lamentation'
(1503) spoken by Queen Elizabeth, the mother of Henry VIII, on her
deathbed, though this is of a less penitential character, for Elizabeth died
in childbed, not in exile.[11] There is, however, the prominent *ubi sunt*
motif, again applied to the royal palaces:

> Where are our Castels, now where are our Towers,

Goodly Rychmonde sone art thou gone from me,
At westminster that costly worke of yours,
Myne owne dere lorde, now shall I never see.   (36–9)

There is also a series of 'farewells' and 'adieus', this time directed mainly
at members of the royal household, and there is again the Christian
ending:

to the alone,
Immortall god verely three and one,
I me commende   (81–3)

Some of these lamentations are very close to actual events, and this
demands, at least in the case of controversial figures, a certain amount
of discretion.[12] In one case the lamentation was actually written by the
person concerned herself: Catherine Parr, the last wife of Henry VIII,
wrote, on the instigation of her family, a *Lamentation of a sinner* (1547),
'bewraying the ignorance of her blind life', as the subtitle points out. It
is a prose document of mainly historical interest that was reprinted
several times in the sixteenth century, not last in Thomas Bentley's *Monument of matrons* (1582). Dynastic and denominational considerations
rule in this abstract confession; the queen, whose sins remain indistinct,
steps back behind her husband, who is presented as *defensor fidei* of the
new, Protestant faith:

But our Moyses, & moste godlye, wise gouernour, and king hath delyuered vs
out of the captiuitie and bondage of Pharao. I meane by this Moyses, king Henry
the eight, my most soraigne [sic] fauourable lord and husbād, one (Jf Moyses had
figured any mo then Christ) through ye excellēt grace of god, mete to be an other
expressed veritie of Moses cōquest ouer Pharao. And I mene by this Pharao the
bishop of Rome, who hathe bene, and is a greater persecutor of all true christians,
thē euer was Pharao, of the children of Israel.   (D6r–v)[13]

There are several more lamentations of this kind ascribed to (but not
written by) the other, more unfortunate queens of King Henry VIII,
some of them of more poetical interest, particularly those written by
George Cavendish, who is better known for his *Life of Cardinal Wolsey*.
Cavendish wrote a number of *Metrical visions* which remained in manuscript until 1825 when Samuel Singer attached them to his edition of the
Cavendish biography of Wolsey. It was Singer, too, who gave them their
title 'Metrical visions'; Sir William Dugdale, who owned a copy of the
manuscript, more aptly called them 'Elegieciall [sic] Poems upon sundry
persons' in a Prologue;[14] Cavendish himself speaks of 'tragedy' (line 50)
and 'whofull playnt' (58). These poems are of special interest for several
reasons: they show the influence of (and occasionally borrow from)
Lydgate's *Fall of princes*, and they were written at about the same time
as the earliest Complaints for the *Mirror for magistrates* – their latest

editor, A.S.G. Edwards, thinks they may have preceded them.[15] In any case Cavendish was the first to introduce portraits of heroines drawn almost from life into his gallery of princes: Anne Boleyn, Katherine Howard, the Viscountess of Rochford, the Countess of Salisbury, and Jane Gray. Anne Boleyn is given pride of place among them; Cavendish held her in special regard (there are fragments of a biography in the same manuscript with the *Visions*).

In some respects, Anne Boleyn's Complaint is similar to the Lament of Elianor: there is a four-fold 'Ffarewell' (624–6; cf. Jane Gray, 2,265–6), and the regret – this time uttered by the narrator – over a royal mansion lost (635). Anne's contrition appears to be quite as deep as Elianor's, but it is mixed with resentment about the way the world has dealt with her reputation:

> The world vnyuersall / hathe me in dysdayn;
> The slaunder of my name / woll aye be grean,
> And called of eche man / the most vicious quen.   (523–5)

This regard for wordly fame is the secular equivalent to the concern about the soul's afterlife expressed in the older lamentations; Cavendish connects it with a motif that points back to classical literature dealing with comparable figures, the motif of the anticipated epitaph:

> My Epetaphe shall be. / the vicious quen
> Lyethe here of late / that iustly lost hir hed
> By cause that she / did spott the kynges bed   (593–5)

There are similar ante-humous epitaphs in Ovid's poems; and there is an equally laconic epitaph which Cresseid orders for herself in Henryson's *Testament*.[16] Anne does not try to whitewash her reputation; her attitude is not purely personal. The main purpose of her Complaint is still to give warning to other women, though this is done in homely, almost Chaucerian terms:

> Geve non occasion / a sparke to kyndell flames
> Remember this sentence / that is both old and trewe
> Who wyll haue no smoke. / the fier must nedes eschewe   (621–3)

Cavendish adds a political dimension which is absent from the Elianor lament: Anne has to accept her death sentence as just, and this acceptance supplants the religious resignation which concluded the lamentations I have mentioned earlier on:

> Marcy noble prynce / I crave for myn offence
> The sharped sword / hath made my recompence   (629–30)

In spite of Anne's acceptance of her punishment, the poem contains an apologetic element. We see Anne Boleyn only as defendant, not as evildoer, and even if the sentence were meted out by a council of gods (as in Henryson's *Testament of Cresseid*), its harshness and her meekness would raise compassion, if only because of her hopeless situation.[17] The fact that the Complaint makes us look at a case like Anne Boleyn's from only one side combines with the bias given in a first-person narrative and intensifies the overall asymmetrical effect. Even Cavendish, who had no personal reason to sympathise with Anne Boleyn, finds words of pity for her in the end:

> My hart lamentid / by carefull constraynt
> To se ffortune / conceyve / such an occasion
> A quene to ouerthrowe / frome hyr Royall mancion   (633–5)[18]

It is with sentiments like these that Cavendish's treatment of women taken from English history points in the direction of later poems in the same tradition. One of these poems is the Complaint George Ferrors wrote on Elianor Cobham for the third edition of the *Mirror for magistrates* (1578), after the walls of that male stronghold had been broken by Thomas Churchyard's 'Shore's wife' (1563).[19] I will come back to Churchyard's pioneering work in my next chapter; but let me point out a few of the changes the lamentation undergoes if transformed into the more sympathetic Complaint. Ferrers probably knew the anonymous 'Lament of the Duchess of Gloucester'; his Elianor takes leave of her favourite palace with the by now familiar words: 'Farewel Grenewych my Palace of delyght' (line 274). He took over several other motifs as well, but altered them to quite new effects.

The prime motive in the first part of his Complaint is that of pride, themoving vice behind many of the masculine figures in the *Mirror for magistrates*. Elianor owns up to this weakness from the outset of her Complaint. Her confession does not, however, develop into a string of self-accusations as it does with, for example, Anne Boleyn or Catherine Parr. In Ferrers' hands the freely-admitted fault becomes a means of excusing the culprit and of winning her sympathies. A 'yes-but' pattern evolves which structures other Complaints, too. Yes, Elianor admits, she had recourse to magical practices, but only for divinatory, not for treasonable purposes;[20] yes, her punishment 'came partly by deserte' (254), but it was much too severe, and it was inflicted for devious reasons. Elianor claims to have been used as a pawn in a political move against Duke Humphrey, and the man behind this move was Cardinal Beaufort, the real villain of the tragedy. Beaufort is the object of a series of maledictions in the centre of the poem (176–203). For his sake Elianor wishes she were a witch (which she is not, of course): she would raise hell to give him his deserts (204–17). In the anonymous 'Lament' it is Elianor who casts herself in the role of a pre-Spenserian Lucifera

('Lament', 29–30); in Ferrers' Complaint it is the cardinal who is denounced as 'Proude Lucifer' (190), and as 'Baal & Belligod' (198) to boot. There is no question that a judgment instigated by this 'Deuil incarnate' (201) is anything but just. In the 'Lament' Elianor had praised her judges, in her Complaint she denounces them: this antinomian tendency is another feature of women's Complaints:

> For Lawiers turned our offence to treason
> And so with rigor, without ruth or reason
> Sentence was gyuen that I for the same
> Should do penance, and suffer open shame.   (130–3)

The motif of shame takes on a new quality, too, in the new surroundings. It is deserved and serves as a warning in the 'Lament'; in the Complaint it is felt to be a humiliation which is aggravated by the fact that the penance forced on Elianor has become the subject of ballads sung by minstrels and old women. This humiliation, which heroines like Chaucer's Criseyde and Shakespeare's Lucrece anticipate in their worst fears (*Troilus and Criseyde*, V, 1,058–61; *Lucrece*, 813–19), is here reported as fact: Complaints, we remember, are spoken from beyond the grave, and a lost reputation is one of the most potent motifs behind them:

> myne enmies made a Iest
> In minstrels ryme myne honour to deface.
> And then to bring my name in more disgrace
> A song was made in manner of a laye
> Which old wyues sing of me vnto this day.   (157–61)[21]

In the 'Lament', the minstrels are part of the worldly joys Elianor has to abjure ('ffarewell, all mynstralcy and song', 121), which means that she has enjoyed that world; in her Complaint they are part of an inimical world whose slanders have to be put right, i.e. she has become a kind of otherworldly figure.

The enmity of a world full of political intrigue throws Elianor back on her personal relationship with Humphrey. The memory of his love takes on the quality of a solace which is comparable to the consolations offered in similar cases by the Church. But the heroines in Complaints move in largely secular surroundings; this is made obvious in the 1578 volume of the *Mirror for magistrates*, the edition in which Ferrers' Complaint first appeared. To this volume Sackville contributed his 'Induction' which places the *Mirror* in a pseudo-classical framework and makes its figures ascend from a Senecan Underworld. Elianor is thus, like her fellow-sufferers, shut off from the comfort that the heroines of the lamentations found in their religion. Her last thoughts turn towards Humphrey who has also died at the hands of their enemies and now appears to her in a dream in the hour of her death (as Ceyx does to Alcyone, 285–7; cf.

Metamorphoses, XI, 655–6). Her last hopes are of an earthly, not heavenly, bliss:

> That my pore corps mought here haue lien with his
> Both in one graue, & so haue gone to blysse.   (314–15)

These hopes are lost, as the reader knows: Elianor is left in the situation of Ovidian heroines, 'with wast woordes to feede [her] mournful mynde' (298).

I shall now turn to Mrs Shore, the unhappy near-contemporary of Elianor, whose life as a fallen woman went through similar stages of intrigue and scandal, and whose literary career went well beyond the honour of being accepted in the company of fallen men in the *Mirror for magistrates*.

The sainted whore

Mrs Shore in Sir Thomas More's *The history of King Richard III*

Ferrers' Elianor Cobham expressed some doubt about the propriety of her appearance 'Amongst princes' (2), although Mrs Shore had preceded her in the second edition of the *Mirror for magistrates* (1563). This edition contained a Complaint of 'Shore's wife' under the title of 'Howe Shores wife, Edwarde the fowerthes concubine, was by King Richarde despoyled of all her goodes, and forced to do open penance'.[22] The author was Thomas Churchyard, and he, or one of the editors, must have had similar doubts about its inclusion in the *Mirror for magistrates*: in a note to a list of his writings published in 1593 Churchyard says that he wrote the Complaint 'in King Edwardes daies', that is, probably for the first edition of the *Mirror for magistrates*, which was suppressed in 1554 or 1555.[23] In this note Churchyard shows some concern that the works he mentions, and in particular *Shore's wife*, be recognised as his own. Complaints à la Mrs Shore had become a vogue by then, and Churchyard felt obliged to give his version a lift to adapt it to fashionable society; he added twenty-one stanzas of mainly decorative material and brought the poem up to fifty-six rhyme royal stanzas.

We can only speculate about the reasons why the poem was left out of the first edition of the *Mirror for magistrates*; it may have been the doing of Baldwin, the chief editor, with whom Churchyard was on uneasy terms throughout his writing career.[24] Another possible reason is that the editors of the first edition of the *Mirror for magistrates* shared the doubts which Sir Thomas More had expressed when he included an account of the fate of Mrs Shore, the concubine of King Edward IV, in his *History of Richard III*:

I doubt not some shal think this woman to sleight a thing, to be written of & set amonge the remembrances of great matters: which thei shal specially think, y' happely shal esteme her only by y' thei now see her.   (*Richard III*, p. 56)[25]

More may have met her in person, and if his portrait is to be trusted, she had come down in the world indeed; he compares reports of her youthful appearance with what she looked like in her later days:

Proper she was & faire: nothing in her body y' you wold haue changed, but if you would have wished her somewhat higher. Thus say thei y' knew her in her youthe. Albeit some that now se her (for yet she liueth) deme her neuer to haue ben wel visaged. Whose iugement semeth me somwhat like, as though men should gesse y' bewty of one longe before departed, by the scalpe taken out of the charnel house: for now is she old lene, withered, & dried vp, nothing left but ryuilde skin & hard bone. And yet being euen such: whoso wel aduise her visage, might gesse & deuise which partes how filled, wold make it a faire face.   (pp. 55–6)

Mrs Shore must have been an old woman at the time when More wrote this; in an early manuscript of the Latin version of the *History* (MS Arundel 43, written after 1513) she is called 'septuagenaria'; the chronicles of Harding and Hall (1548) give the eighteenth year in the reign of Henry VIII (i.e. 1526–7) as the date of her death.[26]

Though More's description shows some personal interest, his main purpose in this passage is political: he wants to raise compassion for Mrs Shore in order to incite contempt for Richard III who stooped so low as to use her as a means to his malicious and avaricious ends: he confiscated her possessions to swell his coffers, and he accused her of fornication to question the legitimacy of Edward's offspring. Richard is to look like a monster of hypocrisy or, worse still, a false Messiah:

And for thys cause (as a goodly continent prince clene & fautles of himself, sent oute of heauen into this vicious world for the amendement of mens maners) he caused the bishop of London to put her to open penance, going before the crosse in procession vpon a sonday with a taper in her hand.   (p. 54)

Everyone laughs at the charges laid against her, particularly that of fornication, and Thomas More, too, views Mrs Shore's faults with a very clement eye. Her adultery, he says, was the consequence of an all too early marriage ('they were coupled ere she wer wel ripe', p. 55); her attraction rests in her wit rather than mere good looks – this works against the suspicion commonly raised against courtesans that they ensnare their victims by artful, often cosmetic means. Mrs Shore is, in short, lovable rather than amorous, and everyone knows that the punishment inflicted on her was dealt for dishonest reasons. No wonder, then, that her public penance at St Paul's turns into a personal triumph:

> her great shame wan her much praise, among those y^t were more amorous of her body then curious of her soule. And many good folke also y^t hated her liuing, & glad wer to se sin corrected: yet pitied thei more her penance, then reioyced therin, when thei considred that ye protector procured it, more of a corrupt intent then ani vertuous affeccion. (p. 55)

The prestige that More's treatment lends to the concubine becomes apparent if we compare her behaviour at court with that of Elianor Cobham. The main charges levelled against Elianor in both the 'Lament' and the Complaint were pride and ambition. More takes pains to point out that Mrs Shore is free of both these vices. Although she has risen from an even lower stratum of society than Elianor, she remains modest and generous and uses her influence with the king 'to many a man's comfort & relief' (p. 56). The contrast between her former affluence and her present poverty serves as an effective ending of More's account, and an elegantly phrased reflection on the ingratitude of former friends:

> for at this daye shee beggeth of many at this daye liuing, y^t at this day had begged if she had not bene. (p. 57)

With his sympathetic sketch of Mrs Shore's life Thomas More established a pattern which was emulated in the service of other 'holie whores' like her.[27] They are made the victims of tyrants (who may take on the guises of corrupt judges or jealous queens), they are surrounded by bad counsellors like nurses, parents or priests, and they are, in the end, forsaken by their friends like Mrs Shore. Their punishments are out of proportion to their sins, their reputations the result of slander. Nevertheless, the wronged mistress has only a supporting role in Thomas More's *History*. She serves to expose the misgovernment of a tyrant. The leniency with which her faults are glossed over do not exculpate her completely, and More is far from challenging existing moral principles. What he aims at is curbing despotism, not giving rein to libertinism. The virtues he stresses in Mrs Shore, her humility and liberality, are chosen to set off the vices of Richard. It was not before Mrs Shore was lifted out of the confines of classical historiography that qualities like her beauty or her passion could be taken seriously in their own right. This opportunity arose in the more open forms of history-writing that were developed in popular historiography. The Complaints in the *Mirror for magistrates* were such a form, and Thomas Churchyard was the man to use it on behalf of Mrs Shore.

Thomas Churchyard, 'Shore's wife'

One of the main achievements of the *Mirror for magistrates* and probably
its chief virtue in the eyes of dramatists like Shakespeare is its variety of
aspects. The Complaints are spoken by different characters, and written
by different authors, the *Mirror for magistrates* contains a wider variety
of tones and points of view than the ordinary chronicle or verse history,
and the editors grew more and more aware of the possibilities this
arrangement offered. Occasionally they discuss these possibilities in the
prose headlinks which are attached to the Complaint. Among other
things the question of decorum is dealt with in these discussions, with
the result that every speaker of a Complaint is allowed his own voice.
Richard III, for example, whose Complaint precedes that of Mrs Shore
in the 1563 edition of the *Mirror for magistrates*, presents himself in a
particularly gruff voice, and this is defended by one of the contributors
in the headlink to 'Shore's wife':

> The cumlyness called by the Rhetoricians *decorum*, is specially to be observed
> in al thinges. Seyng than that kyng Rychard never kept measure in any of his
> doings, seing also he speaketh in Hel, whereas is no order: it were agaynst the
> *decorum* of his personage, to vse eyther good Meter or order.[28]

To offset this rough Complaint, Mrs Shore's 'tempered tounge'
(line 167) is given leave:

> And to supplye that whych is lacking in him, here I haue Shores wyfe, an eloquent
> wentch, whyche shall furnishe out both in meter and matter, that which could
> not comlily be sayd in his person.   (p. 372)

She uses her eloquence, of course, to plead her own case and to blame
her persecutor.

In the *Mirror for magistrates* of 1587 the temperament and calling of
the poets involved in the enterprise are taken into account, too. In this
edition the prose headlink of Churchyard's Complaint is – somewhat
inconsistently – spoken by Mrs Shore, and she disqualifies Baldwin from
the task of writing a woman's Complaint because he is 'a Minister and a
Preacher: whose function and calling disdaynes to looke so lowe, as to
searche the secrets of wanton women'; Churchyard is better suited
because he is a 'martiall man, who hath more experience both in defending of womens honour, and knowes somewhat more of theyr conditions
and qualityes' (p. 372). Although this bantering is probably occasioned
by more or less friendly differences between Churchyard and Baldwin,
it again stresses the importance these authors attributed to questions of
decorum in the widest sense of the word.

The differences of tone and the change in perspective brought about
by the introduction of 'Shore's wife' into the *Mirror for magistrates* is

considerable. It facilitates the changes towards a more domestic perspective which anticipates, as Hallett-Smith has pointed out, tactics and tendencies later used in Thomas Heywood's domestic dramas and, one might add, later still in 'she-tragedies' such as Nicholas Rowe's *Jane Shore* (1714).[29] Churchyard has received high praise for these changes, but praise from the historian's rather than the critic's standpoint: there is so much left of the 'Minister's and the Preacher's' voice in Mrs Shore's Complaint that it is often hard to decide whether it was design on the part of the author or just pressure from his chosen medium which moved him in a new direction.[30]

The overall effect is mixed; there are contradictions on almost every level of the poem. Some of the images we have met with in earlier elegiac literature reappear, but strangely twisted. The familiar simile of the beleaguered fortress, for instance, is here applied to the advances of the lover-king, and this seems appropriate because, as Esther Beith-Halahmi calls to mind, King Edward was 'as famous for his military prowesses as for his amorous conquests'.[31] Mrs Shore is, of course, taken by storm, and she does not put up much of a defence. The simile, normally used to present either the victim of an assault or an unassailable virgin, is here made to serve weaker ends: on the one hand it is to underline Mrs Shore's contention that it would have been useless to resist so powerful a prince ('Loe, there the strong did make the weake to bowe', 77); on the other she does not deny that she willingly bowed to Edward's will ('For I agreed the fort he should assaulte', 84; cf. 150–4).

The confession of weakness is more than another instance of the tactics of concession employed by her sisters in distress. Shore's wife is familiar with the ways of the world to an inordinate degree; this is evident from her use of the sort of worldly-wise sayings which were a favourite device, as we have seen, in Chaucer's Dido tales. In the 'Legend of Dido', however, the heroine was too good for this world; in Churchyard's poem this relation has become ambiguous. Mrs Shore confesses from the start (with characteristically heavy accent):

> This wandryng worlde bewitched me with wyles,
> And wonne my wittes wyth wanton sugred ioyes   (8–9)

But then she seems quite happy to be 'in earthly pleasures clad' (216), and her final attempt to dissociate herself from 'this world, and all his wanton wayes' (391) is not entirely convincing. Despite the commonplace *Mirror for magistrates* admonitions, directed at 'Princes all, and Rulers everychone' (337) and, as an afterthought, at 'both maide and wyfe' (388), one lesson taught by this Complaint is this: 'Thus bound we are in worldly yokes to drawe' (33). Mrs Shore is a child of Mundus and Natura who bestowed her with the gifts of wit and beauty, and she still seems proud of these assets which have, after all, won her the favour of a mighty prince. The charge of witchcraft would not seem unfitting if laid at the feet of this charming woman, but it is not raised at all in Churchyard's poem.

The indulgence that a woman such as Mrs Shore can count on is partly due to what used to be called feminine charms; it is also due to the Pulcinella career she enjoyed. Churchyard makes use of this last element, too, by stressing her lowly origins and comparing her to a 'Goddesse' (217) at the height of her success. Her bourgeois background serves as an excuse for her pliability at the hands of the royal suitor; the eminence to which she rises before her fall is exploited for the conventional moral lesson that it is best to keep a low profile in this world. This lesson is first clad in philosophical terms (with a reference to Aristotle's teaching that virtue is a mean between two extremes), then with a simile from nature:

> The setled minde is free from Fortune's power,
> They nede not feare who looke not vp aloft,
> But they that clyme are carefull every hower,
> For when they fall they light not very softe:
> Examples hath the wysest warned ofte,
> That where the trees the smallest braunches bere,
> The stormes do blowe and have most rigor there.   (239–45)

This, again, is a confused version of a well-known emblem. Usually it is the tall tree, an oak or a cedar, which is unfavourably compared to a shrub or a reed: the trees are exposed to the strongest storms and therefore break sooner than the shrubs which are flexible or sheltered. The emblem usually serves to propagate humbleness and submission, and this may be the lesson Churchyard had in mind. He develops it, however, to teach that one is safest on the lower branches of a tree – 'Where is it strong but nere the ground and roote?' (246) – and thus mixes two sets of concepts, the one advocating strength, the other pliability.[32] The best that could be said, and has been said, about the result of Churchyard's wavering between higher and lower modes of morality is that the speaker herself is torn between different impulses, and that her voice is, following decorum's laws, a quavering one, as Richard's was of necessity gruff. For this, however, there is too much preaching and ministering in the Complaint, particularly in a diatribe against Fortune (8–28) and a warning to rulers (337–57).

Churchyard is not always as awkward in his use of imagery and sentiment. He can give a conventional image a poetical touch of his own, as when Mrs Shore accuses the friends that corrupted her youth of having 'bent the wand that might have growen ful streight' (140). He is best, however, in passages where he can show himself to be the chivalrous man experienced in 'defending of womens honour' (p. 372) that Mrs Shore had made him out to be, and he has an eye for the moving detail. His most memorable picture is the one of Mrs Shore roaming the streets with a clack-dish:

> A lynnen clothe was lapt about my heare,
> A ragged gowne that trayled on the ground,
> A dishe that clapt and gave a heavie sound,
> A stayeng staffe and wallet therewithal,
> I bare about as witnesse of my fal.   (367–71)[33]

He leaves the reader with this image of his heroine, except for a closing stanza that asks women to take heed of Mrs Shore's example and to defy this world 'and all his wanton wayes' (391). He does not follow up this last *contemptus mundi* thought with a look beyond this world. Churchyard is not a religious writer; the slightly flattering portrait that Mrs Shore gives of him in her headlink is quite correct in this respect: he is 'a writer of good continuance, and one that dayly is exercised to set out both matter tragicall, and other prophane histories and verses' (p. 372). I will examine another of his profane tragedies later on in chapter 6.

Anthony Chute, *Beauty dishonoured*

There are disturbing elements in Mrs Shore's life such as the corruption of youth and the curse of beauty which Thomas Churchyard touches on but does not develop beyond the trite didactic precepts usually shown in the *Mirror for magistrates*. At about the time when Churchyard took his Complaint of 'Shore's wife' out of the *Mirror for magistrates*, brushed it up and published it under his own name in *Churchyard's challenge* (1593), Anthony Chute took up the story and developed it into a remarkable and independent Complaint, *Beauty dishonoured: Written under the name of Shore's wife* (1593), revolving around these disturbing elements. Chute, together with Trussell, Heywood and Middleton, is of a generation which we have come to know as the Sons of Will on account of their imitations of Shakespeare's passionate *Venus and Adonis*. Like them, Chute gives his poem the Shakespearean stamp by calling it 'the first inuention of my beginning Muse'.[34] Some of his inspiration may also have come from Samuel Daniel, whose *Complaint of Rosamond* had come out a year before. The publication of Daniel's Complaint certainly spurred on Churchyard, and he 'somewhat beautified [his] Shores wife' (*Challenge*, S4v). A great part of Churchyard's effort went indeed into a description of the beauty of his heroine, and he set it expressly above that of Rosamond:

> The damask rose, or Rosamond the faire

That Henry held, as deere as Jewells be,
Who was kept close, in cage from open ayre:
For beauties boast, could scarse compare with me   (*Challenge*, T2r)

The luxuriousness of the description is an element from the erotic epyllion and seems hardly appropriate for Mrs Shore, neither dead in her 'shrowdeing sheete', as in the *Mirror for magistrates* (p. 372), nor alive, when she 'delited not men so much in her bewty, as in her plesant behauiour', as in Thomas More's description (*History*, p. 56). As the title of the poem suggests, Chute also tries to make Mrs Shore's beauty one of his themes, but he does so not only by cosmetic means, but by heightening beauty to an almost spiritual quality on the one hand, and by probing its destructive depths on the other.

The authors of erotic epyllia were all drunk with the beauty and passion of Shakespeare's *Venus and Adonis*; the almost incoherent beginning of Chute's poem may serve as an instance:

> SIgh, sad musde accents, of my funerall verse,
> In lamentable grones, (wrought from true pietie)
> Sing you the wept song, on her wronged hearce
> [. . .]
> Weepe pen in warme blood, to the world approuing
> How faire, how good, how deare, old age did way her.
> > Bleed teares, weepe bloud, pen, sing, sighe on her hearce
> > Her gratefull obsequies in a funerall verse.   (A3r)

The uncertain tone and the metonymic shifts look forward to the style of Middleton's *Ghost of Lucrece*; they also point to the subject of the poem: the mystery that beauty is doomed to infect and corrupt itself. It is not an ordinary theme, and Chute knows this:

> The high-musde period of the storie reader,
> (Wondring or warre, or matter causing terror)
> Omits her fortune, to her fates arreader,
> (Precisly censuring bewtie by her error)
> > So she that euen the fairest she surmounted,
> > Now of the fairest, is the fowlest counted.   (A3r)

The sense of these lines is obscured by an erratic syntax and equally erratic spelling. What Chute seems to be saying is that poetry of the *Mirror for magistrates* kind (being high-browed and censorious) is unable to do justice to a woman like Mrs Shore, who is marred by a fatal flaw rather than a common vice. This interpretation is substantiated in Chute's dedication of the poem to Sir Edward Winckfield in which he dissociates himself from Italian and French poetry, particularly the religious epic. Even more than Thomas Churchyard he professes to be a poet of the elegiac and of the profane:

SYR since such is the industrious nature of our owne Poetes, as though Italie sleepes in the charme of a sweet Hierusaleme, and France waxes proud in the weeke labours of her toyling-mused *Bartas* (the first as conceiptiuely Allegoricall, as the other is laboursome significant) yet our owne clyme, challendging vnto her selfe hardly a second esteeme, to the first: and hauing produced such witty, & so happy conceiptes, as wandering in the secresie of some passionate Elegies, blush at their owne apparence: How might I be esteemed guiltie of myne owne disgrace, that daring to make my selfe priuie to the knowledge thereof, should not sticke, to argue my selfe improuidēt, in not bequeathing to silence the first inuention of my beginning Muse? (A2r)

The notion that beauty's error is something given, not comitted, is confirmed towards the end of the poem when Mrs Shore complains of an '*error* [. . .] *in natures will*' which afflicts improvident creatures like her (F3r). This tragic flaw in the nature of the beautiful is Chute's main concern; as suggested in the stanza quoted above, he sets his poetry of error against the terror treated in other poetry, or, to translate his poetics into the Aristotelian terms he may have had in the back of his mind, he will stress pity, not fear in his tragedy of Mrs Shore.

The setting of Chute's poem is terrible enough, though. Mrs Shore is presented on her death bed, with Death in person stalking about her room eager to claim her life, but loath to destroy her beauty. In the *Mirror for magistrates* Mrs Shore, like all the speakers of the Complaints there, came from the dead, wrapped in a shroud and, presumably, even less sightly a view than More's *septuagenaria*, 'old lene, withered, & dried vp' (*History*, p. 55). In Chute's poem she retains her beauty right to the end, and even Death is arrested at the sight:

> Then through transparance of the white was left her,
> Freshly peeres secret glorie of her bloud,
> When euen that death, of life that would haue reft her
> With feare and reuerence amazed stood,
>   Doubting, though at the last gaspe she did lye,
>   A bewtie so deuine could neuer dye   (A4v)

The last line of this stanza forms a refrain in the closing parts of the poem and rings in variations of 'life' and 'death', 'live' and 'die' a knell through the agonising final stanzas. Death takes Mrs Shore's life but not her beauty. When the red has fled her face and she resembles a withered lily, her beauty is of a perfect white (G2v), and the fame of this beauty, we are assured in the last line of the poem, will survive: '*Death vow'd her body should be eyed neuer, / Yet life hath vow'd her fame should liue for euer*' (G3v). Beauty in this poem gains the immortalising force that is ascribed to belief in a religious context.[35]

The lingering of Death at the sight of Mrs Shore's beauty gives the delay necessary for the deliverance of the dying woman's long Complaint which revolves around the detrimental effect that beauty had on her life. The epic opening of the poem and its sixain stanza form, both features of the erotic epyllion, might lead one to expect extensive descriptions of this beauty in the ornamental fashion peculiar to that genre. There are, in fact, some epic similes and mythological ornaments to nourish this expectation. But there is nothing like the sense of lushness and sensuality prevailing in Shakespeare's *Venus and Adonis* or Marlowe's *Hero and Leander*. The impression given by Barbara Brown of 'a rambling descriptive poem, full of self-conscious lyricism, classical references, and endless invocations of the Muse' is, I think, misleading.[36] There is an element of self-awareness in the poem, but this is of the reflective kind peculiar to Complaints. Mrs Shore is turned into an introspective heroine, and Chute uses the self-consciousness inherent in the form of a Complaint to a degree unprecedented in the genre. In particular in the domestic scenes from Mrs Shore's unhappy early married life, he brings to life what Louis Zocca has called 'the eternal type, the beautiful woman, married to a brutish husband'.[37] He achieves this largely by concentrating on emotional reactions, not exterior events, and Esther Beith-Halahmi is right, I think, in praising the 'psychological acuteness' which he shows in the process.[38]

Chute follows Mrs Shore's development from bashful country beauty (he does not mention her city background) to courtly coquette with a number of telling incidents. The key event and turning point in her career is the arranged marriage with an elderly husband. Chute pursues the theme of the forced marriage – a favourite topic of satirical literature and conduct books – in a series of stanzas spoken by his heroine in the third person which breaks up the first-person perspective of the Complaint, and this seems to meet the demand for an impersonal tone in didactic literature. Esther Beith-Halahmi gives instances of such literature and interprets the change in grammatical person as a change from the subjective to a more objective mood: Chute seems to be 'entering the lists of the moralists'.[39] One could, however, give this breach of perspective a more sympathetic interpretation. Immediately after her digression into the third person Mrs Shore is made to say that her marriage estranged her from her former self:

> Loe so vnited to a discontent,
> Departed from my selfe, to live t'vnkindnesse
> Too soone my ill-bestowed youth did repent
> My parentes auarice, and desaster blindnesse,
>   That could not see the loathing that is bred,
>   In discord iarring of an vnkind bed: (B4v)

This change may have found expression in the grammatical shift. This interpretation, which may look over-subtle, is supported later on (*'I that from me, my selfe, my selfe had sold'*, C4r), and similar instances of self-estrangement are given in comparable cases, by Thomas Middleton's Lucrece, for example, or by Gervase Markham's Marie Magdalen: they result from the state of forlornness in which heroines of the elegiac tradition are usually placed.

That Chute is indeed capable of reproducing subtle psychological effects by poetic means is proved most impressively in the stanzas that describe the cankerous growth of Mrs Shore's dissatisfaction in her marriage which Esther Beith-Halahmi has traced with sympathy in her analysis of the poem (pp. 152–3). Mrs Shore herself seems frightened by the change this dissatisfaction effects in her character, and this gradually moves her into the situation of an outsider who, like the suitors beginning to cast greedy eyes on her, expects her to give way under the pressures of unsatisfied passion at any moment. She begins to pry on herself, and this leads to the passage in which she, in retrospect, generalises her experience in the manner of a conduct book:

> *Marke how the down cast lookes her eyes reflect,*
> *Argues her life, sequestred from her mindes ease:*
> *And euery gesture, secretly detect,*
> *The note of silent paßion neuer findes ease:*
>   *And though she seemes vnwilling to bewray it,*
>   *Yet in that seeming so she seemes to say it.*
>
> *She sits and heares, euen paßionatly attentiue,*
> *How better fortunes ioy the happie wed,*
> *When in a sodaine thought hartely pensiue*
> *She castes her eyes vp, and she shakes her head*
>   *VVhilst many thoughtes concurring all in one*
>   *Makes her greeu'd soule yeeld forth a deadly groane.*   (B4v)

The change to the third person reflects her passage from innocence to experience, and this reflection is highly characteristic of the 'pensive' mode of the Complaint.

It does not do justice, then, to the subtlety of such passages in Chute's poem to consign it to a satirical or didactic tradition.[40] On the contrary, Chute corroborates his initial statement that his heroine is not to be judged by *'precisly censuring'*, and this has further implications. If Mrs Shore's fate is to be understood neither in political terms (as in More's *History* – the historical background is barely mentioned in Chute's poem), nor in moral terms (as in Churchyard's Complaint) – in what way can it be understood? We are taken back to the 'error' which, the poet suggested, is inherent not only in nature (the nature of a woman in particular, according to the convictions of the time), but also in the seemingly

divine. It is exactly the angelic appearance of womanly beauty which
breeds its own corruption. Chute takes hold of this thought early in his
poem in a slightly garbled stanza:

> *Nor let my bewtie be impeacht with this,*
> *That I was woman like, though Angell fayre,*
> *For him doth puretie fortunately blisse,*
> *That is not blemisht with some blacke impayre:*
>   *For this we see almost in things deuine*
>   *T'is quickly stayned is the purest fine.*   (C1v)

He resumes the theme later on, after the death of Edward which sends
his heroine into '*Blacke desolation*', '*forlorne dispayre*' and '*Eternall
blackness*' (E4r), and mentions again something like the '*precise censuring*' of the beginning in a series of remarkable stanzas which I ask
leave to quote at length:

> *Sayd ere* Philosophie *hell was confind*
> *Below the yearth where neuer any were?*
> *O if it be so, yet withall I finde,*
> *That hell's aboue the yearth as well as there*
>   *And neuer could Philosophie approue,*
>   *That there was one below but one aboue.*
>
> *T'is but th'inuention of th'highe-witted wise,*
> *Allow'd of any there, more then t'expresse,*
> *Th'extreame of tortures, that might tyrannise*
> *Them being dead, that liuing did transgresse:*
>   *Nor haue they left vs any confirmation,*
>   *But deem'd surmises of imagination;*
>
> *This t'was rayn'd on the yearth, and prayd on me,*
> *T'was this which I esteem'd a heauen before,*
> *And more infernall cannot any be,*
> *For hell is but extreame, yet this was more:*
>   *And we ner know what t'is in heauen to dwell,*
>   *Vntill we know what t'is to liue in hell.*
>
> *O could my wordes expresse in mourning sound,*
> *The ready paßion, that my mynde doth trye,*
> *Then, greefe all eares, all sences would confound,*
> *And some would weepe with me, as well as I:*
>   *Where now because my wordes cannot reueale it*
>   *I weepe alone inforced to conceale it.*   (F2 r–v)

The desolation speaking from these lines is similar to what we have
noticed in Middleton's *Ghost of Lucrece*; it is worthy of note, however,
that we have not an ancient, but an English heroine in this poem, and
not classical, but Christian concepts of heaven and hell in the back-

ground. Esther Beith–Halahmi rejects the sentiments expressed in lines like these as spurious because Mrs Shore's 'misery is in large measure merely physical and external' (p. 132). It seems to me, however, that the anguish expressed in the Complaint has its spiritual side and is all the more convincing for leaving aside the possibility of a recompense paid in some metaphysical coin.

It is perhaps unwarranted to presume that Mrs Shore acts as a kind of mouthpiece for the author of her Complaint. There is, as in the *Mirror for magistrates*, the excuse of decorum which allows the poet to dissociate himself from the character he created, and the situation of Mrs Shore, '*All solitarie, alone, forlorne*' (G1r) could be said to have induced despair or even mental derangement. Poets such as Middleton, Chute, and Marlowe, however, belonged to a generation which knew doubts and despair and sought refuge in their art. Unfortunately, we know nothing about Anthony Chute except that he died early,[41] though let us hope not as early and as basely as D.F. Rowan supposed when he referred to his only poem:

the quality of the verse lends credence to the story that the author died in the year of its publication; whether by his own hand or as the result of a public stoning is not known.[42]

He certainly deserves better than that.

The beautiful and the blameless: Fair Rosamund and chaste Matilda

Samuel Daniel, *The complaint of Rosamund*

Mrs Shore, the bourgeois concubine of Edward IV, became one of the most popular heroines of English history, rivalled only by Rosamond Clifford, the mistress of Henry II. Hand in hand these two walk through poetry and drama, from early ballads to chapbooks and filmscripts, as *The unfortunate royal mistresses, Rosamond Clifford and Jane Shore*.[43] If Jane Shore has the advantage over her rival by a short head, this may be due to her lowly origin with its Pulcinella appeal. Another point in her favour, mentioned by Samuel Pratt, is the fact that she did not oust the legitimate queen (who is not even mentioned in the poetical versions we have been discussing).[44] Rosamond Clifford's is an altogether more aristocratic case. 'The bloud I stain'd, was good and of the best, / My birth had honour', she says in her Complaint – small wonder that she appealed to more highly strung poetic temperaments like that of Samuel Daniel.[45]

Thomas Churchyard and Anthony Chute were struggling poetasters compared with Daniel and his connections to the Pembroke, the Cumberland, and later to royal circles. Daniel's poetry, much more than Anthony Chute's, was of a courtly disposition;[46] his *Complaint of Rosamond* was published together with a cycle of Petrarchan sonnets titled *Delia* in 1592, and closely connected with the high-flying and flattering sentiments displayed in such cycles. The courtly influence on the Complaint makes itself felt so strongly that Homer Nearing classified it as 'a hybrid between historical tragedy and the amatory vein'.[47] *The Complaint of Rosamond* was a great success (there was a second edition in the year of its first publication), and it set a fashion of independent 'Mirrors for Fair Ladies' in the 1590s.[48] *The Complaint of Rosamond* has proved Daniel's most popular poem to date; it has borne out Edmund Spenser's prediction that he would most excel 'in Tragick plaints and passionate mischance'.[49]

In Daniel's poem Rosamond rises from the underworld like a ghost in the *Mirror for magistrates* (after it had been classicised by Sackville's Induction). Throughout it is difficult to place the poem exactly between the cultures. The 'horror of infernall deepes' of its first line cannot be hell, although Rosamond has come to confess a sin and her fall is later on compared to that of Eve (332, 456, 747–9);[50] Rosamond says that she is waiting to be transported to Elysium, but lacks the fee demanded by Charon: the sighs of a lover sympathising with her fate.[51] Unlike Shore's wife, her sister in distress, she has so far been denied such compassion, although hers is the nobler fall and the better cause:

> No Muse suggests the pitty of my case,
> Each Pen doth ouerpasse my iust complaint,
> Whilst others are prefer'd, though farre more base;
> *Shores* wife is grac'd, and passes for a Saint;
> Her Legend iustifies her foule attaint.
> > Her well-told tale did such compassion finde,
> > That she is pass'd, and I am left behinde.   (22–8)

She hopes that the Delia of Daniel's sonnets (which in the 1592 edition preceded the Complaint) will commiserate her fate if the poet brings it to her attention, and that she will send her to her rest.

As usual with Petrarchan ladies in sonnet cycles, it is hard to tell who the Delia of the sonnets is; Daniel says no more than that she is a country beauty, 'left t'adorne the West' (532). The poem is, however, aimed at an addressee like her: it is dedicated to that great patroness of poets, Lady Mary Herbert, née Sidney, Countess of Pembroke, to whose literary circle Daniel belonged. The third edition of the *Complaint of Rosamond* was published together with Daniel's drama *Cleopatra* (1594), which he wrote as a companion piece to Lady Pembroke's *Antonie*, and in the French classicist style which she promoted in England. Publications like these were directed, like much of the courtly literature of the time, at a well-situated, well-educated predominantly female public; there grew in these circles, apparently, a taste for softer poetry to complement the rigid tragedies, a demand for the sentiments of 'tender care, / And pitty' (57–8) which found expression in imitations of Ovidian heroical letters (like Daniel's 'Letter from Octavia') and in women's Complaints. Another caterer to this taste was Samuel Brandon, who published a double letter, 'Octavia to Antonius, Antonius to Octavia', together with his classicist drama *The virtuous Octavia* (1598). There is a remarkable parallel to this development a hundred years later when 'tenderness' became a much-discussed critical term, and the native heroic tragedies were complemented by imported Ovidian literature like the *Lettres portugaises* or the various *chroniques scandaleuses* around the turn of the seventeenth century.

Daniel's audience is courtly, but with a sentimental taste for the countryside which was, at the same time and in the same circle, also the basis for pastoral poetry.[52] The pastoral background, which is only hinted at in Chute's *Beauty dishonoured*, plays an important part in Daniel's Complaint: Rosamond is a girl from the country, brought up in pristine purity, and this affects both the sense of beauty and of morality in the poem. Rosamond displays a strong sense of sin throughout her Complaint, but her faults are always set against an originally, and radically, pure character; she will, in the end, be 'repurified' (10) with the help of that mysterious West Country beauty Delia, and she will gain her 'sweet Elisian rest' (9) – a compensation for the 'pure fields' she has been 'vnparadis'd' from (456–7) by becoming the lover (she never uses a baser term) of the king. The classicist and the sentimental background of the Pembroke circle tempers in Daniel's Complaint the judgments passed on sinners such as Rosamond in *Mirror for magistrates* literature.

With a background like this, Rosamond will not express the same sense of despair or even damnation as Middleton's Lucrece or Chute's Mrs Shore. There is much talk of shame and disgrace in her Complaint, but the terms apply to the sphere of beauty as well as to that of religion. It is significant that the word 'adulterate' is used for cosmetic, not for carnal practices in Rosamond's description of herself:

> Such one was I, my beauty was mine owne,
> No borrowed blush which bank-rot beauties seeke:
> That new-found shame, a sinne to vs vnknowne,
> Th'adulterate beauty of a falsed cheeke:
> Vilde staine to honour, and to women eeke   (141–5)

A woman's honour is stained by false cosmetics, not false morals. Conversely, the term 'grace' runs through different shades of meaning in the poem, from a vaguely theological sense (Rosamond deplores that she lacked the grace to use her gifts from Nature and Fortune, 80–1), to the dubious 'grace' poured over Mrs Shore in Churchyard's 'Legend' (25–6), and the dear 'notes of former grace' which not even ugly death can drive from Rosamond's discoloured cheeks (843–4) and which King Henry wants to preserve at all costs.[53]

Rosamond can talk of her beauty without blushing because this is 'simple beauty' (156) and she is, at least in the beginning of her career, unaware of its effects (one of the happier results of the court-and-country contrast underlying the poem). Her beauty nevertheless reigns supreme wherever it shows, even in those parts of the poem where its bearer tries to denounce it:

> Ah beauty Syren, faire enchaunting good,
> Sweet silent Rhetorique of perswading eyes:
> Dombe eloquence, whose powre doth moue the bloud,
> More then the words or wisdome of the wise;
> Still harmony, whose Diapason lyes
> > Within a brow, the key which passions moue,
> > To ravish sence, and play a world in loue.   (127–33)

Daniel makes the most of the world-well-lost or conqueror-conquered theme; 'imperious beauty' (73) vanquishes King Henry at a glance: 'A Crowne was at my feete, Scepters obey'd me' (163). In Rosamond's Complaint the great king, and the whole of the dynastic action in the background, dwindles to such small proportions that Rosamond herself, assuming for a moment an objective stance, feels obliged to excuse his neglect of imperial duties (in Virgil, we remember, it was either the epic narrator or Hermes, the mouthpiece of Jupiter, who reprimanded both hero and heroine for being neglectful, 'regnorum inmemores', *Aeneid*, IV, 194):

> Yet must I needs excuse so great defect;
> For drinking of the *Lethe* of mine eies,
> H'is forc'd forget himselfe, and all respect
> Of maiesty, whereon his state relies:
> And now of loues and pleasures must deuise.   (204–8)[54]

One of the laws in the world of Rosamond is that love and majesty dwell ill together (868), and whenever beauty and duty compete (as they do as rhyme words in a closing couplet in lines 167–8), beauty prevails. Clearly, the law governing this Complaint is not that of the epic; if given the traditional choice of 'hic amor – haec patria', Rosamond's Henry would vote for love. Daniel pushes this temporary abdication of the king to such lengths that it affects his character in the end. Henry is in danger of looking like a nearly impotent elderly ruler who deserves more pity than respect. Rosamond is his sole joy in a life of broil at home and strife abroad (819).

This reduction of the hero is not rectified in the course of the poem as it is at the end of Virgil's Dido episode. Some of the most moving scenes in the poem are those of the king grieving for the loss of his joy. In fact, Daniel finds it difficult to maintain the constellation usually given in women's Complaints when a seducer is opposed to his victim: both king and concubine seem to have fallen prey to irresistible forces, and Daniel has to introduce two other characters as evil agents at crucial points in Rosamond's career to establish the customary contrast of innocence and corruption: one is a matron which King Henry uses as a female pander to lure Rosamond into his bed (she is Daniel's invention, though the wicked duenna is, of course, a familiar figure), and the other Queen Eleanor (who had been made responsible for Rosamond's death in Robert Fabyan's *Chronicles* of 1516).[55] These act as devil and as tyrant in Rosamond's account, the parts traditionally reserved for men, and this serves as a means of saving her reputation by contrast: she may be the frailest of women (as she freely admits), but there are much worse examples of her sex.

The encounter with these women gives Daniel opportunities to dramatise the plight of his heroine. In the confines of a Complaint, a monologue spoken from beyond the grave, this is largely a matter of dramatic tensions within the speaker who relives a situation, but with the benefit, if it can be called a benefit, of hindsight. Daniel uses the possibilities this situation offers to memorable effects. Rosamond vividly remembers, for instance, the dilemma in which the procuress left her when she brought her an invitation from the king. She felt then like a latter-day Lucretia:

> But what? he is my King, and may constraine me,
> Whether I yeeld or not, I liue defamed.
> [. . .]
> And if I yeeld, tis honourable shame,
> If not, I liue disgrac'd, yet thought the same.   (344–5; 349–50)

The offer was not accompanied by threats, however, but by a costly present, and looking back now, Rosamond knows that her decision to yield was not forced: her feeling like a martyr was an act of self-dramatisation. Daniel makes his heroine relive the vacillations of her youthful mind, but he also lets her see them in the light of her older self.

The basic retrospective situation of the Complaint might lead to no more than the conventional 'Utinam ne' or 'Hadde I wist' of classical or medieval poetry, but Daniel gives it an additional twist by suggesting that experience has not made Rosamond much better or much wiser. This is most conspicuous in his handling of the obligatory formal description.

The costly present of the king was a small casket inlaid with Ovidian mythological scenes (the coquettish equivalent to the shield of Ulysses); it shows, for instance, the abduction of Amymone and the transformation of Io; both these scenes are, of course, premonitions of Rosamond's own fate. In retrospect, Rosamond sees the connection, but on the eve of her seduction she did not – and would it have made any difference?

> These presidents presented to my view,
> Wherein the presage of my fall was showne,
> Might haue fore-warn'd me well what would ensue,
> And others harmes haue made me shun mine owne.
> But Fate is not preuented, though foreknowne.
> > For that must hap, decreed by heauenly powers,
> > Who worke our fall, yet make the fault still ours.   (414–20)

Far from exposing Rosamond's folly, these reflections put her in a line with mythological heroines who fell victim to heavenly powers: there is as little use in resisting Henry as ever was in resisting Jove.

Rosamond's recollections of the meeting with her rival, Queen Eleanor, which were enlarged in the later editions of the Complaint, run in a similar direction. Rosamond is all victim in this scene; Eleanor the victor. The queen, who is compared to a 'Tygresse' (589), speaks her death sentence with 'hellish breath' (617) and is 'proud with victorie' (632) after the confrontation.[56] Rosamond is left in the situation of an Ovidian or Chaucerian heroine, 'alone, of all the world forsaken' (633). And again she begins to dramatise her situation by assuming an appropriate role, this time that of Ariadne, and by imagining that she has 'to die forlorne/In Desarts where no eare can heare [her] mourne' (657–8). Her hiding place in Woodstock has been compared to a labyrinth (484–90), but it bears no resemblance to Naxos or some other desert place; on the contrary, Henry has taken pains to make it a garden of delight, 'With sweetest flowers that eu'r adorn'd the ground' (480).

Much of the attraction of Daniel's *Complaint of Rosamond* lies in contradictions and self-dramatisations like these. If they were planned (and they probably were), Daniel has tried to trace in them the movement of a troubled or simply clouded mind between past and present, pride and penitence, and he has tried to solve one of the major problems of this sort of Complaint: to present a conscience at once simple and wise, innocent and full of remorse. To achieve this, he had to break through the moral framework that surrounded similar Complaints in the *Mirror for magistrates*; the Complaints John Higgins contributed to its later editions show the difference. There still is some out-of-character moralising in Daniel's *Complaint of Rosamond*, but it also shows a heightened sense of the appealing qualities of the pitiful, and an open eye for the beautiful.[57] For Daniel, beauty is eminently a quality of the female sex; he does not try to solve the problems it creates when it leads its bearers into conflicts with the traditional virtues of that sex; he is content to let Rosamond point out the dilemma:

> O Beautie thou an enemie profest
> > To Chastitie and vs that loue thee most,
> > Without thee, how w'are loath'd and with thee lost?   (684–6)

Like his King Henry, who reads obsequies to the 'Wonder of beautie' (848), he sets up a monument to one of beauty's martyrs:

> And after-Ages Monuments shall finde,
> > Shewing thy beauties title, not thy name,
> > Rose of the world, that sweetned so the same.   (859–61)

In this epitaph Henry (and through him Daniel) answers one of the prayers repeated by many of love's martyrs, and often directed at a poet, namely to have their reputations saved, but he does it not in the accepted way by directing his heroine's view towards some other world, but by allowing her to look back to what she achieved in this one. And Daniel corrects in these lines a most uncourteous play on Rosamond's name in the process. The closing line about the Rose of the world alludes to the epitaph said to have been inscribed on Rosamond's tomb in Godstow Abbey:

> Hic jacet in tumba Rosa mundi non rosa munda.
> Non redolet sed olet quod redolere solet.[58]

It may be one, and not the least, of Daniel's achievements that Rosamond has been remembered as the Fair ever since.

Michael Drayton, *Matilda*

It is hard to tell what Drayton thought of Daniel's treatment of Fair Rosamond; he clearly alludes to his rival's poem in the beginning of his *Matilda*, an imitation of the *Complaint of Rosamond*, and there is reason to believe that he quotes the reserved judgment of 'some Matrons' on Rosamond in the same spirit as Augustine quoted a 'certain disclaimer' of Lucretia:

> Faire *Rosamond*, of all so highly graced,
> Recorded in the lasting Booke of Fame,
> And in our Sainted Legendarie placed,
> By him who strives to stellifie her name,
> Yet will some Matrons say she was to blame.
> > Though all the world bewitched with his ryme,
> > Yet all his skill cannot excuse her cryme.   (29–35)[59]

In his preface, directed at 'The honourable gentlemen of Englande, true favorers of Poesie', he expresses doubts or even disgust about what he calls adulterous literature in his own voice and in no uncertain terms:

And yet, such is the folly and shamelesse impudencie of some, (as wee see every day,) which in their wanton and adultrate conceits, bring forth such ugly Monsters, as a modest and sober eye, can hardly abide to view their deformities. Then it is no mervaile though the divine Muses, take so small delight in our Clime, finding their sweet and pleasant fields, which should be holy and sacred, defiled, and polluted, with such lothsome ordure.   (p. 211)

The language is stronger even than that in Augustine's attacks on worldly literature. It reminds one of the zest with which religious, and particularly Puritan, critics challenged erotic poetry of Ovidian origin.[60]

Though Drayton's attack may not be aimed at Daniel personally, it goes in his direction in general. Drayton feels called on to champion a new, less worldly feminine ideal. His heroine is to be as fair as Rosamond, but also chaste, and Matilda, the girl who withstood the wooing of a king, answers this ideal; the subtitle of his Complaint calls her 'the fair and chaste daughter of the Lord Robert Fitzwater', and the second epithet pushes the first towards its more spiritual meaning of 'unspotted' and away from 'beautiful' in the ordinary sense.[61] The contrast between Drayton's and Daniel's understanding of what is fair and what is chaste is made explicit throughout Drayton's poem, starting with the location: Daniel's Rosamond sacrifices her body in an almost pagan ritual on her couch in the labyrinth of Woodstock:

> That body which my lust did violate,
>   Must sacrifice itselfe t'appease the wrong   (628–9)

Matilda offers nothing but incense on her deathbed in the monastery of Dunmow, where she has fled to escape the entreaties of King John; the scenery is changed from worldly to spiritual surroundings:

> I offer heere upon my dying bed,
> This precious, sweet, perfumed sacrifice:
> Hallowed in my almighty Makers eyes   (920–2)

A scent of incense hangs over Drayton's poem from the start.[62] The whole of the Complaint, Matilda claims, should form a fragrant skein around her hearse; one is led to wonder if this is not meant to perfume over the slanderous *Rosa munda* lines:

> You blessed Impes of heavenly chastitie,
> You sacred Vestalls, Angels onely glory,
> Right presidents of imortalitie,
> Onely to you I consecrate my storie.
> It shall suffise for mee if you be sorie.

If you alone shall deigne to grace his [i.e. Drayton's] verse,
Which serves for odours to perfume my hearse.   (15–21)

The perfume of Petrarchism, however, is all but dispersed in Drayton's poem; one should note that not another Delia, but Vestals and Angels preside over her Complaint.[63] Its author is not out to win the favour of some capricious lady but to erect a monument of chastity. This is an altogether more weighty task; the honour of an ancient family is at stake, as the subtitle tells in capital letters of 'THE TRVE GLORIE OF THE NOBLE HOVSE OF SVSSEX', not the name of an erring beauty. Glory and its paraphernalia play an important part throughout the poem. In the beginning Matilda asks to be crowned with 'Conquerors Lawrell' (24), in the end this demand is met and she feels that her 'glorious life' and 'spotlesse Chastity' (925) have won her immortal fame:[64]

With Laurell, these my browes shall coronize,
And make mee live to all posterities.   (930–1)

There is an aristocratic attitude behind such lines which is based on Christian principles and contrasts sharply with Daniel's half pagan cult of beauty. Drayton's poem moves on an epic plane midway between Spenser and Milton. This is in accord with the definition of a legend which Drayton gives in the preface of a later edition of the poem:

But the principall is, that being a *Species* of an *Epick* or Heroick Poeme, it eminently describeth the act or acts of some one or other eminent Person

('To the reader', *Legends*, 1619)[65]

In *Matilda* Drayton is concerned with the establishment of the ideal woman in a Christian world; the classical drapery thrown around Rosamond and her sisters in the elegiac line is substituted in Drayton's poem by semi-religious canopies. Matilda is in a state of grace all her life. Her beauty is a gift not of nature, but of heaven, and its fame spreads to heaven, not abroad (all movement seems to be directed vertically in the poem):

From hence my praise began to prove her wing,
Which to the heaven could carry up my fame   (134)

Unlike Rosamond, she receives the antidotes together with the attractions of her gift: beauty loses its poison, if it ever had any, at the very beginning of her career. Even before King John, her would-be seducer, can test her firmness, Matilda is given dissuasive arguments by the dozen:

'Lacivious will, the sences doth abuse,
'Birth is no shaddow unto tyranny,
'No scepter serves dishonour to excuse,

'Nor kinglie vaile can cover villanie   (260–3)

Matilda has the maxims that other heroines buy dearly with experience at her fingertips, and she tells them like so many beads on her rosary. Rosamond, for example, comes to the precept that 'Kings cannot priui-ledge what God forbade' (*Rosamond*, 700) only in her last hour.[66]

The string of adages in Drayton's poem from which I have quoted is indicative of the orthodox character of the whole; in early editions such corns of wisdom were apostrophised for readers not interested in the chaff, and sometimes they were taken out and collected in commonplace books.[67] It goes without saying that Matilda's peace of mind is only slightly ruffled by the advances of the amorous King John; the *bellum intestinum* he stirs up in her soul ('And in my soule a sudden muti-nie', 436) is soon quelled with the help of heavenly powers ('Grace divine from highest heaven came', 446). Matilda's life runs along the lines of a saint's *vita*, her convictions are never really shaken – in this respect she is even more secure than the Biblical heroines I shall discuss in my next chapter. Both the Old Testament Susanna and the New Testament Mag-dalen feel sometimes lost on their way through the sea of life (Susanna's exclamation when confronted with the Elders, 'angustiae sunt mihi undique', is transferred to the Magdalen in the *Omelia Origenis*), but Matilda's heart 'rides at ease' (478) in the midst of temptations and attempts at her virtue. It is, by moral necessity, a heart of stone in a breast of flint (680–1), informed by a strength and will-power that is designed to put to shame the malleable women we have met with in similar poems of the elegiac tradition. Even Shakespeare's heroic Lucrece conceded that 'Men have marble, women waxen, minds' (*Lucrece*, 1,240); Matilda is above such weakness, as her will-power is above that of a tiger's:

> 'Tygars are tam'd with patience and with skill,
> 'All things made subject, but a woman's will.   (685–6)

Again one is reminded of Daniel's *Complaint of Rosamond*, where the furious Eleanor was compared to a tigress ('Looke how a Tygresse', etc., *Rosamond*, 589), and it becomes increasingly evident that Drayton's poem is meant to supplant the feminine ideal presented in the elegiac tradition with a positive heroic counterpart.

This, however, runs counter to some of the formulae, if not the very form of the Complaint. The well-worn phrases of helplessness, like the ancient 'quid faciam' (What might I doe?', 619, 641) are suddenly out of place; Matilda is not to be counted among love's (or any other worldly power's) victims, and deferential labels like the medieval 'Silly, helplesse mayde' (619, cf. the 'silly Lambe', 642) will not stick on a heroine who accepts the cup of poison that King John forces on her in the end with an almost cavalier flourish:

> Taking the poyson from his deadly hand,
> Unto the King caroust my latest draught (883–4)

Little is left of Ovidian motifs in Matilda's legend. There are reminiscences of the letter of Phyllis to Demophoon: a poignant epigraph, for instance (line 868), and a stinging question mark which Matilda sets after King John's martial exploits ('Then of this conquest let thy Soveraigne boast', she tells the envoy who brings the poisoned drink, 869; cf. *Heroides*, II, 63–74).[68] But there the similarities end. Phyllis fell victim to Demophoon not only physically but also morally; she is on the defensive, whereas Matilda triumphantly proves her moral superiority. A potentially Ovidian heroine is aggrandised to heroic proportions in Drayton's poem, and Matilda gives a foretaste of the transformations heroines like her underwent in Drayton's *Heroical epistles*.

Drayton has been called an 'English Ovid', mainly in praise of his imitations of the *Heroides*, but even there the epithet is misleading: Drayton takes over little more than Ovid's letter form – or rather the form of the double letter with its corrective tendency – and a number of motifs; he is far from imitating Ovidian asymmetry and sentiment.[69] As I have mentioned above, he explains in the preface 'To the reader' of his *Heroical epistles*, the 'heroical' of its title euhemeristically; here is the passage in full:

And though (heroicall) be properly vnderstood of demi-gods, as of *Hercules* and *Aeneas*, whose parents were said to be the one celestial, the other mortal, yet is it also transferred to them, who for the greatnes of mind come neere to Gods. For to be borne out of a celestial *Incubus*, is nothing els but to haue a great and mighty Spirit, far above the earthly weakenesse of men, in which sence *Ovid* (whose imitator I partly professe to be) doth also vse heroicall. (1598 ed., A2r)

This is a proper explanation of the term, but hardly apposite to Ovid's heroines, who are never free of human weakness. They tremble in the shade of heroic events or try to undermine the heroical status of their male counterparts. This cannot have escaped a learned reader such as Drayton. His explanation is another instance of the sort of creative misunderstanding we also find in authors of the twelfth century Renaissance who managed to adapt the Ovidian style to their Biblical epics. If anything, the *Heroides* show that Ovid has a predilection for *libertinae* such as Phaedra, Helen or Medea – girls and women who do not hesitate to sacrifice their honour to their passion. Drayton prefers 'Vestall maydes' (738) such as Matilda, who value their honour above everything or else are repentant 'maides misled' (Daniel's term in *Rosamond*, 556)

such as the Rosamond of his *Epistles*. Whenever Drayton treats his heroines in the manner of the Ovidian *Heroides*, discrepancies between style
and character arise, most notably in his letter of 'Matilda to King John',
where he invests the steadfast nun with all the trembling passion of a
Byblis, extending two lines from Ovid's *Metamorphoses* to four in Matilda's letter:

> I write, indite, I point, I raze, I quote,
> I enterline, I blot, correct, I note,
> I hope, despaire, take courage, faint, disdaine,
> I make, alledge, I imitate, I faine   ('Matilda to King John', 35–8)[70]

A hundred lines further on the same Matilda breaks into a rebuke of
'Lascivious Poets' (135) who care too much for fallen women such as
Myrrha, Scylla, Leucothoe – and Byblis, whose letter served as a model
for parts of her own. In the letter of 'Mistress Shore to king Edward the
fourth' there is a similar diatribe against '*Romes* wanton OVID' (103–4)
which makes the assumption even more unlikely that Drayton imitated
the Roman in spirit as he did, occasionally, in letter. The epithet 'English
Ovid' would much better fit Drayton's rival Daniel, who treated his Rosamond with the kind of sympathy for which lascivious poets are blamed
by Matilda who, in her 'Letter to King John', also wonders why Rosamond did not take the veil as she did when assailed by an amorous king:

> Had ROSAMOND (a Recluse of our sort)
> Taken our Cloyster, left the wanton Court,
> Shadowing that Beautie with a holy Vale,
> Which she (alas) too loosely set to sale   (165–8)

There is little doubt that these lines were written with Daniel's *Complaint
of Rosamond* in mind, particularly since Drayton harps on the one asset,
beauty, which Daniel's Rosamond valued so greatly. With the best of
intentions, no doubt, Drayton prepares the way for poets like Richard
Brathwait who take up such ironies as the curse of beauty satirically and
treat figures like Rosamond and Mrs Shore as trulls. Brathwait's *The
golden fleece* (1611), for example, contains a moralistic 'madrigal' which
toys with Rosamond's epitaph and turns Matilda's pious thought into the
impossible wish that she had never been born:

> If Rosamond had euer beene an hower,
>   Nere bene interred in her bed of earth,
> If she had euer kept such vitall power.
>   As to smell sweet with her mellifluous breath.
> She had beene well excused to chuse that state,
>   Which should be neere ecclipsde by mortall date.
>
> But she poore wench did flourish for a while,

> Cropt in the primrose of her wantonnesse,
> And she that did the noblest thoughts beguile,
> Is now conuerted into rottennesse.   (F8v)[71]

Moralism verges on morbidity in epitaphs like these, and Drayton's asceticism also comes dangerously close to this borderline. His Matilda mortifies herself by entering the convent of Dunmow, and she does it expressly to bury her beauty:

> I leave the Court, the Spring of all my woe,
> That Court, which gloried in my Beauties pride,
> That Beauty, which my Fortune made my foe   (464–6)

It is hard to escape the inference that this is meant as a corrective to Rosamond and Drayton's poem as a *remedium amoris* against Daniel's erotic verse.

The ascetic tendencies in Matilda's Complaint put Drayton in a position close to the religious reaction against the wave of Ovidian poetry. The basis of his poem is not, however, Puritan (or religious in any denominational sense), but idealistic with religious overtones. He imitates Ovid, as he says himself in his preface to the *Heroical epistles*, only partly (Heinrich Dörrie would not speak of imitation at all in his case, but of adaptation);[72] he does not try to emulate Ovid's poetry but to surpass it or to fortify it with spiritual values – small wonder then, if the new wine sometimes strains the old bottles. Drayton's product is at once homely and refined; his matter is taken from British history, and refined with Christian spirituality. The competitive spirit of the enterprise shows through in several places. Drayton's figures have to compete with their classical counterparts: Matilda is a second, but better, Lucretia ('I as fayre and chast, as ere was she' (42), though the reference is to Shakespeare's *Lucrece* rather than to Livy or Ovid.[73] Robert Fitzwater, her father, is another Virginius. If he cannot match the Roman's severity – he cuts rather a timid figure – this is due to a reversal of roles which is peculiar to this kind of counter-Complaint. To mark the difference between the all too feminine heroines of the elegiac tradition, heroines such as Matilda are steeled to masculine virtues, and men are almost necessarily emasculated in proportion. It is not merely a matter of plot, then, if Sir Robert is not allowed to kill his daughter as Virginius does; it is also a matter of principle.

Drayton's precept of female heroism was taken up and developed by later authors in the epistolary as well as in the epic traditions. One of these followers was the emigrant John Dickenson, who wrote a neo-Latin short life of Matilda in his *Parallela tragica* (Leyden, 1605), placing her side by side with Sophonisba. In a forerunner to this Plutarchan collection Dickenson had praised Matilda's 'virtus mascula' (*Speculum tragicum*,

Leyden, 1605, P1r). David Murray put this virtue to the test in his epic version of the Sophonisba story (*The tragical death of Sophonisba*, 1611); later still, it was given the most rigorous definition by George Rivers in a summary to his collection *The heroinae* (1639):

THE Heroïna *hath nothing of woman in her but her sex, nothing of sex but her body, and that dispos'd to serve, not rule her better part.* [. . .] *Her soule is her heaven in which she enjoyes æternall harmony: her conscience is her Sanctuary, whither, when shee is wounded she flies for refuge. Her affections and paβions, in constant calme, neither flowe nor ebb with Fortune;* [. . .] *Outward happinesse she owes not to her Starres, but her Vertue that rules her Stars. If shee bee lash'd by Fortune, it is but like a Toppe, not to bee set up, but kept upright.* [. . .] *She understands not the common conceit of love, nor entertaines that familiarity with man that hee may hope it.* [. . .] *If Love enter her breast, it is in the most noble way directed to the beauty, neerest the most perfect beauty. If shee marry, it is onely to propagate; the very act tending thereto shee singles from the thought of sinne* [. . .] *Shee is temperate, that her soule may still be Soveraigne of her sense. Shee entertains pitie as an attribute of the Divinitie, not of her sex. Shee is wise, because vertuous.* (I2r–3v)

Drayton is not quite as rigorous as Rivers; the influence of the heroic ideal, however, pervades his poem and shapes his characters. In his Matilda it is the father, not the daughter, who shows signs of weakness when fortune lashes out. Fitzwater feels 'accurst' (960) and falls into the kind of despair we have seen associated with heroines such as Lucrece:

> Yee powers Divine, if you be cleane and chast,
> In whom alone consists eternitie,
> Why suffer you, your owne to be disgra'st,
> Subject to death and black impuritie? (967–70)

He soon recovers at the thought of the glory Matilda's death must bring to the family and the good influence it may have on the whole of England. This thought inspires Matilda's last moments, too. She faces death calmly and even rejoices not only in the knowledge of having 'liv'd and dyed a Mayd' (889), but also in the hope 'That by [her] death, [her] Soveraigne may survive' (907). Drayton uses the opportunity for a prophetic glance at a happier England of the future:

> *England,* when peace upon thy shores shall flourish,
> And that pure Maiden sit upon thy Throne (1,030–1)

The fate of Matilda is thus linked with the fate of England, and the whole poem takes a turn away from the personal to the public. Matilda has proved what Dickenson in his *Speculum* calls her patriotic spirit, 'animus patria dignus sua', and it is this spirit of heroism and patriotism that marks much of Drayton's later poetry. In 1627 he published another historical legend under a title which raises expectations of a poem in the elegiac strain, *The Miseries of Queen Margarite, the infortunate wife of that most infortunate King Henry the sixth*. The very first lines, however, put this poem firmly in an epic tradition, and this is where it stays:

> I sing a woman, and a powerful Queene,
> Henry the sixt, the King of *Englands* Wife[74]

This is the same epic formula that Protestant poets used to set their Biblical heroines apart from the Byblis-Myrrha-Phaedra line; Thomas Hudson translates the beginning of Du Bartas' *Judith* as 'I sing the vertues of a valiant Dame', and Robert Aylett opens his epic *Susanna* with 'I Sing the honour of that noble Dame'. I shall return to these Biblical heroines presently; but first I will take a look at the miseries of some English queens in the elegiac tradition.

Queens regnant and consort: Elizabeth Gray and Queen Elizabeth

Thomas Sampson, *Fortune's fashion*

When put to the test between the rival claims of private or of public obligations, concubines such as Rosamond and Mrs Shore opt for personal values such as love or beauty, and the first-person Complaint supports this subjective approach. With a queen this is bound to be different: the more important her role in history and the closer she comes to political issues still virulent, the clearer public concerns will claim their rights and the more objective values will come into the foreground. Such simple considerations of decorum play their part when it comes to choosing the medium for a piece of historical poetry. It seems only appropriate that Churchyard chose an elegiac Complaint for Mrs Shore, the passive victim of historical manoeuvres, and Drayton the epic form of a verse chronicle for the valiant activities of Queen Margaret of Anjou. With regard to origin and status, Lady Gray, the widow who became King Edward's consort, is placed somewhere between Mrs Shore and Queen Margaret: 'I know I am too mean to be your queen, / And yet too good to be your concubine', she says of herself in part three of Shakespeare's *King Henry VI*, (III, ii, 97–8). When Thomas Sampson, therefore, sat down to write a poem on Elizabeth Gray, he had the choice between both forms; he decided in favour of a *Mirror for magistrates* Complaint and called his poem *Fortune's fashion: Portrayed in the troubles of the Lady Elizabeth Gray* (1613), thus addressing the widow rather than the queen in his heroine.[75]

The poem opens in the familiar Senecan manner: Elizabeth appears, as the narrator explains in his prose argument, wrapped in her winding-sheet:

You see her newly risen out of her graue, and in the extremity of her griefe speaking as followeth.   (A3v)

What follows, however, is not exactly a Complaint in the manner of either Baldwin or Churchyard. In spite of her appearance Elizabeth lacks the spirit of revenge or even the wish to recover her reputation. And there is, of course, little of the energy that drives Queen Margaret. The political moves around Elizabeth are sketched into the Complaint with a few strokes ('To Lancaster . . . To London . . . To Burgondie' in the compass of half a dozen lines, C1r); in contrast to Drayton's *Queen Margarite*, a 'bone-dry chronicle' in Homer Nearing's estimation,[76] the War of the Roses which rages in the background serves only as a back-cloth to the 'pensiue stage' (*Fortune's fashion*, D4r) on which Elizabeth acts out her fate. On the other hand, there is little mythological embroidery or romantic interest in the poem (despite the epyllian sixain stanzas), and this, again, is only appropriate: when Elizabeth entered the public stage and was wooed by Edward she was already a widow. Elizabeth describes the courtship of the king in rather conventional terms: the nautical metaphor dramatised by other heroines in distress is toned down to a quiet cruise:

> A King to woo his subiect in such sort,
> As no dishonor by his loue might rise:
> Blame me not then, if to that princely port,
> I was contented to be led as prize:
>   Where honor grac'd with regall maiestie,
>   Was Pilot to my ship in ieopardie.   (B1r)

This is a far cry from the Lady Gray who matches Edward's equivocations in the stichomythic wooing scene of Shakespeare's play (*3 King Henry VI*, III, ii); what Elizabeth loses in wit and glamour, however, she gains in sincerity. She is a Chaucerian Good Woman, unworldly and completely guileless. She does not even show a cat's paw towards her female rivals, as she might have done in an Ovidian epistle. There is no jealousy between her and the mistress of her husband: Mrs Shore is barely mentioned in her Complaint – we are on our way towards the domestic solution of the problem in part two of Thomas Heywood's tragedy, *King Edward IV*, where queen and concubine are reconciled in a sentimental scene.[77] The placatory attitude may be based on the lowly origin which associates Mrs Shore and Lady Gray, their bourgeois or baronial backgrounds; the main reason for the reticence of such figures is, however, their final state of helplessness. Abandoned by their royal lover or husband they move on a plane with forsaken women of all ranks and times. Sampson's Elizabeth, like Ovid's Dido, is in a state of humiliation, and decorum demands an appropriately humble style, the *stilus humilis*, not the *grandis* ascribed to heroines such as Shakespeare's Margaret or the Virgilian Dido.

Sampson's Elizabeth is almost awkwardly aware of this situation and what is expected of her, and she uses well-worn phrases such as the 'quo fugiam' formula to express it:

> But whither wade I now? I must not rage,
> Though extreame griefe doth make my heart to vexe,
> And passe decorum for a pensiue stage   (D4r)

Elizabeth humiliates herself to the point of self-effacement. Not only amorous, but also political passions are cut down to domestic size. The queen is truly what Gloucester in Shakespeare's play only claims to be, 'too childish-foolish for this world' (*Richard III*, I, iii, 142), and her simple nature makes her an unwitting, almost witless victim of the men around her, 'Vlysses-like' Warwick (B2v), Cardinal Bourchier and, above all, Machiavellian Richard.

The unselfishness of Elizabeth remains in character because her main role is that of a mother, not a mistress. Her chief concerns are her children, seven in all from first and second husbands. That is not quite as many as Hecuba had, but her ordeals are similar to those of the Trojan queen: she is forced to hand over and lose one after the other to the world of men. The process is, ironically, helped on by her trusting nature as in the case of the princes Richard and Edward, whom she puts into the hands of Cardinal Bourchier. The crowning irony comes in the end with the loss of her daughter Elizabeth: she complies with Richard's demand for her daughter's hand in order to save their lives, though she secretly supports the cause of Richmond and prays for the tyrant Richard's fall. After Richard's death on Bosworth Field she rejoices in Richmond's victory and his conciliatory marriage with her daughter – only to learn that she is to be banned from the court and to lose her possessions because of her connivance with Richard's plans. Only the lack of an accusation of lechery or witchcraft denies her equal footing with Mrs Shore.

The question of how much sympathy Elizabeth is able to secure depends largely on the reasons given for her dealings with Richard. In Edward Hall's chronicle (which is based on Sir Thomas More's *History of Richard III*) her acquiescence is put down to the inconstancy natural to all womankind; moreover, Elizabeth is said to be 'blynded by avaricious affeccion and seduced by flatterynge words'.[78] In the second wooing scene of *Richard III* Shakespeare leaves open the question of whether Elizabeth's acceptance of Richard's offer is real or feigned. He puts the 'donna è mobile' insinuation into King Richard's mouth, 'Relenting fool, and shallow, changing woman!' (IV, iv, 431), an insinuation at least as old as

Virgil's *Aeneid*, as we know, where Mercury applies it to Dido, 'varium et mutabile semper / femina' (*Aeneid*, IV, 569–70). Sampson, having chosen the form of Complaint, lacks the distance of either the epic or the dramatic poets; he uses the personal (and partial) perspective to disclose Elizabeth's true motives and to refute the historian Hall's and possibly the dramatist Shakespeare's views.[79] His Elizabeth justifies her activities (or rather her inactivity) not only with the political argument of having chosen the lesser evils, but also by admitting the subjective motive of plain fear, and again she does it in a common formula followed by a common sentiment:

> Alas, what could a silly woman do?
> My female frailtie might haue coloured this:
> I feard to taste the furie of my foe,
> Because my strength was all too weake for his:
>> I timorously did feare the bloudie slaughters,
>> That he might do to me and to my daughters.   (F2r)

This is an inferior motive, not as base as the insinuations of Hall, but well below anything a Matilda or a Margarite would have considered.

The explanation of Elizabeth's behaviour with purely personal motives and with the simplest of reasons does not offer a new view of the history of the War of the Roses. Sampson knew his historical sources well, as his 'Argument for the better vnderstanding of the Readers' (A3r–v) shows; in a way the apologetic tendency of Elizabeth's Complaint even anticipates the more accurate and generous appreciation of her position which in historical works gained ground only a hundred years after the appearance of his poem, but this does not make his poem a piece of historiography. Rather it is an experiment in looking at history from a neglected point of view. Elizabeth is an unpolitical figure, and her main characteristic is her 'maternal gentleness', as Homer Nearing has called it in his thesis on English historical poetry of the period (p. 59). Sampson makes her act out the role of a victim of historical events beyond her control to the point of self-effacement and eventually self-destruction. It is hard to say whether Sampson had a political motive for driving her to such extremes. Nearing believes that the submissive attitude of the heroine is to be seen as a bow towards Jacobean absolutism. But I doubt if King James would have felt flattered by being implicitly compared with a tyrant like Richard. And if the poem were to expound the virtue of obedience, this virtue should have its rewards; Elizabeth, however, loses everything in the end.

The moral stance of the poem can just as well be accounted for by referring to generic laws inherent in the Complaint: its aversion to the heroic ethos of fortitude leads here into the opposite state of fear, and this is so basic a force that it almost forestalls questions of morality. Fear is no more a vice than simple trust, its complement, is a virtue. There are, therefore, no profound moral lessons to be drawn out of the story Elizabeth has to tell. The maxims we are given look familiar, like the one at the beginning of the poem, a variation of the well-worn oak-and-reed emblem:

> The Cottage seated in the dale below,
> Stands safe, when highest towers do ouerthrow.   (A4r)

At best, maxims like these have a consolatory effect; in a context which seems to demand action, or at least indignation, they look tame to the point of irony, as in the case at hand: the Elizabeth we meet in Sampson's Complaint tries to keep away from the towers, but is in the end immured in a convent which, for her, is little better than a dungeon:

> With wounded heart, the remnant of my dayes,
> In th'Abbey of Bermondsey in teares I spent: (F2v)

In a tragedy, ironies like these might lead to questioning fate and the gods; Sampson's poem ends in resignation. Elizabeth's point of view is that of popular poetry – the milkmaid's view of history:

> If such the world in former times hath beene,
> That highest states most subiect were to fall:
> How true said she, that late was Englands Queene,
> When she her selfe at that time was in thrall,
>> Loe yonder milk-maid liues more merrily,
>> Then I, that am of noble progenie?   (F3r)

Elizabeth uses the same sentiment in Shakespeare's *Richard III*, but to oppose Gloucester;[80] it does not daunt him, of course, but she has put up a fight.

Christopher Lever, *Queen Elizabeth's tears*

The late queen of England to whom Sampson's Elizabeth alludes is, as Sampson makes clear in a marginal note, her namesake Elizabeth I, and her time of thrall are the years she spent under arrest in Woodstock and the Tower of London at the instigation of her sister Bloody Mary ('It was the saying of Queene Elizabeth, when she was prisoner in the time of Queene Mary', F3r). For her chronicler, Christopher Lever, the secluded situation of the princess must have seemed close enough to Fair Rosamond's stay at her Woodstock labyrinth to qualify young Elizabeth for a poem reminiscent of Daniel's *Complaint of Rosamond*. He did not make it a first person Complaint, though, and for very good reasons. Some of these reasons came with the subject matter: there is, for example, the obvious difference that Rosamond was shut away by her lover-king for amorous purposes, and Elizabeth by her sister-queen for political purposes. Another difference lies in the fact that Rosamond ended her life at Woodstock; for Elizabeth, the years of isolation at Woodstock and in the Tower of London were only episodes in her career before she gained the epic status of a Virgin Empress. The whole of this career was suitably celebrated in the grand style by Richard Niccols in his 'England's Eliza, or: The victorious and triumphant reign of that virgin empress of sacred memory, Elizabeth, queen of England, France and Ireland'. Niccols published this poem in 1610 as an appendix to his, the last augmented, edition of the *Mirror for magistrates*. It is a work of epic proportions which, with its 463 rhyme royal stanzas (plus 272 lines of Induction and a six-line epilogue, both in heroic couplets), exceeds by far the limits of a Complaint in the *Mirror for magistrates*. A Complaint is usually undivided, and this sometimes gives it an appropriate out-of-breath, or last-breath, semi-dramatic appearance. Niccols's poem asks for a longer breath, and consequently for divisions; he mentions in his 'Epistle to the Reader' that he at one stage planned to have it divided into cantos or books.[81] This would have made evident the proximity to epic poems such as Drayton's *Barons' wars*, which was cast in *ottava rima* and arranged in cantos in 1603.

The verse historian William Warner may have had this sort of epic in mind when he challenged the poets of his day to produce 'a legend of her [i.e. Elizabeth's] life' in his *Continuance of Albion's England* (1606). Homer Nearing believes the challenge was mainly directed at Drayton;[82] it was, however, Christopher Lever who responded with a legend in the spirit of Drayton's *Matilda* called *Queen Elizabeth's tears: or, Her resolute bearing the Christian crosse, inflicted on her by the persecuting hands of Stephen Gardner, Bishop of Winchester, in the bloody time of Queen Mary* (1607). The hagiographical title indicates that Lever's poem is even closer to the original meaning of the word 'legend' than Drayton's own *Matilda*; it also adopts, as we shall see, some of the ingredients of a religious legend. Lever thus goes one step further in reversing a process which was started by Chaucer when he profaned the term in his legendary of Cupid's saints and which culminated in the concubines' Complaints of the 1590s. While Drayton had already tried to stop the process with his chaste *Matilda*, Lever goes beyond this. There is no erotic interest at all in his poem (this would have detracted from the memory of the 'Virago, virgo, dea' apostrophised in the complimentary Latin verses attached to the poem, A2r); he presents a worldly princess with all the paraphernalia of a Christian martyr.

Lever's poem presents a secular saint's life, and this proves an obstacle to the personal interest which a Complaint, by simple force of its subjective point of view, usually arouses. Not only is there no hint at an erotic entanglement; the family rift between the half-sisters Elizabeth and Mary, which might have served as a substitute for the familiarity characteristic of the elegiac tradition, is constantly widened to take in the larger dynastic and denominational issues in the background. What remains of the elegiac mode is the limited scope: we are not given a complete life, but only the Woodstock and Tower episodes, that is those stages in the life of the saint which alone justify the doleful title of the poem. In a proper Complaint stages like these lead to a heroine's fall, the episodes follow a line descending to the final scene of desolation; we remember Mrs Shore in the streets of London, Rosamond in the labyrinth at Woodstock, Elizabeth Gray at Bermondsey Abbey. The listener or reader knows that worse, or the worst, is imminent – heroines of the *Mirror for magistrates* type sometimes carry the instruments of their various deaths onto the scene. These instruments may be comparable to the attributes of Christian martyrs, but they are not carried as signs of triumph over death or a tyrant. Foreknowledge in these Complaints serves to sharpen the sense of the inevitable end and to heighten the pity roused by heroines who otherwise are likely to meet with no more than a 'serves her right' shrug. In Drayton's legend of Matilda, on the other hand, which is designed to command admiration rather than commiseration, the pitiable state of his heroine is relieved by an outlook on the altar erected in her honour by King John after her death: Matilda is raised to the honour of a patron saint (with an eye already on the saint to come in the person of Queen Elizabeth); this ending moves her Complaint close to a saint's legend of which such veneration after death forms an integral part.

Lever's Elizabeth, now, is sanctified already in the beginning of the poem. She does not, like her sisters in the *Mirror for magistrates* tradition, rise from her grave; the narrator has seen her in a heavenly vision, accompanied by saints:

> Among the number of these holy Saints,
> A happy lady, where all happies are   (B1r)

While less happy ladies show the instruments of their deaths, Elizabeth carries the insignia of her majesty; a globe at her feet makes her look like another Virgin Mary:

> Within one hand she held an armed blade,
> (Whereon was writ her many victories;)
> The other with much reuerence she laide,
> Vpon the Booke of heauenly mysteries;
> [. . .]
> Before her feete a Globe of earth was cast,

> Scepters, and Crownes, and markes of high estate,
> Yea Kings themselues and Potentates were plac't,
> In humble ranke before this Magistrate   (B1v)[83]

At this point the narrator halts (reminded, perhaps, of the title of his poem) and turns, with appropriate modesty, to the subject of his poem, Elizabeth's earthly trials:

> My selfe that haue these admirations seene;
>   In humble verse her suffrings doe relate,
>   That dare not meddle with her time of State.   (B2r)

There is a similar protestation of modesty at the end of the poem. This chimes in, of course, with considerations of decorum which demand a plain style for Complaints.

Sampson's poem retains some lustre, however, from the heroine's crowning achievement anticipated in the initial vision, and one of the aims of the narrator is to keep this glorious vision in view. He asks his readers to uphold the honour of Elizabeth, which he thinks is on the wane after her death; in his preface he reminds them of their patriotic duty:

honour her remembraunce, whome all the best in the world do honour with admiration, which thou also wilt doe, if thou beest either honest, or truely English.   (inserted leaf a1r)

The Virgin Queen obviously poses problems quite different from those of a heroine whose honour is in doubt or threatened or has to be established against public opinion, the prime motive in a Complaint. One of the difficulties is the question of perspective. A princess whose habit has been described as being 'all day, and nothing night' and bearing the motto of '*Defendor of the Faith*' (B1r) can hardly be presented as a passive victim only who spends her days in dungeons of varying shades of darkness. Consequently, Lever gives us not only the static picture of Elizabeth complaining in Woodstock or the Tower. He also presents the historical background and chronicles the events leading from the death of Edward VI to these solitary scenes: Elizabeth's banishment, her arrest, trial and eventual confinement. The agent behind these events is the Bishop of Winchester rather than the sister queen: Gardner is the Machiavell of the poem, with an equally villainous Pope in the background; the blood that soils the reign of Mary springs from Rome:

> These Instigators fill her hands with blood,
> (In all respects but this a vertuous Queene)   (B3r)

Here we have an instance of a deferential attitude towards the throne, and this time it is more likely to be dictated by reasons of state than in

Sampson's Complaint of Elizabeth Gray. The strained relation between
the different daughters of Henry VIII was, of course, a much more sensitive issue than that which concerned their great-grand aunt, and it was
not yet settled with the accession of King James.

Such reasons apply to an even greater degree to their cousin Mary
Stuart, who was also made the subject of a lengthy anonymous Complaint, *The Legend of Mary, queen of Scots*, which was never printed but
is preserved in a number of manuscripts.[84] In this poem, which is to a
great part written from Mary Stuart's point of view, the queen of Scots
treats Elizabeth with much respect and accepts even her own execution
as justified: she sacrifices her body on the altar of political prudence: 'I
did my corps bequeath, / To make a sacrifice for pennance due'
(1,226–7). The difference between these politically motivated poems and
Sampson's Complaint of Elizabeth Gray is a matter of ethics, or rather
different levels of ethics which correspond to the status of the heroines.
In the *Legend of Mary, queen of Scots* Mary Stuart meets her cousin
Elizabeth on an equal, stateswoman-to-stateswoman footing. This lifts
the Scottish queen out of her traditional roles as rebel or as martyr: she
is able to look calmly at her fate and to accept her infamous death as a
matter of course: she would, for reasons of state, have done the same
with a political enemy.

Lever also lifts his heroine to a higher, although different, level. During
the reign of Bloody Mary, Elizabeth was too young to be presented as a
reigning princess. But Lever never presents her as a helpless victim of
political circumstances, as another Elizabeth Gray. Even in her different
prisons the princess always keeps her head, and what she lacks in political
power she makes good in spiritual strength. She spends her times of
confinement edifying and elevating her mind by spiritual exercises and
(in contrast to Elizabeth Gray) thus masters her misfortunes:

> Here might she spend her holie meditation,
> (As sure she did much holier than I write)
> She alters not with Fortunes alteration:
> Resolue had made her sufferings her delight   (B3v)

Elizabeth's meditations are at the heart (or should one say the head) of
the poem. They are reported in direct speech and thus come closest to
the form of a Complaint (the longest of them covers 37 of the 202 rhyme
royal stanzas of the poem). But not even in these solitary meditations is
Elizabeth left alone. She never experiences the spiritual forlornness of
Middleton's Lucrece or Chute's Mrs Shore, and there are, of course,
neither husband nor children whom she might miss as Elizabeth Gray
does. Her complaints are no soliloquies, but prayers or meditations, parts

of a constant dialogue with her God. Even if He should nod and her enemies prevail she knows her soul is safe:

> Be it that Gods preuenting eie should sleepe,
> And that their purpose haue desired end:
> That Soule they take from me they cannot keepe,
> Which to a mighty Lord I recommend   (B4v)

This trust in God distinguishes the princess from most other heroines of the elegiac tradition. Classical figures such as Lucretia could not have it, but even the New Testament Magdalen lacks it in the eyes of the church-fathers; 'moeret desperatione corporis non reperti', says Maximus of Turin of Mary's weeping by the open grave of the risen Christ, and Ambrose thought this typical of a woman's weakness of faith which rests too much with bodily, as opposed to spiritual values: 'Quae non credit, mulier est, & adhuc corporei sexus appellatione signatur.'[85] Elizabeth is able to face losses of the corporeal kind with equanimity: she is not in love and she does not care for beauty, and again her words to that effect, a series of *contemptus mundi* arguments, might be addressed to one of her weaker sisters in distress:

> Is beauty then of that high consequence,
> Wherein I may disswasiue reason finde?
> Is that faire shadow of that excellence,
> That for the face I should exchange the minde?
> Beauty that blindeth many, cannot blinde
>   My Reason so; for Beautie's but a floure,
>   Which being pluckt it fadeth in an houre.   (C2v)

Saints such as Elizabeth are founded on metaphysical principles, and physical assets, including life, mean little to them – Elizabeth is armoured with Christian virtues and despises the world and the flesh, not to mention the Popish 'diuel', Gardner (E2r):

> What is my life the world should enuie so?
> (Alas) a little puffe of breathing aire   (B4r)

These ascetic or heroic qualities do not turn Elizabeth into a heroine of the amazon sort, however. Lever takes great pains to make visible the frightening circumstances under which she has to prove her fortitude, and he succeeds in showing how they affect her as a 'seely woman' (E3v) not naturally predisposed to meet them, most impressively during her arrest in the Tower of London, where she is sealed off in a sunless 'priuate roome' (F4r), surrounded by men of arms and ammunition:

> To see the men of warre to be her garde,
> The dismall place she was to enter in;
> The heaps of Ammunition in the yarde,

The noyse of fetter'd prisoners from within,
To see these markes of warre and prisoning,
  Were much vnfitting objects for the sight,
  Ladies (not loue) but feare to be in the fight.   (F3r)

What Lever stresses and Elizabeth ponders over in her meditations, is
the necessity to bear the afflictions of this world and not to yield to
despair; it is, in a word, the virtues of patience and fortitude which
Elizabeth represents. She expounds these virtues with arguments taken
from ancient sources, both classical and scriptural. In a passage which
sounds like a treatise on moral philosophy there are hints at Plato's hor-
ses-and-chariot simile about the reining in of the passions ('For heady
Passion's like an vntam'd beast', C1r) and Aristotle's *mesotes*-theory
('This violence exceedes his vertuous meane', C1r), and the Stoic ideal
of apathy ('Griefe should be borne with much indifference', C1r) – it is
a passage which would seem wildly out of character if we did not know
that Elizabeth actually translated the *Consolatio philosophiae* of Boethius, which was also written in prison and which incorporates a great
deal of classical philosophy, though she did this in her later years.[86]
  The virtue of patience is more than once set against the passion of
grief, and this seems to be a major concern of the author. Grief is not
one of the Christian cardinal sins,[87] and at first sight the artillery of
philosophical arguments directed against it seems uncalled for. The fact,
however, that a relative of grief is invoked, in Latin, on the title-page of
the poem, 'Nocet indulgentia nobis', underlines the importance it must
have for Sampson. We have noticed that fear is the controlling emotion
in Sampson's *Fortune's fashion*, and grief and related emotions like fear
left their impression on most of the poetry in the tradition of Ovidian
querelae which we have analysed. By making the maxim 'Nocet indulgentia nobis' his personal hallmark (it is also on the titlepage of his later
poem called *A crucifix; or, A meditation upon repentance and the holy
passion*, 1607) Sampson apparently contradicts this poetry in general,
and the Italian influence of *Lagrime* poems in particular which mingled
with this tradition and which will be considered in the next chapter.
  There is some evidence, then, that Lever led a personal crusade against
lachrymose poetry of different kinds, and that he chose 'Nocet indulgentia nobis' for his battle cry. He had allies in this crusade, Protestants such
as Thomas Hudson, who wrote an epic, *Judith* (1584, after Du Bartas),
and may have sung it to King James,[88] and classicists such as David
Murray, a Scotsman, who in his *Sophonisba* (1611) tried to revive an
ancient sense of heroism. Though these poets battled on different fields,
their efforts combined into a campaign against the weakness of Ovidian
and Italian poetry that characterises a large part of Jacobean narrative
verse. Like Drayton, Lever represents the patriotic English wing of this

campaign. There is, however, nothing partisan about his ethic stance. If looked at more closely, the passion of grief which he opposes is the old spiritual sin of despair. This was always thought to be deadlier than the deadly sins, and as we have seen the heroines of Complaints are indeed in danger of falling into despair. Keeping this background in mind, the concern shown in Lever's poem seems less exaggerated:

> The Griefe of mind is that intestine warre
> That stirres sedition in the state of man   (C1r)

Tears could be called a symptom of this illness, and *Queen Elizabeth's tears*, which leads up to Christian resolution, is a treatise written against the unwholesome wet tradition. It does not come as a surprise, then, that Elizabeth, in spite of the tearful title, sheds but few tears in the poem. Lever mentions Elizabeth's 'religious teares' (B2r) in the beginning of his poem; these he wants to preserve. The princess weeps only once, however, when moved by the courageous conduct of the Earl of Sussex who dares to oppose a royal command by carrying a letter of hers to Queen Mary. Otherwise Elizabeth overcomes moments of weakness by reminding herself and those around her of her noble bearing ('We that are princely minded cannot fear', D3r) and her divine protection ('And when religious griefe bedims our eie, / The Angells come to wipe and make them drie', F3v). In contrast, the angels that appear to Mary Magdalen fail to bring consolation.

This almost-martyr is as resolute, then, as the stricter church-fathers wished the Magdalen had been or the strictest Protestant poets made Susanna out to be.[89] The tears of the Magdalen were read as signifying a lack of trust in God; Elizabeth in the end endures the strongest tribulations and overcomes her grief:

> How ere it be, my comfort is in heauen,
> That makes me powrefull to support my griefe;
> God that is iust, to my iust cause hath giuen
> Patience, by which the wronged haue reliefe   (E1v)

The idea of a Christian heroism informs even a set piece of the rival epyllion tradition which Lever inserts in his poem, the formal description of a piece of art: it becomes instrumental in strengthening Elizabeth's fortitude. In her dark room in the Tower, the sort of surroundings that plunges heroines of Complaints into unrelieved despair, she comes across a tapestry, not of destruction, as in Shakespeare's *Lucrece*, but of salvation:

> As thus her griefe vnrested had her Grace,
> To euery place she casts her searching eie,
> Fearing some hidden danger in the place:

> Where in the hangings wrought, she did espie,
> How *Daniell* in the Lyons Denne did lie,
>> Which counterfet of griefe she stands to see;
>> Griefe is best pleasd with like societie. (F4r)

The association with Daniel assures her of her noble blood and her noble cause ('As I, so *Daniel* was of noble blood / Both I and *Daniel* haue like holy cause', G1r), and Lever makes her switch to the plural which nicely expresses both majesty and company:

> We are not then alone, why grieue we thus?
> For *Daniel* and the Lyons be with vs (F4v)

Elizabeth, like Daniel and Susanna, has become what theologians call a heroine of the 'deliverance type'.[90] Soon after this illuminating scene she is released from her prison, and later vindicated by her repentant sister Mary (the conversion miracle in her legend). Lever can end his counterfeit-complaint on a confident note:

> So God was pleasd with prouidence and care,
> This vertuous holy Lady to defend. (G4v)

5 Susanna and the Magdalen: religious epyllia and Complaints

Compassibile enim est muliebre genus, & natura flebile
Chrysostomus, *Homilia 85 in Joannem*

Ovidian poetry, epyllia as well as Complaints, presented a challenge to zealous Christian authors of both Catholic and Calvinist creeds. Some of the poems in these lines looked downright pagan, at least to devout readers, for instance Marlowe's *Hero and Leander*, and even the most ascetic of the Complaints, such as Lever's *Queen Elizabeth's tears*, were based on a Boethian rather than specifically Christian ethos. For a religious poet there were different ways of meeting this challenge: he could try to beat his worldly rivals out of the field, or he could try to join their game and gradually convert them. Joshua Sylvester is such a religious poet; he gave Michael Drayton his title of an 'English Ovid', and it may have been a doubtful compliment, for in his translation from Du Bartas' Old Testament epic *The second week or childhood of the world* (1598) Sylvester admonished Drayton and Daniel to look up to more worthy subjects:

> My deere sweet Daniel, sharpe-conceipted, breefe,
> Ciuill, sententious, for pure accents chiefe:
> And our new NASO, that so passionates
> Th'heroik sighes of love sick Potentates
> May change their subject, and advance their songs
> Up to these higher and more holy things[1]

Du Bartas and his translator were Protestants; at the other end of the religious spectrum we find the Jesuit author of a Catholic New Testament epic, *Saint Marie Magdalen's conversion* (1603), dissociating himself from worldly poetry altogether:

> Of *Helens* rape, and *Troyes* beseiged *Towne*,
> Of *Troylus* faith, and *Cressids* falsitie,
> Of *Rychards* stratagems for the english crowne,
> Of *Tarquins* lust, and lucrece chastitie,
> > Of these, of none of these my muse nowe treates,
> > Of greater conquests, warres and loues she speaks.

154

A womans conquest of her one affects,
A womans warre with her selfe-appetite,
A womans loue, breeding such effects,
As th'age before nor since nere brought to light,
    Of these; and such as these, my muse is prest,
    To spend the idle houres of her rest.   (A3r)[2]

Both critics then go on to write epyllia on Biblical subjects, the Calvinist
preferring Old Testament stories, the Catholic New Testament figures.
Their positions are typical for the different directions the Biblical narrative takes in Elizabethan literature. Surprisingly, perhaps, the division
corresponds to the pattern we have seen emerging in the Ovidian tradition: we find epyllia which deal with 'lust and [. . .] chastitie' as in the
story of Susanna, and Complaints which register the movements of a
doubtful soul such as that of Mary Magdalen, 'A womans warre with her
selfe-appetite'.[3] The Ovidian influence is visible in both directions, and
has been in similar poems from the Middle Ages. I will trace the development of the Protestant epyllion and the Catholic Complaint following
poems and treatises on the figureheads of Reformation and Counter-
Reformation womanhood, Susanna and the Magdalen.

The Old Testament heroine: Susanna in medieval and Renaissance verse

The apocryphal Susanna story fills only an episode in the book of the
prophet Daniel. The tale of the tribulations of the fair and pious daughter
of the tribe of Juda is related in 64 verses as an example of the providence
of God; it culminates in the trial scene which shows Daniel in his epony-
mous role as instrument of divine retribution: Daniel literally means
'God's justice'. The action is hastened to this culminating point; there
are no descriptions and no retardations. Even the tribunal with its cross-
examination is treated in a peremptory manner: the 'wise youth' Daniel
foreknows everything, and the foolish elders hardly put up a defence;
their conviction is a matter of course.[4]

The heroine Susanna has no more than a supporting part to play in
her story. She is the daughter of righteous parents and the wife of an
honourable husband. In court, too, she seems less a person in her own
right than a member of her family. Her beauty is remarkable only for
starting off the action; the dilemma imposed on her by the elders is
treated in one verse, its solution in the next, her lament in two more.
The thanksgiving for her deliverance is offered by her relatives; the last
verse speaks of the greatness of the prophet:

> Helcias autem et uxor eius laudaverunt Deum pro filia sua Susanna,
> cum Ioakim, marito eius, et cognatis omnibus, quia non esset inventa

in ea res turpis. Daniel autem factus est magnus in conspectu populi, a
die illa, et deinceps.   (*Vulgata*, Dan. 13.63–4)

Susanna in medieval Latin verse: Petrus Riga and Alan of Melsa

Despite its sparse rendering in the Old Testament, the story of Susanna
has all the ingredients of a titillating Ovidian tale: the bathing scene, the
dilemma and the trial would have appealed to the master of eroticism,
psychology and rhetoric. It is not surprising, then, that authors of the
'Ovidian' High Middle Ages took up the story of Susanna and adorned
it with flowers culled from Ovid's works. One of these authors, Petrus
Riga, is said to have composed a version of her story in about a hundred
elegiac distichs. He wrote it early in his poetic career, around 1175; one
is tempted to think he was as young as the authors of Elizabethan epyllia
we have met before. He incorporated an extended and allegorised version of the poem later on in his *Aurora*, a collection of biblical verse tales
on an epic scale.[5]

The earlier version of Petrus Riga's 'De sancta Susanna' is concentrated on a single scene at the place of judgment. The events in the garden
are reported and corrected from different points of view, first by one of the
elders, then Susanna, then Daniel. In the epic version this piecemeal
presentation is abandoned in favour of a more balanced, but still dramatic
structure with two locations (garden and court) and a more detached
narrator leading from the one to the other. The changes of perspective,
however, provided some of the attractions in the earlier version; the
bathing scene in the garden in particular gains a sort of heated intensity
by being related as seen through the eyes of one of the elders first, then
by Susanna. In the voyeur's report one can almost literally feel the sultry
atmosphere of a summer afternoon creep into the narrative as he relives
the experience. The elder seems incensed by the wish to be in the position
of the lover he invents to deceive the judge. He describes Susanna's
clothes and her cosmetics, and then asks why she came to the bath alone,
and so conspicuously dressed:

> Cur sic? ut placeat magis, ut magis urat amantem;
> > Plus igitur placuit, plus suus arsit amans.
> Arsit et accessit, os ori, brachia collo
> > Junxerunt, pudor est ordine cuncta sequi.   (61–4)

It is a very subtle exercise in Ovidian psychology which loses some of its
effect as soon as the description is put into the mouth of a disinterested
narrator.

In contrast to the heated discourse of the elder, Susanna expresses herself in the cooler medium of water imagery. Her dilemma, for instance, which resembles that of Lucretia (to commit or to be accused of adultery), is rendered in the sort of Scylla-and-Charybdis simile we have found in erotic epyllia, but extended to spiritual heights and depths:

> Navis quo fugiet geminis impulsa procellis?
>   Hinc mihi nulla salus, hinc fuga nulla patet.
> Sirtes incurret fugiens mea cymba Carybdim,
>   Et mea fata cavens in mea fata ferar.
> Peccem? peccantem me puniet ira Gehennae;
>   Clamem? clamantem puniet ira senum.
> Sed si vestra, senes, manus in me saeviat, iram
>   Leniat inferni verbere trita caro;
> Ut damnum carnis animam lucretur, ametque
>   Portum caelestem naufraga vita mihi.   (173–82)

The topos is too common to be traced to any particular source; other additions to the Bible story are taken directly from Ovid: there is a garbled quotation from the equally agitated 'Letter of Phaedra to Hippo-lytus' in the *Aurora* version of the story,[6] and some of the arguments used by the elders in their efforts to flatter or threaten Susanna into submission are taken from Lucretia's tale in the *Fasti*.[7] Whereas, how-ever, the Roman *matrona virilis* gives in to the tyrant, the single Susanna triumphs over two tempters:

> Dixit et obsistit et preualet una duobus
>   Seuis blanda uiris femina iusta reis.   (183–4)

But Peter does not aim at setting Biblical against pagan virtue like the early church-fathers. He exploits the delicate and the drastic potential of the story, and sometimes both at once; his characterisation of the elders' worldly preferences, salmon rather than Solomon, was later extended to the practices of medieval monks.[8] The fate of Susanna, and the lessons to be drawn from it, are subordinated to rhetorical effects, and so are theological and historical implications. The poem may have been a five-finger exercise of young Peter, a *prosopopeia* as set in medieval schools, but it shows the hand of a future poet.

At about the same time as Petrus Riga, an English monk, Alan of Melsa (i.e. Meaux on Humberside) wrote another 'Tractatus metricus de Susanna'. The metre is elegiac again; Alan's poem is much longer, however, and comprises about 200 distichs. Not only because of this length, but also because of its decorative and descriptive material this poem can be regarded as a forerunner of the Elizabethan Biblical epyllion.[9]

Alan gives his tale a moralising framework: the narrator poses as a penitent sinner who ponders over the story of Susanna and marvels at the fact that she, a woman exposed to the temptations of world and flesh, was able to withstand while he failed; she must be the Phoenix of her sex:

> Pretitulatur opus Susanne causa uirilis:
> [. . .]
> Feminei sexus Susanna fit unica fenix,
>   Quam non extulerunt copia, forma genus.   (39, 47–8)

The Phoenix is, of course, sexless: Susanna's heroic stand places her outside the pale of her sex – in that she resembles Ovid's *matrona virilis* Lucretia and other women we have met in the worldly heroic tradition, for example Boccaccio's Elissa, who is allowed to figure in the *De casibus virorum illustrium*. Boccaccio praises Dido, too, for her manliness, 'O mulieris virile rubor', because she held off the importunate Iarbas, and in *De claris mulieribus* he compares her with Susanna.[10]

Unlike Petrus Riga, Alan is interested in this kind of intercultural competition: he compares Susanna to Penelope and he ranks her with and above Helen of Troy and Lucretia of Rome. This interest seems rooted, however, not so much in Alan's ambition as moralist than as epic poet. He allows his elders, for instance, to compare themselves to Hercules and Solomon, and he introduces classical gods and goddesses into his Old Testament poem, regardless of propriety. Hymen is invoked at Susanna's nuptials, Fama dares not detract her, Lachesis and Fortune manipulate her fate. Not only the Olympian machinery, but also the luxurious descriptions of Susanna's palace, of her garden with its birds and plants and, of course, of her beauty, are worthy of an epyllion.[11] The narrator seems constantly in danger of losing his head, or at least the thread of his tale, in all this luxury; now and then he gets completely lost and has to call himself back to the moral significance of his story:

> Vicit amor legem, racionem forma, senectam
>   Flamma, caro mentem uicerat, Eua uirum.   (201–2)

Were Eve replaced by Dido, this would read like an allegorical interpretation of Book IV of Virgil's *Aeneid*, complete with the traditional equation of woman with beauty and the flesh; Alan seems to have forgotten that this time a woman is the protagonist. We have here, in a nutshell, one of the main difficulties that Christian epic poets such as Du Bartas or Milton had to overcome: it is difficult to bring the beautiful to terms with the ascetic.

Alan's wish to take in as many Classical elements as possible extends into the sphere of philosophy and gains cosmic dimensions in a magnificent apostrophe which Susanna addresses to heaven when confronted with the elders in her garden:

At pater architipo complectens omnia cosmo,
   Omnibus ydeas pretitulante noym,
De nichilo formans animas producis ad yle
   Corpora, coniungens dissona lege pari,
Qui facis ut pariant elementa tribus tria feta,
   Aer equor humus pisces uolucre fera,
De fornace trahens Ebreos eripuisti,
   Fluctibus equoreis hoste cadente suo:
De fornace precor me tolle libidinis, ut non
   Me trahat in facinus territa morte caro.   (273–82)

This is a far cry, indeed, from the single prayer in the Bible and from the Susanna whose reticence Augustine so warmly praised in contrast to the clamouring elders:

Clamabant qui Susannam accusabant, et ad coelum oculos non levabant; ille tacebat, et corde clamabat: unde illa meruit exaudiri, inde isti puniri.[12]

Alan aggrandises the simple prayer with a mixture of Platonic and Aristotelian terms ('ydeas', 'noym', 'hyle'), regardless again of dramatic situation or, indeed, theological soundness. There is only one moment during the trial scene when Alan presents something like the dumb and dazed heroine of the Biblical story, and this is when she is almost stifled by inquiring relatives, and it is at this moment that he uses the 'ter conata loqui' (an epic formula) of the *Fasti* legend of Lucretia (II, 823) and accompanies it with appropriate gestures:

Queritur unde gemit, cur plorat, que lacrimarum
   Copia, que gemitus causa, quis auctor erat.
'Pres' prius et 'biteros' repetens dum cincopat, uno
   Singultu nequiit dicere presbiteros.   (287–90)

But Susanna soon regains her eloquence and acts out the scene in prima-donna style.

The split word or phrase is a stock element in epic and in elegiac poetry, for instance in romances of the period, where it is used mainly in love scenes. Something of the spirit of romance governs Alan's 'Tractatus metricus', too:[13] Daniel acts as *deus* (or *manus Dei*) *ex machina*, and Susanna, soon relieved of her manacles, vocally and otherwise, leaves the scene in triumph, while the narrator takes his *congé* with only a formal bow in the direction of a moral interpretation of his epic tale:

Exultat populus, meruit Susanna coronam,
   Leta domum rediit, et periere senes.   (401–2)

Robert Roche, *Eustathia*

The epyllion, like the romance, has a leaning towards the comic, in
Susanna's case towards a kind of divine comedy in which every move is
watched over by the all-embracing father of her invocation. Other medieval and early Renaissance treatments of her story bear out this tendency:
the anonymous *Pistil of Susan* comes complete with a sword-brandishing
guardian angel (lines 318–20); in Thomas Garter's *Comedy of Susanna*, a
late example of the Biblical morality play (or an early one of the domestic
play), there is a Vice who is hanged with a joke on his lips and a Susanna
whose chief concern is the servant question. After the Reformation, the
expansion of religious controversy into the field of literature brought
about a change towards a new seriousness in the handling of stories such
as Susanna's. Du Bartas led the way; the first part to be translated of
his versified Bible history was in Thomas Hudson's *Judith*, which was
published in Edinburgh in 1584. Joshua Reynolds' translations of
all the *Divine weeks and works* began to appear in London in
1592 and were completed with the first collected edition in 1605.[14] The
evolution of the minor religious epic thus coincided with the development
of the different strands of Ovidian poetry, and the imitations inspired by
the example of Du Bartas in England had to compete with the erotic
epyllion on the one hand and the tragic Complaint on the other.
   Susanna soon became the patron saint of Protestant devotional literature and was set against the *libertinae* of the erotic tradition. The first to
take up the Ovidian challenge in earnest – that is, on a greater scale than
Robert Greene's *Mirror of modesty* (1584), a prose tract in Euphuistic
style, or ballads such as 'The constancy of Susanna' – was Robert Roche.
He was a clergyman who published his poem *Eustathia: or The constancy
of Susanna* in 1599, while he was at Oxford. He went back to the West
country soon after and died as Vicar of Holton in Dorset.[15] Roche chose
the stately rhyme royal for his poem and added to the gravity of the metre
by telling his readers that he had been about to try his hand at pastoral
poetry when his mother (slightly veiled under the name of Thestylis) died
and he changed both style and subject matter. His poem, then, comes
close to an elegy in the obituary sense of the word, and it is not only
modesty which makes him dissociate himself from other poetry of the
elegiac kind:

   Expect not heere, th'invention, or the vaine,
   Of Lucrece rape-write: or the curious scan,

Of Phillis friend; or famous fairy-*Swaine*;
Or Delias prophet, or admired man.
      My chicken fethered winges, no ympes enrich,
      Pens not full sum'd, mount not so high a pitch.   (A3r)

The muted tone is resumed in the end: the poem closes with an extended
memento mori passage spoken by Susanna on her death-bed. It is a
passage which mixes domestic realism and possibly a personal remi-
niscence with a solemn parody on the love-and-death bed scenes we have
found in Ovidian Complaints, for instance Chute's *Beauty dishonoured* or
the *Complaint of Rosamond* by Daniel (who is, of course, 'Delia's prophet'
in the quote above).

As the solemn ending with Susanna's death suggests, Roche does not
feel bound to the course of events as given in the Bible, but follows
Susanna's life from birth to bier; the didactic intention of his poem leads
him away from the more dramatic design of the story in the Book of
Daniel. In structure his poem comes close to that of a saint's life. He
stretches the short story in the Book of Daniel to the length of about 400
seven-line stanzas (not counting a lengthy induction, an inlaid prayer in
ballad metre and an epilogue). If the length seems epic, the style is not.
Roche is intensely wary of the pitfalls which made Alan of Melsa stumble,
and he uses the means usually employed to swell the epic discourse very
sparingly. This, again, is an outcome of the didactic aim of the poem
which is written large over his heroine's education: 'Be graue, not gay'
(B4v). Worldly pleasures are to be avoided, and so is everything that
might give rise to them. Susanna's beauty is therefore unveiled only to
serve as a warning for fair women:

      Her *Amber* tresses, made a seemely shew;
      Her milk-white skin, adorned natures skill,
      Yet all did vanish, as the liquid devv,
      VVhile *Chastitie* remaines eternall still,
      VVhy then are vvomen vvedded to vaine vvill?
            That for a wanton momentanie pleasure,
            They (wilful) vvast an everlasting treasure.   (D3r)

Even a praise of matrimony (which accords with the Protestant pro-
gramme of the author) must not promise too much joy; it is dampened
with a reminder of the pains of childbirth.

All the sensual details of Susanna's story that were lovingly dwelt on
not only by poets but also by painters in the later Middle Ages and
early Renaissance (one need only think of Altdorfer and Tintoretto) are
pruned back to Biblical blandness by Robert Roche. The garden, often
the place to show off her beauty, shrinks to the measurements of a monastic
herbary:

> A fine contrived plot and passing faire;
> Hem'd in with stately walles vvhich lik'd her vvell,
> (Chast cloistred nymph, within so sweete a cell)   (D5r)

Roche's Susanna takes her bath only to comply with her religious duties, 'She serues her God, with solitarie muse' (E5v). It is somewhat misleading, then, when Lily B. Campbell counts this poem among the 'Divine erotic epyllia' in chapter 12 of her study of Elizabethan *Divine poetry and drama* (pp. 125–7). There are religious poems which exploit the erotic potential of stories such as Susanna's – for example Francis Sabie's short epyllion *David and Bathsheba* (1596), which has an opulent garden and a matching bathing scene ('Then nimbly casts she of her Damaske frocke', etc., F1v). The relation of Roche's *Eusthatia* to Sabie's *David and Bathsheba* is comparable to that between Shakespeare's *Lucrece* (of which there are several echoes in Roche's poem) and his *Venus and Adonis*.

Roche's Biblical saint is immured in her virtue, and this virtue suffers no scratch in the course of her career, least of all from the elders who, after a sound verbal thrashing from Susanna, are so contrite that one can hardly believe they ever yielded to temptation at all. In spite of the strictly moral concern of the author, then, there is little moral tension in the tale, and there is not much human concern, either; it is significant that the only cry of anguish comes from the narrator:

> Thou God which dost, fell tyrans rage detest,
> VVhy suffrest thou such wolues, to tyrannise?
> VVhy are thy seely lamkins so opprest?   (D4r)[16]

Susanna herself stays calm and collected throughout the tale, very much as Augustine liked to see her.

It is part of the concept Susanna is made to serve if the protagonists in Roche's poem move with a certain stiffness. As the title says, Susanna stands for 'Eustathia', and that means 'firmness'. The action moves rather stiffly, too, with prayers and expostulations at every turn. Only once does it leap into life in a domestic interlude following the garden scene. Susanna runs indoors after her confrontation with the elders, and is comforted by her husband. She is afraid of telling him the whole truth, and partly blames her servants for being slow to bring the soap she had sent for; that is why she was alone and exposed to the advances of the elders:

> And as we blame misfortunes, in their bringers,
> Shee blames her maides, as fawtors of her wrong,
> Shee feeles impatient fittes, and they her fingers,
> That durst neglect their due returne so long,
> Whose sad excuse, (permixt with teares amonge,)

To seeke the thinges, her selfe had laide amisse,
Return'd her selfe the blame, that wrong'd her blisse.   (F6v)

That fit of impatience and the zeugmatic itch in her fingers show Susanna
and her author at their most sympathetic. It also gives evidence of
another tendency in the story towards domestic realism which, however,
Roche seldom allows to prevail over his religious idealism. Nevertheless,
he has succeeded in his modest aim of setting up an epitaph in the family
tomb by praising a private rather than a public virtue in Susanna's constancy.

Robert Aylett, *Susanna*, and George Ballard, *The history of Susanna*

When, a quarter of a century after Roche, Robert Aylett took up the
subject of Susanna, he had a more ambitious aim in mind. Aylett came
from the landed gentry and went into the legal profession, with an eye
on advancement in the civil service. F.M. Padelford, who has closely
studied Aylett's career, believes that his poetical works were written
mainly to promote this aim.[17] Aylett was not a politician, but as a civil
servant under Bishop Laud (and later Cromwell) he was necessarily
involved in the political commotions of his time. The title of his poem
Susanna: or the arraignment of the two unjust elders (1622) already hints
at a shift of interest from the private to the public issues behind the Bible
story. The motto on the title page stresses the point:

> DEVT.16.20. *That which is iust and right shalt thou follow, that thou
> maist liue and enjoy the Land which the Lord thy God giueth thee.*

To dispel any remaining doubts, Aylett prefixed his poem with an allegorical interpretation of the apocryphal story which firmly places the
public virtue of justice at the centre of interest:

> I Chaste *Susanna*, here interpret Right,
> Or Iustice; cleare, as pure celestiall Light   (A2v)

With regard to form, Aylett follows even more clearly than Roche the
epic example set by the English imitators of Du Bartas; his opening lines
echo those of Hudson's *Judith* ('I sing the vertues of a valiant Dame' etc.)
which were later adopted by Sylvester in his translation of *The divine
weeks*:

> I Sing the honour of that noble Dame,
> Who for true vertues sake despised shame   (A3r)

Like Sylvester and Roche he then goes on to dissociate himself from
pagan rivals of his heroine, in particular Lucretia, whom he silences with

Augustine's 'Si adulterata, cur laudata; si pudica, cur occisa' (*De civitate Dei*, I, xix):

> *Lucrece* be mute; if chaste, why should thou die?
> If not, why should we praise thy chastitie?   (A3r)

The altercation with these rivals is resumed later on with the more poignant argument already quoted that Susanna needs no stiletto to defend her honour (B5r).

Though only about half as long (1,470 lines), Aylett's poem is an altogether lavish affair compared with Roche's version of the same story, and it is appropriately written in heroic couplets. Like Roche, Aylett emphasises the domestic role of the heroine, but the surroundings are completely changed: Aylett's heroine begins her day with an elaborate *levée* which starts off like an erotic epyllion, but the author takes care to be suggestive only in a spiritual sense:

> Now scarce his steedes had *Phoebus* watered,
> And for long iourney ready harnessed,
> And fair *Aurora* vsher of the day
> Made haste; because *Sol* went his longest way,
> When chaste *Susanna* from sweete side arose
> Of *Ioachim*, and putting on her cloathes,
> She meditates on roabe of righteousnesse,
> Wherewith the bridegroome his belou'd doth dresse:
> His merits made her owne by imputation,
> In spirituall birth, not fleshly generation.   (A8r)

She ends her day with an evening stroll in the garden she herself designed in Spenserian opulence:

> Amongst the fruits of her Industriousnesse,
> Who neuer eate her Bread in idlenesse,
> Shee plants an orchard fruitfull, rich, and faire,
> Whither she with her *Lord* doth oft repaire,
> Themselues awhile from worldly cares to free,
> And on their handy *workes Gods* blessing see.
> There might they please, smell, touch, eate, taste, and sight,
> With flowers, fruits, and musiques sweete delight   (A5r)

Aylett evidently tries to combine the profitable and the delightful, abstract virtue and its material, even sensuous rewards. He is much less wary than Roche of the more decorative elements of his art; even the most artificial part of an epyllion, the formal description (which Roche omitted from his *Eustathia*) is put to good use when Susanna is shown at her needlework:

> She for her husband workes a cap or band,
> To make him be more honour'd in the land,

Where thou might see, with cunning needle told,
The subtile serpent simple *Eue* infold
[. . .]
Here in the bush a spotlesse lambe doth lye,
Willing, to saue young *Isaacks* life, to dye;
A figure of that lambe that offered
His life to saue vs all in *Isaacks* seede.   (B1r–v)

The elaborate description works on several levels of meaning at once: it
shows Susanna as an accomplished housewife (spinning or knitting have
been signs of domestic skill in women since Penelope and Lucretia, and
particularly in wool-producing and wool-processing England);[18] it surpasses such worldly artefacts as Rosamond's curious casket or Hero's
silken scarf by being more useful and presenting worthier subjects;[19] it
foreshadows future events (Susanna will be tempted like Eve and rescued
like Isaac by divine intervention – the familiar image of the lamb underlines the correspondence); and it gives the action a typological significance (Susanna is, like Isaac, a prefiguration of Christ). It is a many-
layered insertion which gives the story of Susanna a depth often lacking
in the more superficial secular epyllion.

   This gain in depth, however, is bought with a loss of sympathy for the
leading characters. Their every single move is strenuously transported
onto a level of spiritual significance. Little room for doubt is left,
emotions are immediately checked by reassuring deliberations, if not by
the characters themselves, then by the omnipresent narrator. And not
even the narrator is given leave to develop too much empathy; in the
trial scene he has to check himself on discovering that, for a moment, he
thought it possible that Susanna might be brought to death:

> Oh Heau'ns! chaste *Susan* die? Thou maist cōplaine,
> That thou thine heart has clensed then in vaine,
> In vaine hast wash'd thine hands in innocence,
> And day and night endured chastisements:
> But vnderstanding well the fearefull end
> Of those that so malitiously intend,
> How they consume and perish suddainly,
> Shee onely thus aloud to God doth cry.   (C2v–3r)

It is a thought that must not be allowed to gain ground, and, of course,
Susanna is relieved immediately after her prayer by Daniel's intervention.
The moments of anguish are cut short in this epic; in a Complaint they would
have been prolonged, the uncertainty of the situation and the doubts of the
protagonist would have been exploited.

   What Aylett gains in his poem, then, is a certain height rather than
depth. Where a Complaint would probe the emotional response of a
character such as Susanna, his religious epic constantly tries to lift her

into doctrinal significance. Stylistically, this leads to an allegorical way of speaking: it is the sort of style we have found straining against the form of the Complaint in Drayton's *Matilda* and Lever's *Queen Elizabeth* with their single-minded, unshakeable heroines. These Complaints, however, propounded more or less personal virtues (chastity and fortitude); Aylett is not content to give his story this kind of moral significance. He adds a political dimension and runs the risk of overloading his vehicle in the process. The way he treats the tribal differences in the background of the Bible story, for instance, makes one suspect an allusion to the schism between the Christian churches of his time. In the trial scene one of the elders is addressed by the judge Daniel:

> Then *Daniel* said, Oh thou of *Canaans* seede,
> And not of *Iudas*, Beauty hath indeede
> Deceiued thee, and lust doth eu'n thy heart
> And all the powers of thy soule peruert:
> Thus you with *Israels* daughters dealt before,
> And they for feare haue plaid with you the whore;
> But *Iudas* daughter, *Ioachims* chaste bride,
> Could neuer such foule wickednesse abide.   (C6r)

Juda is the tribe of David and of Jesus; the difference between Israel and Juda was taken up in the religious disputes of the time by contendents such as Richard Hooker and transferred to the churches of Rome and of Geneva.[20] Aylett makes his political implications explicit a little later on in an epic simile which brings the Gunpowder Plot on to the Biblical scene:

> And as when *Faux* that arcenall full fraught
> With treason, mischiefe, and rebellious thought,
> (Plotting the death and vtter desolation,
> Of King, Priests, Nobles, and of all our nation,
> Because like *Susan* here we did deny,
> To leaue our Lord, and to accompany,
> With *Iezabel* in foule abhomination,
> With whom earths Princes commit fornication,)
> Condemned was by Iudges iustest dome,
> Lo all the people doe together come,
> With ioyfull hearts, vnto his execution,
> Where he receiueth iustest retribution:
> Eu'n so when *Daniel* [. . .]   (C7r)

In a similar manner Chapman had built into his continuation of Marlowe's *Hero and Leander* (1598) an allusion to the Essex expedition to Cadiz, and thus spiked the erotic epyllion with allegorical elements.[21] In both cases, there may be a certain amount of personal ambition behind the allusions to the politics of the day. Aylett dedicated his *Susanna* to a young nobleman of his native county, the Earl of Warwick, whom he apostrophises as '*Another* Daniel *for iudging right*' (A2r); for himself Aylett tacitly claims the role of a counsellor on the proper way of carrying out the laws of God. Aylett's epyllion ends with an elaborate moralisation containing personal hints like these combined with an outlook on Daniel's career at the Persian court (and a reference to Joseph's at the Egyptian, C8v). Susanna's person recedes into the background; Aylett aspires to greater things. A year after *Susanna* he found a subject more suitable to his ambition and published a short epic on the Biblical Joseph; in 1638 he took another step towards the full-scale Biblical epic with a poem of 3,400 lines on King David in which the epyllic interest is confined to an inlaid report on the Bathsheba story.[22]

1638 is also the year in which another *History of Susanna* was published. Its author, George Ballard, was apparently unaware of any previous attempts at the subject, for he wonders in his 'PROPOSITION Apologicall to the Learned Readers' that 'her Legend hath (so long / Poets so plenteous) never yet been sung' (A7v). His ambitions as a poet are at least as high as those of Aylett, but they are pious rather than political. He dedicates his poem to the Countess of Northumberland (Aylett had addressed the Earl of Warwick first, and then his spouse) and probably has in mind a more private audience than Aylett. The *History of Susanna* is arranged in seventeen sections of 50 to 100 lines in heroic couplets; each section is followed by a meditation of about 50 more lines; a set of these would provide food for an evening's reading and reflection.

Despite the devotional purpose of the poem, the ornaments are those of a Christian epic: there is an invocation of the 'Great God of *Moses*, God of Muses, too' (A2v) which asks for the same inspiration that fired the prophet Daniel, and the dedication tries to establish Susanna as a female Hercules: 'Her countenance in the cradle, manifested infallible tokens, to character succeeding honour' (A4v). In his 'PROPOSITION Apologicall' the author laboriously entrenches himself opposite the classical tradition; his main antagonists are, apparently, epyllia on subjects taken from the *Metamorphoses*:

> No storie of transformed Dames (of old)
> By Poets changed into stars of gold,
> Into cleere Fountains, Birds, and branches green,
> Nor of the Pagan-prays'd *Ephesian* Queen,
> Who (naked) bath'd with Virgin-Nymphs of Wood
> In bubling streame; whose Nymphs about her stood,
> Like Iv'ry pales (in vain) to hide their Dame,
> From *Cadmus* Kinsman, that a Hart became:
> No laud of her; but I Encomiums sing,
> Of new *Titania* bathing in a Spring;

More constant, chast, more beautifull divine:
Of whom *Diana* was a former signe.   (A7r–v)

The idea of a quasi-typological relation between classical and Biblical
heroines (Diana being 'a former signe' of Susanna) indicates that the
difference between old and new poetry is not unbridgeable; Ballard's
procedure is comparable to that of medieval authors who made the substance of Ovid's stories presentable by trimming them with moral glosses
(the story of Orpheus provides an excellent example; see for instance its
interpretation in Chaucer's *Boece*, Book II, Metrum 12, or Henryson's
Tale of Orpheus and Erudices). What Ballard does is to take a morally
irreprehensible substance (such as the story of Susanna), and to present
it in Ovidian style. The medieval mixture was an *Ovide moralisé*, his is a
Bible ovidisé. Ballard's story of Susanna comes complete with an *aition*
in the epyllion manner: the curative effects of St Winifred's well are
attributed to the tears of 'Saintly *Susan*' (E7r). To heighten its sensuous
appeal he need not even step out of the Old Testament: the *Canticles* is
as good in this respect as anything in Ovid, and Ballard (like Du Bartas
before) follows Solomon's example. The description of Susanna's beauty
in section 2 may serve as an example:

> Some said her necke a turret seem'd of one
> Smooth pollisht snow-white Alabaster-stone [sic]:
> And that the same (for evermore) inzon'd
> A Carquenet of costly diamond.
> Her paps two Swan-down worlds, that each containes
> Like Rivolets, bright Azure branched veines   (B6r)

When it comes to the machinations of the elders, the author looks up
from his story and dissociates himself from the proceedings with as much
indignation as Ovid shows in his stories of Philomela or of Myrrha. Where
Ovid shows disgust with the barbarian practices in Thracia or in Cyprus,
Ballard gives vent to his anti-Roman and anti-Popish sentiments; the
'*boldest whores*', he claims, are those '*uptrain'd in stewes at* Rome'
(Medit. XI, G3r);[23] after their execution his elders join '*triple-crowned
Popes*', '*shavelin Priests, and cowled Friers*' (I1v) in hell. If this appears to
look back to an uneasy combination of classical and Christian elements
characteristic of earlier Tudor literature – the hellish company is the same
the elders find in Richard Robinson's satire *The reward of wickedness*
(1574) – other signs point forward to a more harmonious fusion of such
elements. On the whole, Ballard's poetry strives to praise and to edify.
It moves on a high poetic level and thus points forward to the religious
epic of Cowley and of Milton, the 'More learned men', one might
extrapolate, he asks in his 'PROPOSITION' to 'come and mend' his poem
(A8r).

In spite of its satirical elements, Ballard's poem is less polemic and less public-spirited than Aylett's. His Susanna is not the unflinching heroine one might have expected. Ballard finds room for empathy, particularly in the meditative parts of the poem, and Susanna is shown to be in tears more often than Roche or Aylett thought compatible with their sterner concept of her character. When she is placed under arrest we find her, to quote one of Ballard's less felicitous coinages, 'pickled up in tears' (F2r), and her friends adding to the brine. Later on the narrator joins in, and has to admonish himself:

> Hence gentle eyes, your teares again will drown
> Her story, teer-already [sic] overflown.   (F5r)

This is a new trait in the Protestant heroine, a trait which has been copied from her Roman Catholic counterpart, the Magdalen, who is introduced in the next chapter.

The New Testament penitent: the *Omelia Origenis de Maria Magdalena* and its influence

Susanna's strength lies in her fortitude, her trust in a providential universe in which, ultimately, virtue and justice prevail. She proves her virtue in the temptation scene – this is her personal trial – and justice is proved in the court scene, the public trial presided over by the God-sent Daniel. Susanna moves in a world without tragedy; there is no need for a stiletto, all you need do is overcome your fear and be quick-witted enough to cry for help or use your brains to expose the slow-witted villains.

Perseverance is one of the strengths of the Magdalen, too – or of the Mary we meet at the empty sepulchre of Christ in the twentieth chapter of the Gospel of St John. This Mary was soon identified with the sinner in the house of the Pharisee (Luke 7.36–50) and the sister of Lazarus (John 11.1–45). She is the only one of Christ's followers to stay at the tomb all through the night before his resurrection: 'Maria autem stabat ad monumentum foris, plorans' (*Vulgata*, John 20.11).[24] Her fortitude moved even the austere Augustine to wonder at this reversal of sex roles: 'Viris enim redeuntibus, infirmiorem sexum in eodem loco fortior figebat affectus.'[25] In a sermon he goes on to direct a few embarrasing questions at the other disciples, with a pun at their front man, Peter: 'Ubi petra? Ubi firmitas petrae?'[26]
In another sermon he goes on to direct a few embarrasing questions at the other disciples, with a pun at their front man, Peter: 'Ubi petra? Ubi firmitas petrae?'[26]

There seems to be strength of body as well as of mind in Mary Magdalen. Later on in the graveyard scene she asks the risen Christ (whom she mistakes for a gardener) to tell her where to find the corpse, for she would like to carry it off ('Ego eum tollam', John, 20.15); an anonymous admirer of the twelfth-century marvels at the woman's trust in her muscle:

O mirabilis mulieris audacia! O mulier non mulier . . . O mulier, magna est fides tua, magna est constantia tua![27]

Mary's perseverance at Gethsemane does not, however, turn her into a *matrona virilis* like Lucretia; her constancy is not rooted in a moral attitude or based on superior faith as in Aylett's Susanna. Rather it rests in her affections or, as some of the early interpreters saw it, in her feminine, not her masculine nature. That is why the first word the risen Christ addressed her with was 'woman', as Ambrose explains, and for him that word 'woman' is virtually synonymous with 'weakness of faith':

Dicit ei Jesus, Mulier. Quae non credit, mulier est & adhuc corporei sexus appellatione signatur.[28]

Mary's faith is deficient because she does not recognise the risen Christ and still hankers after his body, not his spiritual appearance. Her belief is of a low order, as another church-father puts it, because she is ignorant:

Fides enim humilis et ignara, quaerit quod nescit, obliviscitur quod docetur.[29]

If one takes into account the profane meaning of 'fides', fidelity in a love relationship, it becomes apparent how close this attitude of the church-fathers is to the fatherly message which Jupiter conveys to Aeneas about Dido and her lack of understanding for his higher mission. Behind this kind of criticism lies the assumption of the weakness of the sex, a weakness that the more ascetic fathers interpret simply as a weakness of the mind. John Chrysostom puts it rather bluntly thus: 'Imbecillis enim naturae erat, & de resurrectione nondum norat'.[30] Theophylactus of Achrida is more lenient and sees her purged of her obnoxious affections in the end:

(muliebre enim genus affectionibus magis obnoxium, & ad lacrymas propensum) [. . .] Purgata igitur per affectionum depositionem, videt Jesum simul deum & hominem.[31]

But these are only the less gallant interpretations of Mary's reactions at the grave; there are others which view her behaviour through more benevolent eyes. Theophylactus with his notion of a catharsis through the emotions stands on the threshold to the more lenient attitude of the later Middle Ages. In that view the Magdalen's weakness of mind is made good by the strength of her soul. The possibility of attaining belief by way of the affections is opened up by Gregory the Great who takes a detour via the *Song of Solomon* and identifies the Magdalen's love with the 'sancta desideria' of the Church: 'Hoc amore arsit, quisquis ad veritatem pertingere potuit',[32] and this way is preferred by the monks and mystics of the twelfth century such as Anselm of Canterbury and, above all, Bernard of Clairvaux. In the end it is exactly Mary's deficient presence of mind, one of the qualities distinguishing her from Susanna, which endears her to preachers of the monastic reform. Her 'imbecility' becomes an engaging 'simplicitas cordis' and almost an attribute of holiness. We have noticed a similar sentiment in Chaucer's attitude towards the 'silliness' of his saints of Cupid.

An outward sign of Mary's weakness can be seen in her tears: she stands at the sepulchre weeping. It is not surprising that the more ascetic of the church-fathers I have quoted disapproved of these tears. They pointed to the scriptural context, where Mary is twice asked what she is weeping for, first by the angels at the sepulchre and then by Christ himself ('Mulier, quid ploras?', John 20.13, 15), and they interpreted these questions as reproofs ('Angeli lacrymas prohibebant', 'Non lacrymas nudas Deus, sed fidem exigit').[33] Others allowed the Magdalen to weep her fill; in fact, Bernard of Clairvaux conjectures that she would have filled the sepulchre with her tears had she believed that this might bring back the corpse: 'Si fieri posset pro redimendo corpore, sepulcrum lacrymis implevisset'.[34] In the late Middle Ages the redemptive force of Mary's tears is taken for granted, and in the *Lacrimae* poetry of the Counter-Reformation they will swell to veritable seas and spill all over Europe and into England. In the following chapters I will follow the conflux of this maudlin flood with the other wet tradition of the Ovidian Complaint.

Omelia Origenis de Maria Magdalena

It is no accident that some of the most intense tracts on Mary Magdalen were written in the Ovidian twelfth century. The puzzled figure at the empty tomb, with her colourful past and uncertain future might have served as another lost lover for the *Heroides*. The situation of the Magdalen quite naturally leads writers who try to enter her feelings to employ rhetorical and poetic means similar to those found in heroical epistles, even if they do not consciously follow Ovid's example.

One of the first to exploit the human interest (as opposed to the doctrinal content) in the Magdalen at the tomb is an Anonymus who was for a long time mistaken for Origen of Alexandria, and later for, among others, Anselm of Canterbury. The latter guess was closer to the truth, for the tract was written towards the end of the twelfth century, and in the style of much of the Marian literature of that time. But it was the earlier one that stuck to the text, and its author is still referred to as the Pseudo-Origen. The title of the tract varies, too; sometimes it is called *De Maria Magdalena*, sometimes *De planctu beatae Mariae Magdalenae*; the shortest title is *Omelia Origenis*, and this is the one I shall use.

The variations in the title point to difficulties in assigning the tract to a definite genre, and this is indicative of its contents which read at times like a sermon, at others like a meditation. The *Omelia Origenis* has been preserved in two versions which differ mainly in their incipits. The one starts with a reference to the feast in hand, 'In praesenti solemnitate', which may refer either to Easter Thursday, the day the Gospel of the women at the tomb was traditionally read, or to the Feast of St Mary Magdalene (22 July); the other goes straight to the subject at hand, 'Audivimus, fratres, Mariam ad monumentum foris stantem'.[35] Addresses such as 'fratres' and 'dilectissimi' and references to the gospel-text throughout give the second version all the credentials of a sermon delivered in, for instance, a convent community. In both versions, however, the emotional commitment of the preacher so often washes over the sermon's homiletic intent that it creates the impression of a very personal involvement in the situation. There are long passages written in a kind of *style indirect libre* where the speaker makes his audience believe that they are listening to a first person complaint of the Magdalen.

The subject of the sermon is the Gospel of St John, 20.10–16; it does not cover the whole span of the episode, (20.10–18), and this is significant because the *Noli me tangere* reproof in 10.17 is barely mentioned, and the anticipation of Christ's ascension is left out altogether. The preacher creates a little drama out of the first encounter with the risen Christ, and he makes the most out of the misunderstandings that arise in this scene. He traces Mary's feelings up to the encounter, and then tries to understand the strangely muted dealings of the risen Christ. On the whole, he takes sides with the uncomprehending Magdalen, and repeatedly intervenes on her behalf. Mary is shown to be guided by love and sorrow from the beginning of the extraordinary events: 'Amor faciebat eam stare, & dolor cogebat eam plorare' (p. 580). All her moves are explained as resulting from these emotions, the signs of strength as well as those of weakness: the courage which enabled her to keep the wake at the tomb, and the slowness with which she takes up the news of the resurrection. The author does all he can to exculpate her from the doubts cast on her character by over-strict interpreters. He knows these doubts, and can for a moment take on the role of an Augustine questioning Lucretia when he asks Mary how she could possibly mistake Christ for a gardener:

O Maria, si quæris Jesum, cur non cognoscis Jesum? Et si cognoscis Jesum, quid quæris Jesum?
(583)

But on the whole his part is not that of prosecutor but of counsel. He defends Mary's error, which was traditionally taken to betray her inferior understanding, and appeals to her ultimate judge:

Igitur misericors & juste judex, amor, quem habebat in te, & dolor, quem habebat pro te, exuset eam apud te, si forte erret de te: nec attendas ad mulieris errorem, sed ad discipulæ amorem: quae non pro errore, sed pro dolore, & amore plorabat
(583)

He likewise defends her from the charge of betraying a lack of faith by shedding tears about Christ's resurrection. This, too, he explains with an extraordinary love which made her mind go blank at the loss of her master:

sensus nullus in ea remanserat, omne consilium in ea perierat, spes omnis defecerat: solummodo flere supererat. Flebat ergo quia flere poterat. (581)

The sentiment reminds one of Ovid's Ariadne who was also left with nothing to do but cry ('quid potius facerent quam mea lumina flerent', *Heroides*, X, 45); in fact, Mary's disconsolate weeping (she refuses to be consoled by the angels) associates her with classical heroines such as Ariadne rather than with the Biblical Susanna. In a way, her speechless confusion puts Mary at the opposite end from the articulate Susanna, who is able to pray and, in later versions of her story, to preach in her extremity. The author of the *Omelia Origenis* allows his heroine a complaint instead of a prayer, and takes one phrase from the Biblical Susanna, but it is the one which expresses her dilemma ('angustiae sunt mihi undique'); otherwise, the complaint is filled with the semi-articulate exclamations of despair we have found in classical as well as medieval complaints: 'Heu me miseram quid agam', 'Sed quid faciam', 'Quo me vertam?' (582).

In her despair Mary is driven to inordinate lengths, considering that the *Omelia Origenis* is an exegetical and a devotional exercise and meant to strengthen the faith in its audience. The way she is said to turn away from the angels, for example, is hardly warranted by the Gospel text; rather it is comparable to Dido's 'taedet caeli convexa tueri':

Proh dolor! qualis est ista consolatio? qualis est ista visitatio? Onerosi sunt mihi omnes consolatores: gravant me, & non consolantur. Ego autem quæro creatorem, & ideo mihi gravis est ad videndum omnis creatura. (582)

The speaker, far from condemning Mary's despair, defends it with equally unorthodox means. He takes up, for instance, the reproof that Ambrose and Chrysostom saw implied in Christ's question 'Mulier quid ploras' and turns it against the questioner:

Tu scis quia te solum quærit, te solum diligit, pro te omnia contemnit: & tu dicis, *Quid quæris?* Dulcis magister, ad quid quæso provocas spiritum hujus mulieris? ad quid commoves animam ejus? Tota pendet in te, tota manet in te, tota sperat de te, & tota desperat de se.   (582)

In a very subtle move the Magdalen's despair with its implication of the ultimate estrangement from God and salvation is changed into self-effacement. Earlier on, Mary's inconsolate state of mind is called 'excessus mentis' (582), and this is the term employed by mystics to denote the state of obliteration prerequisite for the spiritual union with God. It is a staggering reversal if compared with earlier comments on the Magdalen's weakness of mind and lack of understanding. After this reunion it seems fit that this preacher closes his sermon on the intimate note of the recognition scene ('Dixit ei Iesus: Maria. Conversa dixit ei: Rabboni', John, 20.16), and to brush over the 'Noli me tangere' of the following verse. The occasion for the rebuff that lies in this verse, Mary's wish to kiss her master's feet, he interprets favourably as a gesture of impatient love. He completely ignores the ascension, which Christ announces in the same verse and which will move him out of bodily reach for ever. The scene is left on the earth, and the sermon closes with a commendation of Mary's 'simplicitas cordis' (584).

The complaint of the lover of Christ Saint Mary Magdaleyn

There is a hint in the *Legend of good women* that Geoffrey Chaucer may have written a translation of the *Omelia Origenis*. In the 'Prologue' Alceste counts it, among 'other besynesse' of the poet, as one of the works suited to placate the irate God of Love:

> He made also, gon is a gret while,
> Orygenes upon the Maudeleyne.   (G 417–18)

If the hint is as correct as that to the Life of Cecily which is mentioned in the same breath, the work has been lost at an early date.[36] The hint to the translation encouraged later editors of Chaucer's poems to fill the gap with a Complaint of Mary Magdalen by an unknown hand. The first of these editors was Richard Pynson, who prints it as a religious complement to the equally apocryphal 'Letter of Dydo to Eneas' in *The book of fame* (1526?), the second part of his three-volume edition of the works of Chaucer. Pynson was not the first to print the poem, though: there is a single copy of an earlier print by Wynkyn de Worde (RSTC 17568, Huntington Library). The copy is impaired, the title page is missing; in the colophon the poem is called *The complaint of the lover of Christ Saint Mary Magdaleyn* (the title I shall use); it was printed around 1520 and may have served Pynson as copy text for his edition of the 'Lamentation of Mary Magdaleyn' as he calls it in his Chaucer edition. The Complaint was later taken over into William Thynne's 1532 and Thomas Speght's 1598 editions of the works of Chaucer. Speght gave a reference to the source of the Complaint on the margin of his edition: 'This treatise is taken out of S. Origin, wherein Mary Magdalen lamenteth the cruel death of her Saviour Christ.'[37]

There is, indeed, little to remind one of Chaucer's style in the *Complaint of Mary Magdaleyn* except, perhaps, the rhyme royal stanza. The descent from the *Omelia Origenis*, however, is unmistakable, despite the fact that there are few verbal parallels. The author retains the habit of sprinkling Vulgate verses into his text ('Thus I muste bewayle / Dolorem meum', 32),[38] but he feels under no exegetic or paraenetic obligation and concentrates on the Magdalen's emotions. No one interferes with her Complaint, which is extended to over 700 lines. There is a comparable passage in the *Omelia Origenis* beginning with a 'Proh dolor', but this covers less than a fifth of the whole sermon – the rest is spoken by a preacher who – however sympathetic in his attitude – has to try to fit Mary's complaints into the great order of the Paschal proceedings. This need to keep the work of salvation in view leads the author of the *Omelia Origenis* to insert a number of preemptive bows in the direction of the redeemer in his sermon (for example, 'non possum omnino excusare hanc discipulam tuam', p. 583), and though he goes on to do exactly that, namely excuse his defendant, there is at least a hint at the unorthodoxy of Mary's position.

The form of the first person Complaint removes this difficulty, but it also adds to the isolation of the Magdalen who is now confined to the static scene given in John 20.11, 'Maria autem stabat ad monumentum, plorans'. Not only is there no outlook towards the ascension and the completion of the scheme of salvation (this was, as I have shown, cut off already in the *Omelia Origenis*); the conciliatory end of the episode is also outside the poem's range: what action there is stops at the moment the risen Christ appears before Mary. Her former and her later life, her roles as *mulier peccatrix* and *apostola apostolorum*, which provided plenty of material for the legendary tradition, never come into view. There is a reference to Lazarus, the brother of one of the Maries who were blended into the Magdalen, but this is part of a cry of anguish: Mary wishes she were delivered of her death-like sorrow as he was raised from the dead. She also wishes she were a recluse in the wilderness, and this looks like a reference to Mary's later career in the legendary tradition, when she became amalgamated with the Egyptian Mary. But the hint is never followed up, and the wish is universal: it might as well stem from Old Testament prophets (e.g. Isaiah), the Apocalypse (Rev. 12) or, indeed, from earlier Complaints in the Ovidian tradition. Daniel's Rosamond, we remember, imagines in her palace at Woodstock that she may have to die in a desert place (*Complaint of Rosamond*, 657–8).

The Complaint does take in some memories of the events around the Passion, and this puts it in the neighbourhood of laments of the Virgin Mary, such as were widespread both in the twelfth and the fifteenth centuries, when the *Omelia Origenis* and the *Complaint of Mary Magdaleyn* were written. Set pieces from this tradition are taken over into the Magdalen's Complaint: there are imprecations against the Jews (106–40, 218–80), and there is an enumeration of the Seven Sorrows in a passage concerned with the Virgin Mother (442–76).[39] There is also an obvious resemblance between the situations of the mother and the lover of Christ, the one staying under the Cross ('stabat mater dolorosa'), the other at the tomb ('stabat ad monumentum, plorans'). But there are also differences: the scene at Calvary, for instance, tends to be more demonstrative than the one at Gethsemane. The finger-pointing verbal gestures of reproach directed at the Jews and the displaying of the Seven Sorrows (with reference to sword-wounds) testify to this tendency. The scene under the cross is also not as desolate; the Virgin is never quite alone; even if she is not surrounded by other mourners such as the two Marys and John the disciple, she is left (though this may seem a scarce consolation) with Christ's corpse. This last difference is made clear by the Mary of the *Complaint of Mary Magdaleyn*:

> Cause of my sorowe / men may vnderstonde
> (Quia tulerunt dominum meum)
> Another is / that I ne may fonde
> I wotnere / Vbi posuerunt eum
> Thus I muste bewayle / Dolorem meum
> With herty wepyng / I can no better deserue
> Tyl dethe approache / my herte for to kerue   (29–35)

The titles of some of the poems in the tradition of the Marian laments indicate the less isolated position of the Blessed Virgin, for instance the *Dialogus beatae Mariae et Anselmi de passione Christi*: there is always someone to talk to; if needs be, the author is partner in Mary's pain. With the Magdalen, this is different: 'But there is no wight gyueth attendaunce' (95), she is made to say in her Complaint, and this is why the stock elements from the Marian laments which are spoken with a view to the Biblical background of the individual loss, do not integrate very well into her Complaint. Mary Magdalen lacks this wider perspective, as she lacks succour and consolation. In particular, she feels left alone by her 'prince of Israel':

> Jesus of Nazareth / my gostly socour
> My parfyte loue / and hope of al honour   (13–4)

In the context of the *Complaint of Mary Magdaleyn* it sounds strange already if Mary, as in the lines just quoted, shows any knowledge of the 'ghostly' background of her situation because otherwise she has little insight into the soteriological implications of her personal experience. Even the heroines much further from the scenes of salvation like Lever's Queen Elizabeth display more trust in a providential arrangement of events (and this is confirmed by Old Testament examples), or they hope for a compensation for their sorrows in their afterlife like the penitent souls in Breton's passion poems (and are granted glimpses of paradise). The Magdalen of the *Complaint* remains confined to her earthly situation, and the thought of the angels in paradise adds only to her sense of forlornness:

> The ioye excellent of blyssed paradyse
> Maye me alas in no wyse recomforte
> Songe of angel nothyng may me suffyse   (295–7)

If this passage sounds again like Dido's world-weary aversion to the stars, there are more reasons in the *Complaint of Mary Magdaleyn* for the association than in the *Omelia Origenis*, where Mary was also impatient with the visiting angels. The Magdalen of the *Complaint* is turned into a romantic lady as Dido was in the romances of the Middle Ages.[40] Mary twice calls her story an 'auenture' (36, 78) and sees it governed by 'chance' (which is not usually a ruling force behind Biblical events). She repeatedly calls Jesus her 'paramour' (216, 291, 678) and when she appeals to her absent 'lorde', the ambivalence of the term is exploited, as in the reproach 'I se right wel my lorde hath me forsake' (87) – rather a bold appropriation of the question from the Cross.[41] Like Chaucer's Anelida Mary complains that her lover has born away the key to her happiness (293–4; cf. *Anelida and Arcite*, 323–4); like Chaucer's Dido she fears that her fate 'shal be tolde in euerlastyng remembraūce' (82), and she wishes, like tragic heroines of all times, that she were never born, 'Alas to this wo that euer I was bore' (621).

The sometimes striking fusion of romantic with Biblical material culminates in the last wishes laid down near the end of the poem in a kind of will which reminded Rosemary Woolf of Henryson's *Testament of Cresseid* and Boccaccio's tale of Ghismonda.[42] Mary asks to be buried in the same tomb with her lover and devises an epitaph also reminiscent of Ovidian examples:

> Here within resteth a goostly creature
> Christes trewe louer / Mary Magdalayne
> Whose hert for loue / brake in peces twayne   (635–7)

Her heart is to be enclosed in a box of balm, and presented to her lover

as a last token of her faith. This is only the final flourish of a theme that
has been developed throughout the poem: Mary's heart has been invoked
in ever changing variations in nearly every stanza, and in some of them
several times. As in Middleton's *Ghost of Lucrece*, this is a consequence
of the emotionalisation of the objective material of the story (historical
there, Biblical here). Like Lucrece, Mary acts her ghostly Complaint on
the stage of her heart, and like the Renaissance scene the medieval one
is covered in blood and tears:

> Myne herte I fele nowe bledeth inwardly
> The blody teares I may in no wyse let   (366–7)

The Complaint does not end with the novellistic idea of the faithfully
preserved heart, however, but with a farewell song; it contains terms of
endearment reminiscent of the Canticles, while the series of 'Adieus'
might be taken from a contemporary historical lament:

> A due my lorde / my loue so faire of face
> A due my turtel doue so fresshe of hue
> A due my myrthe / a due al my solace
> A due alas / my sauyour lorde Jesu
> A due the gentyllest that euer I knew
> A due my most excellent paramour
> Fayrer than rose / sweter than lylly flour   (673–79)

Although the reader of a Complaint like this enjoys a wider vision than
its speaker and knows about the outcome of the Gospel story, the end of
the poem still holds more bitterness than sweetness because the heroine is
denied even a glimpse of hope: 'Wherefore my lyfe must ende in bytter-
nesse', are her own words (696). The poem ends with another striking
appropriation of Biblical phrases, two more of the last words from the
Cross:

> My lorde / my spouse: Cur me derelequisti
> Sith I for the suffre al this distresse
> What causeth the to seme thus mercylesse
> Sith it the pleseth of me to make an ende
> (In manus tuas) my spirite I cõmende.   (710–14)

Such is the contrafactive force of the Complaint that there is just the
'seme' of line 712 to prevent the divine comedy from being turned into
a human tragedy.

A short look at the way the Magdalen's life is dealt with in late medieval
drama and epic will sharpen the sense of how remarkable an achievement
the *Complaint of Mary Magdaleyn* is and how strongly the elegiac restric-
tions cast over a story like hers work towards giving it an unorthodox
bias. In Mystery plays of the Passion Mary Magdalen is usually assigned

a role within a salvational framework: she serves as a witness of Christ's crucifixion and his resurrection. The Digby play of *Mary Magdalene*, for example, spans the whole of Mary's life, and this leaves only little room for her personal feelings.[43] The large scale of the action is indicated by the fact that it encompasses Rome and Jerusalem, Heaven and Hell as well as the saint's life. In the first part of the play Mary's life as a sinner is dealt with in the manner of an elaborate Morality (with Satan and the deadly sins in leading parts), in the second her legendary life after the resurrection comes into the foreground. The Passion, with Calvary and Gethsemane, is the culmination and the turning point, but not much more than a point, in a series of world-moving events; there is no time to mirror its effects on the bystanders at any length. In one scene Mary Magdalen is escorted to the tomb by Peter and John, they are soon joined by the other Marys, and the swiftness of the action allows not even for the traditional laments which are incorporated in the Shrewsbury fragments of plays on *The Burial and Resurrection*.[44]

In Nicholas Grimald's neo-Latin tragicomedy *Christus redivivus* (Cologne, 1543) the scene is laid in Golgotha and the action is concentrated on the Passion.[45] The first act is filled with laments in the manner of a Senecan tragedy, with the Magdalen leading a choir of plaintive voices, but these laments serve wholly homiletic purposes: Christ's miracles are remembered, the Jews are indicted, and there is again no room for Mary's private cares. She would play the Philomel and complain all night:

> Heû me, quid obsecro misera, misera,
> Quid agam tandem aliud misera, misera,
> Quam quod furtim erepta sibi querens pignora,
> Philomela & noctu factitat & interdiu?   (lines 103–6)

But she is rudely checked by Nicodemus:

> Maria, caue Maria, ne insanis clamoribus
> Coelestis patris iras adversum te incites.   (109–10)

Once more the humanist exacts a more reasonable behaviour with the severity of a church-father.

Lewis Wager's interlude *The life and repentance of Marie Magdalene* also subordinates the heroine's behaviour to doctrinal considerations.[46] In his play the action is concentrated on the early parts of Mary's life, up to her conversion (the interlude does not cover the whole of the Gospel story, as Helen Garth suggests; the Passion is left out altogether).[47] Mary's conversion is used to demonstrate the Calvinist doctrine of the justification by faith rather than by works. The doubtful and desperate Mary at the tomb accords ill with this concept, and her inordinate feelings are sacrificed to orthodoxy.

Setting out the exemplary and the orthodox is what most of the saint's legends also ask Mary Magdalen to do when they describe her life at length in the manner of the *Legenda aurea*. The events reported by John the evangelist are cut short in the interest of Mary's life before and after the resurrection. This is true not only of medieval legends (beginning with the ninth-century *vita* of Hrabanus Maurus), but also of later Lives written with missionary zeal by Jesuits, for example, Joseph Cresswell's(?) *Saint Mary Magdalen's conversion* (1603) and John Sweetnam's *St Mary Magdalen's pilgrimage to paradise* (1617) – propagandist literature probably printed in France, at Douai or St Omer, but smuggled into England. Both poems are set against the Ovidian tradition and focus the attention of their readers on devotional matters – the process of repentance and penitence in the case of *Marie Magdalen's conversion*, the exemplary life in that of *Mary Magdalen's pilgrimage*. The more doctrinal of the two is Cresswell's. An indication of that is its style which looks back to the allegorical medieval *psychomachia*. Sweetnam's more meditative poem may have been influenced by the *Omelia Origenis* tradition, in particular in a Complaint inserted in the 'Fourth Dayes Iourney' stage of the pilgrimage which shows the Magdalen at the sepulchre (G4v–7v). This Complaint is appropriately set in twenty-one rhyme royal stanzas and adopts many of the sentiments exhibited in the *Omelia Origenis*, but adorns them with a more poetic language, as in this opening:

> VVHEN Christ that Orient pearle, and shining sunne
> VVhas drowned in VVestern streames vpon the Crosse,
> Then Magdalen her flouds of teares begun
> To shew her loue, and to bewayle her losse:
> Thus gold appeares, when purified from drosse.
>   How at the monument she did deplore,
>   Shall be her monument for euermore   (G4v)

The outbursts of poetry and passion subside, however, in the prosaic account of Mary's apostolic mission which fills the second half of the treatise and is, of course, closer to the missionary heart of its writer.

A similar zeal inspired the Protestant Thomas Robinson to produce his *Life and death of Mary Magdalen* (1620). The poem presents a curious mixture of *psychomachia* and religious epic and is apparently aimed at a popular audience.[48] Heaven and earth are moved around Mary's conversion, and a war is fought on the battlefield of her soul. The legend was probably devised to counteract the elegiac Magdalen literature of the Counter-Reformation, and therefore staged up to heroic proportions; the best that can be said of it is B.O. Kurth's compliment that it helped pave the way towards the Miltonic epic. I shall move back now in the opposite direction.

Robert Southwell, *Marie Magdalen's funeral tears*

The elegiac tradition derived from the Pseudo-Origen's *Omelia* had continued to flow throughout the earlier Renaissance. Apart from Latin editions there were several translations of the *Omelia Origenis* in the sixteenth century. Two early printed versions are preserved, one fragmentary (*An homily of Mary Magdalen* [1555]), the other a complete translation of the 'In praesenti' version (*An homily of Mary Magdalen, declaring her fervent love and zeal towards Christ*, 1565). Towards the end of the century another English version appeared under the title of *Marie Magdalen's funeral tears* (1591). This much augmented paraphrase of the *Omelia Origenis* was printed in London anonymously. Its author, Robert Southwell, the poet and Jesuit missionary, was imprisoned the year after its publication and prosecuted for high treason. This sensitive political background did not affect the treatise's success with the public. At least two more editions were out before Southwell was executed in 1595.[49] Like other missionaries, Robert Southwell had been prepared for his fatal mission on the Continent at Jesuit colleges in Douai and Rome; this is one reason why his treatise on the Magdalen, together with its brother-piece, *St Peter's complaint* (1595), is often assigned to the Italian tradition of *Lagrime* poems, and Erasmo de Valvasone's *Lagrime della Maddalena* is often named as a possible model.[50] In fact, Mario Praz has proved the influence of Luigi Tansillo's *Lagrime di San Pedro* on Southwell's *St Peter's complaint*.[51] There is evidence, however, that *Marie Magdalen's funeral tears* derives directly from a Latin version of the *Omelia Origenis* – to be precise, from an 'In praesenti' version of the sermon: two fragmentary draughts in Southwell's hand, which are preserved in the library of Stonyhurst College (MS A.v.4; an extensive early draft on fols. 56r–60v, 62r [fol. 61 is an inserted leaf], and a fragment of seventeen lines from a later, rhetorically expanded version) prove this beyond doubt.[52] The early draught clearly shows the poet struggling with a Latin copy text; it begins:

In this present solemnity hauynge <to speake> <utter> to speake in <the hearynge> [Janelle transcribes 'the fearynge'] this audience of your charityes we ar put in mynde how that Mary Maudelyn <louynge our lord aboue all creatures, when his oune disciples fled> <as in loue of Christ so> as she surpassed many in loue so passed she <most> Christs oune disciples in loyalty.[53]

This corresponding version of the *Omelia Origenis* begins:

In praesenti solennitate locuturi auribus vestrae charitatis, dilectissimi, adducimur ad memoriam, quomodo beata Maria Magdalenae Dominum nostrum super omnia diligendo, discipulis fugientibus, eum ad mortem euntem sequebatur.
(*Bibliotheca Patrum*, vol. V, p. 580)

Southwell's English may seem shaky in these drafts, his version of the sermon, however, fits in well with the Ovidian poetry in vogue at the time when he started on his mission in England: the Complaint literature may have reminded him of his early exercises in 'Ovid's strain', as Janelle characterises them, and perhaps in Seneca's, too, if a fragment in four-teeners inscribed 'Amemmon' in Stonyhurst MS A.v.4, fol. 61r, is his and alludes to Seneca's play.[54] In any case Southwell's training in classical and medieval Latin literature was an excellent preparation for the task of turning the *Omelia Origenis* into the 'prose poem' it eventually became.[55]

Southwell introduced his treatise on *Marie Magdalen's funeral tears* in a letter of dedication which is an important document in its own right. Like so many other letters prefixed to poems and treatises in the Complaint tradition it is directed at a woman, a Mrs D.A. whom Christopher Devlin, Southwell's biographer, identifies as Dorothy Arundel, daughter of the recusant Earl of Arundel, whose domestic chaplain Southwell had become in 1589.[56] Southwell discusses in his letter the problem of love poetry in a Christian world; he deplores, like the Protestant critics we have met, the rapid spread of erotic literature and asks himself what should be done to stop its further growth. Unlike his colleagues from the other side of the religious fence, however, he does not suggest it should be weeded root and branch, but rather, to extend the metaphor, that more profitable shoots should be grafted on its tree. This tree is the passion of love which, to him, is not an evil in itself: it can be used to bear spiritual fruit:

For as passion, and especially this of loue, is in these daies the chiefe commaunder of moste mens actions, & the Idol to which both tongues and pennes doe sacrifice their ill bestowed labours: so is there nothing nowe more needefull to bee intreated, then how to direct these humors vnto their due courses, and to draw this floud of affections into the righte chanel. Passions I allow, and loues I approue, onely I would wishe that men would alter their object and better their intent. For passions being sequels of our nature, and allotted vnto vs as the handmaides of reason: there can be no doubt, but that as their author is good, and their end godly: so ther vse tempered in the meane, implieth no offence. Loue is but the infancy of true charity, yet sucking natures teate, and swathed in her bandes, which then groweth to perfection, when faith besides naturall motiues proposeth higher and nobler groundes of amitye.   (A3v–4r)

For him the Magdalen gives an example of a passionate nature grown to perfection, and even its defects turned to good. I ask leave to give another lengthy quotation from Southwell's remarkable letter:

Such were the passions of this holy Sainte, which were not guides to reason, but attendantes vpon it, and commanded by such a loue as could neuer exceede, because the thing loued was of infinite perfection. And if her weakenes of faith, (an infirmity then common to all Christes disciples) did suffer her vnderstanding to be deceiued, yet was her will so setled in a most sincere and perfect loue, that it ledde all her passions with the same bias, recompensing the want of beliefe, with the strange effectes of an excellent charity. This loue & these passions are the subiect of this discourse, which though it reach not to the dignity of *Maries* deserts, yet shal I thinke my indeuors wel apaide, if it may wooe some skilfuller pennes from vnworthy labours, eyther to supply in this matter my want of ability, or in other of like piety, (wherof the scripture is full) to exercise their happier talents. I knowe that none can expresse a passion that hee feeleth not, neyther doth the penne deliuer but what it coppieth out of the minde. And therefore sith the finest wits are now giuen to write passionat discourses, I would wish them to make choise of such passions, as it neither should be shame to vtter, nor sinne to feele.   (A5v–6r)

With this apology Southwell surpasses even his benevolent medieval model, the *Omelia Origenis*. The Pseudo-Origen retained some reservations about his defence of the Magdalen, presumably because it was based on empathy alone; he found it hard to disperse the doctrinal doubts about the unreasonable, because emotional, basis of Mary's faith; we remember his uneasy 'non possum omnino excusare hanc discipulam' (*Omelia Origenis*, ed. Combefis, p. 583). Southwell tries to supply his apology with a framework strong enough to contain even the excesses of Mary's emotions. He achieves this by abandoning the scholastic notion that every excess is an evil, and shifting allegiance towards the Franciscan concept which allows even an excessive passion to be sublimated into something good if it is directed at the absolute goodness of God. It is the sublime end which sanctifies passion, but even so passion loses much of its evil aspect. Southwell views passion as created by God, and therefore good as long as it is not deflected towards base objects. He thus lays an intellectual basis not only for his treatise, but for emotional religious poetry as a whole, and he helps to bridge the gap between worldly and heavenly love.

Southwell's treatise on *Marie Magdalen's funeral tears* is built on this basis; it is an exercise in the containment of emotional language by rhetorical means. His prose is highly polished, the frequent use it makes of parallelism and antithesis shows some influence of the mannered style made fashionable by John Lyly and his followers. Herbert Thurston called the treatise 'Euphuist', Helen White 'metaphysical', but its style is never as witty or clever as these labels suggest, and it is not as learned: there is nothing like the Classical or scientific arsenal which the Euphuists and the Metaphysicals used to exhaustion.[57] Their influence is felt in Thomas Lodge's prose lament *Prosopopeia: the tears of the holy, blessed, and sanctified Marie, the mother of God* (1596), which is also said to be influenced by Southwell's treatise; a very conscientious learnedness shows through the affected modesty of Lodge's introduction:

To good men therefore let this suffice, that in imitation of no lesse than fiue & twenty ancient, holy, and Catholique Fathers of the Church, I haue enterprised this Prosopopeia: [. . .] Some (and they too captious) will auowe that Scriptures are misapplied, fathers mistaken, sentences dismembred. [. . .] To leaue them satisfied therfore, let this suffice, I haue written nothing without example, I build no waies on mine owne abilitie.[58]

By comparison, Southwell's learning is light: he makes do with the bare six or seven verses of the Gospel. Over these he pores and ponders with the utmost attention. His rhetoric is made to follow the ups and downs of emotions raised in a sympathetic reader who examines Mary's actions, words and gestures as reported by St John. The author tries to dramatise the potentially meditative situation by frequently addressing his subject as if his Magdalen had stepped out of the Bible and into his study. The situation approaches that of the *Mirror for Magistrates*, but Southwell does not feel free to make the Magdalen give us her own Complaint, and he does not enter upon a proper conversation with his heroine as some of the medieval Passion poems did, for instance the *Dialogus beatae Mariae et Anselmi de passione Christi* mentioned above.[59] His Marie remains confined to the Gospel words. The result is an oblique mode consisting of a long series of rhetorical questions which the author has to answer himself, and attempts at entering into the thoughts of his heroine. The abundance of questions sometimes has the same drilling effect that we have found in the interrogations of Augustine:

O *Marie* is it possible that thou hast forgotten Jesus? faith has written him in thy vnderstanding, loue in thy will, both feare and hope in thy memorie: and how can all these registers be so cancelled, that so plainly seeing, thou shouldest not know the contentes.   (G3r)

But, of course, the answer given is much more understanding:

But there is such a showre of teares betweene thee and him, and thy eyes are so dimmed with weeping for him, that though thou seest the shape of a man, yet thou canst not discerne him.   (G3v)

The more or less mute role the Magdalen plays in the scene at Gethsemane forces the interpreter of her performance to pick up the minutest hints that might be of help to interpret her motives. Gestures and facial expression are made to supplement the few words given in the textbook. The language of the eyes becomes even more important in Southwell's treatise than in other poems of the Complaint tradition, and, of course, the tears mentioned in the first verse of the episode in a kind of stage direction, flow freely throughout the scene, and they are interpreted more sympathetically than ever:

But thy loue had no leysure to cast so many doubts. Thy teares were interpreteres of thy words, and thy innocent meaning was written in thy dolefull countenance. Thy eyes were rather pleaders for pity, then Heralds of wrath; and thy whole person presented such a paterne of thy extreame anguish, that no man from thy presence could take in anie other impression. And therefore what thy wordes wanted, thy action supplied, and what his eare might mistake, his eye did vnderstand. (H2v)

The treatise thus becomes a eulogy on the tears of the Magdalen, the same tears that had been used as evidence for the prosecution in some of the more ascetic tracts are now made to plead in her defence:

But feare not *Mary* for thy teares will obtaine. They are too mighty oratours, to let any suite fail, & though they pleaded at the most rigorous bar, yet haue they so perswading a silence, and so conquering a complaint, that by yeelding they ouercome, and by intreating they commaund. They tie the tongues of all accusers, and soften the rigour of the seuerest Judge. Yea, they win the inuincible and bind the omnipotent. When they seeme most pittiful, they haue greatest power; and being most forsaken they are most victorious. (H7v)

With a praise of tears like this Southwell marks the extreme opposition to the Marian writers suspicious of an emotional approach to the Gospel. These writers had weighty doctrinal reasons why the Passion should not be regarded as too sad and too personal an event: it brings redemption for the whole of mankind; it is the culmination of the Gospel (and Gospel means 'glad tidings'), and at least in Roman Catholic doctrine, the Virgin is assigned an active role in the work of redemption.[60] There were also reasons of decorum to be considered: how human should the mother of God appear?[61] And there was Biblical evidence that could be adduced to ban tears from under the Cross. Not only early church-fathers, but also later theologians such as the Lollards and the Puritans pointed to Christ's admonition, 'Nolite flere super me' (Luke 23.28); Ambrose made negative evidence serve the same purpose: 'Stantem illam lego, flentem non lego', was his curt conclusion drawn from the Gospel text.[62]

With the Magdalen the case is different; she is expressly associated with tears, not only in Gethsemane (John 20.11), but also, if one accepts the identifications, in the house of the Pharisee (Luke 7.38,44) and on the death of her brother Lazarus (John 11.33). The difference between the Maries is still in evidence in Thomas Lodge's Marian lament *Proso-*

popeia, though there are tears in its subtitle. Lodge was a convert from Ovidian literature (and to Roman Catholicism) and might have felt no scruples to present a Virgin Mary in the Roman style. But his Mother of God apologises to her son before she indulges her grief at his death, and she stresses her steadfastness under the cross: 'When the earth trembled, I was not troubled, when the pillars of heaven were shaken, I sounded not, they fell, I stood.' (p. 29) In effect this runs counter to the narrative situation of the first person mode of a *prosopopeia*. For reasons of doctrine or of decorum the Virgin must not be confined to a narrow perspective, and before she can bewail the loss of her son she assures him that the weakness of her flesh will never make her forget what her spirit knows: that there is no loss to bewail.

No my charitie shall not let me, my love shall suffer my griefe to exceed her, and reason shall surrender his Lordship to passion, sufficeth it my son, that in spirit I assure mee of thy life, yet in flesh whilest thou art absent, & dwellest with death, let mee bewaile thee, (for humane weeknesse requireth a little more weeping.   (pp. 111–12)

No such excuses are necessary for the Magdalen: she is a living example of the weakness of the flesh, and the poet can depict her grief with all the details of a Gothic or a baroque painting. Southwell makes use of this licence. Not only Marie's tears, but every other means of expressing grief is employed. The age-old device of the broken speech which we have met already in Alan of Melsa's *Susanna* and which Anselm of Canterbury uses in his *Oratio ad Sanctam Mariam Magdalenam* is rolled out into an extended conceit which leaves the heroine, unlike Susanna or Lucretia, virtually dumb:

Loue would haue spoken, but feare enforced silence. Hope frameth the words, but doubt melteth them in the passage: and whē her inward conceits striued to come out, her voice trembled, her tongue faltered, her breath failed. In fine teares issued in liew of words, and deep sighes in stead of long sentēces, the eie supplying the mouths default, and the heart pressing out the vnsillabled breath at once, which the conflict of her disagreeing passions, would not suffer to be sorted into the seuerall sounds of intelligible speeches.   (I3r)

It is in such dumb rhetoric that Southwell excells, and in this respect the third-person perspective he retained from the *Omelia Origenis* comes to his aid. He can avoid one of the difficulties in first-person Complaints: his heroine is not forced to express her own bewilderment in so many words, and the unthinking, all-feeling nature of the Magdalen can be described in a less affected manner. Southwell presents her, in fact, as even more dumbfounded and down-to-earth than the Pseudo-Origen, who closed his sermon on the happy note of the recognition scene in

John 20.16. Southwell follows his Marie beyond this point and plunges her into the deepest disappointment occasioned by the interdiction in the next verse: 'Noli me tangere'. Being of a humble and earthbound disposition, Marie is unable to understand this veto, and she is slow to overcome her disappointment. Not even the role of *apostola apostolorum* assigned to her afterwards is much of a consolation. On her way to spread the glad tidings of the resurrection to the other disciples she loses herself in memories of past pleasures. In her *excessus mentis* she dreams of physical, not mystical, contact with Christ:

Sometimes shee forgetteth her self, and loue carrieth her in a golden distraction, making her to imagin that her Lord is present, and then shee seemeth to demand him questions, and to heare his answeres: she dreameth that his feete are in her folded armes, and that hee giueth her soule a full repast of his comfortes. But alas when she commeth to her selfe, and findeth it but an illusion, she is so much the more sorie, in that the onely imagination, being so delightfull, she was not worthie to enjoy the thing it self.   (I7v–8r)

In the end, however, Southwell manages to have the dream come true, though in an unorthodox manner, by harmonising two versions of the Easter story: he blends Matthew's report of the incident on the road to Galilee (Mat 28.9) into that of John. He thus arranges another meeting between Mary and Christ, and this time Mary is allowed to have her embrace – a happy ending by sentimental, though less by doctrinal, standards.

[Gervase Markham], *Marie Magdalen's lamentations*

It must have been obvious to Robert Southwell himself that his treatise on the tears of the Magdalen would make an excellent subject for a Complaint in the style of the profane poetry which he wanted to redirect to worthier ends. Soon after the publication of *Marie Magdalen's funeral tears* (1591) he showed how to do it in his *Saint Peter's complaint* (printed in 1595, but written shortly before his arrest in 1592), which turns Luigi Tansillo's third-person narrative *Le Lagrime di San Pietro* into a first-person Complaint. In the mid-nineties there were prose imitations of the *Funeral tears*, Nicholas Breton's *Mary Magdalen's love* (1595), and Thomas Lodge's *Prosopopeia* (1596) which, as we know, is a lament of the Virgin Mary.[63] But it was not before 1601 that a metrical Complaint was made out of Southwell's treatise, *Marie Magdalen's lamentations for the loss of her master Jesus* (a second edition was published in 1604). The author is probably Gervase Markham, certainly not one of the 'finest wits' whom Southwell had asked in his dedication to change sides from

profane to religious poetry, but neither is he the 'base fellow' Ben Jonson
is said to have dubbed Markham.[64] He calls himself 'Collin' at the end of
his own verse preface, which probably is a very early instance of the
word in the sense of husbandman and would then give a hint to his
identity: Gervase Markham was (and is) better known for his writings on
the art of husbandry and horsemanship than for his poetry.[65]

Markham's muse may have been 'russet-clad', as Grosart has described
her,[66] but Markham was not unprepared for the task of versifying
Southwell's treatise. He had written a *Mirror* type historical tragedy, *The
most honourable tragedy of Sir R. Grinuile, Knight* (1595), and he had
translated the Song of Solomon into a half pastoral, half Petrarchan idiom
in *The Poem of Poems: or Sion's Muse . . . devided into eight eclogues*
(1596). His acquaintance with Southwell's works is also attested by a
poem in the *Lagrime* tradition, *The teares of the beloved: or The lamentation of Saint John* (1600), a brother-piece to *Saint Peter's complaint*.
The Southwell connection of Markham's *Marie Magdalen's lamentations*,
however, has rarely been noticed, though Herbert Thurston had pointed
out in 1895 that 'the great bulk of it is simply a skilful rendering into
metre of selected passages from the *Funerall tears*'.[67]

It is, indeed, an obvious connection, though more in letter than in
spirit. In his poetical preface Markham enters the lists as a champion of
his lady with the customary rhetorical flourish in the direction of less
devout contenders:

> Each soule misled can shape a pensiue passion,
> Can billow forth a sea of ceaslesse tears,
> Can pine with griefe, and all to winne compassion,
> Of some light loue, that murders what she heares,
> > But to that bond, that loues and saues his friends,
> > No soule (alas) or sighe, or teare once sends.   (1604 ed., A4v)[68]

Markham's dependence on Southwell is very pronounced already in his
preface. Like Southwell, he deplores that poets of renown prefer to write
profane poetry, and he shows how to use some of the devices employed
in historical complaints for worthier purposes:

> THe happiest soule that ever was invested,
> In sinne-staind skin awakes my woe-fed Muse,
> To sing her love (whose love is now celested)
> Sith graver pens so good a worke refuse,
> > To wet the world with her sinne-washing teares,
> > Which well destil'd, each cloudie conscience cleares.
> > > (1601 edn, A3r)

The sin-stained skin is reminiscent of the blood-stained garment of a
heroine in the *Mirror for magistrates* tradition, but Markham turns it

inside out (or rather outside in) by concentrating on the movements of his heroine's soul. This introversion, as well as the indefinite phrasing (Mary's name is not yet mentioned) shows affinities with the more ethereal souls complaining in Protestant imitations of Southwell's prose poem which will be discussed below.

Markham's *Lamentations* are as close to Southwell's *Tears* as the arrangement of the treatise in sixain stanzas allows. Southwell's wording hardly needed any touching up to adapt it to a more poetic form, it was poetical enough without rhyme or metre. What additional effects there are in Markham's version come mainly from the change to a first-person Complaint. It is an indication of how close Southwell's empathetic treatise came to the inside view demanded by the different form that this change was possible with so few alterations. The personal view comes to dominate the poem, although Markham interrupts the uninhibited flow of Southwell's treatise by arranging it in seven lamentations of varying lengths, one each for the seven verses of the Gospel which report the Gethsemane incident (John 20.11–17). Nicholas Breton had used the same arrangement in his prose imitation *Marie Magdalen's love* (1595), which also dwells, as it says in a subtitle, *Vppon the twenty Chapter of Iohn from the first verse to the eighteenth* (A3r). Breton had kept, however, the third-person address and had developed its doctrinal contents. His treatise is much more orderly than Southwell's passionate *Funeral tears*; after giving the Gospel text it dissects each verse almost word for word in the academic style of a sermon by Lancelot Andrewes:

DEerely beloued in our Sauiour *Christ*: In this first verse I find foure cheefe note: to bee well marked, and kept in memorie: First the person named, who it was, and of what condition: secondlie, the time, Thirdlie the place, and fourthly what was there seene and done. The person was *Marie* a woman [. . .]   (A3r–v)[69]

Markham's schematic plan might have pushed him in a similar direction, and thus have obstructed the erratic movement of the original or channelled it in the direction of some doctrinal aim. But he leaves his heroine floating on her sentiments and sensations even more freely than she does in Southwell's treatise. In the end he almost drowns her in a flood of despair which Southwell's different mode of presentation had held back. Mary even contemplates suicide like a classical heroine and seems to shy away from it for physical as much as for metaphysical reasons:

> And yet (even this) too happy a choice vvould be,
> For me, so vile, so base, unhappie vvretch:
> For if to chuse my death it lay in me,
> How soone should I that execution catch?

> How vvilling vvould I be to stop lives breath,
> If I might point the manner of my death?   (B4v)

The expression 'point' might even contain a hint to the 'stiletto' solution of the problem which Aylett's Susanna discards with much more confidence.

The first-person perspective of the Complaint has also a certain depressing effect on the sentiments uttered by the Magdalen, and some of the impression of 'baseness' may well be due to this effect. This becomes obvious in Marie's reactions on the various supernatural visions she has in the churchyard of Gethsemane, and mostly in her encounter with the risen Christ. Vision is not the strongest point in Marie's constitution, not even in its physiological sense. She prefers to move on the lower levels of the hierarchy of the senses. This is brought out forcefully in a stanza which traces Marie's reaction to the *noli me tangere* verdict down to the lowest level, the sense of touch:

> To see him therefore, doth not me suffice,
> To heare him doth not quiet vvhole my mind,
> To speake vvith him in so familiar vvise,
> Is not ynough my loose-let soule to bind:
>   No, nothing can my vehement love appease,
>   Least by his touch my vvo-worne heart I please.   (F4v)

This is, of course, in keeping with the way the Magdalen's love was induced: not through the eyes, as in Petrarchan or other idealised love relations, but through the touch of her lips, as she remembers:

> My lips impression humbly seal'd the same,
> With reverent stamp, which frõ˙ my sick soule came.
>
> They vvere the dores that entrance first did give
> Into his favour   (G4r)

The influence of the elegiac mode also comes to bear on passages which present Mary lost in thought or with her mind wandering. There are several such passages of illusion or despair, beginning with statements such as 'And all in darknesse I desire to dwell' (B1v) and 'I am not vvhere I am' (C4r). They are more convincing in the Complaint than in a homily because they now come from Mary herself, not from an observer. Heroines of Complaints are generally apt to fall into nightmarish or wistful reveries. Whole parts of the Complaints I have dealt with in earlier chapters are written in this illusory mode; I shall come back to this generic element in my final chapter.

One cannot be quite sure if all the effects made possible by the personal perspective of the Complaint were sought after by the poet, but they do work mostly to the poem's advantage. Some of the thematic changes which Markham introduced have less felicitous effects. His Magdalen is endowed with a profound sense of guilt alien to Southwell's apologetic treatise (and the tradition of the *Omelia Origenis* as a whole). This sense of guilt gives the poem a strong penitential aspect which has been read into Southwell's *Funeral tears* as well and has served to align this treatise with Counter-Reformation campaigns in general and Southwell's English mission in particular. Around the turn of the century, it is argued, English Catholics were in particular need of penitential exercises because the scarcity of priests made regular confessions almost impossible. In this situation the ruling of the Council of Trent, that private contrition might serve as a substitute for the absolution by a priest, was a great relief, and so *Lagrime* poems, which helped to create a penitential mood, were put to almost sacramental use.[70]

However pertinent this argument may be to other *Lagrime* poems, it hardly applies to Southwell's *Funeral tears*. Apart from the fact that most of the elements of the treatise are much older than the Council of Trent (1545–63), the tenor of Southwell's text is not penitential but pathetic. If there is a clear-cut moral or spiritual application, it is given by the Pseudo-Origen already in terms of affective rhetoric:

> Sequamur igitur, fratres, huius mulieris affectum, ut perveniamus ad effectum   (*Bibliotheca Patrum*, vol. V, p. 584)

It seems to have been effective, too: Pierre Janelle has recorded the fact that Dorothy Arundel, to whom Southwell's treatise was dedicated, entered a convent and died a Benedictine nun at Brussels.[71] Southwell's Marie does not weep for remorse but, like Markham's, *for the loss of her master Iesus*. This makes it even more difficult to account for the intrusion of a penitential element in the Complaint Markham made out of Southwell's treatise. As far as we know, Markham was not a Roman Catholic. Why should he add an element of Jesuit propaganda which the Jesuit Southwell had left out?

The answer to such questions must lie in a different corner altogether. There is the formal influence to be considered: *Mirror for magistrates* Complaints often contained a strong self-accusing element, and this may have coloured Markham's Marie to the extent that she feels not only unhappy, but in addition 'vile' and 'base'. Moreover, the women in this secular tradition were mostly fallen women of some sort. And Mary Magdalen also is, to use another melodramatic term, a woman with a past, and Markham may have been reminded of this past by the *Mirror for magistrates* model. But I suspect that Markham is influenced by his religious background as well. The Pseudo-Origen, who concentrated on the scene at Gethsemane, virtually ignored Mary's life as a sinner because it is not recalled in John 20, and he was interested in compassion, not in accusation. In the late medieval *Complaint of Saint Mary Magdaleyn* Mary was made to play the part of the forsaken lover who is more sinned against than sinning, and like the medieval Dido unable to understand why she should abandon her love for the sake of an idea of destiny that escapes her simple understanding. After the Reformation, different doctrinal positions made themselves felt, and poetical treatments of the Magdalen became less naive. As we have seen already in our short over-view of the dramatic and epic versions of her story, Protestant writers tended to stress the conversion of the sinner Mary, and therefore took in more of the earlier parts of her history, in particular the scene in the house of the Pharisee as related by Luke 7.36–50. This automatically shed more light on Mary's dubious past, and her sins were not as easily washed off as in the maudlin poems of the Counter-Reformation. What in the *Lagrime* tradition with its concentration on the absolution could be treated as a happy sin and a more personal equivalent to Eve's *felix culpa*, became much more of a burden in the Protestant literature which lacked this penitential background. In *Marie Magdalen's lamentations* there are occasional hints that Markham may be shifting the human accent of the *Omelia Origenis* towards more doctrinal grounds, but these are soon corrected by the catholicism of his preceptor, Southwell.

Protestant repentant souls

The process of making the Magdalen less catholic in the wider and the narrower senses of the word was advanced by Protestant poets who, like Gervase Markham, had connections with the literary circle around Sidney's sister, Mary Herbert, Countess of Pembroke. The most prolific of these poets, Nicholas Breton, calls her 'Nourisher of the Learned and fauorer of the Godly' in the dedication of his *Divine poem, divided into two parts: The ravished soul and The blessed weeper* (1601), and with reason. The countess encouraged not only experiments with classicist drama but also the development of devotional poetry and had herself completed her brother Philip's translation of the Psalms.[72] It was part of the family heritage: her niece, Sir Philip Sidney's daughter Elizabeth, to whom Markham dedicated his metrical version of the *Song of songs*, wrote religious poetry, too. In this respect the Sidneys were not an excep-tional family; as can be gathered from dedications and prefaces, devotional poetry must have provided a considerable part of the family reading, and in particular for educated women, throughout the country.

It also spread into the most ambitious political circles of the capital. The Earl of Essex, always subject to fits of despondency, developed a taste for devotional poetry (which he may have passed on to his follower Gervase Markham) and probably wrote one of the most significant poems of this kind, *The Passion of a discontented mind*. This was until recently attributed to Breton on stylistic and external grounds (a copy of the 1602 edition of the poem was bound with several of Breton's poems in a volume of 'N. Breton's works'); evidence from two manuscripts of the poem, British Library Sloane 1779 and Folger Library V.a.164, which was presented by Steven W. May in his edition of the poems of the earl, seems to prove that Essex wrote it after his trial, between 21 and 24 February (he was executed on 25 February), in the Tower of London, seized by 'a confessional fever', as May puts it, induced by his chaplain, Abdie Ashton.[73] If this evidence holds, the poem is a marvel of self-effacement: there is scarcely a single line containing a specific hint at the person of its author or the occasion of its composition.

Extreme self-effacement is, however, one of the features already of the earlier penitential poems in the Protestant tradition, in particular the devotional poems and treatises which Nicholas Breton wrote for the Pembroke circle. One of these is not only dedicated to Mary Herbert but put into her mouth: *The passions of the spirit* (1594), which in some manuscripts bears the title *The countess of Pembroke's passion*.[74] Considering the speaker it is not surprising that the passions displayed in this poem are of a more ethereal kind than those we have met with in either the secular or the sacred traditions examined so far. But it is not only respect for his patroness which makes Breton refine the passions in his poetry. Several of his other poems betray his ethereal aspirations, from his *Pilgrimage to paradise* (1592) to his *Divine considerations* (1608). Taken together, they give the impression of being parts of the prolonged battle against devotional poetry of the Magdalen variety which we have seen raging already in the background of Lever's poem on princess Elizabeth. Breton does not meet his rivals head-on by creating a decidedly Protestant heroine like Susanna, but conducts his campaign alongside or even behind enemy lines, draining their territory of its emotional resources and redirecting them towards his own ends.

In his early devotional poetry Breton moved along the lines of Southwell's *Marie Magdalen's funeral tears*. Breton's prose tract on the Magdalen *Marie Magdalen's love* (1595), is so close to Southwell's treatise that Thomas Corser thought he must have been a recusant in disguise, and A.B. Grosart excluded it from the canon of Breton's works for religious reasons.[75]

I have argued above that the affinity between the two Magdalen treatises is one of letter rather than of spirit. The pronouncements on the art of poetry in Breton's *Marie Magdalen's love*, however, are similar to Southwell's in *Marie Magdalen's funeral tears*, and Breton repeats them throughout his poetical works. They are also taken up, and given a less tolerant turn, by the earl of Essex in *The passion of a discontented mind*:

> O that the learned Poets of this time
> (Who in a love-sicke line so well indite),
> Would not consume good wit in hatefull Rime   (lines 31–3)

He takes up the subject again at the end of his Complaint, and what sounds as shrill as the voice of a Puritan opposing all worldly poetry may well have been the earl's adieu to this world; in the printed version of his Complaint the last stanza begins:

> *I* sing not *I*, of wanton loue-sicke laies,
> Of trickling toyes to feede fantasticke eares   (379–80)[76]

Under the circumstances the earl's insistence on the originality of his Complaint, brought forth with the same sort of national pride that Drayton displays in his historical poetry, may gain in poignancy, but not in truth:

> No farre fetcht story haue I now brought home,
> Nor taught to speake more language than his mothers,
> No long done Poem is from Darknesse come
> To light againe, it's ill to fetch from others:
>   The song I sing, is made of heart-bred sorrow,
>   Which pensive Muse from pining soule doth borrow.   (373–8)

The sentiment (against worldly poetry, and against foreign poetry) is all too familiar, and it is nourished by foreign sources, if not by Southwell, then by DuBartas. The point is, however, that the earl's insistence on the originality of his story is quite beside the point, for he does not pursue a recognisable story. This is made obvious in an oblique reference to the *Mirror for magistrates* in the beginning of his Complaint. His discontented mind arises from an indistinct limbo like a contrite ghost in the *Mirror for magistrates*:

> FRom silent night, true Register of mones,
> From saddest soule, consum'd with deepest sins,
> From hart quite rent with sighs and hevy grones,
> My wailing Muse her wofull worke beginnes:
>   And to the world brings tunes of sad despaire,
>   Sounding nought else but sorrow, griefe, and care.   (1–6)

Recollections of Rosamond's appeal to the poet, 'in thy wofull song [. . .] register my wrong' (Daniel, *Complaint of Rosamond*, 34–5) and Lucrece's apostrophe to Night, 'Dim register and notary of shame' (Shakespeare, *Lucrece*, 765) spring to mind. Like Southwell, Essex uses the costumes of secular poetry to deck out his new type of Christian hero or heroine.[77] With these precedents in view it becomes the more obvious that there are no references to any specific historical person or situation in the Complaint. Essex follows a purely spiritual concept of devotional poetry, and the garments from the historical Complaint prove somewhat heavy for the ethereal spirit he introduces in his poem. Lucrece and Rosamond are persons of flesh and blood, their lives are tied up with some recognisable historical framework, even if they speak as ghosts in a *Mirror* type Complaint. The same applies to the Magdalen: she may seem oblivious to the great events around her, but the biblical background is there and adds to the importance of her despair. With the lamenting souls of Essex and of Breton this is different. They are lifeless in a more abstract way because they apparently never had a definite place in space and time. It may be hard to imagine a ghost emerging *Mirror*-like onto an imaginary stage, but it is much harder to visualise one of these disembodied souls, for instance the Discontented Mind:

> with sorrow-rented hart,
> With blubbred eyes, & hands uprear'd to heauen;
> To play a poore lamenting Mawdline's part,
> That would weepe streams of bloud to be forgiuen			(61–4)

Middleton's Lucrece and Southwell's Magdalen might be expected to weep 'streams of blood', but with pale abstractions such as the Discontented Mind this seems incompatible. The authors must have felt this lack, and they try to make up for it by making their souls play the 'Mawdline's part'. They 'sit with Marye, at the grave', as in Breton's *The passions of the spirit* (stanza 65) or at Christ's feet as in Essex' Mind, but they can do so only figuratively:

> O, heare me, Lord, in bitternesse of dole,
> That of my sinnes do prostrate heere complaine;
> And at thy feet, with Mary, knocke for grace,
> Though wanting Marie's tears to wet my face.			(189–92)

This last quotation is significant in more ways than one. Breton's penitent souls (like Essex' repentant Mind – the terms seem significant, though probably Essex did not choose his title) have no tears, and they knock for grace, whereas Southwell's Mary asked for love. The presence of the Magdalen in this Protestant Magdalen poetry is reduced to a few appearances, and these mainly in her role of penitent sinner, not as disappointed lover.[78] In their efforts to refine the Magdalen into something more divine than Southwell's or Markham's saint, they are forced to eliminate her human traits and to drive her out of the sensible and tangible world altogether.

This is obvious even in one of Breton's poems which introduces the Magdalen in person, *The blessed weeper*, published together with *The ravished soul* in 1601 and dedicated to the Countess of Pembroke. *The blessed soul* is written in the form, and this time the metre, too, of a *Mirror for magistrates* Complaint (forty-nine rhyme royal stanzas). The poet overhears a 'silly woman weepe' (D4r)[79] whose name is revealed only in the last stanza; he finds her at Gethsemane, but he only hints at the situation:

> The place, neere which she sate, was like a graue,
> But all vncouer'd, and the bodie gone: (D4r)

The first-person Complaint soon moves into rather abstract protestations of grief; the identity of the 'I' emerges only after three stanzas of moaning:

> I wretched, I, the out-cast of all grace,
> And banisht for my sinne, from heauenly bliss   (E1r)

The woman presents herself as a penitent grieving not, like the Magdalen of the *Omelia Origenis* tradition, for the loss of her love but for having fallen out of grace. Her plight is of a spiritual, and a Protestant, kind. She has no material claims to make, and she constantly refers to herself in terms of her soul ('wretched soule', E1r; 'naked soule', E1v; 'wounded soule' E4r; 'wicked soule', F1r; etc.). She seems full of remorse, but in a peculiarly abstract way. When she recalls a particular Biblical incident, for instance the meeting with Jesus in the Pharisee's house, surely a scene full of physical and emotional contact, she resorts to expressions of verbal communication:

> He felt my teares, though no man heard my weeping,
> And gaue me grace, though no man for me mou'd him;
> Which made me know, he had my soul in keeping,
> Though sinne too long, too far from me remou'd him.
> For sinne once fled, how deare in soule I lou'd him,
>   His words can witnesse, that my soule did tuch,
>   Much is forgiuen her, for she loued much.   (E3v)

Even the *Noli me tangere* scene in Southwell's treatise has more tangible emotion than this *Quoniam dilexit multum* incident. It is in keeping with the expurgation of her story in Breton's poem that his soul of the Magdalen expresses her relationship with Christ only in terms of family ties 'Child' – 'Father' (E1v), 'Seruant' – 'Lord' (E2v), 'Sister' – 'Brother' (E3r), or all together:

> To lose a Father, Maister, Brother such,
> Child, Seruant, Sister, how can I weepe too much?   (E3r)

In a way, this domestication of the story and the attempt to treat history in personal terms is in a line with developments we have observed in other fields of the literature of Complaint. One might argue that the concentration on the spiritual concerns of the individual soul is the logical consequence of a process of internalisation inherent in the form. If this is so. Breton has touched the limit of this process in his *Blessed weeper*, and gone beyond this limit in his other Complaints of completely disembodied minds and souls. At this limit the personal perspective, narrowed to a point outside of time and space, widens again to the impersonal point of view which takes in the universal Christian truth of the salvation. Despite their protestations to the contrary, these Protestant souls are never really at a loss; they may feel like fallen angels, but they always know the paradise open still and ready to take them in again. This gives all of these poems a hopeful aspect, even if contradicted by facts, as in the case of the Earl of Essex (and even he may have written his poem under the impression that his release was imminent).[80] Christian hope informs these poems not only in the end, as in Southwell's treatise, but throughout the protestations. Breton's Magdalen knows she is saved long before the end. Her soul is elevated when her heart begins to sink:

> Although my heart in comfort be acold,
> My soule doth tell me that these teares of mine
> Shall all be dri'd vp by his hand diuine: (F1v)

The rebuff of the *Noli me tangere* does not fit into this concept; Breton's Mary has been in search only of her 'soules delight' (F3r), and her soul is secure in her master's hand. Breton does not mention the command and has Mary renounce voluntarily all but a bashful glimpse, not even at Christ's body, but at his eyes, and these eyes are already transfigured, and alive only in the spiritual sense of The Book of Life:

> I will not presse one foote beyond the line
> Of thy loues leaue, vouchsafe me but a looke
> Of that sweete heauenly holy eye of thine,
> Of my deere Loue the euer-liuing Booke:
> VVherein my teares haue such true comfort tooke,
>   That, let the world torment me nere so sore,
>   Let me see thee, and I desire no more.   (F3v)

Compared with Southwell's unruly, full-blooded Marie, this is rather an anaemic Magdalen. Part of the disappointing effect of poems such as *The blessed weeper* may be due to Breton's limited poetical talent, or to his excessively scrupulous religious attitude, or, perhaps, to an anxiety not to discomfort his readers whom he reassures in his foreword:

> If you note it well, you may finde matter of comforte, and nothing to the contrarie: God truely glorified, in his manifould blessinges: and many greatly blessed, that being endued with his Graces, by faithe taketh hould of his mercies: the Athists [sic] confounded in their follies: and the vertuous blessed in their election.   (A2v)

With regard to the questions of genre raised in this study, it is more important to note that there are limits to the narrowing of perspective and that Complaints cannot well do without some kind of material background. Otherwise both the human interest begins to flag and the artistic tension to sag. This background of reality need not be taken from the higher strata of important historical or Biblical events; it can also be taken from lower life, scenes from the life Mary lived at Magdala, for instance, before she entered the Biblical scene. Such scenes are in the background of our last strain of Complaints.

Violenta and Amanda: the novellistic Complaint

It is the pathos of the stews

Spectator, 7 Jan. 1837

The stately novella: Boccaccio's 'Tancredi' in England

In a way, the subjectivity of Complaint literature makes it the most objective narrative genre next to drama because the author is able to hide behind his character; this is one reason for the rediscovery of the mode in Browning's dramatic monologues and Joyce's interior monologues. Molly Bloom is a descendant of not only Homer's but also Ovid's Penelope, even if she finds little to complain about: realism, the unheroic point of view, has become the norm, pathos turned into ethos, tragedy into comedy.

In early literature, too, the real world (that is the world governed not only by heroic, or even honourable norms) is a world of comedy. Women belong to this world of reality according to ancient decorum of both pagan and Christian origin. Aristotle's *Poetics* and St Paul's 'Epistle to the Ephesians' give evidence to this effect. In terms of literary decorum this means, to put it crudely, that where women take over, comedy begins; for narrative poetry, the epyllion gives numerous examples of comic elements, be they intended, as in Shakespear's *Venus and Adonis*, or unintended, as in Trussell's *Raptus I. Helenae*. The tragic Complaints which I have analysed so far infringe on these gender-based rules of decorum in so far as women of lowly origin and concerned with private cares are taken seriously.

With the Italian novella late medieval literature developed a special narrative medium for the presentation of realistic material in the comic mode. Love in its less elevated form is prominent in the novella, and women are often at the centre of interest in both active and passive roles. It is only natural, therefore, that writers working in the Complaint tradition should have been alerted to the possibilities inherent in the new genre. The impact, however, of the first wave of Italian novelle was rather small. It is doubtful, for example, to what extent Chaucer, with his excellent Italian connections and a taste for the lower strata of literature, knew Boccaccio's *Decameron* – if he knew it at all. To him and to his contemporaries, Boccaccio is chiefly known for his erudite *exempla* and as a writer of high romance. Throughout the fifteenth century Boccaccio remains the author of such works as *De claris mulieribus* and *Filostrato*, as Chaucer himself is mainly praised for his *Legend of good women* or his *Troilus*. This may well have been due to the lack of high poetic seriousness in both their mixed-bag collections, the *Decameron* and the *Canterbury tales*, and it may have proved an obstacle to the conversion of novelle into Complaints, too.

The kind of woman presented in a novella is ill suited to Complaints of the types we have analysed so far because these Complaints require, as I have shown, important historical events in the background to elevate their more or less helpless victims to tragic importance. These Complaints depend, in other words, on a strong contrast between a grand plane of action, and a smaller plane of suffering. In the more realistic novelle the action moves on a domestic plane throughout. The women acting on this plane do not face imperial pressures as do Dido or Rosamond. They are at least equal to their opponents, and they are much too practical to be easily victimised. Even if they find themselves tempted or bullied, they are not easily awed or terrified into submission. The tale of *The wright's chaste wife* (c 1462), an English novella based on Legend 69 ('De castitate') from the *Gesta Romanorum*, is a case in point: the wife of the title, though left alone for weeks by an itinerant husband, is never at a loss in defending her chastity against the most pressing suitors; on the contrary, she is able to take advantage of the menfolk by tricking them into captivity and setting them to task with, of all things, needlework. The novella is, as its subtitle says, *A merry tale*, and the provincial Penelope at its centre a study for such quick-witted heroines as Willoby's *Avisa* (1594) or Richardson's *Pamela*.[1]

There are women like the wright's wife in Boccaccio's *Decameron*, but they were not deemed worthy of independent treatment in England. The first tales to be detached from the collection were those of 'Tancredi' (or 'Guiscardo and Ghismonda') and 'Titus and Gisippus'. They both deal with love and friendship of the most magnanimous sort and may owe their wide dissemination and higher estimation to the fact that they were translated into learned and international Latin by Leonardo Bruni in 1436.[2] Of the two, the Tancredi novella is of particular interest for this study because its protagonist, the princess Ghismonda, who refuses to renounce her love to the low-born Guiscardo, is one of Cupid's martyrs. Her story was translated into English around the middle of the fifteenth century by Gilbert Banester from a French version of the Latin text. The translation is preserved in two manuscripts which both acknowledge the kinship of the story with those in Chaucer's *Legend of good women*: in the British Library Add. MS 12524 it is attached to Chaucer's 'legend of ladyse' and given an appropriate heading, 'Incipit llegenda Sismond'; in the Rawlinson MS C 86 kept in the Bodleian Library it is set side by side with the 'Legend of Dido'.[3]

Banester thus adapts his story outwardly to the *Legend of good women* frame; he also borrows material from other Chaucerian poems. His Sismond is modelled after the lady in the *Book of the duchess*.[4] Her beauty is said to outshine that of the heroines in the 'Knight's tale':

> Passing Penelope and lucres off face,
> Ypolita and Emyles hire yonge suster withall   (Add. MS, 47–8)

Banester generally tries to heighten his characters to the status required in a medieval tragedy: his Tancred and Sismond are of royal blood, Guystard is promoted to knighthood and proves their equal in highmindedness. In the interest of this status all the petty details of the story are dropped: there is no intrigue, no hidden letter inviting Guystard to Sismond's room, nor a secret passage conveying him to her arms. The same respect is paid to the moral status of the protagonists. A decidedly patriarchal morality is observed. Sismond is not allowed to challenge the authority of her father by insisting on her own choice of a lover and she agrees with his command not to remarry. The Ovidian motif of a woman preferring her *amor* to her filial or conjugal *pietas* is not developed. In breaking her vow, Sismond becomes the victim not so much of her father's tyranny but of her own rashness – a solution that runs counter both to the source and to the spirit of the *Legend of good women*.

A second adaptation of the story of Guiscardo and Ghismonda must have been written shortly after Banester's version. Wright dates it on internal evidence towards the end of the reign of Richard III (1485).[5] It is preserved in a manuscript, Trinity College, Cambridge, MS R.3.19, which again attests the story's affiliation with Chaucer's legendary, and at the same time hints at the generic problems evident in Banester's version: it contains copies of both the *Legend of good women* and the 'Monk's tale'. The author is unknown; like Banester, he worked from a French version of Bruni's Latin translation of the Tancredi novella. He also must have had Banester's poem at hand because he took over his predecessor's ending of the tale (which was easy because they both used rhyme royal stanzas). A somewhat polished version of this second adaptation was published with *Certain worthy manuscript poems of great antiquity* in 1597 and inscribed 'The stately tragedy of Guistard and Sismond'; for the sake of distinction between the two versions and for reasons of convenience I shall adopt this later title and quote from the printed version.[6]

The title 'Stately tragedy' is well chosen because the adaptor has tried, like Banester, to give the story the greatness of a tragedy in the moralising

Fall of princes manner. It is to serve as a warning to beware of tyranny and may have been directed at the arch-tyrant of the age, Richard III. This background almost necessarily puts Sismond into the situation of victims such as Mrs Shore and Queen Elizabeth and allows for a number of Ovidian or Chaucerian elements in the story: the description of Sismond's beauty is more detailed, her secret letter to Guistard is spun out into an Ovidian epistle, and the debate with her father is less one-sided than it is in Banester. In style, too, the 'Stately Tragedy' shows elements of both a mirror for princes and a mirror of souls. Of course, Tancred is the prince whose fall from paternal love to fury gives an example of tyranny. The adaptor keeps the signs of weakness he possessed already in Boccaccio's novella (his tears about Ghismonda's trespass and his perplexity at the situation she has created). He turns Tancred, moreover, into an archetype of the sentimental tyrant who weeps and whips in turn and acts out his cruelty in a backhanded way.

In the debate about her freedom of choice Sismond comes to dominate. In this respect, too, she is different from Boccaccio's robust virago. In the *Decameron* Ghismonda faces her father unabashed ('non come dolente femina') and promises to act in a heroic spirit, with greatness of soul ('con fatti fortissimamente seguire la grandezza dell'animo mio'), while her father weeps like a beaten child ('piagnendo si forte come farebbe un fanciul ben battuto').[7] In the adaptation Sismond shows a less heroic temper; at one point she admits that her 'heart was not so big to make resistance' and thereby expressly denies the *grandezza* she has in the *Decameron*. She does not need to aggrandize her stature in the English version because her father debases himself by adding meanness to his cruelty and accusing her of behaving like a common prostitute:

> When ye like women of a brothel and prostrage
> Tok what com to hond as the chaunce would fall
>
> ('Stately Tragedy', 542–3)

This allows Sismond to adopt the role of the woman defamed beyond measure such as Henryson's Cresseid or Churchyard's Mrs Shore: she may have sinned, but is more sinned against. The whole debate thus gradually changes into an accusation of the father, not so much because Sismond's arguments are right, but because her father has put himself in the wrong. The headstrong combatant in Boccaccio's version who fights for her somewhat dubious right of natural love is turned into the slighted sinner of the apologetic Complaint.

There are several such softening touches in the adaptation, most notably the secret letter I have mentioned already. It ends, broken-voiced and self-forgotten, like an epistle in the *Heroides* line:

> She wrot ther By your owne, and made no mention

Of her name: till after a gret stound
With sighing sore she added to, Sismond.   (299–301)

There follows a dream vision which foreshadows the ghastly end of Guistard and puts Sismond completely out of her mind. It is reminiscent both
of Ovid's or Chaucer's Alcyone and of the Lady of Sorrows. The latter
association is supported by the prayer that follows the vision:

And sodenly with that out of her slepe she stert
As a woman from her self, she was so sore dismaid,
She thought of very deth the sword went to her hert,
And thus weeping by her selfe she prayed:
O myrrour of all women Mary she seyd,
From all shame and velony my loue & me defend,
And helpe that my dreme to me none pretend.   (505–11)

Ghismonda, then, becomes a much more vulnerable person in the
hands of this English adaptor, a martyr of love rather than the proud
mistress of her fate she is in Boccaccio's novella. It is only fitting that in
the English version she is transported to a lovers' elysium after her death:

That as I trust she is in blesse celestiall,
As of faith and troth all louers surmounting,
She was a mirrour vnto women all,
Example of true and stedfast loue giuing   (989–92)

In the end the tale moves into the realm of the *Legend of good women*
and Sismond is judged by Cupid's law. It is the same law that governed
the fifteenth-century poems which we have come to know in other com-
partments of this study: the 'Letter of Dydo to Eneas', the 'Complaint
of the lover of Christ' and the 'Lament of the Duchess of Gloucester'.
All these poems are anonymous, and all of them were at some time
associated with the *Legend of good women*. This need not argue for a
common author (be he Chaucer or Sir Richard Roos), but it does argue
for the ongoing influence of the Ovidian and Chaucerian tradition in
the latter half of the fifteenth century. This influence extended into the
following century. Most of the poems just named found their way into
the early printing houses. The 'Stately tragedy' arrived somewhat late; it
was reprinted at the height of the Ovidian season in 1597, but there was
an earlier deputy in William Walter's *Guystarde and Sygysmonde*, again
a translation from the Latin and also written in rhyme royal, which was
printed by Wynkyn de Worde in 1532.

The sensational novella: adaptations of Bandello's tales

The special esteem the story of Guiscardo and Ghismonda enjoyed in England may be due to the fact that it contains a number of elements unusual in a novella – in particular the 'hic amor, haec patria' conflict at the heart of the story with its possibility of an in-depth study of the heroine's motifs. In effect the 'legenda Sismond' enjoyed a career independent of the *Decameron* all over Europe. In Italy, it is sometimes coupled with Enea Silvio Piccolomini's poem *De duobus amantibus* (1444), which Joseph Raith has called the first 'modern' novella because of its psychological depth.[8] The fare offered in a novella is normally of a much coarser fibre, and authors of a less refined temperament, given the subject of the Tancredi story, would have concentrated on the cutting out of Guiscardo's heart rather than the movements in Ghismonda's soul. The first requisite of a novella is that it reports on an extraordinary event and concentrates on the crisis of an action – often the topsy-turvy action of erotic fabliaux. Most of Boccaccio's novelle in the *Decameron* adhere to this rule, and even where he strives for the problematic and the tragic, as he does in the tales of the Fourth Day which opens with the Tancredi tale, the violent parts of the action with its surprising turns occupy most of the narrator's interest.[9]

With Boccaccio, this concentration on the external aspects of a story is tempered by his humanist outlook and his wide range of styles. With his followers in the novella tradition, a deterioration towards the merely sensational set in, and it was collections of the second generation like the *Novelle* of Matteo Bandello (written in the first half of the sixteenth century) that were imported wholesale from Italy in the latter half of the century. They usually took their way via France, where they were enriched with classical and romantic material, and labelled 'tragic', as in the case of the *Histoires tragiques* of Pierre Boaistuau and François de Belleforest (1559–82). Wrapped up in cautionary forewords these novelle were then marketed by the dozens in English translations; the most popular collection was William Painter's *The palace of pleasure* (2 vols 1566, 1567) which contains extended versions of sixteen of Boccaccio's and twenty-five of Bandello's tales.[10]

In spite of the careful wrapping, the sensational contents of these later tales look through their titles, and this was, of course, part of the advertising. In the case of Bandello's story of Didaco and Violenta, for instance, the violent action is indicated in the name of the heroine already.[11] At the beginning of the tale, however, Violenta does nothing to live up to her name. The story moves rather smoothly on the same plane as Boccaccio's 'Tancredi' novella – or rather on the same planes, because it also uses an uneven match as central motive. The roles of the couple are reversed, though: low-born Violenta is secretly married to the noble Didaco. They both enjoy their union until Didaco plans a marriage of convenience with a woman of equal rank and offers his first wife to keep her as a mistress. Upon this Violenta instantly turns into a fury; she kills her husband, mutilates his corpse and throws it contemptuously into the street.

The story of Violenta presents a brutalised version of the heroic way out of the dilemma that heroines are faced with in both the epic and the elegiac tradition. Ovid's elegiac heroines such as Dido and Briseis volunteer to serve as mistresses in their letters; they are prepared to compromise their honour in favour of their love.[12] Epic heroines such as Progne and Medea go for revenge,[13] and this is what Violenta does: she follows her sense of honour which is as savage as that of her mythic sisters. The ensuing slaughter looks the more shocking since it occurs in the city of Valencia, not any barbarous country, and is meticulously planned. It is in keeping with the cold-blooded nature of Bandello's heroine that she shows no sign of fear or remorse and urges her judges to sentence her to death. The sense of morality in the audience is served in a matter of fact report of the judicial proceedings up to Violenta's beheading 'for her excessiue crueltie', and the assurance that the story was told after the best authorities.[14]

Thomas Achelley, *A Spanish gentlewoman named Violenta*

About ten years after its first publication in England, Thomas Achelley took the story of Didaco and Violenta out of Painter's *Palace of pleasure* and turned it into a verse tale as long and as loud as its title suggests: *A most lamentable and tragical history, containing the outrageous and horrible tyranny which a Spanish gentlewoman named Violenta executed upon her lover Didaco, because he espoused another being first betrothed unto her* (1576), Achelley reinforces the advertisement in his dedication to Sir Thomas Gresham, and he garnishes it with a few learned references to mythic tales of similar horror:

TO discourse of the furious tirannie of the boocherly *Medea*, in dismembring the innocent infante *Absyrtus* her owne naturall brother, and scattering his martyred limmes in the hie waye where her father shoulde passe, were but a loste labour. Or to vnfold the horrible crueltie of the beastly *Progne*, in murthering her owne chylde *Iphis*, and rosting his fleshe, to present the same to her husbande *Tereus* in a Banquet, were but vaine taken traveyle, and time altogether mispended, which might otherwyse haue beene farre better employed. Those are but Ethnicke examples, farre fette, and a wonderfull waye distant from our climate both by Sea and Lande: and committed among such barbarous people, that had no knowledge of any God nor yet of any sparke of Ciuilitie.

Neyther shall wee neede to traueyle so farre for the matter. Let vs but cast our eyes ouer the sea here into Spaine, that lyeth in the hart of Christendome, where God is knowen and honoured, mutiall amitie frequented, and all kinde of good order and ciuilitie obserued, and let vs see what hath there happened. Surely, an example so terrible, that it would moue any true Christian to teares, yea and make his haire stand vpright, for horror, in thinking of so detestable a fact:

(A3 r–v)

Like the patriotic Drayton, Achelley wants to outdo the ancients, but he deals in horrors rather than in heroes and he spots them in an enemy country, Spain. The method is as gratuitious as the one Ovid employs in his *Metamorphoses* when he places the story of Progne in faraway Thracia and dissociates himself from the barbarity of the region.[15] Like Ovid, his first aim is to raise hairs, his second to move to tears. On the other hand he exploits what the matter-of-fact presentation of Painter (and Bandello) had only implied: the additional shock provided by the fact that the events related are real, and closer to home since they occurred in a Christian country.

Achelley's tale is written in fourteeners, which is most appropriate since it makes possible heroic strides as well as balladic jolts. Didaco's love is of the heroic kind; he is a warrior, and compared with the greatest heroes such as Hercules and Hannibal. He falls in love only through the machinations of a Venus who is jealous of Mars. She sets Cupid to work who shoots one of his fatal arrows, and Didaco breaks into a violent love-complaint:

> *O heauen*, o earth, o Joue aboue,
>   What meanes this sodayne stroke?
> Did euer poore *Didaco* yet
>   Thy power diuine prouoke?
> What sodayne marirdome [sic] is this?
>   What pinching pangues of hell?
> The fates agaynst the freedome, of
>   *Didaco* doe rebell.   (B8r)

In this tale, then, Didaco turns out to be love's martyr; the constellation reminds one of the erotic epyllion where even gods fall prey to coquettish maidens such as the Apollo in Richard Barnfield's *Cassandra* (1595) who is made a 'silly god that thinks none ill' (D6r) by the princess, though he has introduced himself with all his titles, as 'God of Musique, and of Poetry: / Of Phisicke, Learning, and Chirurgery' (D5r). The difference is that Didaco is most cruelly martyred in a real sense; after the murder his body is so mangled that no one is able to recognise 'the sillie martirs face' (F3v). Violenta, too, is anything but coquettish. Her servant Iamque compares her to heroines from Ovid's *Heroides*, and she writes

a letter to Didaco, but then she acts out her butcherly part most cruelly.
The letter is in prose and lures him to his death-trap; it does not serve a
softening purpose as inlaid letters sometimes do in extended versions of
novelle.[16]

Achelley's Violenta is modelled on the Medea of the *Metamorphoses*,
not the *Heroides*; she is much harder even than Boccaccio's Ghismonda,
and cuts her lover's heart out herself. The end of the tale is so violent
that the narrator feels obliged to prevent her misdeeds from befouling
the whole of her sex:

> You Ladies all whose weeping eyes,
>   This hystorie peruse:
> At rareness of this monstrous fact,
>   No marueyle though ye muse.
> But as the splendant blasing lampe,
>   Doth neuer burne so bright:
> As when a darkesome shade doth seeme,
>   For to eclipse his ligh. . [sic]
> So you, deere dames whose vertuous minds,
>   Abandon all such wayes:
> By contrarie of this foul facte,
>   Deserue immortal prayse.   (F3r)

Achelley here addresses the public he apparently had in mind when he
wrote his adaptation of the novella: in spite of the dedication to Sir
Richard, poems such as *A Spanish gentlewoman named Violenta* were
presumably written for gentlewomen rather than gentlemen.[17] This could
also be said of other prose novelle which had their heyday in the 1570s.
Sometimes the intended public is acknowledged, as in George Pettie's
Petite palace of Pettie his pleasure [1576], a collection of mainly classical
tales (among them versions of the Progne, the Scylla and the Procris
stories from the *Metamorphoses*) which is expressly directed 'To the
gentle Gentlewomen Readers' (A2r). An exception is George Whetstone's *Rock of regard* to which I now turn.

George Whetstone, *The disordered life of Bianca Maria*

Whetstone addresses his *Rock of regard* (1576) 'To all the young Gentlemen of England' (x2r), and several of these gentlemen have contributed
commendatory verses to the collection. It is a many-layered piece of
rock, however, containing among 'diuers other morall, natural & tragical
discourses: *documents and admonitions*' (subtitle, x1r) several Complaints spoken by women. Some of these Complaints are short, like 'Creβids complaint' (Argument B1r; Complaint B1v–3v) and 'The pitious

complaint of Medea' (E6r–v), which shows the heroine as love's victim, exiled in an imaginary desert:

> AMid the desert woods, I rue and shew my fate,
> Exild (O wretch) frõ courtly ioyes, bereft of princes state,
> O loue, from whence these plagues proceede,
> For seruice true, is this thy meede?   (E6r)

One of these Complaints, 'The disordered life of Bianca Maria' (Argument xx3r–v; Complaint A1r–B1r) is of considerable length (sixty-eight rhyme royal stanzas, plus an inlaid letter of six sixains); together with 'Creβids complaint' (twenty-two rhyme royal stanzas) it belongs to the first part of *The Rock of regard* subtitled *'the Castle of delight*: Wherein is reported, the wretched end of wanton and dissolute liuing' (x1r). There are three more parts; together they form the *paysage moralisé* of the *Rock of regard*: there is a 'Garden of Vnthriftinesse' with a prose novella of Dom Diego and Ginevra and the Complaint of Medea, an '*Arbour of Vertue*' and an '*Ortchard of Repentance*'. The order mirrors the different stages of a Rake's Progress, as Whetstone explains in his '*generall aduertisement* vnto the Reader':

thinke that the good and the badde in this booke, is to forwarne youth, and to recreate the stayed: & thinke that my beginning with Delight, running on in Vnthriftines, resting in Vertue, and ending with Repentaunce, is no other then a figure of the lustie yõkers aduentures   (x3v)

The story of Bianca Maria, the dissolute countess who instigated the murder of her husband, is one of Bandello's *Novelle* (vol. I, no. 4); according to Koeppel it was his 'most odious and most popular'.[18] The tale had been adapted by William Painter in his *Palace* (vol. II, no. 24) and by Geoffrey Fenton in his *Tragical discourses* (1567, no. 7); it served as a source for John Marston's tragedy *The insatiate countess* (1613). Whetstone turned it into a tragical Complaint.

In spite of the framework and the introductory letter, the bloody Mary of this Complaint does not address the younkers of England, but ladies of rank who she tacitly implies are in danger of being morally debased like herself:

> Good Ladies first, to you this tale I tell,
> To you as chiefe, this drirye plaint I preach,
> Your hie estate, your vices cannot quell: (A1r)

Bianca Maria is of base birth herself; her father was the usurer Giacomo Scappardone, and she only married into the aristocracy. The social argument is not, however, used to the heroine's credit, as often in Complaints and domestic tragedies. Bianca Maria's corruption is not brought about by the courtly atmosphere or the advances of a courtier. On the contrary,

her several aristocratic husbands are as discreet about her wanton ways
as possible. Rather it is her base nature which asserts itself time and
again and eventually corrupts her aristocratic lovers, too. Compared with
Boccaccio's 'Tancredi' novella, the question of rank and morality is put
upside down; Ghismonda proves her great soul in adversity, Bianca
Maria her base one in spite of prosperity: sooner make a lamb intimidate
a wolf than change a base mind, as Maria puts it in an extended simile.
A sidenote is more succinct: 'Kitt will to kinde' (A1v).

The lambs in Bianca Maria's story, as in that of Violenta, are the
men. In Achelley's broadside-ballad this reversal of traditional sex
roles added to the sensational impact of the novella. In Whetstone's
Complaint it runs counter to the tendency of his chosen form; the somewhat confused animal imagery in the simile mentioned is only one indication of the difficulties he encountered. In a Complaint the woman is
the lamb, of course, and the image is meant to give her confession an
engaging note. With Bianca Maria the reverse is the case. She is her own
severest judge and heaps accusation after accusation upon herself – she
sees her life from the outside and comments on it in the hard-as-rock
morality of the framework in which her Complaint is set. This alien
perspective transforms all the ingredients which in other Complaints
serve an emotive purpose. An inserted letter, for example, is an indict-
ment of Bianca Maria's treasonous nature, and she subscribes to it whole-
heartedly. In this letter the customary list of love's martyrs is turned into
a catalogue of harlots when Maria says of her lover Valperga (with an
involuntary inversion in the term 'heave up' where 'debase' seems called
for):

> Hee heaues mee vp to filthie *Faustines* state,
> A *Layis* byrde, for *Masseline* a mate,
> A filth, a flurt, a bitch of *Megraes* kinde,
> A rigg, a rampe, and all that came to minde   (A4r)

Even Violenta was associated with heroines from the *Heroides* and the
Metamorphoses – Bianca Maria refers to Ovid only as author of the *Ars
amatoria* (with another inversion in 'cleanly'):

> Immodest rigg, I *Ouids* counsell vsde,
> Where cleanly, I did couler shame with sleightes   (A3v)

The inventory of such inversions could be extended to the pathetic prop
of the forsaken bed which Bianca Maria mentions in an *ubi sunt* catalogue
and promptly turns into a piece of evidence against herself.

> My lothsome couche, presenteth to my vewe,
> My beds of doune: with thought of sweete delights,
> Thus day and night, my wilfull harme I rewe:

> Ech thought of grace, my conscience guilt affrights,
> Yet (loth to die) against repentaunce fightes,
> Till due desert, by lawe and Iustice lead,
> Did dome my misse, with losse of my poore head.   (A8v)

Law and order bring to an end Bianca Maria's disordered life, and this shows in the style and structure of the poem. Thematically, too, the Complaint is ruled by justice, not mercy like most other Complaints, and justice of the strictest kind: 'Bloud cries for bloud' (A1r), Bianca Maria had announced in her very first sentence, and that is why she willingly climbs the scaffold from which the Complaint is supposed to be spoken (xx2v). The sensational aspects of the case in hand, as well as the crudity of the lesson to be drawn from it, place this Complaint in the vicinity of the confessions that were hawked in the streets after a hanging at Tyburn or a beheading at the Tower. The psychological realism which is promoted in Complaints of the apologetic tradition is here replaced by the circumstantial realism of a murder case. The introspective form is used for extrovert, demonstrative purposes, and this puts a strain on the whole of the performance. Bianca Maria reviews her disordered life along the straight lines of a trial; a little more insight in the moral disorder of her 'mightie litle hart', as she calls it (A6v), would have been more convincing. As it stands, the fate of this *femme fatale* is apt to arouse neither pity nor horror, and one suspects that it did little to warn the young gentlemen of England, except of the dangers lurking in hot-blooded countries such as Italy, and to assure their ladies of the benefit of their own more temperate climate.[19]

The sentimental novella: reformed whores in Renaissance literature

Thomas Churchyard, *A dolorous gentlewoman*

The poet to apply the rules of the compassionate Complaint to the life of an Italian courtesan was Thomas Churchyard, who, as we know, had helped to launch the genre on its career with his Complaint of an English concubine, 'Shore's wife', which first appeared in the *Mirror for magistrates* in 1563. In 1579 Churchyard published a collection of his own under the title of *A general rehearsal of wars*. The contents of this volume are martial only in its main part, a manifold *ars militaria*, with 'fiue hundred seuerall seruices of land and sea: as sieges, battailles, skirmiches, and encounters', etc. (subtitle, *1r); the rest of the volume is padded with 'some Tragedies and Epitaphes', among them 'A pitefull complaint, in maner of a *Tragedie, of Seignior Anthonio dell Dondaldoes* wife, somtyme in the duke of Florences Courte' (x2v), which apparently follows up the earlier 'Shore's wife'.

Churchyard claims to have translated the story of Donaldo's wife from the Italian, but the original has yet to be found. Part of the action reported in the Complaint is placed at the court of Florence, but no duke is named, and there is no touch of a Medici atmosphere. The exotic props are kept to a minimum and they do not look genuine. It is probable that Churchyard, who was always struggling for survival, labelled a piece of his own invention according to the Italianate vogue of the time. When this vogue had ebbed away, he had little difficulty in changing the scenery: in his later collection called *Churchyard's challenge* (1593) he published a revised version of the poem under the title of 'A Tragicall Discourse of a dolorous Gentlewoman' (Gg3v–L11r), and transferred the action to England. It took just a few additional lines (the total is 118 rhyme royal stanzas in the later version) in which the city of Bath is as casually mentioned as the court of Florence was in the earlier version.

Churchyard does not intend to entertain or to caution the lusty younkers of England as does Whetstone. His Complaint is 'dedicated to all those Ladyes that holdes good name precious' (Subtitle, Gg3v) – not gentlewomen only, for Churchyard seeks as wide an audience as possible, and he may have left the dolorous gentlewoman anonymous (and placed her at the city of Bath, which was not yet a fashionable watering place) for that purpose. In fact, the appellation 'gentlewoman' seems hardly appropriate for the lady complaining, neither with regard to the situation we find her in (she is forced to beg in the streets like Mrs Shore, whose Complaint precedes her's in *Churchyard's challenge*, S4r–X1v), nor from her origin or career. She must have grown up in affluent surroundings for she confesses that she was spoilt in her youth, but the husband she chooses apparently lives the life of a merchant.

The circumstances of her marriage play an important part in her Complaint, as marital problems tend to do in earlier English narratives with women protagonists, from the 'marriage group' in Chaucer's *Canterbury tales* to Richardson's *Clarissa*. The Gentlewoman takes her time before making her choice of a husband at the age of twenty-two, and Churchyard uses the opportunity to insert a piece of useful, well-balanced advice: girls should not be allowed to have all their ways, but fathers should not suppress their daughters' wishes, either. This hortatory part gives the poem the aspect of a conduct book and prompted Willard Farnham to the remark that the subsequent tragedy 'might be called 'domestic' '.[20]

The epithet 'domestic' would better fit Anthony Chute's *Beauty dishonoured*, in which the conduct-book element is developed into a domestic variant of the theme of *tyrannis*. In Chute's Complaint young Mrs Shore is forced into a loveless marriage, and this is the beginning of her tragedy. In Churchyard's Complaint of the Gentlewoman the conduct book advice is not really apposite: the lady is allowed her own choice, and her husband is as indulgent with her whims as her father was. In the beginning of her marriage these whims are harmless and mainly directed at costly clothes; later on they expand to the illicit: she abuses the freedom her husband's wealth and his business trips offer for an occasional love affair. When the merchant is called to a war (the martial framework makes itself felt) she bridges the longer absence by taking a permanent lover. When her husband comes home she is expecting a child which she tries to foist on him. He sees through the fraud, but is easily appeased. It takes him some time to realise that she will in the end ruin them both; even after a period of separation which she has used to turn the family home into a brothel he tries to win her back – his patience is more than angelic.

It is this incredibly patient husband who gives the Complaint of the Gentlewoman a human interest that Bianca Maria's confession under the gallows lacks. Paradoxically, it also lends some probability to the changes worked in the fortunes of the heroine. When her husband eventually loses faith in her she is utterly lost and has to fall back on her natural gifts: her looks which no longer can sustain her. She scrutinises her mirror image and gives us her features in a catalogue which reverses the catalogue of beauties we traditionally find in an erotic epyllion:

> The crooked backe, must bolstred be by arte,
> The tawny skinne, must shine by some trim knack,
> The twinkling lookes, for sport must play their part
> The perwickes fine, must curle wher [sic] haire doth lack
> The swelling grace, that fils the empty sacke:
> And ietting pace, with lims stretcht out ful streight,
> To patch out pride, are matters of great weight.   (Kk4v)

This reflection from the mirror brings Bianca Maria to her senses, and to reflection in the figurative sense; even her moral defects now feel like spots on her once beautiful face:

> For my conceite, is such a deadly dark,
> That where I goe, or walke in any place,
> Me thinkes my faults, are written in my face.   (Ll1r)

The total dependence on physical appearance, the realisation (in front of a mirror) that with beauty waning her capital is being used up, and the remorse that is felt as a brand (i.e. a physical mark) – these elements are developed into the features of many a fallen woman in later literature. We find all of them, and the infinitely patient, though uncomprehending, husband, too, in Arthur Wing Pinero's domestic tragedy of *The Second Mrs Tanqueray*, a kept mistress in her former life.[21] Churchyard introduces these features only in the end of the Complaint, and they come too late to offset the long passages of superficial comments on the lady's long slide down the primrose path of dalliance. In the end she lands herself literally in the mire:

> I loued not one, but lusted after all,
> The puddell foule, was fittest for a gigge:
> The fountaine faire did drinke like bitter gall,
> In filthy mud I wallowed like a pigge.
> About the streets was gadding gentle rigge.
> With clothes tuckt vp to set bad ware to sale:
> For youth good stuffe, and for olde age a stale.   (Ii1r)

Still, together with the domestication of the subject, the final search for subcutaneous truth distinguishes the Gentlewoman's Complaint from the mere surface reaction of the Bianca Maria type and shows some of the possibilities of the mirror held up by a not quite lady-like gentlewoman.

Gervase Markham, *The famous whore, or noble courtesan*

When the second generation of novelle reached England in the 1560s, single representatives of the first found their way onto the English stage: *Gismond of Salerne*, adapted from Boccaccio's 'Tancredi' novella by Robert Wilmot and others, was first acted in 1567–8 at the Inner Temple and revised at a peak period of revenge tragedy in 1591–2. The sensational heroines of the second generation had their entrances on the Jacobean stage, in plays such as Websters *Duchess of Malfi* (1612–13) and Marston's *Insatiate countess* (1613). One of the poets to respond to the Jacobean taste in Italianate blood-and-tears tragedy was the prolific Gervase Markham who, as we have seen, responded to the influence of Italianate lachrimose poetry with his *Marie Magdalen's Lamentations* (1601). In 1609 Markham published a Complaint with the somewhat irresolute title of *The famous whore, or noble courtesan*. The subtitle places the poem more firmly in an Italian setting than its predecessors: 'Conteining the lamentable Complaint of PAVLINA, the famous Roman Curtizan, sometimes M[es] vnto the great Cardinal *Hypolito, of Est*'.

Markham's originality lay in the field of husbandry; most of his poetical works are adaptations; one should expect, therefore, this Complaint to be derived from an Italian novella, or possibly a French translation of such a source, but none has been found yet. The author does not mention an authority (but then he did not mention Southwell, whose *Funeral Tears* he closely followed in his *Lamentations*). Markham had dealt with second-hand Italian literature before: his *Rodomonth's Infernal* (1607) is based on an adaptation of parts of the *Orlando furioso* by Philippe Desportes.[22] He may have known Ariosto's original as well; in her Complaint Paulina compares her deflowering by a 'groom as base as earth' (B1r) to an episode from the *Orlando*:

So *Medor* wanne *Angelica* by chance,
From all the noble Palladines of France.   (B1r)

His acquaintance with Ariosto's epic might have led Markham onto the scene of his Complaint: Ariosto wrote his *Orlando* while he was employed by Ippolito d'Este, and Markham may have come across some background material concerning the lavish life of the Cardinal while working on the epic.

The connection with Ippolito invests the story of Paulina with a historical interest which must have had a special appeal to a post-Reformation Englishman; the fact that the Cardinal is mentioned in the subtitle would support this appeal and indicate that the name of Ippolito d'Este (who died in 1520) still rang a bell in the ears of prospective readers. Markham does not, however, exploit the possibility of castigating one of the most profligate Italian churchmen; there is an exclamation of resentment when Paulina remembers how she was pandered to the Cardinal in her early teens:

O you Church mirours say, why do you liue
Thus loose, that should vs better instance giue?   (B2r)

But this is qualified by the practical thought that celibacy virtually forces Roman priests into bypaths like this – a thought which is in keeping with Markham's common sense attitude and the (at the time of her Complaint) seasoned mind of the courtesan.

Ippolito, or Popish practices in general, are not the butt of Paulina's Complaint. On the contrary, the Cardinal is described as a remarkably generous admirer of his young mistress. He tries to make Paulina's life as enjoyable as he can, and he marries her off to a young nobleman when he feels no longer up to her increasing demands on his virility. The agreeable character of the Cardinal may be due to Ariosto who decorated his *Orlando* with flattering remarks on his patron, or to the sympathetic sketch of young Ippolito in Castiglione's *Il cortegiano*; it is more likely, however, that the laws of a courtesan's confession demand such kind antagonists to set off the culprits in the foreground. We had a similar constellation in the tales of Violenta, Bianca Maria and Churchyard's Gentlewoman (alias Signora Dondaldo): these women are defined first and foremost by the one physical feature in which they – according to common belief – outstrip men, namely their insatiable sexual appetite, and this naturally results in relationships with domineering wives (or lovers) and incompetent men. This generic law appears to be so strong that in Paulina's Complaint it not only inverts the victor–victim relation usually observed in this form, but makes a doormat of a notorious tyrant. It is the same law of the tyranny of love which informs the erotic epyllion but is there resolved in comedy or metamorphosis. Here it is debased to the tyranny of lust and leads those wielding the tyrannic power to disaster.

Both the genres of erotic epyllion and of the courtesan's confession are rooted, of course, in the belief in an ideal order of things which places men above women as it places reason above passion. At one point in her Complaint Paulina expounds this order by alluding to the first disobedience and fall of man:

> O liberty thou serpent subtil vile,
> How many of my sex dost thou beguile!
> [. . .]
> Wise are wee when we in obedience stand,
> And best we rule when others vs command.   (B3r)

Paulina thus becomes an instrument in the service of a morality which had been questioned, at least in its severest strictures, by her sisters in the elegiac tradition. She is made to denounce the principle of liberty by which she lived, and this stands in the way of a more sympathetic treatment of her experience. In this context, 'liberty', of course, is still far from being a positive term. Even a hundred years later Defoe's Roxana is doubly checked when she professes the principle of 'liberty' to escape the bonds of matrimony. She has to reveal that in reality she acts on account of material interests, 'I was inflexible, and pretended to argue upon the Point of a Woman's Liberty', and she is put right by her wooer, the Dutch merchant: 'Dear Madam, you argue for Liberty at the same time that you restrain yourself from that Liberty, which God and nature has directed you to take'.[23] The clumsiness that mars passages like these results from the form of the first-person narrative: the heroines have to judge their own case from the standpoint of a superior morality; in the last resort, this is, of course, the standpoint of the authors, who make their characters mouthpieces for moral pronouncements. Markham distrusts his instrument as much as Defoe and tries to make his meaning doubly sure: in default of a Dutch merchant, he adds authorial comments on the margin of his poem. These comments sometimes take on a decidedly misogynic air. There is, for instance, a passage in which Paulina reports (in her coarsest strumpet voice) how she cursed her husband when he finally left her:

> May heauens worst plague his ingrau'd bones torment,
> And all besides that hold his president.   (C1r)

In this curse 'heauens worst plague' probably means a venereal disease which she may have passed on to him. Markham adds a marginal note: 'A right passion of a woman and it is called amongst the Italians a curtezans blessing.' There are similar notes, as we have seen, on the margin of Whetstone's *Bianca Maria*.

Comments such as this point to another feature of the courtesan's confession. It professes to be a moral and a cautionary tale. To achieve a deterrent effect, the authors feel obliged to display the dark side of a courtesan's career as drastically as possible, and sometimes the superior moral attitude is weighed down by a preponderance of unsavoury detail. It is, however, this wealth of detail which makes confessions like Paulina's Complaint valuable documents in the hands of those interested in (or simply fond of dabbling in) the more intimate aspects of cultural history. In the nineteenth century works such as Markham's *Famous whore* were published in private press editions by Frederick Ouvry, the eminent antiquarian and friend of Charles Dickens, and probably not only for reasons of their scarcity. Markham seems fascinated, too, by the exotic, and also the sordid aspects of the environment in which his heroine moves. Paulina describes, for example, in great detail the ways and wiles of a courtesan and shows an unusually observant eye for local colours. This 'Ethnicke' interest (to use an expression of Thomas Achelley's) sometimes clashes with the chosen perspective. On the one hand, Markham must not assume his readers to be conversant with Paulina's milieu (the printer, however, expects them to be familiar with English prostitutes and asks them to be courteous to the 'famous strange whore' ('The Printer to the Reader', A3r); on the other hand it would look out of character if Paulina were to explain what must be obvious in her surroundings. To solve this difficulty, Markham again takes recourse to the margin and adds a note of explanation here and there. He tells his readers, for instance, that every respectable Italian prostitute employs three men: a 'Curso' to sustain her, a 'Bravo' to defend her, and a 'Bello' to love her.[24] Explanations like these make the Complaint sound like a soliloquised tale from Aretino's *Ragionamenti*, and the author indirectly acknowledges the affinity: Paulina invokes Aretino's, not Ovid's *Art of Love* as her textbook:

> Briefly, I knew all *Aretine* by rot,
> And had him read and in acquaintance got,
> So that his booke-rules I could well discouer
> To euery ignorant, yet wanton louer,
> Yea thousand waies I knew by learning deepe,
> *Venus* to wake, which else had beene a sleepe.   (C4v)

Towards the end of the poem, with Paulina's career reaching its ebb, the surface realism of the Complaint takes on a shocking character. Paulina describes how she fell from the position of a courtesan to that of a common prostitute and dwells at length on how her lodgings, her customers, and her ailments went from bad to worse. Ironically, her fall is brought about by a 'Bello' whom she is no longer able to keep. The turning point in her career is a scene in which she brews, Medea-like, a love potion with the most revolting ingredients (including 'virgin parchment' and '*Mensis profluuium*', E2r). It does not work, and she is left without means or lover. Soon afterwards a new Pope tries to cleanse the city of Rome of prostitutes, and Paulina finds herself out of her house, and out of work, and on the road – a victim of Paul IV as Mrs Shore was of Richard III. Paulina comments on the moral effect with a Ciceronian 'O tempora, o mores':

> O times, O manners, o vnluckie age,
> O *Rome* once master, now worse than a page!   (F1r)

The Complaint thus ends on an almost ludicrous note which brings back however, regardless of whether Markham wanted this outcry to ring true or false, the antinomian potential inherent in the form. If this ending had been prepared more carefully, Paul's purification campaign might well have looked like the hypocritical penitence Mrs Shore was subjected to by Richard. The components to give the poem a different direction were there: Paulina is sold as a child by her mother, she is robbed by a lover and penalised by a tyrant. A more sympathetic hand might have turned Paulina into one more of love's martyrs. Markham's heroine, however, wavers, like the title of her Complaint, between noble courtesan and famous whore.

Thomas Cranley, *Amanda: or The reformed whore*

One of the characteristic traits of figures such as Violenta or Paulina is their activity; in this they are different from their English counterparts such as Rosamond or Mrs Shore. The structure of the novella is extrovert and asks for rapid action, that of the Complaint is introvert and bent on reflection. As Markham's Paulina shows, it is hard to reconcile these different tendencies. The women of the elegiac Complaint usually see themselves as victims, often as victims of male oppression; in the harlot's confessions this constellation is reversed, and the manipulative faculties of women are exaggerated to mock-heroic disproportions. This inversion of accepted roles is most obvious in a complaint by Thomas Andrewe, *The unmasking of a feminine Machiavell* (1604) which ascribes the role of the tyrant to the wife of a man who appears, like Ariadne, 'In a vast desert all alone' (B1r) to deliver his Complaint.

Such inversions serve a moralising purpose: the perversion of what was thought to be the natural, god-given order of things is emphasised. Markham followed a similar aim with his *Famous whore*, except that in Paulina's final barking at the moon above papal Rome she seems transformed into a latter-day Hecuba. In all probability, however, Markham was far from condoning his heroine's fate and the final gesture was meant to disclose a deluded mind. Nevertheless, there is something pathetic about this end, and even on the lowest plane of dealing with female fates the by now familiar division between the heroic and the elegiac becomes visible. There is a kind of negative heroism on the one hand, meant to inspire not admiration but horror of its Machiavellian threat to the most sacred authorities, and a sort of adulterated pity on the other, a sentimental concern with victims of their own undoing, a concern that sets in only after they have landed in the stews or on the streets. This dissociation is widened in later literature. One further stage in the development of such heroines is the opposition of female characters in tragedies of the eighteenth century, with victims on the one, and fiends on the other hand. Examples are the heroine of Nicholas Rowe's *Jane Shore* (1714), who dies with a prayer on her lips, and the demonic Millwood in George Lillo's *London merchant* (1731), who goes to the gallows with a curse.

As Rowe's tragedy shows, the sentimental approach is easier if the heroine is presented only in the latter stages of her development. Markham's Paulina gives a complete *curriculum vitae*, and the author is mainly interested in the outrageous and titillating aspects of her life; though her end is pitiful, it cannot delete the degrading impressions left by her dissolute life. This, however, is not necessarily so. Another prostitute, aptly named Amanda, found a priestlike figure to accompany her in the latter end of her life in Thomas Cranley, who wrote an apparently popular piece which was twice printed towards the end of our period, first as *Amanda: or The reformed whore* (1635), then as *The converted courtesan: or The reformed whore* (1639). Its lasting appeal is attested by the fact that it, too, was chosen for a private press reprint by Frederick Ouvry in 1889, a time of high concern over the reformation of Amandas.

Cranley's story of Amanda is again presented with a wealth of detail which, were it directed at the same gentlemen as Markham's *Famous whore*, would have had a thoroughly familiar look. It is placed in the heart of the City of London and makes up for its lack in exotic appeal by its realism. The author knows very well what he is doing, both with respect to his poetics and to his material. His Latin motto is *Admiranda canunt, credenda aliquando Poetae*, which he translates as 'Poets doe tell of strange things not a few, / Yet often times those things, though strange, are true' (titlepage, A1r). Cranley is anxious to make his poem credible; he deliberately descends onto a lower plane of realism in order to create a sense of truth rather than of admiration, and he moves into spheres of reality which he knows from personal experience. As he announces on the titlepage, he was a prisoner at the time his booklet went to the press: 'Composed, and made by *Thomas Cranley*: Gent. now a Prisoner in the Kings-bench'. This might be taken as a trick to create credibility or to promote sales were it not confirmed by an episcopal *Imprimatur*:

Iuly 1. 1635

Perlegi hoc opusculum cui titulus (Amanda, or the reformed whore) *quod continet folia 52° aut circiter, in quibus nihil reperio quo minus cum utilitate publica imprimi queant, modo supprimantur quae deleta sunt, & intra sex menses proxime sequentes reliqua typis mandentur.*
      GVILIELMVS HAYVVOOD. RR.P.Arch. Cant. Cap. Dom.   (A2v)

Permissions such as these were not yet required for profane texts; Haywood, one of Laud's domestic chaplains, mainly checked books suspected of overly Roman Catholic leanings, and unless Amanda was mistaken for a veiled Magdalen of Roman origin the book went through the censor's office of Lambeth Palace because its author was awaiting trial at the nearby King's Bench prison.[25] This lends credibility, too, to the account given in the beginning of the book of how the narrator met Amanda while in custody at the Fleet prison. At the time the book was written the Fleet was still a 'prisone for gentylmen' (Sir John Falstaff, one will remember, is sent there after Prince Hal has become King Henry), not the debtor's prison of ill repute it became in 1641.[26] If they could afford to pay for it, prisoners were allowed considerable freedom to move about and be entertained – not only by loose women, but also by respectable ones with perhaps an eye on what was called a Fleet marriage.[27] All of this could apply to Cranley himself, who is called 'gentleman' on the title page and may well have been the prisoner who one day watched an Amanda go about her business from the window of his lodgings in the Fleet as related in his tale. His descriptions are so accurate that Dobb not only takes it for granted that his story is authentic, but also recommends his report as a 'mine of information on the privileges of Fleet prisoners at that period'.[28] This prisoner becomes acquainted with the girl and tries to dissuade her from her dissolute life. He writes her several verse letters; the longest is addressed 'To the faire *Amanda*' and fills the bulk of the book with its 190 rhyme royal stanzas (D3r–I4r). This verse letter is stylised out of the realistic setting, of course, and so is Amanda's answer, inscribed 'The Penitentiall answer of the reformed *Amanda*' (104 stanzas, K1r–M4v) and the two concluding stanzas by the narrator (M4v). The prose introduction and the short prose headings to these letters thus serve no other purpose than the argument to an Ovidian pair of epistles.

The self-appointed shepherd-prisoner in Cranley's book has found his lamb when it was almost lost in the undergrowth of the city. This saves us a detailed account of Amanda's former life. There is little action and no real development; Amanda's conversion is effected in no time, between the two long letters. As in the *Heroides* tradition, the movements of the protagonists are confined to the smallest of rooms: the prisoner's cell and the prostitute's bedroom. These rooms, however, in particular Amanda's boudoir, are described with the same wealth of intimate detail we have found in Markham's *Famous whore*. Though the author dissociates himself from Ovid's erotic tales (Pygmalion, Venus and Adonis, Salmacis and the Hermaphrodite are mentioned specifically, E4v), there is a certain sensuousness in these descriptions (nourished from Ovid's *Remedia amoris* and *Medicamen faciei* rather than his *Metamorphoses*) which only rarely lapses into the bad taste of Markham's (or, for that matter, Swift's) misogynic realism:

> At windowes end, are certaine glasses set,
> Fill'd with rare water, for to make thee faire.
> At tother end, lockt in a Cabinet,
> Are dainty powders for thy hands, and hayre.
> White prick-seam'd Gloves of Kid full many a paire.
>> With them are bags of precious sweete perfume;
>> And Masticke patches for to stay the rhume.   (E4r)

From time to time the windows are opened, and we catch a glimpse of the surroundings of the Fleet and Amanda's former haunts around the city (Westminster, Clerkenwell, the Strand, Shoreditch, Lambeth, Hackney – the girls had to change quarters frequently for fear of raids), or we take a look into the possible future for a girl like her if she were captured and sent to Bridewell for correction: Cranley describes the practices there with what might be thought the inventiveness of a de Sade were they not in all probability true:

> I see (me thinkes) a solemne Congregation
> At Old-Bridevvell, of grave, and solid men,
> Sitting together there in consultation,
> What punishment shall be inflicted then
> On thy polluted corps, and thou agen
>> Standing neere to them in another roome,
>> Trembling with feare, attending of thy doome.
>
> The Iudges on thy pennance there agree'd,
> For executing of their strict command.
> According as they had before decreed,
> A Beedle comes, and takes thee by the hand
> To bring thee forth, and lets thee understand,
>> That thou for all thy bravery, and cost,
>> Must walke with him unto the whipping post.
>
> Whither he brings thee, straightwaies without staying,

Puls off thy robes, and lockes thy hands up fast.
Then to his office, without long delaying,
Thy clothes pul'd down, starke naked to thy waste,
He thereby lets thee understand the taste,
> *Of his smart Whipcord, where there doth imprint*
> *Each lash a seame, and every knot a dint.*

For flourishing with hand above his head,
And shaking of his four limb'd instrument,
In the descent, so learnedly they spread
About thy shoulders, that incontinent
Thy dainty skin, is all sanguinolent,
> *And so he deales his lashes one by one,*
> *Till the set number of his stripes are done,*

Thus being of thy silkes, and Sattins stript,
Exposde to publique shame, and so disgrac'd.
And for thy impudent abuses whipt:
A poore blew gowne upon thy backe is plac'd,
And Canvas coyfe upon thy head unlac'd.
> *Where in that guise thou marchest from the stocke,*
> *And then dost practise Hempe, & and Flax to knocke.*   (I2r–v)

There is a similar warning in one of Thomas Killigrew's almost contemporary comedies, where a character is told that anything 'is better than Bridewell hemp, brown bread and Whip-cord'.[29]

The long description of Bridewell practices is taken from the prisoner's letter to Amanda, and it seems to add only a particularly colourful streak to the boudoir tapestry usually displayed in harlot literature. It also seems designed to feed a superficial curiosity on the part of its reader rather than to serve the moral purpose of deterring Amanda from pursuing her career any further. Cranley does not go about his business as sanctimoniously as might be expected; in his Go-little-book preface he stated expressly that he would rather like the booklet to give pleasure than profit only:

> That may please some, which will not profit all,
> Although my lines are not didacticall.   (A3r)

In the beginning of his letter the narrator gives as his chief motive the pity inspired by first the body, and then the soul, of his catechumen:

In pity therefore of thy wretched state,
And meerely in compaβion of that face,
I vow'd my best, thy life to renovate,
And see if in thy brest there were a place
That would give entertainment unto grace.
> *For doubtlesse in my heart I should condole*

The losse of such a body and a soule. (E1v)

The thread is taken up by Amanda in her reply, which is full of penitence and despair. With its lack of spiritual hope it resembles Magdalen Complaint in more respects than those Amanda mentions:

> *My spotted life hath made me sathans denne,*
> *Fuller of fiends then* Mary Magdalene.
>
> *Her sinnes I doe commit, but want her sorrow,*
> *Of all the ill she had I am possest,*
> *I get the bad, the good I cannot borrow:*
> *I have her vices all, but want the rest.*
> *Her worst acts I embrace, but leave the best.*
>   *My Saviours feete I wash not with my teares,*
>   *Nor (with her) doe I wipe them with my haires.*
>
> *I want the gifts of grace that she had given,*
> *And her repentance, my hard heart to move.*
> *I cannot apprehend the joies of heaven,*
> *Nor love my Saviour with her ardent love,*
> *My hearts desire with hers flies not above.*
>   *I feele no spirituall comfort in my soule,*
>   *Nor can I thoroughly my state condole.* (K4r)

She appeals to the friend not to forsake her, and there might have been a possibility of these two finding a kind of salvation on a private basis. But Cranley opts for a spiritual solution after all. Amanda is converted, asks for a Bible, leaves the house only for church services and dies a couple of years later with a prayer on her lips. It is the solution cherished in plays of fallen women throughout the centuries; they all die with their eyes lifted towards heaven and expecting their final forgiveness there, even if the person they injured here on earth has long forgiven them: from Mrs Frankford in Heywood's domestic tragedy *A woman killed with kindness* (1603) to Mrs Shore in Nicholas Rowe's *Tragedy of Jane Shore* (1714) to the melodramas derived from Mrs Wood's *East Lynne* (1861). It is not only an English solution: Dumas added a spiritual dimension in the dramatic adaptation of his Magdalen novel *La dame aux camélias* (1852) by concluding on a Biblical note: 'Dors en paix, Marguerite! il te sera beaucoup pardonné, parce que tu as beaucoup aimé!'[30] While one suspects Cranley of having glanced at Lambeth when he devised the ending of his Amanda, one must admit that his book looks forward to many another Amanda with Magdalen affiliations.

7   Commiseration and imagination: reflections on the elegiac narrative mode

> Or is it the lamenting Elegiac; which in a kind heart would move rather pity than blame?
>
>   Sir Philip Sidney, *Apology for poetry*

The tragic potential in Complaints

Tragedy curtailed: pity rather than fear (or admiration)

In Thomas Heywood's *Apology for actors* (1612) Melpomene, the Muse of tragedy, takes the stage in the manner of a ghost from the *Mirror for magistrates*;[1] it seems appropriate, then, that the epitheton most often applied to the Complaints discussed in this study is 'tragic'. Richard Robinson says of his Complaint of Medea: 'This history is merveylously tragicall, and a good example for VVomen' (*The reward of wickedness*, 1574, F2v); Thomas Churchyard calls his adaptation of a novella 'A pitefull complaint, in maner of a *Tragedie, of Seignior Anthonio dell Dondaldoes wife*' (*A general rehearsal of wars*, 1579, x2v), its extended version 'A Tragicall Discourse of a dolorous Gentlewoman' (*Churchyard's challenge*, 1593, Gg3v); Thomas Lodge his historical poem *The tragical complaint of Elstred* (1593); Thomas Middleton his *Ghost of Lucrece* (1600) 'Lucrece' tragedy' (line 12), Thomas Sampson his Complaint of Elizabeth Gray a 'tragicall history' (*Fortune's fashion*, 1613, A2r). The qualification is extended to epyllia of the classical kind like Sir David Murray's *The tragical death of Sophonisba* (1611), and even a Biblical heroine such as George Ballard's Susanna speaks of the 'Tragedy' she must 'selfe-act in death and dust' (*The history of Susanna*, 1638, G2v).

In part the latitudinarian concept of tragedy behind these definitions dates back to the Middle Ages when a tragedy was, to quote Chaucer's Monk, 'a certeyn storie, [. . .] Of hym that stood in greet prosperitee, / And is yfallen out of heigh degree / Into myserie'' ('Monk's tale', 1973–7). The medieval concept is latitudinarian with regard to form, not content; not every subject is qualified: the sad stories the Monk goes on to tell speak of 'popes, emperours, or kynges' (1986). We are moving in

223

a man's world; the subtitle places the Monk's collection of tragedies in a predominantly masculine tradition initiated by Boccaccio: 'Heere bigynneth the Monkes Tale De Casibus Virorum Illustrium'. The one woman to have found her way into the club of kings is Queen Cenobia, but the narrator goes out of his way to make us forget her less heroic assets. He stresses her royal descent and her martial achievements ('So worthy was in armes and so keene, / That no wight passed hire in hardynesse', 2,249–50) and he questions her womanly qualities ('I seye nat that she hadde moost fairnesse', 'From hire childhede I fynde that she fledde / Office of wommen', 2,253, 2,255–6). The feminine complement of the Monk's collection, 'the Seintes Legend of Cupide', had been set apart before by the Man of Law and related to Ovid's *Heroides* ('Man of Law's tale', 53–76).

This predilection for the martial and the manly in the world of tragedy is shared by that other monk, John Lydgate, who also introduced such women in his *Fall of princes* only as conform to the Amazon ideal or qualify as *matronae viriles* such as Dido (the mistress of Carthage, not of Aeneas) or Lucretia of Rome. Lydgate bequeathed this heroic spirit to the most influential English collection of *de casibus* tragedies, the *Mirror for magistrates*, which, in its first edition of 1559, contained only Complaints by famous men and none by women, not even Amazons. When eventually the barrier was broken down in the second edition of the *Mirror for magistrates* (1563), not by a Cenobia-like queen but a concubine of low birth, Churchyard's 'Shore's wife', there were protests, most vociferously from Giles Fletcher's Richard III:

> *Shores* wife, a subject, though a princesse mate,
> Had little cause her fortune to lament.
> Her birth was meane, and yet she liv'd with State,
> The King was dead before her honour went.[2]

These invectives are followed by censures against Daniel's Rosamond and Lodge's Elstred, concubines like Mrs Shore and also subjects of Complaints in the *Mirror for magistrates* tradition.

By the end of the sixteenth century the barrier for women entering on a career as tragic heroines had become even higher than before. The influence of classicist theories of tragedy which added to the *a priori* condition of a certain status considerations of the appropriate effect a tragedy should have. Moralising Aristotle's notion of catharsis, Sir Philip Sidney praises 'the high and excellent Tragedy'

> that, with stirring the effects of admiration and commiseration, teacheth the uncertainty of this world, and upon how weak foundations gilden roofs are builded[3]

The terms 'admiration' and 'commiseration' both intensify the emotional effect denoted by their Greek equivalents. 'phobos' ('fear', 'concern') is heightened into admiration, 'eleos' ('pity') into commiseration; the tension becomes visible which will eventually break up the Aristotelian twin formula and develop into the rift between heroic and domestic tragedy.

Sidney's terms 'commiseration' and in particular 'admiration' are already removed to a certain extent from their original meaning. They have gained a demonstrative quality which deviates from the individual concern probably meant to be aroused in a Greek tragedy, and this concern for public virtues intensifies the reservations against the presentation of women as protagonists to be found already in Aristotle's *Poetics*. Despite the example of their Queen, who was idealised into asexual virginity and almost out of humanity, the Elizabethans' idea of femininity pointed towards more private roles of wife and mother; even fallen women were, as Shakespeare's Lucrece puts it in one of her laments, 'the private pleasure of some one', and should not become, like Helen of Troy, 'the public plague of many moe' (*Lucrece*, 1,478–9). As a norm, Elizabethan women found themselves defined by their sex and confined to their domestic duties (though not, perhaps, as strictly as their Victorian descendants). It is not by accident that so many Complaints are spoken in private rooms, and in particular in bedrooms.

There is, of course, a deep irony in the fact that even as women fulfil their sexual roles this brings them down in the world of decorum-bound poetry. They disqualify for parts in all the higher orders of such poetry, be it Petrarchan sonnets, or Spenserian epic, or the high and excellent tragedy. Virginity seems to be a prerequisite for these parts. Such rules of decorum are not the invention of medieval ascetics; they are rooted deeper even than the Christian aversion to the world of the flesh and the devil and may be based on archetypal notions which I am unqualified to assess – I can only describe their literary connotations. Geoffrey Chaucer, one of the least ascetic of medieval authors, applies these rules not only to his virgin martyr Cecilia, who refuses her husband Valerian his marital rights and warns him of an avenging angel (one suspects Chaucer's sympathies to be with Valerian, who demands 'Lat me that aungel se', 'Second Nun's tale', 164), but also to Cenobia, who allows her husband Odenatus to lie with her but once or twice,

> for thus she seyde,
> It was to wyves lecherie and shame,
> In oother caas, if that men with hem pleyde. ('Monk's tale', 2,292–4)

Chaucer may be tongue-in-cheek in these instances, and one suspects that in such passages he tried to expose the extremes of modesty dictated to women in the decorum-ruled higher forms of narratives. These rules allow only for love of the Platonic kind in tragedies and legends. Making love in the modern, unromantic sense is banished to genres like the fabliau or the farce. Even if a heroine merely suffers it, that rules her out of the higher orders of literature and banishes her to those called 'low mimetic' by Northrop Frye.[4] Chaucer knew the rules, and he had to devise a new kind of legend for his martyrs of love, the *Legend of good women*. Churchyard did something similar later on, when he removed his Complaint of 'Shore's wife' out of the *Mirror for magistrates* because he realised it constituted a new genre.

The rules applying to the heroic and ascetic tradition are outlined in no uncertain terms by George Rivers when this tradition was gaining the upper hand in the course of the seventeenth century:

THe *Heroïna* hath nothing of woman in her but her sex, nothing of sex but her body, and that dispos'd to serve, not rule her better part. [. . .] She understands not the common conceit of love, nor entertaines that familiarity with man that hee may hope it. [. . .] If shee marry, it is onely to propagate; the very act tending thereto shee singles from the thought of sinne.   (*The Heroinae*, 1639, I2r–3v)[5]

Love, then, if consummated, not directed at some ideal, is common. This looks Platonic, but Aristotle, too, had his doubts about love and woman as subjects for a tragedy; apparently not even the passionate women tragedies of Euripides, which he knew, could convince him of their suitability (see chapter 15 of his *Poetics*).[6] Arbiters of the epic held similar reservations with regard to pathetic heroines. Servius, the eminent fourth-century grammarian and influential commentator on Virgil dispraised the most popular Book IV of the *Aeneid* on the grounds that it treats of affection and therefore verges on the comic:

est autem totus paene in affectione, licet in fine pathos habeat, ubi abscessus Aeneae gignit dolorem. Sane totus in consiliis et subtilitatibus est; nam paene comicus stilus est; nec mirum ubi de amore tractatur[7]

Servius would have disapproved of Leo's dictum that the story of Dido and Aeneas is the only Roman tragedy worthy of the title. For high-minded critics women like Dido were unable to command the admiration reserved for epic and tragic heroes. They may be able to command, for a short while, emperors or emperors to be and thus prove the power of love, but eventually they have to stand back and leave their lovers to their imperial duties – or else be blamed for standing in their way. At best they are the subjects for poems 'on an humbler theme . . . / A Melancholy tale of private woes', as Nicholas Rowe classes the subject of his *Fair penitent*. By the time Rowe wrote the prologue to this play (1703), the dissociation of the emotions ascribed to a tragedy by Aristotle had set in and Rowe was about to specialise on arousing commiseration in a series of she-tragedies, one of them his *Tragedy of Jane Shore* (1714).

It is commiseration of a kind different from the pity associated with tragedy in the classical sense. Though imbued with an almost religious intensity by Rowe (his Jane Shore is compared to the Magdalen in the final scene of her tragedy), commiseration is a private feeling (Jane Shore takes leave of her husband in that final scene). For Sidney, high tragedy is concerned with public issues, where pity is of doubtful value, and so is the epic. Spenser, too, seems suspicious of the effects of pity in affairs of state: Mercilla, one of the embodiments of Queen Elizabeth in the *Faerie queene*, is allowed only a few secret tears when sitting in judgment over Duessa (alias Mary Stuart); they have to be wiped away with imperial purple:

> But she, whose Princely breast was touched nere
> With piteous ruth of her so wretched plight,
> Though plaine she saw by all, that she did heare,
> That she of death was guiltie found by right,
> Yet would not let iust vengeance on her light;
> But rather let in stead thereof to fall
> Few perling drops from her faire lampes of light;
> The which she couering with her purple pall
> Would haue the passion hid, and vp arose withall.
>
> (*Fairie queene*, V, ix, 50)

Compassion counts among the passions to be avoided in the field of public duties, and justice comes before mercy. Mercilla acts as a judge in the passage quoted, and a judge in particular must not be carried away, as Archbishop Sandys put it in a sermon of 1585: 'The judge may not give place to commiseration: his place is a place of equity, not of foolish pity.'[8] Pity is not only foolish but potentially dangerous; it can be aroused by sirens intent on glancing a hero off the path of duty. Guyon is warned to shun such sirens by Spenser's Pilgrim:

> when she your courage hath inclind
> Through foolish pitty, then her guilefull bayt
> She will embosome deeper in your mind,
> And for your ruine at the last awayt.   (*Faerie queene*, II, xii, 29)

The same analogy was used, as we have seen, against Elianor Cobham in the anonymous 'Complaint for my lady of Gloucester' and later on against Jane Shore and others; these sirens and witches, however, are the subjects of women's Complaints which are being written alongside the *Faerie queene* and by poets also working in the heroic tradition such as Daniel and Drayton, and in these Complaints they are given more than a fair hearing and more than a few secret tears. They follow their own set of rules, based, as it were, on an inversion of 'Quod licet Iovi':

Io is allowed what Iuno must condemn. Sidney acknowledges the different laws reigning in the lamenting Elegiac, 'which in a kind heart would move rather pity than blame', though in his view the elegiac, too, must be restricted to what is just and what is right. He praises it 'either for compassionate accompanying just causes of lamentation, or for rightly painting out how weak be the passions of woefulness':[9] one should keep in mind that he is out to defend poetry against the allegation that it incites passionate instead of reasonable responses. His colleagues working in the elegiac line are under no such obligation. They write Complaints for Rosamond or Mary Stuart, professed sirens and sinners, and hardly repentant ones at that.

The new set of rules applies not only to worldly poetry, but also to divine, and Complaints can look back not only to classical masters of the elegiac mode like Ovid, but also to medieval ones like the Pseudo-Origen, who in his *Omelia* had pleaded for mercy instead of justice for the erring Magdalen:

igitur misericors & juste judex, amor, quem habebat in te, & dolor, quem habebat pro te, excuset eam apud te, si forte erret de te: nec attendas ad mulieris errorem, sed ad discipulae amorem: quae non pro errore, sed pro dolore, & amore plorabat[10]

In Southwell's treatise *Marie Magdalen's funeral tears*, which is based on the *Omelia Origenis*, tears are allowed to plead and are sure to succeed with the highest judge: 'But fear not, *Mary*, for thy tears will obtaine. They are too mighty orators.'[11]

In all of the different fields investigated in this study the elegiac mode is set against the heroic, heroines are set against heroes, and commiseration against admiration. The private point of view is at least temporarily allowed to dominate, subordinate characters are, for once, allowed to defend their case. In Daniel's *Complaint of Rosamond* it is a concubine against a queen, in Chute's *Beauty dishonoured* a wife against her husband, in Sampson's *Fortune's fashion* a mother against a host of politicians, in Markham's *Marie Magdalen's lamentations* the lover against the Messiah. The women of Complaints are up against adversaries of inhuman or superhuman powers – the powers we are asked to admire in heroic forms of poetry. In the literature of complaint we are asked instead to immerse in feelings, and to stay submerged: there is little striving after the uplifting or cleansing effect expected from epic or tragic poetry. The emotions of pity, grief and fear which dominate in Complaints are traditionally regarded as inferior; the Pseudo-Longinus considers them too mean to raise the soul to sublimity (*On the sublime*, chapter VIII). Heroines in the higher regions of poetry find an outlet for their grievances in heroic deeds (and be it suicide), or at least to vent their fury like

Euripides' Medea or Virgil's Dido. The monologue of Scylla in Ovid's *Metamorphoses*, for instance, develops into fury, 'consumptis precibus violentam transit in iram' (VIII, 106); the lament of Spenser's Britomart dissolves in the encounter with Marinell, 'Her former sorrow into suddein wrath' (*Faerie queene*, III, iv, 12, 6). Heroines in the elegiac tradition lack courage, hope and counsel, and sometimes even speech, to relieve their situation, and the listener is asked to commiserate:

omne consilium in ea perierat, spes omnis defecerat: solummodo flere supererat. Flebat ergo quia flere poterat.[12]

Losing heart and searching soul: tragedy on the inner stage

The feeling the listener to a woman's Complaint is asked to share is, above all, one of helplessness. We usually find the complainant in a situation of impasse, unable to act or even to move at will. It is, in the extreme, the situation Aristotle ascribes to women in general in chapter 15 of his *Poetics*, and the main reason for his doubts about their suitability as protagonists in a tragedy. Aristotle had defined tragedy as the 'representation of an action that is worth serious attention' (chapter 6), and women's lives are, 'in general, insignificant' (chapter 15). Furthermore, a tragic action, for Aristotle, 'is that which reveals in personal choice the kinds of things a man chooses or rejects' (chapter 15), and this, again, is denied to women – if not women in general, then certainly the sort of women speaking in Complaints.

Actions and decisions want room, but room, both in its literal and in its figurative sense, is what complainants lack. They are confined in their actions; decisions are taken or have been taken by their antagonists. Some of their most frequent exclamations, 'quid faciam' or 'hadde I wist' or their modern equivalents, bear witness to this confinement; Helmut Hross, in his dissertation on forsaken women in Latin poetry, inscribes two of his chapters with similar formulae from the *Carmen* No. 64 by Catullus which provides the *locus classicus* for situations like theirs: the island of Naxos, where Ariadne is left behind by Theseus.[13] Most of the women whose Complaints we have analysed find themselves sooner or later in similarly desolate surroundings: Philomel in the forest of Thracia, Rosamond in her labyrinth, the Magdalen facing the empty tomb, Bianca Maria the gallows. The heroines of Complaints in the stricter form of the *Mirror for magistrates* fare little better: they speak from beyond their graves, if not, like Sampson's Elizabeth Gray, out of it: 'You see her newly risen out of her graue, and in the extremity of her griefe speaking as followeth' (*Fortune's fashion*, A3v).

The situation in which we find these women, then, is one of the utmost passiveness; they suffer or have suffered their fates, and passive suffering, as Yeats is said to have remarked, is not a theme for poetry.[14] It is certainly not a subject fit for tragedy in the classical sense. Complaints do not present tragic complications, but at best situations overcast by a sense of tragic loss. Their structure is static, actions are only remembered or reconsidered. The sense of desolation evoked in Complaints is even stronger than that in Ovid's *Heroides*, where the letter-writers have moments of hope. In epic and dramatic poetry scenes of lament are bound up with actions; some of the Senecan tragedies, for instance, which have left their mark on the *Mirror for magistrates*, begin with lengthy laments. Julius C. Scaliger prescribes such a beginning in his draft for a tragedy of *Ceyx and Alcyone*, 'Primus actus esto conquestio', and this was imitated by Elizabethan and Jacobean classicists. Plays written under French influence such as Thomas Kyd's *Pompey the Great* (1594, a translation of Robert Garnier's *Cornelia*), Samuel Daniel's *Cleopatra* (1594), and Samuel Brandons *Octavia* (1598) contain strings of lamentations; Lady Elizabeth Carew's *Tragedy of Mariam* (1613) has a first act lament which exactly answers Scaliger's prescription.[15]

Dramatic laments, however, like epic lamentations, initiate an action, or comment on it, but plays or epics do not end with them. The elegiac poet takes up the loose ends of stories left in tragedies and epics, like Henryson adding his *Testament of Cresseid* to Chaucer's *Troilus and Criseyde* (this was in turn finished off, probably by William Fowler, in a 'Last Epistle of Creseyd to Troyalus'), or Middleton giving the *novissima verba* to the ghost of Shakespeare's Lucrece. The procedure is similar to that chosen by Ovid for his *Heroides*: the letter-writers there are put in situations taken from ancient epics or tragedies, and they are left alone. This, too, was imitated by Elizabethan writers in the elegiac mode: Samuel Brandon publishes a double letter, 'Octavia to Antonius, Antonius to Octavia' with his *Tragicomedy of the virtuous Octavia* (1598), Daniel adds a 'Letter sent from Octavia to her husband Marcus Antonius into Egypt' to his *Tragedy of Cleopatra* (1599). The speakers of laments are never as isolated as letter-writers or the speakers of Complaints. The execrations of Queen Margaret in Shakespear's *Richard III*, for example, are hurled against the tyrant and, if they do not hurt on the spot, they at least come true in the end.[16] Furthermore, the laments in this play have, as has often been observed, a ritual quality: the queens find support and comfort in each other's wailings. In the field of religious drama, this choric effect is matched by the groups of women lamenting under the cross; the 'lugete' or 'plange mecum' formulae indicate their corporate quality. In contrast, the isolation in Complaints such as that of Elizabeth Gray or Jane Shore is unrelieved, and the tyranny they indict is the more terrible for not being visible on the stage. The Magdalen, too, is left alone at the tomb in the *Omelia Origenis* tradition, and her isolation is intensified rather than diminished by the various abortive attempts at communicating with the angel or the 'gardener' or the *noli-me-tangere* Christ.

Epic lamentations are as firmly woven into action as dramatic laments. Usually they lead up to a resolution to act. The lament of Britomart, for instance, in Spenser's *Faerie queene* (III, iv), though spoken against a Naxos-like background ('vpon the rocky shore', stanza 7), is cut short not only by Britomart's manly courage ('She shut vp all her plaint in priuy griefe; / For her great courage would not let her weepe', stanza 11), but also by the arrival of Marinell which causes Britomart's 'former sorrow' to dissolve 'into suddein wrath' (stanza 12). Richard Heinze has shown that, in spite of the to-and-fro in the heroines' deliberations, such monologues in epic poems as those of Medea or Scylla in Ovid's *Metamorphoses* (VII, 11–71; VIII, 44–80) result in definite and rational resolutions. He has contrasted them with the inconclusive wavering of Tarpeia's complaint in Propertius (Elegy IV,4) or the Pseudo-Virgilian *Ciris*.[17] He could just as easily have chosen letters from the *Heroides* as counterparts.

great epics of the English Renaissance as Spenser's *Faerie queene*, but also in epyllia. The essentially reasonable and conclusive nature of such monologues is clearly discernible in Murray's *Sophonisba*, where the decisive monologue of the heroine is conducted in the well ordered ranks of a *bellum intestinum*, with no uncertain outcome:

> Yet in this sad and silent agonie,
> While life and honor furiously contend,
> Enters braue Courage with audacitie,
> And giues this inward strife a fatall end,
> And Honors high attempt doth so commend,
>   That in despite of what her life could say,
>   Makes her resolu'd to die without delay.   (C7r)

The same spirit of honour decides, as we have seen, the 'see-saw pathopoeia', as Anthony LaBranche has termed it, of the laments in Shakespeare's *Lucrece*.[18] The contemplation of scenes on the battlefield of Troy spurs Shakespeare's heroine into action, her final suicide is not, I think, undertaken 'out of a kind of despair', as Ian Donaldson sees it.[19] In her last words, Lucrece gives an exhortation to all knights and an example for all ladies: her end is meant to make sense. The opposite view is taken by Middleton's Lucrece: she has fallen into despair, as I have tried to show, and there are neither words nor actions in her Complaint to relieve it. The epic and the elegiac points of view are complementary, or rather: the one seems to generate the other, the classical epic Ovid's

Heroides, the Germanic epic Old English elegies, Chaucer's *Troilus and Criseyde* Henryson's *Testament of Cresseid*, Shakespeare's *Lucrece* Middleton's *Ghost of Lucrece*, and so on.

Being condemned to passivity and driven into isolation, the women of Complaints are thrown back on their own resources, and that means mainly their passionate feelings. These feelings are pent up like those of Ovid's Hermione, who feels ready to burst:

> rumpor, et ora mihi pariter cum mente tumescunt,
> pectoraque inclusis ignibus usta dolent.   (*Heroides*, VIII, 57–8)

Hermione's passions may be as violent as those of Virgil's Dido, but there is no room in which she could vent them, no person at whom she could throw them. Pent in their various prison-walls, the looks of these heroines are turned inwards and backwards; theirs are, I think, the interminable debates and the moral uncertainties Donaldson ascribes to Shakespeare's heroine (pp. 43, 44).

The poets in the *Heroides* tradition make use of the more emotional, and less rational, quality of their heroines' discourse to experiment with less firm and less elaborate forms of diction. There is less allegory, for example, in Complaints than in epyllia, and the moral issues debated are less well defined. The *bellum intestinum*, if there is one, is fought out not between vices and virtues or reason and passion, but between different forces of a less spiritual and more emotional or even physical order like duty and desire, or fear of death and motherly care. The dilemmas of this lower moral order are more often doubtful to the end, if not insoluble like the paradoxes of the necessary corruption of innocence and beauty. The infirmity of the moral structure of women's Complaints is not so much a matter of gender (though Elizabethans may have seen it that way), but of perspective. It is the introspective view, not the female voice, which brings about the moral uncertainty characteristic in the best of the Complaints and distinguishes them from the more stable forms of drama and epic.

Wolfgang Iser has outlined comparable distinctions with respect to the influence of Puritan diaries, which are written in similar isolation (if not in prison like Bunyan's *Grace abounding to the chief of sinners*, 1666), on the development of the early English novel. What Iser describes as one of the major effects of the introspective view, namely its humaneness, is anticipated, if not surpassed, in the Complaints we have anlysed.[20] Puritan diaries are written with at least a hope of finding out the ways of God with man and a striving for the *certitudo salutis*. The women in some of our Complaints have long despaired of such aims, and they are reduced to the utterly human cry of Middleton's Lucrece: 'O Divinity, / Where art thou fled?' (92–3). They are overwhelmed not so much by *taedium vitae*, but, in a more spiritual sense than Virgil's Dido, by *taedium caeli*. Even if visited by heavenly messengers such as Mercury or the angel in Gethsemane, they refuse to give up their human perspective. One might claim that these Complaints (or the affiliated forms the elegiac narrative found in the later seventeenth century such as the *Lettres portugaises*) did as much to dissolve the epic frame of thought and expression as the Puritan diaries and thus helped prepare the way for such novels as Defoe's *Moll Flanders* or *Roxana* with their decidedly down-to-earth point of view.

Plain style and broken structure

The modest eloquence of women's Complaints

The fact that the elegiac narrative points forward to both the tragedies and the novels of the early eighteenth century is in accordance with what rhetoricians of the Middle Ages and the Renaissance had to say about the elegiac mode. They took the term 'elegiac' in neither its ancient metrical nor in its modern mournful sense, but used it for one of the major genres of poetry, side by side with the epic and the drama.[21] In Eberhard of Bremen's *Laborintus* the elegiac metre is held to be appropriate for Complaints and placed between verse forms suited for historical and lyrical subjects. In an early gloss to the same tract the term 'Elegia' is set alongside comedy and tragedy.[22] Later on the humanist Lilius Gregorius Gyraldus in his *De poetis nostrorum temporum* places the elegiac between the heroic and the lyrical.[23] To Friedrich Beißner these and other instances suggest that the elegiac was looked at as a mode of expression like the lyrical, the epic and the dramatic rather than a literary genre.[24] In French Renaissance literature the development of an elegiac genre was stimulated by Ovid's poetry (the *Heroides* rather than the *Amores* or the *Tristia*) and settled on a tone of complaint; 'de sa nature l'Élégie est triste et flébile' is Sebillet's definition in his *Art poétique françois*.[25] A landmark in this development is the *Heroides*-translation by Octovien de St Gelais which also served as copy to the author of the English 'Letter of Dydo to Eneas'.[26]

Sidney places his characterisation of the 'lamenting Elegiac' in a line with definitions of the pastoral, the comic, the lyric and the heroic. This indicates a similarly wide concept of the elegiac as those we found on the Continent, at least in theory. But Sidney's is only one definition. There are others in Elizabethan treatises on poetry and rhetoric which vary from the formal to the modal, and the latter ones comprise the playful as well as the passionate.[27] In practice, the term 'elegy' is frequently used to denote the querulous mode of Complaints: George Gascoigne calls his *Complaint of Philomene* (1576) 'an elegye, or sorrowefull song' (Dedication, I4r), Thomas Lodge's Elstred (*Elstred*, 1593) weeps 'Elegies of sorrow' (line 445) with her daughter Sabrina, Anthony Chute speaks of 'passionate Elegies' in the dedication of his *Beauty dishonoured* (1593, A2r), and an admirer of Markham's *Marie Magdalen's lamentations* (1601) describes them as 'seau'n mournfull Elegies' (Ad Autorem', A3r).

More important than these scattered remarks is the fact that the elegiac narrative mode has its own voice and is most readily discernible if this voice is female. In epic and dramatic poetry it is usually drowned or brought to accord with the Olympian grumbling of 'varium et mutabile semper / femina' (*Aeneid*, IV, 569–70) or the devilish chuckling of 'shallow, changing woman' (*Richard III*, IV, iv, 431). However, take Dido out of the *Aeneid* or Elizabeth Gray out of *Richard III* and they almost necessarily speak a language different from the *sesquepedalia verba* of Virgil's epic or the stichomythic verse of Shakespeare's drama. The rhythmic effect may not be exactly the same as that of the uneven distich, Horace's 'versibus impariter iunctis querimonia', but it is, in other respects, just as broken and as limping[28] – and sometimes literally so: one of the most often used stylistic devices is to have the female voice break up under emotional strain and to render its utterance *semifractis verbis*. It is an age-old, and an ageless, device; Heinze contrasts Lucretia's halting speeches in Ovid's *Fasti* with the grandiloquence of Philomela in his *Metamorphoses*;[29] its significance for T.S. Eliot and modern poetry in general has lately been discussed at length by Charles Tomlinson.[30] The broken voice had become a topos in tracts on the Magdalen; Lancelot Andrewes gives it a special term in his 'Sermon on the resurrection' of 1620 when he speaks of her unintelligible answers to the risen Christ: 'This is *solecismus amoris*, an irregular speech, but love's own Dialect'.[31]

In his *Art poétique françois* Sebillet had demanded a simple style, 'de style plus populaire', 'Simplement et nuément', for the elegy, and he had based this demand on Ovid's epistles.[32] English Renaissance poets refer to the rules of decorum when they assign a plain style to elegiac poetry. The manner of a Complaint should be 'correspondant plaine and passionate, much like a mourning garment', says Joseph Cresswell in the foreword to his *Saint Marie Magdalens conversion* (1603, A1v), and we have noted similar claims in secular poems before.[33] Eloquence is a characteristic of seducers like Aeneas and Richard; 'credidimus blandis, quorum tibi copia, verbis', Phyllis writes to Demophoon (*Heroides*, II, 49), and Middleton's Lucrece accuses herself of not having seen through Tarquin's 'colour of deceit' (*Ghost of Lucrece*, 394); the first of these seducers, as we are frequently reminded, was Satan in disguise:

> THe Devill want's no orators in time

Of old, he could make Serpents plead for him
In wily arguments   (Ballard, *Susanna*, E7r)

There is, however, a contradiction of theory and practice not only in epyllia such as Shakespeare's *Lucrece*, where the 'modest eloquence' (563) of the heroine contrasts sharply with the heightened rhetoric of her set speeches, but also in Complaints where more is displayed than the 'sad silence' of tears (Patrick Hannay, *The Nightingale*, line 1,538). In part, the immodest amount of eloquence results from the situation in which Complaints are spoken: shut off from the world of action, the speakers can do little else but 'with wast woordes to feede [a] mournful mynde' (like Elianor Cobham in Ferrers' Complaint)[34] or to address an unappreciative posterity. This gives their speeches an additional, but irresolute urgency, and clashes occur almost inevitably between the outward-looking, rhetorical and the inward-looking, reflective parts of their speeches. And both kinds of addresses require a degree of self-consciousness that can look ill-suited in a situation fraught with frustrated emotions.

The affected simplicity shown in some of the Complaints is a well-known device in forensic oratory. It is prescribed, for instance in Cicero's *Art of rhetoric*, as a means of special pleading in cases where the fault or crime itself cannot be denied. The forensic situation resembles the position of many of the complainants, in particular those of a dubious character such as the concubines. Cicero recommends that in such cases one should plead guilty (the tactics based on the 'ubi confessio, ibi remissio' rule), but claim in addition to have been tricked or pushed into the offence, 'aut stultitia, aut impulsu alicuius [. . .] fecisse quod fecerit' (Cicero, *De inventione*, 106). This is exactly what most defendants do in their Complaints. They call themselves 'silly maid' or 'harmless lamb' and compare their antagonists to wolves or tigers. In earlier usage, the term 'silly' still carries the meaning of innocence, if not blessedness, as in Chaucer's outcry in the 'Legend of Dido', 'O sely wemen, ful of innocence' (*Legend of good women*, 1254). This meaning is revived in an act of special pleading by culprits who ultimately claim to be exempt from the normal strictures of justice. The argument of utter, and irresponsible, simplicity is widely used in literature dealing with women on the defensive, and sometimes with the strongest or the most seductive, from Ovid's Medea ('Haec animum . . . movere puellae / simplicis', *Heroides*, XII, 89–90) to Mary Stuart in the *Legend of Mary, queen of Scots* ('a silly harmlesse lamb', 197), to Dryden's Cleopatra in *All for love* ('A wife, a silly, harmless, household dove', IV, 92), Richardson's Clarissa ('foolish creature that I was, and every way beset', *Clarissa*, vol. I, p. 475) and

William Morris's Guenevere, who pleads in court to have lost her head at least 'half mad with beauty' (*Defence of Guenevere*, line 109).

Classical rhetoric provided precepts how to find emotive words of extenuation and how to adapt them to different cases under such heads as *prosopopoeia, pathopoeia, ethopoeia* and *eidolopoeia*. The influence of such precepts on elegiac literature, and in particular on Ovid's *Heroides*, has been discussed *in extenso* by classical scholars.[35] With respect to the Complaints analysed in this study the term *pathopoeia* (as used in judicial rhetoric) would seem most appropriate since it is related to the figure of *conquestio*, complaint, and aims at arousing compassion in a judge. The distinctions between the different terms, however, were never quite convincing, and they were hopelessly confused in Renaissance treatises.[36] Nevertheless, some of the definitions in Elizabethan rhetorical treatises fit in precisely with what some of the complainants produce, although I do not think the poets used these treatises as textbooks. In some cases it was the other way round; the definition of *prosopopoeia* that Henry Peacham gives in his *Garden of eloquence* (1577) may well be written with one of the *Mirror for magistrates* ghosts in mind:

PRosopeia, the fayning of a person, [. . .] this figure Orators vse as well as Poets, [. . .] and sometime they rayse as it were the deade agayne, and cause them to complayne or to witnesse that they knew.   (O3r)

Peacham's definition of *pathopoeia* seems to describe the apologetic tendency of *Mirror for magistrates* Complaints:

The other is, when the Oratour by lamenting some pittiful case, maketh his hearers to weepe, and also mooueth them to pittye, and mercy, & to pardon offences. To make men weepe, lamentable Hystoryes doe serue, and lykewyse Poets complayntes, may geue good examples to moue men to pittye, and to pardon offences   (P3r)

Aphthonius and the English adaptors of his *Progymnasmata* (rhetorical school exercises) quoted complaints of Hebuca, Andromeda and Medea as examples for the figure of *ethopoeia*.[37] The term *prosopopoeia*, which originally covered only orations by non-human beings or objects, such as animals or towns, lends itself readily to satirical purposes as in Spenser's *Prosopopoia: or Mother Hubbard's tale* which Spenser published together with his equally satirical other *Complaints* (1591). Spenser's usage is conservative, though; Erasmus of Rotterdam had already applied the term to Ovid's *Heroides*,[38] and Thomas Lodge applied it to his prose lament *Prosopopeia: Containing the tears of the holy, blessed, and sanctified Marie, the mother of God* (1596), which, like Southwell's *Marie Magdalen's funeral tears* (1591), is based on medieval treatises on the Passion. Lodge specifically mentions the *Lamentacio Bernardi* in his preliminary letters, but claims to have read the works of twenty-five church-fathers besides; the anonymous *De arte lacrimandi*, subtitled *Prosopopeia B. Virginis* (Harley MS 2274), rather than a treatise on rhetoric, may have provided the title. Later on, Martin Parker, the ballad writer, applied the term *prosopopoeia* to his Philomela Complaint, *The nightingale warbling forth her own disaster* (1632).

Despite these various correspondences (and there are more), the rhetorical handbooks do as little to elucidate Elizabethan Complaints as classical *progymnasmata* do to explain Ovid's *Heroides*, or homiletic manuals do meditations such as the *Omelia Origenis*. Rhetoric is always extroverted, directed at a public, it is calculated for an active effect, whereas Complaints and, to a certain extent, letters and meditations, too, are ultimately introspective or retrospective and, at least seemingly, naive. They are, to use one more rhetorical term, pathopoeic in the literal sense: they stir up emotions and work on the imagination: 'commiseratio' and 'imaginatio' are its most important qualities according to Veltkirchius, who wrote a commentary on the *De copia* of Erasmus (he names Book IV of the *Aeneid* as an example for pathopoeic writing). Erasmus himself had mentioned Phaedra, Medea, and Dido as essentially pathetic figures in his *Ecclesiastes*. Richard Sherry also uses the terms 'commiseratio' and 'imaginatio' to distinguish between two kinds of *pathopoeia* in his *Treatise of schemes and tropes* (1550):

The sixt kynde of rethoricall descripcion is *Pathopeia*, that is expressyng of vehement affeccions and perturbacions, of the whych ther be two sortes. The fyrste called *Donysis*, or intencion, and some call it imaginacion, wherby feare, anger, madnes, hatered, enuye, and lyke other perturbacions of mynde is shewed and described [. . .] Another forme is called *Oictros*, or commiseracion, wherby feares be pyked out, or pyty is moued, or forgeuenes.[39]

The self-reflective structure of Complaints

The emotive quality inherent in certain descriptions serves different aims in poetical and rhetorical usage. A sermon, for instance, like a plea in court, moves to some positive goal, the correction of a vice or the prevention of further crimes, whereas the broken rhetoric of a Complaint moves, as we have seen, in circles or into dead ends. The less straightforward movement of poetic *pathopoeia* renders it rather suspect to the guardians of positive laws or an active faith; it also has its negative consequences for the passive Complaint. The circular movement leads to repetitions and ultimate futility, and one might be forgiven for asking with one of Nicholas Breton's tormented souls what the exercise is good for:

But why shall I tell this tale? who takes pleasure in a Tragedie? [. . .] and can my griefe by any thing eased by laying my miseries before me? why? they say, that the eye sees not, the heart rues not [. . .] and can I chuse to see my selfe? and by sight of my selfe, to bring in memorie the sorrowes that I neuer put out of my mind. What need I then to record, that I cannot but remember?

(*The miseries of Mavillia*, 1597, Aa4r–v)

Apart from these drawbacks, the essentially reflective structure of Complaints has its advantages. It enables a poet to exploit the fields of emotion and of imagination to an extent less easily attainable in more stable or progressive forms. The now obsolete expression 'Brainish' which Drayton uses to censure love complaints in the preface to his *England's hero-ical epistles* (1597)[40] pinpoints this reflective quality exactly. For Drayton, this brainish quality is dangerous; he is suspicious of the corrosive effect of the egocentric movement of the 'amorous Humor' in his epistles and seeks to stay it by interlacing 'Matters Historicall' and, one might add, by counterbalancing the single letters with replies. In contrast with Drayton's pairs of letters, the movement in Complaints like that of his rival Daniel is an unsteady to-and-fro between the rival claims of some universal authority and personal longings, or between rueful memories and doubts about the future. The 'trauailing phansies' of Southwell's Magdalen (K1r) thus waver between love and duty when she is sent on her mission:

Thus dutie leading, and loue withholding her, shee goeth as fast backeward in thought as forward in pace, readie eftsoones to faint for griefe, but that a firm hope to see him againe did support her weakenesse.

(*Marie Magdalen's funeral tears*, I7v)

Middleton's Lucrece is virtually torn apart between past and future: she relives the moment of her shame and nourishes dreams of a paradise regained. The hopes and dreams are occasioned by a present (in the case of this Lucrece, an everlasting present) which seems barred; they are, therefore, futile imaginations, and they intensify the feeling of unfulfilled desire that already constitutes the classical elegy.[41] In Complaints of the *Mirror for magistrates* type, where time is suspended altogether because the speakers come from the dead, this feeling can be condensed into utter despair: not even suicide, the heroical option (and ultimate action) remains open for the *Ghost of Lucrece*. This option forbids itself, of course, for Christian heroines such as the Magdalen; in Markham's *Marie Magdalen's lamentations* she is made to say:

> How vvilling vvould I be to stop lifes breath,
> If I might poynt the manner of my death?   (B4v)[42]

The short-circuit or to-and-fro movement of Complaints which finds its appropriate expression in broken sentences, aimless questions and futile wishes often makes the complainant appear like a person not only distracted but about to disintegrate, 'My wits destraught, . . . / My thoughts let loose and fled I know not where', as Markham's Marie puts it (C4r). The corresponding manner of speech is the broken language, or the language of gestures, often ascribed to these women in distress. The Magdalen of the Pseudo-Origen tradition is a speaking picture of this tendency again: in Gervase Markham's *Lamentations* she distrusts language altogether and at one point is made to struggle through her speechlessness for half a dozen stanzas (F3v–4r).

The retreat from an ordered, but heartless outside world into heartfelt, but chaotic emotions can lead to the brink of madness – madness not in any modern psychological sense, but different older ones: it leads into a situation outside the common bounds of humanity. The howling of Hecuba is but an extreme sign of this exclusion. The more common cipher is the wilderness so often evoked in Complaints. The women need not be placed on an island like Ariadne or in the forests like Philomela to be aware of their exclusion. In English Complaints the wilderness is often only imagined, and conjured up to provide a means of identification with a mythical heroine as in Daniel's *Complaint of Rosamond*. Ovid provided most of the scenery for such imaginary flights, not only with the wilderness of his *Metamorphoses*, but also with the more intimate haunted groves mentioned with a mixture of memory and desire by Dido, Medea, and Sappho in the *Heroides* (VII, 93–4; XII, 67–8; XV, 137–45). An early Gothic example of such scenery is to be found in Alexander Pope's epistle of 'Eloisa to Abelard' (1717) which intensified the eighteenth-century cult of grots and ruins.[43]

The imagined sceneries in Complaints sometimes look like backcloths to early melodramas in which the speakers stylise themselves into the roles of their legendary ancient models. Thus Mary Stuart compares her first meeting with Darnley to the 'bane' Dido received on the arrival of Aeneas:

> From first I saw this new arrived guest,
> (Poor Didoes bane) I lodg'd him in my breast.

Thomas Underdowne somewhat anachronistically introduces the same motif into his otherwise modernised Ariadne story:

> I bancketted this Traytours men,
> I vittayled them with store[44]

There are similar opportunities for wishful or fearful thinking in the religious Complaints we have come across; the soul in Breton's *Passions of the spirit* believes she is in purgatory at one moment, and in paradise the next.

If these identifications seem somewhat theatrical, the loss of home and of identity which occasioned them is better founded. Most of the heroines in Complaints are exiles of some sort; like Ariadne and Medea they have fled (and betrayed) their families to follow their loves and feel doubly betrayed now by their lovers. The motif is applied even to a Christian heroine like Mary Magdalen. She also left her home town, if not her father and mother, to follow her love and feels betrayed in the end; when confronted with the risen Christ, her state of mind is (almost ironically) described in terms of the *excessus mentis* that characterises the mystical union: 'Exanimis' is the expression used in the *Omelia Origenis*;[45] 'I am not where I am', she says in Markham's *Lamentations* (D1r). Other heroines feel exiled even from their former (or better) selves, such as Anthony Chute's Mrs Shore, who passes through several stages of forlornness, from married state ('Departed from my selfe', B4v) to courtly status ('I that from me, my selfe, my selfe had sold', C4r) and on to beggary:

> (Then from the Court, the martirdoome of mee,)
> All solitarie, alone, forlorne, I went   (G1r)

The lack of reality which Eliot, it will be remembered, used as a reflection on all poetry of the pathetic kind is constitutive for the reflective literature of Complaint. This literature has its defects, but it also offers opportunities. The most important of these opportunities lies in the probing of subjective realities less accessible to the more objective modes of epic and drama which Eliot has in mind. There is, however, no definite dividing line between the pathetic and the tragic. When Eliot says of Thomas Heywood that 'he is eminent in the pathetic, rather than the tragic' he seems to imply that the poet working in the more pathetic medium can achieve only a lesser eminence. Eliot's is the classicist's and, of course, the modernist's point of view. For him, the tragic is restricted to tragedies of 'the highest kind', and he distrusts the 'homely pathos' and 'the simple poetry' which A.M. Clark had praised in Heywood.[46] One has to go back to the eighteenth century to find this view of tragedy expressed in the most uncompromising terms, for example by the archclassicist Thomas Rymer. It is well known that Eliot showed more than usual understanding for Rymer's much derided view of Shakespeare's most homely tragedy, *Othello*. Rymer is not content with Aristotle's statement that a tragedy purges the passions like a surgeon; he asked for Plato's horseman, Reason, to rein them in for good:

And besides the *purging* of the *passions*; something must stick by observing that constant order, [. . .] that necessary relation and chain, whereby the causes and the effects, the vertues and rewards, the vices and their punishments are proportion'd and link'd together; how deep and dark soever are laid the Springs, and however intricate and involv'd are their operations.[47]

Rymer and his fellow classicists derive their judgments mainly from Horace, who, for them, contained and complemented Aristotle's *Poetics* and whose 'good fund of strong masculine sense' one of these fellow classicists, Ambrose Philips, set side by side with the gentler style displayed in Ovid's *Heroides* in one of the later contributions to the *Spectator* (no. 618, 10 November 1714).[48] It is with poetry which allows for passions of the softer kind and tries to cultivate them as suggested by Southwell that this study has been concerned. The gentle style of this poetry need not be sentimental, and it has, apparently, survived, if not prevailed. The Complaint-like novels which have appeared in recent years give evidence that it is as persistent as any poetry, and able to penetrate the firmest opposition.

Notes

Introduction

1 T.S. Eliot, 'Thomas Heywood', *Selected essays* (London, 1951), pp. 179–81.
2 See John Nist, 'The art of Chaucer: *Pathedy*', *Tennessee Studies in Literature*, 11 (1966), 1–10; cf. Paul G. Ruggiers, 'Notes towards a theory of tragedy in Chaucer', *Chaucer Review*, 8 (1973), 89–99, and Dorothy Guerin, 'Chaucer's pathos: three variations', *Chaucer Review*, 20 (1985), 90–112, who tries to establish three types of pathetic tales, all with women heroines, in Chaucer's *Canterbury tales* and *The legend of good women*, one modelled on saints' legends, one on romances, and one exploring, by means of irony, its heroines' psychological states. See also Mary-Jo Arn, 'Three Ovidian women in Chaucer's *Troilus*: Medea, Helen, Oenone', *Chaucer Review*, 15 (1980), 1–10.
3 *Canterbury tales*, 'General prologue', 306; quotations from Chaucer refer to F.N. Robinson's edition of *The works of Geoffrey Chaucer*, 2nd edn (London, 1957).
4 *Ovid's 'Heroides'* (Princeton, N.J., 1974), pp. 353–4.
5 'Heywood', p. 179.
6 *The art of English poesy* (1589), II, ii, in *Elizabethan critical essays*, ed. G. Gregory Smith (Oxford, 1904), II, p. 68. Cf. the definitions by George Gascoigne, *Certain notes of instruction* (1575), ch. 14, 'seruing best for graue discourses', and King James IV, *A short treatise on verse* (1584), 'for tragicall materis, complaintis, or testamentis', in Smith (ed.), *Elizabethan critical essays*, I, pp. 54, 222.
7 The erotic epyllion originated in Hellenistic literature, but only a few sketches have been passed down to us; see Marjorie Crump, *The epyllion from Theocritus to Ovid* (1931; rpt. New York, 1978) for the early development of the genre.
8 *English literature in the sixteenth century (excluding drama)* (Oxford, 1954), p. 499.
9 *English literature*, p. 501. The saintly epitheton is used in *Lucrece*, 85; all Shakespeare quotations are taken from the Arden Shakespeare.
10 References to *The complaint of Rosamond* are taken from *The complete works in verse and prose of Samuel Daniel*, ed. Alexander B. Grosart (5 vols., 1885; rpt. New York, 1963), I, pp. 80–113.
11 *Colin Clout's come home again*, 423, 427; Spenser quotations are taken from *Spenser: poetical works*, ed. J.C. Smith and E. de Selincourt (Oxford, 1912).
12 *Minor poets of the Caroline period* (Oxford, 1905), I, p. 615. Several rare pieces of Ovidian narrative poetry have survived in earlier collections like the Caldecott and the Burton volumes or similar volumes in the Malone collection. The Malone volumes are now in the Bodleian Library, Oxford

242

(Bodl, Malone 393 and 436); the Caldecott and the Burton volumes are described by Joseph Quincy Adams in the introduction to his edition of Thomas Heywood's *Oenone and Paris* (Washington, D.C., 1943), pp. xvi–xxiv; for the Caldecott volume cf. M.A. Shaaber's introduction to his edition of John Trussell's 'Raptus I. Helenae', *Shakespeare Quarterly*, 8 (1957), 408. See also the British Library casebook C.39.a.37, which contains, among other Ovidian poetry, Shakespeare's *Lucrece* (1624 edn), John Marston's *Pygmalion's image* (1619 edn) and an adaptation of the story of Myrrha from the *Metamorphoses*, *The scourge of Venus* (1614 edn), by H[enry] A[ustin]. A description of this volume is in P.W. Miller (ed.), *Seven minor epics of the English Renaissance (1596–1624)* (Gainesville, Fla., 1967), pp. xviii–xix, which also contains a facsimile reprint of *The scourge of Venus*, pp. 229–72.

13 John F. Patton, 'Essays in the Elizabethan she-tragedies or female-complaints', PhD thesis, Ohio University, 1969; Gary F. Bjork, 'The Renaissance Mirror for Fair Ladies: Samuel Daniel's *Complaint of Rosamond* and the tradition of the feminine complaint', PhD thesis, University of California, Irvine, 1973; Willard Farnham, *The medieval heritage of Elizabethan tragedy* (Oxford, 1936), p. 311.

14 W.F., 'Ad autorem', *Marie Magdalen's lamentations* (1604 edn), A3r–v; Markham's own terms on A4v and B2r.

15 Chaucer's love-complaints have been traced back to Ovid by Nancy Dean, 'Chaucer's *Complaint*; a genre descended from the *Heroides*', *Comparative Literature*, 19 (1967), 1–27; for earlier literature on the 'complainte d'amour' see F.N. Robinson (ed.), *The works of Geoffrey Chaucer*, p. 789. For the Latin 'planctus' see Hennig Brinkmann, *Geschichte der lateinischen Liebesdichtung im Mittelalter* (1925; rpt. Darmstadt, 1979), pp. 73–7 (on Goliardic *planctus*) and Peter Dronke, *Poetic individuality in the Middle Ages* (Oxford, 1970), ch. 4 (on Biblical *planctus*).

16 Helmut Hross, 'Die Klagen der verlassenen Heroiden in der lateinischen Dichtung', unpublished PhD thesis, University of Munich, 1958; see also Howard Jacobson, *Ovid's 'Heroides'* (Princeton, 1974), p. 342.

17 See W.F. French, *'A mirror for magistrates': its origin and influence* (Edinburgh, 1898); Willard Farnham, 'The Progeny of *A mirror for magistrates*', *Modern Philology*, 29 (1932), 395–410, incorporated in his *Medieval heritage*. See also Lily B. Campbell's editions of *The mirror for magistrates* (Cambridge, 1938) and *Parts added to 'The mirror for magistrates'* (Cambridge, 1946) and the substantial study on the tradition in Edwin D. Craun's unpublished PhD thesis 'The *de casibus* complaint in Elizabethan England 1559–1593', Princeton University, 1971.

18 The quotation is taken from the summary of her PhD thesis 'Angell fayre or strumpet lewd: the theme of Jane Shore's disgrace in ten sixteenth-century works' in *Dissertation Abstracts International*, 32 (1971), 2050 A. The thesis was published under the title *Angell fayre or strumpet lewd: Jane Shore as an example of erring beauty* (Salzburg, 1974).

19 Dörrie's bibliography misses out numerous examples of English heroical epistles, particularly in the eighteenth century. I have called attention to some of the earlier pieces he omitted in my *Frauenklage* (pp. 33, 39, 41, 57, 61, 138). This also contains a chapter on English *Heroides* (ch. C), mainly of

the Renaissance period, which I left out of this revision because the tradition of the English heroical epistle, and in particular its medieval and eighteenth century stages, deserves a study (or two) of its own. There is a spirited essay by Gillian Beer which focusses on one of the later landmarks of this tradition, Alexander Pope's *Eloisa to Abelard*, 'Our unnatural no-voice: The heroic epistle, Pope, and women's Gothic', *Yearbook of English Studies*, 12 (1982), 125–51. Gretl Kutek's unpublished PhD thesis 'Ovids *Heroides* und die englischen Heroidenbriefe von der Renaissance bis Pope' (University of Vienna, 1937) centres on George Wither's *Fidelia*, a pastoral variant of the tradition which falls outside the scope of the present study. I could find no trace of a treatise on English translations of the *Heroides* by Linda Van Norden, 'A rich and exhaustive study . . . still in manuscript' which is mentioned in the California edition of *The works of John Dryden*, ed. E.N. Hooker and H.T. Swedenberg (Berkeley, 1956), I, p. 330; it probably stayed in manuscript.

20 *Telling classical tales: Chaucer and 'The legend of good women'* (Ithaca, N.Y., 1983).

21 Again, I will not enter on a discussion of the adequacy of such terms as 'epyllion'; it is not of classical origin and was rejected by Walter Allen, Jr., in his article on 'The non-existent classical epyllion', *Studies in Philology*, 55 (1958), 515–18, but has proved useful to others, for instance Marjorie Crump in *The epyllion from Theocritus to Ovid*. See also Janet M. Webber's unpublished PhD dissertation on 'The English Renaissance epyllion' (Yale University, 1973), which draws a useful distinction between the frivolous epyllion and the didactic Complaint, but connects only the former with Ovid.

22 'Ovids elegische Erzählung', in Richard Heinze, *Vom Geist des Römertums*, ed. Erich Burck (4th edn, Darmstadt, 1972), pp. 308–403. The article was first published in *Berichte und Verhandlungen der Sächsischen Akademie der Wissenschaften zu Leipzig. Philologisch-historische Klasse*, 71 (1919), 7. Heft. The quotation is part of a preliminary definition of elegiac as opposed to epic narrative on p. 314 of the reprint.

2 Dido and Elissa

1 The etymology of Dido's name, 'Dido id est virago Punica lingua', is in the commentary on the *Aeneid* by Servius, 'Ad Aen. I, 340', *Servii Grammatici qui feruntur in Vergilii carmina commentarii*, rec. Georgius Thilo et Hermannus Hagen (1881; rpt Hildesheim, 1961), I, p. 120. Justinus tells the story of Elissa in his *Epitoma*, XVIII, iv–vi; his excerpts are taken from the lost *Historiae Philippicarum* of Pompeius Trogus. Earlier traces of the legend are to be found in the works of the Sicilian historian Timaios of which only fragments are extant. The remarks on Dido's hospitality are in Ovid's *Metamorphoses*, XIV, 78, and Boccaccio's *Genealogia deorum*, VI, liii.

2 Medieval versions of the legend of Dido up to Chaucer are summarised in L.B. Hall's 'Chaucer and the Dido-and-Aeneas story', *Medieval Studies*, 25 (1963), 148–59.

3 Hieronymus, *Adversus Jovinianum*, in *Patrologia latina*, ed. J.P. Migne et al., 23 (1845), cols. 270–6; English translation in *Chaucer. Sources and backgrounds*, ed. Robert P. Miller (New York, 1977), pp. 415–36.

4 The tears were, however, more or less enforced, 'Tenere cogebar Aeneae

nescio cuius errores, oblitus errorum meorum, et plorare Didonem mortuam, quia se occidit ab amore, cum interea me ipsum in his a te morientem, deus, vita mea, siccis oculis ferrem miserrimus'. *St Augustine's Confessiones*, tr. and ed. William Watts (London, 1950), I, p. 38.

5 There are plenty of instances in the second, medieval part of an unpublished PhD thesis by Anna Dermutz, 'Die Didosage in der englischen Literatur des Mittelalters und der Renaissance' (University of Vienna, 1957). The exemplary tradition is amply documented in an article by Mary Louise Lord, 'Dido as an example of chastity: the influence of example literature', *Harvard Library Bulletin*, 17 (1969), 22–44, 216–32; Adrianne Roberts-Baytop gives a summary of both the romantic and the didactic strains in the chapter on 'The pre-Renaissance', in her *Dido, queen of infinite literary variety* (Salzburg, 1974), pp. 1–9; the Ovidian Dido of Chaucer's *Legend of good women* has been read as an example for the lack of equality between the sexes by George Sanderlin, 'Chaucer's *Legend of Dido* – a feminist exemplum', *Chaucer Review*, 20 (1986), 331–40.

6 The anachronism was known well before Petrarch's time; it is mentioned by John Ridevall in his commentary on Augustine (see Beryl Smalley, *English friars and antiquity* [Oxford, 1960], p. 130). The implication that Virgil and Ovid damaged Dido's reputation by making her the mistress of Aeneas is already contained in a poem usually ascribed to Ausonius which is based on a Greek epigram and was translated by Sir Thomas Wyatt (No. CLI in Joost Daalder's edition of the *Collected poems*, London, 1975, p. 193; cf. H.A. Mason, *Editing Wyatt*, Cambridge, 1972, pp. 176–7). For the anti-Virgilian tradition, see Gerald Morgan, 'A defense of Dorigen's complaint', *Medium Aevum*, 46 (1977), 77–9, and Craig Kallendorf, 'Boccaccio's Dido and the rhetorical criticism of Virgil's *Aeneid*', *Studies in Philology*, 82 (1985), 401–15.

7 See Craig Kallendorf's article on 'Boccaccio's Dido'. One should not forget, however, that Boccaccio wrote not only in this learned Latin, but also in the romantic vernacular tradition. He had treated Dido as a pathetic victim of love in his vernacular works, particularly *Fiammetta* and *Amorosa visione*, and only later developed the more learned and moralistic approach of his Latin works; in the *Amorosa visione*, for example, the forsaken Dido is allowed to complain of her fate together with other Ovidian heroines such as Phyllis, Briseida and Hypsipyle (Cantos XV–XXIV; see Piero Boitani, *Chaucer and the imaginary world of fame*, Cambridge, 1984, pp. 94–5). Boccaccio tried to reconcile both versions in his *Genealogie* and in his commentary on Dante.

8 *De casibus illustrium virorum*, quoted from Louis B. Hall's facsimile reproduction of the Paris edition of 1520 (Gainesville, Fa., 1962), p. 58.

9 It is reprinted in Douglas Gray's *Oxford book of late medieval verse and prose* (Oxford, 1985), pp. 64–8. Alain Renoir compares Canace's lament on the death of her son with that of Chaucer's Griseldis on the loss of her children, in 'Attitudes towards women in Lydgate's poetry', *English Studies*, 42 (1961), 1–14.

10 See Carl Vossen, 'Der Wandel des Aeneasbildes im Spiegel der englischen Literatur', unpublished PhD thesis, University of Bonn, 1955, p. 35; cf. *Realencyclopaedie*, II. ser, vol. 16 (Stuttgart, 1958), col. 1373.

11 Quotations are from the Tusculum edition, *Vergil: Aeneis*, 3rd edn, ed. Johannes Götte (Munich, 1971).

12 Richard C. Monti, *The Dido episode and the Aeneid: Roman social and political values in the epic* (Leyden, 1982), review by Erich Segal, *Times Literary Supplement*, June 11, 1982, p. 634.

13 Howard Jacobson, *Ovid's 'Heroides'* (Princeton, N.J., 1974), pp. 76–84; W.S. Anderson, 'The *Heroides*', in *Ovid*, ed. J.W. Binns (London, 1973), pp. 49–68.

14 Quotations are from the Loeb edition, *Ovid: Heroides and Amores*, ed. Grant Showerman (London, 1914).

15 The enumeration of kindnesses extended to faithless lovers is traced back to Homer's Calypso (*Odyssey*, V, 116–44) and Euripides' *Medea* (465–519) by Helmut Hross in 'Die Klagen der verlassenen Heroiden'.

16 Reuben A. Brower, *Hero and saint: Shakespeare and the Graeco–Roman heroic tradition* (Oxford, 1971), p. 132, and Howard Jacobson, *Ovid's 'Heroides'*, pp. 396–7, have dealt with Ovid's paradoxical fusion of vice and virtue.

17 *Virgil and his influence* (Bristol, 1984), 'Introduction', p. 6.

18 See I.K. Horvath, 'Impius Aeneas', *Acta Antiqua*, 6 (1958), 385–93.

19 *Classical influences on English poetry* (London, 1951), pp. 159–60.

20 *Telling classical tales: Chaucer and the 'Legend of good women'* (Ithaca, N.Y., 1983). For a more balanced recent assessment of the 'pervasive irony view' of Chaucer's *Legend of good women* see Janet M. Cowen, 'Chaucer's *Legend of good women*: structure and tone', *Studies in Philology*, 82 (1985), 416–36.

21 An exception is Bruce Harbert's calmly revisionary article 'Chaucer and the Latin classics' in *Geoffrey Chaucer*, ed. Derek Brewe (London, 1974), pp. 137–53.

22 R.L. Hoffman, *Ovid and the 'Canterbury tales'* (Philadelphia, Pa.,1966); J.M. Fyler, *Chaucer and Ovid* (New Haven, Conn., 1979); R.W. Frank, Jr, *Chaucer and 'The legend of good women'* (Cambridge, Mass., 1973); Lisa Kiser, *Telling classical tales*: the further we get from the positivist studies of the turn of the century, the more generous the allowances appear to be which are made for Chaucer's erudition; I have argued for a return to more positivist approaches in an article on 'Gower, Chaucer and the classics: back to the textual evidence' (in *John Gower: Recent Readings*, ed. Robert F. Yeager, Kalamazoo, Mich., 1989, 95–111).

23 This traditional view has recently been put forward most strongly by J.A.W. Bennett in *Chaucer's 'Book of fame': an exposition of "The house of fame"* ' (Oxford, 1968); see, for instance, his introductory remarks, p. xi.

24 *Confessio amantis*, VIII, 2,266; *The house of fame*, 1,487. Quotations from the *Confessio amantis* are taken from G.C. Macaulay's edition, *The English works of John Gower* (Oxford, 1900–1).

25 Derek Pearsall, 'Gower's narrative art', *Publications of the Modern Language Association*, 81 (1966), p. 478.

26 There is, in fact, little evidence that he knew any of his works; see my article, 'Gower, Chaucer and the classics'.

27 *Confessio amantis*, IV, 85, marg.

28 I have borrowed the paraphrase from B.A. Windeatt's *Chaucer's dream poetry: Sources and analogues* (Woodbridge, 1982), p. 69.

29 See particularly the chapter, 'The image of man', in his *Ricardian poetry* (London, 1971), pp. 93–129.

30 *The book of the duchess*, 1,024–6.

31 *John Gower: Moral philosopher and friend of Chaucer* (New York, 1964), p. 150. For statistical evidence of Gower's borrowings see Eric Stockton's edition of *The Latin works of John Gower* (Seattle, Wash., 1962), p. 27, and F.C. Mish's unpublished PhD thesis, 'The influence of Ovid on John Gower's *Vox clamantis*', University of Minnesota, 1973.

32 'Gower's narrative art', p. 481. Pearsall analyses a number of Ovidian tales from Gower's *Confessio amantis*; see also Arno Esch, 'John Gower's Erzählkunst', in *Chaucer und seine Zeit*, ed. Arno Esch (Tübingen, 1968), pp. 207–39, and ch. 6 of my *'The middel weie': Stil-und Aufbauformen in John Gowers 'Confessio Amantis'* (Bonn, 1974).

33 The Maeander–Menander confusion about the second line of 'The Letter of Dido' is not uncommon in medieval manuscripts of the *Heroides*; see Heinrich Dörrie's article on such manuscripts, 'Untersuchungen zur Überlieferungsgeschichte von Ovid's Epistulae Heroidum', *Nachrichten der Akademie der Wissenschaften in Göttingen aus dem Jahre 1960*, Philologisch-historische Klasse (Göttingen, 1960), pp. 113–230 and 359–423. The swan's suicide is described in Vincent of Beauvais, *Speculum naturale*, cap. L, which Gower knew. He may have found it in an explanatory note on the margin of his manuscript; that Gower made use of annotated manuscripts of the *Heroides* has been suggested by Conrad Mainzer in 'John Gower's use of the "Medieval Ovid" in the *Confessio amantis*', *Medium Aevum*, 41 (1972), 215–29; I doubt, however, that he had to go to Italian and French sources to find such annotations; for details, see my article, 'Gower, Chaucer and the classics'.

34 *Telling classical tales*, p. 131. Peter Dronke gives less technical explanations for Chaucer's many *occupationes* in an article on 'Dido's lament: from medieval Latin lyric to Chaucer', which takes the lyrical lament of Dido from the *Carmina burana* as its starting point (in *Kontinuität und Wandel*, Festschrift Franco Munari [Hildesheim, 1986], pp. 364–90).

35 Chaucer uses the same formula in his description of the temples in his 'Knight's tale' (1,914–2,088). Elizabeth Salter has suggested that it may owe something to Dante's 'Io vidi' enumeration of Patriarchs in the Limbo section of his 'Inferno' (IV, 121–51); *Fourteenth-century English poetry: contexts and readings* (Oxford, 1983), pp. 161–3.

36 For the early development of the motif see Francesco Della Corte, 'Perfidus hospes', in *Hommages à Marcel Renard I*, ed. Jacqueline Bibauer, *Collection Latomus*, 101 (Brussels, 1969), pp. 312–21. The *hospitium* motif can be turned in different directions; a simple rhetorical figure will twist friendliness into foolishness or worse. I have already quoted Ovid's and Boccaccio's zeugmatic remarks on the reception Aeneas found in Carthage ('animoque domoque' or 'amicitia et lecto'; see above, p. 17); Gower handles a similar case with characteristic courtesy when he summarises his version of the story of Phyllis and Demophoon (which he took from the *Heroides*): 'Demephon . . . a Phillide Rodopeie Regina non tantum in hospicium, set eciam in amorem, gaudio magno susceptus est' (*Confessio amantis*, IV, 735–40, sidenote). By then, the play on the word 'hospitium' was so well established

that Gower's wording need not point to a particular medieval edition of the *Heroides* (cf. Conrad Mainzer 'John Gower's use of the "Medieval Ovid" ', p. 215).

37 *Chaucer's early poetry* (London, 1963), p. 87; see also Janet M. Cowen, 'Chaucer's *Legend of good women*: structure and tone', *Studies in Philology*, 82 (1985), pp. 434–5.

38 Janet Cowen believes he used the term in a parodic sense only, 'Chaucer's *Legend of good women*', p. 417.

39 See Clemen's analysis of the various debunking techniques Chaucer employs to that end (*Early poetry*, 80–7); cf. J.A.W. Bennett, *Chaucer's 'Book of fame'*, ch. 1, 'Venus and Virgil', pp. 1–51, and Sheila Delany, *Chaucer's 'House of fame'* (Chicago, Ill., 1972), ch. 5, 'Dido and Aeneas', pp. 48–57.

40 The holiness of Chaucer's Dido comes out more clearly in the *Legend of good women*, of course, where it culminates in the narrator's question: if the Creator had to choose a wife, 'Whome shulde he loven but this lady swete?' (1,042). Peter Dronke calls this 'a daring metaphysical conceit' and compares it to 'certain high-flying moments in Dante's early poetry' ('Dido's lament', p. 383). I would base the sentiment on humility rather than on exaltation; see my discussion of 'holiness' in Chaucer's 'Legend of Lucrece' below, pp. 83–7.

41 I.C., *Saint Mary Magdalen's conversion* (1603), A1v.

42 Cf. Alan T. Gaylord's analysis of the opening scenes of the legend, 'Dido at hunt, Chaucer at work', *Chaucer Review*, 17 (1983), 300–15; Gaylord's main interest lies in the prosody of the tale.

43 'Chaucer's *Legend of good women*', p. 427.

44 The 'like-father-like-son' argument is used twice explicitly in Chaucer's version of the Phyllis-and-Demophoon story (*Legend of good women*, 2,398–400; 2,543–7); see Janet Cowen, 'Chaucer's *Legend of good women*', p. 430.

45 See Richard Heinze, *Virgils epische Technik* (1915; rpt. Darmstadt, 1976), pp. 135–6 on the humiliation motif in classical literature. Peter Dronke compares the 'extreme of self-abasement' into which Chaucer transforms his Dido to Ovid's Briseis; he finds it inconsistent with her character (*Heroides*, III, 69; 'Dido's lament', p. 385). Dido's servility is, of course, opposed to the imperial ethos of Aeneas. Alexander Pope stresses the same contrast when his Eloisa prefers to become Abelard's mistress or to earn 'yet another name more free, / More fond than mistress' to being '*Caesar's* empress' (*Eloisa to Abelard*, 85–90).

46 Cf. Shakespeare's description of the equally stealthy approach and exit of Tarquin in *Lucrece*, 729, 736.

47 Forsaken women in the *Heroides* tradition are often shown on or near their beds; see Ovid's Penelope and Ariadne (*Heroides*, I, 7–8; X, 9–14), Chaucer's Lucretia and Ariadne (*Legend of good women*, 1,719–20, 2,210–13), Daniel's Rosamond and Octavia (*Complaint of Rosamond*, 645–51; 'Letter from Octavia', 77–80), etc. The situation is indicative of their essentially domestic and private outlook.

48 See Heinze on Dido's end in the *Aeneid*, *Virgil's epische Technik*, pp. 137–44.

49 The elegiac tone of the legend prompted the scribe of the Rawlinson MS C.86 to give it the title 'The complaynte of Dido'. He ascribed it to Lydgate. See *The Riverside Chaucer*, ed. Larry D. Benson (Boston, Mass., 1987), p. 1,179.

50 The Magdalen-Complaint lived on independently as *The complaint of the lover of Christ Saint Mary Magdaleyn* printed by Wynkyn de Worde, c. 1520.

51 *Sir Richard Roos: Lancastrian poet* (London, 1961), p. 365.

52 'Chaucer and an Italian translation of the *Heroides*', *Publications of the Modern Language Association*, 45 (1930), 110–28.

53 To give but two instances: Cf. *Heroides*, VII, 69, 'coniugis . . . deceptae . . . imago' with Octovien's 'Lymage froide de ta femme deceue' and the 'Letter', 'The colde ymage / of your disceyued wife'; or see Octovien's 'Ton espee qui moccira demain' and the English 'the swerde / that shall kyll me tomorwe' where Ovid has only an indefinite future tense ('lacrimae . . . labuntur in ensem, / qui iam pro lacrimis sanguine tinctus erit', *Heroides*, VII, 185–6). There were ten printed editions of Octovien's *Epistres* before 1526, the year Pynson's *Book of fame* was (most probably) published; copies of four of these are in the British Library (see Christine M. Scollen, *The birth of the elegy in France 1500–1550*, Geneva, 1967, App. II, pp. 157–9). The British Library also has an illuminated manuscript of the translation (Harley MS 4867, erroneously dated fourteenth century in the *Catalogus librorum Harleianae*, III, 213). Another, even more lavishly illuminated manuscript of the *Epistres*, possibly a copy produced for dedication to Louis XII and Anne of Brittany, is kept in the Huntington Library (HM 60).

54 Quotations are from the only copy of Pynson's edition in the British Library, *The book of fame*, F3v–F5r. Douglas Gray has included some excerpts from the poem in his *Oxford book of late medieval verse and prose* (Oxford, 1985), pp. 91–3.

55 Horace, *De arte poetica*, 105–6; cf. Cicero, *De oratore*, III, lix, 221–3. Ovid uses the formula in his tale of Lucretia (*Fasti*, II, 758: 'Et facies animo dignaque parque fuit'); this is taken up by Chaucer in his 'Legenda Lucrecie' (*Legend of good women*, 1,738–9) and extended by Lydgate in his tale of Lucrece (*Fall of princes*, III, 1,037–50). Chaucer uses it more lightheartedly in his *Troilus and Criseyde*, I, 12–14; so does Henryson in his *Testament of Cresseid*, 1–4. For further parallels of this well-worn topos, particularly in Lydgate, see Eleanor P. Hammond's note to Lydgate's *Fall of princes*, VI, 3,144–50, in *English verse between Chaucer and Surrey* (Durham, N.C., 1927), p. 528.

56 Quoted from Kallendorf, 'Boccaccio's Dido', p. 412. Boccaccio may have developed this moralising exegesis under Petrarch's influence; the tradition of learned allegorical interpretations of the *Aeneid*, however, goes back to much earlier commentators; see O.B. Harrison, *The enduring moment: a study of the idea of praise in Renaissance literary theory and practice* (Chapel Hill, N.C., 1962), pp. 24–36.

57 *The Complete Works of Samuel Daniel*, ed. Alexander B. Grosart (1885; rpt. New York, 1963), I, pp. 119–20. The same contrast of witty eloquence and simple trust governs novels such as Richardson's *Clarissa*.

58 There is a similar appropriation of the sword of sorrows in Chaucer's complaint of Anelida (*Anelida and Arcite*, 270–1).

59 The cut is reproduced on the dust-jacket of the German edition of this study, *Die Frauenklage* (Tübingen, 1984).

60 Preserved only in later form; see *The Roxburghe ballads: illustrating the last years of the Stuarts*, ed. J.W. Ebsworth (1886; rpt. New York, 1966), vi,

pp. 547–51; Anna Dermutz dates its composition to the first half of the sixteenth century ('Die Didosage', p. 116).

3 Philomela and Lucretia

1 Heinrich Dörrie gives more examples of such catalogues from Gottfried's *Tristan und Isolde*, Dante's 'Paradiso' and Boccaccio's *Fiammetta* in his *Der heroische Brief*, pp. 350–5.

2 De argumento operis, non opus est multa dicere, cum titulus satis indicet. Nam si è è sacris literis hic aliquid petere licebit, cogita Iosephum quendam alterum adolescentem, Pharaonis vxori quae molesta olim erat & dicebat dormi mecum, hic respondere, & nefandum stuprum recusare.   (x8v)

The comparison to the Biblical Joseph places this letter of response in the vicinity of the *Heroides sacrae* which were at the same time written on the Continent, partly as an antidote to the Ovidian originals. For detailed criticism of Shepery's letter see Wolfgang Mann, *Lateinische Dichtung in England* (Halle, 1939), pp. 137–48.

3 Not even the title *Heroides* or *Liber heroidum* has Ovidian authority; it was added in later manuscripts. Ovid himself speaks only of 'epistulae'; see Walther Kraus, 'Ovidius Naso', in *Ovid*, ed. Michael v. Albrecht and Ernst Zinn (Darmstadt, 1968), p. 89.

4 For a detailed assessment of the double letters see Walther Kraus, 'Die Briefpaare in Ovids Heroiden', *Wiener Studien*, 65 (1950/51), 54–77, and cf. W.S. Anderson's chapter on 'The double letters' in his article 'The *Heroides*', pp. 68–81.

5 'Matilda to King John', 135–56; *The works of Michael Drayton*, ed. J. William Hebel (Oxford, 1932), II, pp. 156–7.

6 The Myrrha-poems are most readily available in facsimile reproductions in an anthology of epyllia, *Seven minor epics of the English Renaissance (1596–1624)*, ed. Paul W. Miller (Gainesville, Fla., 1967). Lodge's *Scilla's metamorphosis* is in three similar anthologies, *Elizabethan minor epics*, ed. Elizabeth Story Donno (London, 1963), *Elizabethan narrative verse*, ed. Nigel Alexander (London, 1967), and *Elizabethan verse romances*, ed. M.M. Reese (London, 1968). The Ovidian epyllia have found plenty of scholarly attention, most recently by William Keach, *Elizabethan erotic narratives* (Hassocks, 1977), and Clark Hulse, *Metamorphic verse* (Guildford, 1982).

7 For an analysis of Ovid's epic (as opposed to his elegiac) style see Richard Heinze, 'Ovids elegische Erzählung', *passim*. See also Reuben A. Brower's chapter on Ovid's epic, 'Metamorphoses of the heroic. i. *Dark philosophie of turnèd shapes*' in his *Hero and saint: Shakespeare and the Graeco–Roman heroic tradition* (Oxford, 1971), pp. 120–41.

8 *Elizabethan narrative verse*, ed. Alexander, pp. 89–92.

9 *Mirrha, the mother of Adonis*, ed. Miller, p. 143.

10 Emil Staiger, *Grundbegriffe der Poetik* (Zurich, 1946).

11 It does not make much difference that these heroines live in the most civilised surroundings of Rome or of London: what matters is that they feel cast out. Shakespeare's Lucrece actually wishes she could join Philomela in 'Some dark deep desert seated from the way' (1,144) after she has pleaded with Tarquin 'in a wilderness where are no laws' (544).

12 See the detailed analysis of the changes the story underwent in Chaucer's hands by R.W. Frank in his *Chaucer and the 'Legend of good women'*, pp. 134–45.

13 *Perihegesis*, I, 41, 8 f.; see Herbert Hunger, *Lexikon der griechischen und römischen Mythologie* (Vienna, 1959), s.v. Prokne, p. 305.

14 *Selections from William Caxton*, ed. N.F. Blake (Oxford, 1973), p. 71. Close verbal parallels suggest that Caxton was working from a copy of the *Ovide moralisé* rather than Pierre Bersuire's *Ovidius moralizatus* or its shortened prose adaptation, as Blake suggests (p. 130).

15 *Agamemnon*, 1,144; *Aeschylus*, tr. and ed. Herbert W. Smyth (London, 1952), II.

16 Parts of the 'Game of chess' section of the *Waste Land*, where the allusion to the Philomela myth occurs, could be taken as a replica of an Ovidian epyllion, suitably shrunk to the proportions of a mantelpiece.

17 *George Gascoigne's 'The steele glas' and 'The complaynte of Phylomene'* (Salzburg, 1975), pp. 57–8.

18 The incidental framework is written in less measured cross-rhymed pentameters. Poulter's Measure is the stately metre of early Tudor poetry. Gascoigne claims to have composed the earlier part of his poem on horseback between Chelmsford and London. In the dedication he asks his patron, Lord Gray of Wilton, 'to gesse (by change of style) where the renewing of the verse may bee most apparently thought to begin', *George Gascoigne's 'Steele glas'*, p. 140.

19 Douglas Bush, 'Classic myths in English verse (1557–1589)', *Modern Philology*, 25 (1927), 47. William Wallace quite rightly points out that Gascoigne's poem 'stands halfway between the medieval mirror complaints and the she-tragedies of the 1590's' (*George Gascoigne's 'Steele glas'*, p. 54).

20 Douglas Bush has shown that Parker's source for the Complaint is George Pettie's euphuistic novella 'Tereus and Progne' in *The petite palace*, D4v–F3v; 'Martin Parker's *Philomela*', *Modern Language Notes*, 40 (1925), 486–8.

21 See M.P. Cunningham, 'The novelty of Ovid's *Heroides*', *Classical Philology*, 44 (1949), 100–6.

22 Erwin Rohde, *Der griechische Roman* (1914; rpt. Darmstadt, 1974), pp. 149–51.

23 *The plays and poems of William Cartwright*, ed. G.B. Evans (Madison, Wisc., 1951), pp. 488–91.

24 *Minor poets of the Caroline period* (Oxford, 1905), I, 'Introduction to Patrick Hannay', p. 615; the score is on p. 620, the poem on pp. 621–42.

25 'Introduction to Hannay', p. 615.

26 He compares instances from Churchyard's 'Shore's wife' and Daniel's *Complaint of Rosamond* in his thesis 'The Renaissance Mirror for Fair Ladies', p. 72.

27 Such striving for synaesthetic effects, often passing over the borders of the artistic medium in hand, is again typical of the epyllion; cf., for example, the Troy painting in Shakespeare's *Lucrece*, where the static scene seems filled with movement rather than with sound.

28 See Clark Hulse's discussion of Ovid's Arachne tale in relation to Spenser's *Muiopotmos* in his chapter on 'Spenser's Ovidian epics', *Metamorphic verse*, pp. 260–1.

29 There is a detailed description of this neglected version of the *Histoire anci-enne* by Clem C. Williams in his article 'A case of mistaken identity: still another Trojan narrative in Old French prose', *Medium Aevum*, 53 (1984), 59–72. Dörrie does not mention it in his short chapter on the *Heroides* (i.e. nos. I, III, V, VII, XIII, XVI, XVII) as supplements to the literature on Troy, *Der heroische Brief*, pp. 345–7. As Professor Williams has kindly informed me, he plans an edition of the *Histoire ancienne*.

30 See Douglas Bush, *Mythology and the romantic tradition* (New York, 1969), p. 301. For examples of the medieval and Renaissance attitude towards Helen see John P. Tatlock, 'The siege of Troy in Elizabethan literature, especially in Shakespeare and Heywood', *Publications of the Modern Language Association*, 30 (1915), 673–770.

31 *Gorgeous gallery*, ed. H.E. Rollins (Cambridge, Mass., 1926), p. 81.

32 Quoted from the reprint in J.P. Collier's *Illustrations of old English literature* (1866; rpt. New York, 1966), II, no. 8, pp. 22–3.

33 M.A. Shaaber (ed.), '*The first rape of faire Hellen* by John Trussell', *Shakespeare Quarterly*, 8 (1957), p. 421.

34 'The first rape of faire Hellen', pp. 407–20. There is a more substantial affiliation of the author with the Jesuit poet Robert Southwell, which Shaaber also deals with in his introduction. Trussell contributed three dedicatory poems to Southwell's *Triumphs over death* (1595) in which he indicates that he was responsible for its publication. This connection is interesting in the light of Southwell's conversion of the erotic epyllion to spiritual use in his treatise on *Mary Magdalen's funeral tears* and his *St Peter's complaint*.

35 The figure of the nurse is not necessarily a comic figure; in Greek tragedies and in Virgil's *Aeneid* she acts on the higher level of a confidant to the heroine; see Richard Heinze, *Virgil's epische Technik*, pp. 127–8.

36 Edited from the unique copy in the Folger Shakespeare Library by Joseph Q. Adams (Washington, D.C., 1943). An early collector bound this copy up with a number of other Ovidian poems (see above, p. 15).

37 Cf. the 'curious workmanship' in the description of Cassandra on her bed in the beginning of Richard Barnfield's 'Legend of Cassandra', which was written in the same year as Heywood's Complaint. Barnfield's poem is a proper epyllion (in 78 sixain stanzas), his descriptions are not as conceitful as Heywood's.

38 *Concerning famous women*, tr. Guido A. Guarini (New Brunswick, N.H., 1963), p. 68.

39 Ed. Henry Bergen (London, 1908), II, pp. 554–5.

40 Excerpts in Geoffrey Bullough, *Narrative and dramatic sources of Shakespeare* (London, 1966), VI, pp. 186–215 (p. 207).

41 *John Dryden: of dramatic poesy and other critical essays*, ed. George Watson (London, 1962), II, p. 167.

42 *Of dramatic poesy*, I, p. 99.

43 *Ibid.*, p. 41.

44 *The lamentation of Troy for the death of Hector, whereunto is annexed an old woman's tale in her solitarie cell*, by I.O. (1594). The ascription was made, on the strength of a cryptic Latin motto in the title, by Elkin C. Wilson in his edition of the poem (Chicago, 1959).

45 The volume is described in J.Q. Adams's edition of Heywood's *Oenone and Paris*, pp. xvi–xxii.

46 See Douglas Bush, *Mythology and the Renaissance tradition* (New York, 1963), p. 309. Bush also names the *Iliad*, Books XXII and XXIV, and a lost ballad, 'The lamentation of Hecuba', as possible influences.

47 Medieval lamentations for the dead and their ancient models are the subject of a study by Renate Haas, *Die mittelenglische Totenklage* (Frankfurt, 1980).

48 'The lamentable end of Julia, Pompey's wife' in *Howell his devices*, C3v–4r. E.C. Wilson did not find a suitable model for Ogle's classical Julia (*Lamentation*, p. 65). H.E. Rollins's conjecture that Ogle was thinking of Arthur Brooke's *Romeus and Juliet* makes little sense.

49 *Mythology and Renaissance tradition*, p. 308.

50 C. David Benson has dealt with the influence of Guido's *Historia* in *The History of Troy in Middle English Literature* (Woodbridge, 1980); for his treatment of battle scenes, see pp. 28–31.

51 'Ovids elegische Erzählung', rpt. in *Vom Geist des Römertums* (Darmstadt, 1972), pp. 341–6. See also part I, 'Prologue: Lucrece in Livy, Ovid, Augustine, and Chaucer', in R. Thomas Simone, *Shakespeare and Lucrece* (Salzburg, 1974), pp. 1–24, particularly 1–14; and ch. 1, 'The shaping of the myth (I): victims and victors' in Ian Donaldson's *The rapes of Lucretia* (Oxford, 1982), particularly pp. 5–12.

52 Ian Donaldson has a chapter on 'Augustine's dilemma', *The rapes of Lucretia*, pp. 21–39.

53 See R.W. Frank, *Chaucer and 'The legend of good women'*, pp. 97–8, n. 8, for a list of medieval comments on Lucretia's suicide, and D.C. Allen, 'Observations on *The rape of Lucrece*', *Shakespeare Survey*, 15 (1962), 89–98, for examples of casuistic treatments of the story.

54 See Dorothy Hammond, 'Lydgate and Coluccio Salutati', *Modern Philology*, 25 (1927), 49–57.

55 This also applies to the reformed theologian: Tyndale is even stricter with Lucretia than Augustine ('She sought her own glory in her chastity, not God's'), and not only with her but with every soul living before the advent of Christ:

Thou mayest hereby perceive, that all that is done in the world before the Spirit of god come, and giveth us light, is damnable sin; and the more glorious, the more damnable; so that that which the world counteth most glorious is more damnable, in the sight of God, than that which the whore, the thief, and the murderer do.

'The obedience of a Christian man', in *Doctrinal treatises and introductions to different portions of the Holy Scriptures*, ed. Henry Walter (Cambridge, 1848), p. 183. See Donaldson, *The rapes of Lucretia*, p. 45.

56 *Seven minor epics of the English Renaissance*, ed. Miller, p. 192.

57 'Gower's narrative art', p. 481.

58 See Peter Szondi, *Die Theorie des bürgerlichen Trauerspiels im 18. Jahrhundert*, ed. Gert Mackenklott (Frankfurt, 1973), pp. 107–8. Szondi quotes from Diderot's *Entretiens sur le fils naturel* (1757).

59 This is one of the stock figures in women's Complaints; Chaucer takes it up in the prologue of his *Legend of good women* where it foreshadows, I think, the cupidity and the sophistry of the seducers in the following tales (F 130–9). It is still met with in such novels of seduction as Samuel Richardson's *Clarissa*

(e.g. II, p. 182, Everyman edn); for its sources see B.G. Koonce, 'Satan the fowler', *Medieval Studies*, 21 (1959), 176–84, and Anthony Kearney, 'A recurrent motif in Richardson's novels', *Neophilologus*, 55 (1971), 447–50.

60 *Chaucer and the 'Legend of good women'*, pp. 93–110; the reference to Augustine is discussed in a footnote, p. 97, n. 7.

61 It is hard to decide whether Chaucer made use of any other source than Ovid's *Fasti*, and which was his exact copy-text; see Frank, *Chaucer and the 'Legend of good women'*, p. 98, n. 9. For Chaucer's handling of Ovid, cf. Norman Callan, 'Thyn owne book: a note on Chaucer, Gower, and Ovid', *Review of English Studies*, 22 (1942), 269–81, and Carol Weiher, 'Chaucer's and Gower's stories of Lucretia and Virginia', *English Language Notes*, 14 (1976), 7–9.

62 *Chaucer and the 'Legend of good women'*, p. 103.

63 *The city of God against the pagans*, ed. George E. McCracken (London, 1957), I, pp. 83–91.

64 Quoted from the edition in the *Bibliotheca Patrum concionatoria*, ed. F. Franciscus Combefis (Venice, 1749), V, p. 583.

65 *Lancelot Andrewes. Sermons*, ed. G.M. Storey (Oxford, 1967); the ascription to Augustine is on p. 209; quotations from the *Omelia Origenis* are on pp. 196, 198, 203.

66 Let me mention but F.T. Prince's Arden edition of *The poems* (London, 1960) from which I quote, and R. Thomas Simone's monograph on the poem and its literary background, *Shakespeare and 'Lucrece'* (Salzburg, 1974).

67 These themes have been treated separately in a perceptive chapter of Ian Donaldson's *Rapes of Lucretia*, ' "A theme for disputation": Shakespeare's Lucrece', pp. 40–56.

68 Heinze deals with asymmetry and subjectivity in chs. 4, 5 and 6 of 'Ovids elegische Erzählung', pp. 338–55; ch. 4 concentrates on the Lucretia legend in Ovid's *Fasti*.

69 C.S. Lewis, *English literature in the sixteenth century* (Oxford, 1954), p. 501.

70 *The rapes of Lucretia*, p. 49.

71 Cf. the description of Cassandra's *levée* in Barnfield's *Legend of Cassandra*:
> VPon a gorgious gold embossed bed,
> With Tissue curtaines drawne against the sunne,
> (Which gazers eies into amazement led,
> So curiously the workmanship was done,)
>> Lay faire *Cassandra*, in her snowie smocke,
>> Whose lips the Rubies and the pearles did locke. [etc.]
> *Cynthia. With certain sonnets and The legend of Cassandra* (1595), D3r.

72 See his chapter on 'Rational soul' in *The discarded image* (Cambridge, 1964), pp. 156–61.

73 C.S. Lewis, for example, finds Lucrece 'too rhetorical in her agonies', *English literature*, p. 501.

74 Heinze uses terms like these to distinguish the style in Ovid's *Metamorphoses* from that of his *Fasti*. He speaks of 'Handlungsmonolog' and 'Zustandsmonolog'; 'Ovids elegische Erzählung', pp. 366–7.

75 'Eyes' are mentioned 75 times in the poem; in comparison, there are 37 occurrences in the whole of *Hamlet*, Shakespeare's longest play. For the importance of facial expression, and particularly the expression of the eyes, in pleading see Cicero's *De oratore*, III, lix, 221–3.

76 For the traditional thinking behind the concept of *amor hereos* see the chapter 'The use and abuse of beauty' in D.W. Robertson's *A preface to Chaucer* (Princeton, N.J., 1962), pp. 65–113, particularly 108–9.

77 The Letter of Briseis is blotted with tears (*Heroides*, III,3), that of Canace with blood (*Heroides*, XI, 1–2); see Eberhard Oppel, 'Ovid's Heroides', unpublished PhD thesis, University of Erlangen-Nürnberg, 1968, p. 22, on the *topos* of the blotted letter in elegiac literature.

78 I will give one early and one later example: Wilhelm Marschall, 'Das Troja-Gemälde in Shakespeares *Lucrece*', *Anglia*, 54 (1930), 83–96, and Clark Hulse's chapter 'The skillful painting of *Lucrece*' in his *Metamorphic verse*, pp. 175–94.

79 *English literature*, p. 499.

80 One should note, however, that in Roman augury congealed blood was taken to bode evil; see, for instance, Lucan, *Pharsalia*, Book I, 614–29.

81 *The rapes of Lucretia*, p. 46.

82 *English literature*, p. 499.

83 *The ghost of Lucrece* (New York, 1937). The edition has an extensive bibliographical introduction and gives both a facsimile and an edited version of the text.

84 The same heated style had been employed before by Anthony Chute in the beginning of his Complaint of Mrs Shore, *Beauty dishonoured* (1593), which will be discussed in ch. 4.

85 There is a similar connection of sword or dagger and pen in the letters of Dido and Canace in Ovid's *Heroides*, VII, 184–6, and XI, 3; Lydgate makes use of it at the end of Canace's complaint (*Fall of princes*, I, 7,022–35).

86 *The ghost of Lucrece*, p. 6, n. 6.

4 Rosamond and the Virgin Queen

1 *Royal faces: 900 years of British monarchy* (London, 1977), p. 19.

2 For the publication history of the *Mirror for magistrates* up to 1587 see the introductions in Lily B. Campbell's editions of *The 'Mirror for Magistrates'* (Cambridge, 1938) and *Parts added to the 'Mirror for magistrates' by John Higgins and Thomas Blenerhasset* (Cambridge, 1946).

3 *The medieval heritage of Elizabethan tragedy* (Oxford, 1936), p. 325; the chapters on the *Mirror for magistrates* and its progeny had appeared in article form in 1926 and 1932.

4 *Mirror*, ed. Campbell, 'George, Duke of Clarence', pp. 220–34; 'King Edward the Fourth', pp. 236–9.

5 *Mirror*, ed. Campbell, p. 236.

6 In the 1571 edition of the *Mirror for magistrates* separate Complaints of Duke Humphrey and Elianor Cobham were announced, but again left out (*Mirror*, ed. Campbell, p. 526). Campbell speculates about the reasons for these omissions in ' "Humphrey Duke of Gloucester and Elianor Cobham his wife" in the *Mirror for magistrates*', *Huntington Library Bulletin*, 5 (1934), 119–55.

7 'An elegy on the deaths of Eleanor Cobham, John Beaufort and Duke Humphrey', in F.M. Padelford and A.R. Benham (eds.), 'Liedersammlungen des XVI. Jahrhunderts, besonders aus der Zeit Heinrichs VIII.: 7. The songs in MS Rawlinson C. 813', *Anglia*, 31 (1908), 325.

8 Lydgate, by the way, who must have been familiar with the facts of the case, kept silent on the occasion of the trial. He had praised Humphrey's marriage to his first wife, Jacqueline of Holland, and may have been the author of a 'Complaint for my lady of Gloucester' (1428), which takes sides with Jacqueline (and popular opinion) against Humphrey. The poem was probably written after Humphrey's desertion of Jacqueline, but before Elianor's trial. Although Elianor is not named in the 'Complaint', she must be the siren and sorceress in its background. The 'Complaint for my lady of Gloucester' is printed side by side with Lydgate's congratulatory verses in Dorothy Hammond's article 'Lydgate and the Duchess of Gloucester', *Anglia*, 27 (1904), 381–98. One should note that the 'Complaint' is a plea for, not by, Jacqueline and therefore not a Complaint in the style of the *Mirror for magistrates*.

9 'The lament of the Duchess of Gloucester', in *Historical poems of the XIVth and XVth centuries*, ed. R.H. Robbins (New York, 1959), pp. 176–80.

10 A similar series of 'Ffarewells' is given to Anne Boleyn and Jane Gray in George Cavendish's 'Metrical visions', 624–6 and 2,265–6. Their Complaints are discussed below, pp. 111–3.

11 Ed. Richard S. Sylvester, *The history of King Richard III and selections from the English and Latin poems* (New Haven, Conn., 1976), pp. 119–22. The poem is bound up with 'The lament of the Duchess of Gloucester' in a Balliol manuscript; see Roman Dyboski's edition of the MS in *Songs, carols, and other miscellaneous poems from the Balliol MS 354, Richard Hill's commonplace-book*, EETS ES 101 (1908), pp. 95–9.

12 A.C. Spearing has pointed out, with respect to Wyatt and Anne Boleyn, the risks of writing amatory poetry around the court of Henry VIII, *Medieval to Renaissance in English poetry* (Cambridge, 1985), particularly pp. 187–8.

13 The *Lamentation of a sinner* was written when Henry was still alive; the comparison between the king and Moses was also drawn by Coverdale in the preface to his translation of the Bible; see William P. Haugaard, 'Katherine Parr: The religious convictions of a Renaissance queen', *Renaissance Quarterly*, 22 (1969), 346–59 (pp. 355–8). A Roman Catholic counterpart to this penitential poem was written by William Forrest, chaplain to Queen Mary, on the life of Katherine of Aragon, *The history of Grisild the second* (1558). It is almost hagiographical in tone.

14 See the scholarly edition of the *Metrical visions* by A.S.G. Edwards (Columbia, N.C., 1980), p. 17.

15 See his articles 'Some borrowings by Cavendish from Lydgate's *Fall of princes*', *Notes and Queries*, 216 (1971), 207–9, and 'The date of George Cavendish's *Metrical visions*', *Philological Quarterly*, 53 (1974), 128–32.

16 See *Heroides*, II, 74; VII, 195–6; *Metamorphoses*, IX, 563; XI, 706–7; *Fasti*, III, 549; *Testament of Cresseid*, 607–9.

17 I have dealt with the sentence passed on Cresseid in an essay, 'Cresseid's trial: a revision', *Essays and Studies*, 32 (1979), 44–56.

18 See *Metrical visions*, ed. Edwards, p. 173, on Cavendish, Anne Boleyn and Wolsey: 'Cavendish's comments on Anne Boleyn must, of course, be seen in the context of his known antipathy toward her because of her role in Wolsey's downfall'.

19 'How Dame Elianor Cobham, Duchesse of Glocester, for practising of witch-

craft and Sorcery, suffred open penance, and after was banished the realme
into the yle of Man', *Mirror*, ed. Campbell, pp. 432–43.

20 Divination seems to have been condoned or condemned only as fallacious;
Sir Thomas More implies in his *Rueful lamentation* that Queen Elizabeth had
recourse to the 'blandishyng promyse' of 'false astrolagy and devynatrice'
(24–5), ed. Richard S. Sylvester (New Haven, Conn., 1963), p. 120.

21 With regard to Criseyde, Henryson had tried to put right some of the blame
that had fallen on the heroine 'throw wickit langage' (*Testament of Cresseid*, 91). Henryson's Cresseid bears some semblance to later 'giglotlike' figures around English courts: she is subject to a cruel sentence and she is
reduced to begging in the streets like Elianor or Mrs Shore.

22 *Mirror*, ed. Campbell, pp. 373–86.

23 *Churchyard's challenge*, ˙1v; the list was interpolated after the rest of the
volume (including title and dedication) had been set.

24 See Campbell's introduction to her edition of *The mirror for magistrates*,
pp. 39–44.

25 *The complete works of St Thomas More*, ed. Sylvester, II; the episode of Mrs
Shore's penance and its background is related on pp. 54–7.

26 According to recent research Mrs Shore was really Elizabeth Lambert who
married William Shore, a London mercer, but had this marriage annulled on
the grounds of her husband's frigidity (the Christian names Jane and Matthew
Shore were given to them in Thomas Heywood's *King Edward the Fourth*,
1599). After her career at court Mrs Shore was married to Thomas Lyneham
or Laynham or Lynom, a solicitor, in the year of her penance (1483). How
she came to be as destitute in her old age as More describes her, remains a
mystery; Thomas Lynom was successful in his profession. See Nicholas
Barker, 'Jane Shore. Part I: the real Jane Shore', *Etoniana*, 125 (1972),
383–91, and 'The story of Jane Shore: a postscript to part I', *Etoniana*, 126
(1972), 410–14. Etonians are particularly attached to Mrs Shore: she is said
to have used her influence with Edward to save the College from destruction.

27 Mrs Shore is derisively called 'an holie whoore' by Richard's page in *The true
tragedy of Richard III* (1594), ed. W.W. Greg (Oxford, 1929), xi, 1,173.
Thomas More recounts that Edward called one of his mistresses 'the holiest
harlot in his realme' (not Mrs Shore; she was 'the meriest'; *The complete
works of St Thomas More*, ed. Sylvester, II, p. 56).

28 Prose 24, headlink to Tragedy 25, 'Shore's wife', *Mirror for magistrates*, ed.
Campbell, p. 371. This headlink was supplanted in the 1587 edition by the
one in which Churchyard asserts his authorship against Baldwin; see the
quotation below.

29 Hallett Smith, '*A woman killed with kindness*', *Publications of the Modern
Language Association*, 53 (1938), 145.

30 The highest praise has come from Esther Beith-Halahmi, *Angell fayre or
strumpet lewd* (Salzburg, 1974). Her chapter on the *Mirror for magistrates*
Complaint is called 'The concubine turned saint: Churchyard's "Shore's
wife" ', pp. 60–110. As an antidote to her sympathetic view of Churchyard's
achievement see Barbara Brown, 'Sir Thomas More and Thomas Churchyard's "Shore's wife" ', *Yearbook of English Studies*, 2 (1972), 41–8.

31 Beith-Halahmi, *Angell fayre and strumpet lewd*, p. 84. Edward's amatory

prowess has become a tag in historiography, from Philippe de Commynes' *Mémoires* to, as we have noticed, the picture book of *Royal faces* (1977).

32 Churchyard is notoriously prone to this muddling use of images; Beith-Halahmi has further instances (*Angell fayre*, pp. 84–92).

33 The beggar's outfit is Churchyard's addition. He may have thought of Henryson's leprous Cresseid, who is forced to beg her living 'with cop and clapper' (387). In a later pamphlet, Robert Tofte mentions Cressida and Mrs Shore and Rosamond Clifford side by side in his *Blazon of jealousy* (1615), N3v.

34 Dedication to Sir Edward Winckfield, *Beauty dishonoured*, A2r. Chute's poem was entered in the Stationers' Register two months after Shakespeare's. The text of the Complaint (without the dedication) is printed in Willy Budig's unpublished PhD thesis, 'Untersuchungen über "Jane Shore" ', University of Rostock, 1908, pp. 89–111. His text has a number of defects; some of these are indicated in Beith-Halahmi's *Angell fayre*, p. 111, which also has the most detailed analysis of the poem so far in a chapter called 'Womanlike though angell fayre: the courtly versions of the Jane Shore myth', pp. 111–76, where it is discussed together with Michael Drayton's pair of letters, 'King Edward the fourth to Mistress Shore, Mistress Shore to King Edward the fourth' from *England's heroical epistles* (1597).

35 Esther Beith-Halahmi reads an inversion of the Christian motif of the death of death into this ending (*Angell fayre*, p. 125); the idea is tempting and would fit in with the profane tenor of the poem; there is, however, no reference to Christian concepts in the immediate context, nor are there Platonic or Petrarchan variations on the immortality theme, and this is in keeping with the down-to-earth perspective of many Complaints. Even the Magdalen in Gervase Markham's *Marie Magdalen's lamentations* dares not look beyond death in her agony: 'And thus (ah thus) I live a dying life, / Yet neither death nor life can end my strife.' (C3v). For her, not beauty, but love is as strong as death; the sentiment from the *Song of Solomon* (8.6) had been applied to the Magdalen in the *Omelia Origenis* (ed. Combefis, p. 581) and in Robert Southwell's prose tract *Marie Magdalen's funeral tears*, B5v. For a contrast see the hopeful play on the life-in-death motif which accompanies the death of a reformed whore in Thomas Cranley's sentimental conversion poem *Amanda* (1635): 'Death vanquisht life, concluding of her paine, / She liv'd, to die, and di'd to live againe' (M4v). In this case the Christian associations are clearly intended. Amanda's last words are 'Jesus receive my soule' (M4v). Markham's poem will be discussed in ch. 5, Cranley's in ch. 6.

36 'Sir Thomas More and Thomas Churchyard's "Shore's wife" ', pp. 47–8. There is, as far as I can see, only the one formal invocation in the poem which I have quoted above, 'Sigh, sad musde accents', etc., and this is directed at the poem itself, not at the Muses.

37 *Elizabethan narrative poetry* (New Brunswick, N.J., 1950), p. 64.

38 *Angell fayre*, p. 130.

39 *Ibid.*, p. 150.

40 Cf. Samuel M. Pratt, 'Jane Shore and the Elizabethans', *Texas Studies in Language and Literature*, 11 (1970), pp. 1,301–2.

41 Chute died in 1595, according to Esther Beith-Halahmi, who also gives a few more facts about his life, among others things that he belonged to the Harvey circle (*Angell fayre*, 118–20).

42 'Shore's Wife', *Studies in English Literature 1500–1900*, 6 (1966), 459.
43 Thus the title of an anonymous chapbook of the nineteenth century. For the ballad tradition of Mrs Shore, see James L. Harner, ' "The wofull lamentation of Mistris Jane Shore": the popularity of an Elizabethan ballad', *Papers of the Bibliographical Society of America*, 71 (1977), 137–49, and Beith-Halahmi's chapter 'The wife turned strumpet: Mistress Shore in the ballads', in *Angell fayre*, pp. 177–230; for the later popular tradition of Rosamond Clifford see Virgil B. Heltzel's chapter on 'Prose fiction – chapbook, novel and tale' in his monograph *Fair Rosamond: a study of the development of a literary theme* (Evanston, Ill., 1947), pp. 39–68.
44 Samuel M. Pratt, 'Jane Shore and the Elizabethans: Some facts and speculations', *Texas Studies in Literature and Language*, 11 (1970), 1,293–306.
45 Her *femme fatale* charm reached out to painters of the Pre-Raphaelite school such as Rossetti, Hughes and Burne-Jones, whereas Mrs Shore inspired the more plebeian young Blake to a watercolour.
46 Beith-Halahmi groups Chute, it will be remembered, with Michael Drayton in her chapter on 'Courtly versions of the Jane Shore myth', *Angell fayre*, pp. 111–76.
47 *English historical poetry 1599–1641* (Philadelphia, Pa., 1945), p. 23.
48 The label is taken from Gary Floyd Bjork's unpublished PhD thesis, 'The Renaissance Mirror for Fair Ladies: Samuel Daniel's *Complaint of Rosamond* and the tradition of the feminine complaint', University of California, Irvine, 1973. Ch. 2 deals with Daniel's poem, ch. 3 with 'The genre of the feminine complaint'.
49 *Colin Clout's come home again*, line 427 (published 1595, but written soon after Spenser's visit to London in 1589–91).
50 Quotations are taken from Alexander B. Grosart's edition of *The complete works in verse and prose of Samuel Daniel* (1885; rpt New York, 1963), I, pp. 80–113. Daniel altered and augmented the original version of his Complaint as it went through several editions, swelling it from 106 to 130 rhyme royal stanzas. The Grosart edition is an unusually accurate reprint of the 1623 edition of *The whole works*, with variants from earlier ones; the short 1592 version is printed, and annotated, in Nigel Alexander's collection of *Elizabethan narrative verse* (London, 1967), pp. 215–36.
51 Elysium is the paradise for love's classical martyrs in the epyllion tradition; Richard Barnfield's Cassandra, for example, finds rest in this 'place for wrongful Death and Martirdum' after she has killed herself (*Cynthia. With certain sonnets and the legend of Cassandra* [1594], in *Some longer Elizabethan poems*, ed. A.H. Bullen [Westminster, 1903], p. 226).
52 The pastoral tradition also produced elegiac poetry, but of a less serious kind, for instance George Wither's epistolary *Fidelia* (1617).
53 Ronald Primeau assumes that passages like these are meant to disclose the fundamental shallowness of Rosamond's sense of beauty. He reads the whole poem in terms of dramatic irony, and while this serves well to dissociate the poem from the simple moralising of *Mirror for Magistrates* Complaints, it serves the heroine rather badly by subjecting her to a much harsher moral verdict than, for example, Mrs Shore; 'Daniel and the *Mirror* tradition: dramatic irony in *The complaint of Rosamond*', *Studies in English Literature 1500–1900*, 15 (1975), 21–36.

54 Both these motifs are elaborated in Thomas May's epic *Reign of King Henry II* (1633), Book II; 'arm'd Pallas' has to remind Henry of his 'affaires of Ireland' (Argument, p. C5r) because Rosamond's 'soveraigne beauty' detains him (pp. D1v–2r).

55 See *Elizabethan narrative verse*, ed. Alexander, p. 333.

56 Thomas Lodge was quick to seize the opportunity held out by such a *scène à faire* between queen and concubine; he made a similar scene serve as centre piece in his *Tragical complaint of Elstred* (1593), and Guendolen, the wronged wife who drowns her rival in the river Severn, fills it with 'heroick sprite' (*The complete works of Thomas Lodge*, ed. Edmund Gosse [1883; rpt. New York, 1963], II, pp. 57–84; p. 74). Like Daniel, Lodge sides with the concubine; in the Complaint of Elstred which John Higgins wrote for the *Mirror for magistrates*, a more orthodox view is taken. The queen is all righteous indignation, and her drowning not only her rival, but also Sabrina, the fruit of Elstred's unlawful union with her husband Locrinus, is fully justified. Higgins' Complaint has the telling title 'Elstride the concubine of Locrinus myserably drowned by Gwendoline his wyfe, declares her presumption, lewde life and infortunate fall', (*Parts added to the 'Mirror for magistrates'*, ed. Campbell [Cambridge, 1946], pp. 87–100); Higgins also wrote a Complaint of Sabrina, *ibid.*, pp. 102–9.

57 See Bjork on Rosamond's 'priviledge of Beautie', 'The Renaissance Mirror for Fair Ladies', p. 82.

58 The epitaph is first recorded in Ranulph Higden's *Polychronicon*, Rolls Series 41, (London, 1882), VIII, p. 54. A.B. Grosart prints slightly different versions of the inscription in his edition of the *Complaint of Rosamond*, p. 80. Trevisa translates the epitaph freely as: 'Here lieth in tombe the rose of the world, nought a clene rose; it smelleth nought swete, but it stinketh, that was wont to smelle ful swete'. The pun on 'mundus' was already in the account Giraldus Cambrensis gives of Henry's illicit relationship in *De principis instructione*, II, iv (ed. George F. Warner, [London, 1891], pp. 165–6). There is no evidence that an epitaph like the one recorded by Higden ever existed: V.B. Heltzel thinks it likely that Higden transferred it from an epigram on Rosamund, the queen of the Lombards who poisoned her husband Alboin to Rosamond Clifford (*Fair Rosamond*, pp. 8–9). There is a report in an early thirteenth century chronicle which says that St Hugh, Bishop of Lincoln, had Rosamond's tomb and her remains removed when he visited Godstow Abbey in 1191 because he found the nuns doing homage at her shrine; see *Gesta regis Henrici secundi Benedicti Abbatis*, ed. William Stubbs (London, 1867), II, pp. 231–2.

59 *Matilda*, in *The works of Michael Drayton*, ed. William Hebel (Oxford, 1931), I, pp. 209–46 (p. 214).

60 Cf. Robert Southwell's much more lenient approach to the problem of erotic poetry in the dedication of his treatise on *Marie Magdalen's funeral tears* to Dorothy Arundell which is discussed in ch. 5. Lily B. Campbell deals with the links between erotic and religious poetry in the first part of her study of *Divine poetry and drama in sixteenth-century England* (Cambridge, 1959). However, she does not mention Drayton's *Matilda*.

61 See R.W. Van Vossen's note on a line from Thomas Heywood's *A woman*

killed with kindness, VI, 180, where the epithet 'fair' carries a similar meaning.

62 Bjork calls Matilda 'sanctimonious' in 'The Renaissance Mirror for Fair Ladies', p. 76.

63 There were stanzas directed at Drayton's Petrarchan Lady Idea in the first version of the poem which Drayton dropped in later editions. The serious aspirations of Drayton's Complaint are also indicated by the fact that it was not, like Daniel's *Complaint of Rosamond* or Lodge's *Complaint of Elstred*, coupled with a sonnet sequence but published first separately, and later together with historical poems. A further instance of this serious intent can be seen in the frequent invocations of Queen Elizabeth ('Beta') in the poem.

64 See also lines 50–6, where the Muses are asked to provide (among other things) 'spreading Palme and never-dying Bay, / With Olive branches'.

65 *Works*, ed. Hebel, II, p. 382.

66 The same moral strength is to be found in the publican's daughter in *Willobie his Avisa*, published in the same year as *Matilda* (1594); Avisa also has 'by grace a native shield' (*The queen declined*, ed. B.N. de Luna [Oxford, 1970], p. 138). In contrast, Rosamond's fallibility is shared by Barksted's Hiren; like Rosamond she knows the fates of such women as Medea and Lucretia but fails to draw the lessons, 'Too many mirrors have we to behold, / Of mens inconstancy, and womens shame', *Hiren*, ed. Miller, p. 188.

67 See Kathleen Tillotson's note in *The works of Michael Drayton* (Oxford, 1941), V, p. 34.

68 In addition, King John's 'victory' over Matilda is contrasted with his father's conquest of kingdoms – another reference to the Letter of Phyllis, *Heroides*, II, 63–74.

69 Richard F. Hardin has cautioned against putting too much weight on the title and has stressed Drayton's historical (as opposed to Ovid's sentimental) turn of mind, 'Convention and design in Drayton's *Heroical epistles*', *Publications of the Modern Language Association*, 83 (1968), 35–41.

70 Cf. 'Incipit et dubitat, scribit damnatque tabellas / Et notat et delet, mutat culpatque probatque' (*Metamorphoses*, IX, 523–4).

71 This is only the ultimate consequence of the ascetic attitude advocated in Drayton's poem. The 'hower' of the first line is probably a singular to 'Horae' in the mythological sense of seasonal goddess (the Oxford English Dictionary has Milton's 'rosy-bosomed Hours' (*Comus*, 1634, line 968) as the earliest instance of this meaning, s.v. 'Hour, 6'. Brathwait was well versed in the elegiac tradition; his *Golden fleece* contains an 'Elegy entitled *Narcissus' change*' and another 'Elegy called *Aeson's affecting youth*'; there are a Pyramus-and-Thisbe tale and a Letter of Hyppolitus in his *Love's labyrinth* (1615), as well as satirical poems on Hero and Leander, Dido and Aeneas and, again, Pyramus and Thisbe in his *Nature's embassy* (1621).

72 *Der heroische Brief*, p. 91.

73 Since Thomas Heywood's tragedy *The rape of Lucrece* (1606–8) came much later, I take the *Lucrece* that Matilda mentions as 'Acting her passions on our stately stage' (40) to be the heroine of Shakespeare's tragic epyllion.

74 *Works*, ed Hebel, III, p. 74.

75 Little is known about the author; there is a Leicestershire connection in the dedication to a Mr Henry Pilkington of Gadsby, and there may be a Cam-

bridge connection in the background: in an epilogue to the Complaint, Sampson upbraids the scholars of Queens' College (which was co-founded by Elizabeth) for not having defended her reputation before he took the task in hand. Sampson's gallant defence has found little grace with the critics. Farnham counts it among the weak third generation of the *Mirror for magistrates* family and classes it with such widely different poems as Patrick Hannay's *Sheretine and Mariana* (1622), a lengthy Complaint about a bourgeois love-triangle situated in eastern Europe during the Turkish wars, and David Murray's *Sophonisba* (1611), a mixture of mythological and historical epic. Homer Nearing gives it more consideration in his *English historical poetry 1599–1641* (Philadelphia, Pa., 1945), pp. 58–61, but the ghost of Richard III looms larger than that of Elizabeth in his, on the whole sympathetic, treatment of the poem. Gary Floyd Bjork dismisses Sampson's poem as a relapse into the *Mirror for magistrates* fashion, unrelieved by the gentle feminine spirit Daniel had infused into the genre of Complaints ('The Renaissance Mirror for Fair Ladies', pp. 206–9).

76 *English historical poetry*, p. 178.

77 *Dramatic Works*, ed. R.H. Shepherd, I, 129; it is a bourgeois solution in a courtly milieu; Esther Beith-Halahmi has dealt with such solutions in her *Angell fayre*, pp. 276–313.

78 See Appendix III in the Arden edition of Shakespeare's *Richard III*, p. 367.

79 There are passages in the Complaint which might point at Shakespeare's handling of the same material in his history plays. Elizabeth's remark, for instance, that she must not act true to 'the imperfection of [her] sexe' by trying to right her wrongs 'by the sharpe and bitternesse of tongue' (D4r) might be aimed at Shakespeare's Senecan heroines, particularly Margaret, 'whose tongue more poisons than the adder's tooth' (*3 Henry VI*, I, iv, 112).

80
> I had rather be a country servant maid,
> Than a great queen, with this condition,
> To be so baited, scorn'd, and storm'd at:
> Small joy have I in being England's queen.   (I, iii, 107–10)

Mary Stuart expresses the same thought in the anonymous 'Legend of Mary, queen of Scots' (*c.* 1601): 'A shepard's life, with calme content of mynde / Is greater blisse, then many Princes fynde.' (Hanna Lohmann, 'John Woodward, The life and tragedy of the royal lady Mary late queen of Scots', unpublished PhD thesis, University of Berlin, 1912, lines 489–90). Cf. King Henry's wish 'To be no better than a homely swain' on the battlefield of Towton (*3 Henry VI*, II, v, 22). Here, as in *Richard III*, this sentiment has no more than anecdotal value, and the fighting goes on.

81 *A Mirror for magistrates* (1610), Eee3v; the beginning of the Epistle is reproduced in Homer Nearing's *English historical poetry*, p. 159; the page with the Epistle (Eee3) is lacking in the British Library copy of the book. Nearing discusses Niccols's poem on pp. 158–62.

82 William Warner, *Albion's England* (1606), Book XIV, ch. 81, B3r; Nearing, *Historical poetry*, p. 156.

83 Elizabeth is indeed several times compared to the 'Virgin-mother' or 'holy Mary' (B1r, C4v); for other instances of the idolization of Elizabeth in Marian terms see the introduction to Robin H. Wells, 'To sound her praise', in his

Spenser's 'Faerie queene' and the cult of Elizabeth (London, 1983), pp. 1–28. Christopher Lever is not mentioned in this study, however.

84 This is the title the poem was given in the first printed edition by John Fry (London, 1810). Hanna Lohmann ascribed the Complaint (on doubtful evidence) to John Woodward.

85 Maximus, *Homilia 85 in Joan. 20.10*, ed. Combefis, V, 586; Ambrose, *Expositio Joan. 20.10*, *ibid.*, V, 584. Augustine censures, as we know, the lack of trust in God in pagan women like Lucretia; *De civitate Dei*, I, xix.

86 Elizabeth's translation of the *Consolatio philosophiae* was made in 1593; see Caroline Pemberton's edition of *Queen Elizabeth's Englishings* (London, 1899), p. ix.

87 Chaucer, however, numbers 'timor' and 'dolor' (or 'drede' and 'sorwe', as he translates them) among the passions and gives warning to 'lat non of thise [. . .] passiouns overcomen the or blenden the'); *Boece*, Book I, Metrum 7, ed. Robinson, p. 329.

88 Hudson was an English musician, but wrote his translation of Du Bartas on the order of King James, to whose household he belonged; see Campbell, *Divine poetry and drama*, p. 96.

89 See, for example, George Ballard in his *Susanna*: 'The subcelestiall armour Saints do weare, / Is resolution' (E7v). The poem will be discussed in the next chapter.

90 'Rettungstypus'; see *Lexikon für Theologie und Kirche*, s.v. Susanna, IX (1964), cols. 1195–6.

5 Susanna and the Magdalen

1 *The divine weeks and works of Du Bartas*, I Part, I Day, II Week, 37–42; ed. Susan Snyder (Oxford, 1979), I, p. 317.

2 The poem was probably printed in Douai; its title gives only the initials I.C. (or J.C.). Herbert Thurston conjectures the author to be the Jesuit Joseph Cresswell, 'Father Southwell the Euphuist', *The Month*, 83 (1895), 241.

3 For the emergence of these religious narratives in the sixteenth century see Lily B. Campbell's *Divine poetry and drama*.

4 Origin and meaning of the story are treated by R.A.F. MacKenzie in his article on 'The meaning of the Susanna story', *Canadian Journal of Theology*, 3 (1957), 211–8. See also Alice Miskimin's introduction to her edition of *Susannah: An alliterative poem of the XIV. century* (New Haven, Conn., 1969), pp. 189–99.

5 J.H. Mozley prints both versions in his 'Susanna and the elders: three medieval poems', *Studi Medievali*, 3 (1930), 30–41. The conjectures about the date of composition and the author's age are taken from Mozley's introduction, pp. 27–8.

6 'Heu pudor, heu facinus, bene clamat Naso, quod omni / Perus adulterio turpis adulter obest' (41–2; for 'Perus' read 'Peius'); see *Heroides*, IV, 34.

7 Cf. 'Susanna', 159–60 and 177–8, with *Fasti*, II, 801–6.

8 'Non alleluia ructare sed allia norunt, / Plus in salmone quam Salamone legunt' 127–8); the lines were taken over by Matthew of Vendôme in his *Ars versificatoria*, ed. Edmond Faral, *Les arts poétiques du XIIe et du XIIIe siècle* (Paris, 1924), p. 169.

9 'Tractatus metricus de Susanna', in 'Susanna and the elders', ed. Mozley, pp. 41–50.

10 'In Didus commendationem', *De casibus virorum illustrium*, ed. L.B. Hall, p. 58; 'The Tyrian Dido or Elissa, Queen of Carthage', ch. XL, *Concerning famous women*, tr. Guido A. Guarino (New Brunswick, N.H., 1963), p. 90. Augustine, too, commends Susanna for her fighting spirit, 'Sermo 343', *Patrologia latina*, vol. 39, col. 1508.

11 Luxurious interiors and exteriors were to become a feature of medieval and Renaissance tapestries and paintings of Susanna in what Louis Réau has called the 'Bible galante' style: 'la leçon morale n'exclut pas une certaine complaisance sensuelle'; *Iconographie de l'art Chrétien*, vol. II, *Iconographie de la bible. I. Ancien Testament* (Paris, 1956), p. 395.

12 *Ennarratio in Psalmum CXXXVII*, *Patrologia latina*, vol. 36 (1845), col. 1775.

13 There is a medieval English version of the story in the style of a bob-and-tail-rhyme romance called *Susannah: or The pistill of Susan*, ed. Alice Miskimin (New Haven, Conn., 1969).

14 *The divine weeks and works of Du Bartas*, ed. Susan Snyder (Oxford, 1979). For details of the influence of Du Bartas see A.L. Prescott, 'The reception of Du Bartas in England', *Studies in the Renaissance*, 15 (1968), 144–73.

15 *Dictionary of National Biography*, vol. XLIX (1897), p. 71; cf. Anthony à Wood, *Athenae Oxonienses* (London, 1813), I, col. 682.

16 The cry has Shakespearean undertones; cf. *Lucrece*: 'Why should the private pleasure of some one / Become the public plague of many moe?' (1,478–9). The wolf–lamb imagery is traditionally associated with the Susanna story; there is an *al fresco* painting in the fourth-century Pretextatus catacomb in Rome showing Susanna between two wolves (*Reallexikon*, III, p. 582).

17 'Robert Aylett', *Huntington Library Bulletin*, 10 (1936), 1–48, and 'Robert Aylett: A supplement', *Huntington Library Quarterly*, 2 (1939), 471–8.

18 A curious instance of this preoccupation is given by Thomas Underdowne in an early version of the Theseus-and-Ariadne story, when the author strongly stipulates in his foreword that Ariadne might have made better use of her wool, and saved herself a lot of trouble, by staying at her spinning wheel; *The excellent history of Theseus and Ariadne* (1566), A4v–5r; the only copy of this adaptation is kept, quite appropriately, at the John Rylands Library, Manchester.

19 See Chapman's continuation of Marlowe's *Hero and Leander*, IV, 37–121, and Daniel's *Complaint of Rosamond*, 379–420.

20 *The Laws of Ecclesiastical Polity*, III, i, 10.

21 'The third sestiad', lines 199–226; *Elizabethan narrative verse*, ed. Alexander, pp. 83–4.

22 *Joseph: or Pharaoh's favourite* (1623); *David's troubles remembered*, published anonymously (RSTC 6316); Padelford ascribed the *David* to Aylett on stylistic grounds ('Robert Aylett', pp. 31–3; cf. Barbara Kiefer Lewalski, '*David's troubles remembered*: An anlogue to *Absalom and Achitophel*', *Notes and Queries*, 209, Sept. 1964, 340–3).

23 Ballard combines his religious with traditional ethnic prejudices in this denunciation. The commonplace of the intemperate southern climate is used

by Edward More to raise the reputation of English women in his *Defence of women, and especially of English women* (1560), A1v–B1r.

24 I quote from the *Vulgata* because most of the literature discussed in this chapter is either medieval or Roman Catholic, and I concentrate on the version of St John (John 20.1–18) because it was his detailed report which fired the imagination (or indignation) of interpreters through the ages. For comments on the significance of the figure of the Magdalen in poetical literature see Hans Hansel, 'Die Quelle der bayrischen Magdalenenklage', *Zeitschrift für Deutsche Philologie*, 22 (1937), 363–88, Helen Garth, *Saint Mary Magdalen in medieval literature* (Baltimore, 1950) and Wiltrud aus der Fünten, *Maria Magdalena in der Lyrik des Mittelalters* (Düsseldorf, 1966).

25 'Tractatus 121 in Joannis Evangelium', in *Patrologia latina*, ed. Migne, 34 (1845), col. 1955.

26 'In diebus Paschalibus, XV', Sermo 244, *Patrologia latina*, ed. Migne, 38 (1845), col. 1148.

27 *Omelia Origenis*, in *Bibliotheca Patrum*, ed. Combefis, V, p. 583.

28 'Expositio Evangelii secundum Joannem', in *Bibliotheca Patrum*, ed. Combefis, V, p. 584.

29 Maximus of Turin, 'Homilia 56: De Maria Magdalena, et de resurrectione Domini, II', in *Patrologia latina*, ed. Migne, 57 (1847), col. 359.

30 'Homilia 85 in Joannem 20.10', in *Bibliotheca Patrum*, ed. Combefis, V, p. 586.

31 'Expositio in Joannem 20.10', *Bibliotheca Patrum*, ed. Combefis, V, p. 599. There is no doubt, however, for Theophylactus that the affections cloud Mary's view: 'Plena enim affectionum erat mens mulieris, non valens sublime quiddam cogitare', *ibid.*

32 'Homilia XXV', XL Homiliarum in Evangelia Liber II, *Patrologia latina*, ed Migne, 76 (1849), col. 1190.

33 Chrysostom, 'Homilia 85 in Joannem', *Bibliotheca Patrum*, ed. Combefis, V, p. 578; Ambrose, 'Expositio Evangelii', *ibid.*, 584.

34 'De Mariae Magdalenae devotione in Christo requirendo, et ejus visione'. Chap. 15 of his *Meditatio in passionem et resurrectionem Domini*, *Patrologia latina*, ed. Migne 184 (1854), col. 765. Cf. the *Lamentacio Bernardi*, which allows the Virgin Mother a similar solace: 'Con I me no beter solas / then for to wepe al my fille' (407–8).

35 Quotations are from the version edited by Combefis, *Bibliotheca Patrum*, V, pp. 580–84. There are other editions of the 'In praesenti' version in Louis Bourgain, *La Chaire française au XIIe siècle d'après les manuscrits* (Paris, 1879), pp. 373–83, and of the 'Audivimus' version in Adolf Patera, *Hradecky Rukopis* (Prague, 1881), pp. 438–449. We still lack a critical edition of this influential tract. For details on the different versions, the discussions about authorship and the manuscript tradition see John P. McCall, 'Chaucer and the Pseudo Origen *De Maria Magdalena*: a preliminary study', *Speculum*, 46 (1971), 491–509.

36 Rosemary Woolf has no doubts about the correctness of the reference; see her article 'English imitations of the *Homelia Origenis de Maria Magdalena*', in *Chaucer and Middle English studies in honour of Rossell Hope Robbins*, ed. Beryl Rowland (London, 1974), pp. 384–91.

37 Quoted from Alexander Chalmers' *The works of the English poets* (London,

1810), I, 532. The various titles have caused some confusion, and later scholarship has done little to answer the questions of who was the author of the
adaptation and how it was transmitted. Tyrwhitt rejected the ascription to
Chaucer (see McCall, 'Pseudo Origen', p. 491); Bertha M. Skeat edited the
text as found in Thynne's *Works*, apparently unaware of earlier prints or
other versions (*The lamentatyon of Mary Magdaleyne*, Cambridge, 1897),
and ascribed it to the fifteenth-century school of Lydgate; Rosemary Woolf
correctly places it in the *Omelia Origenis* tradition, but seems confused about
some of the bibliographical points involved. She believes, for instance, the
Pynson edition of the poem lost ('English imitations', p. 391, n. 18; as stated
above, it is in Pynson's *The book of fame*, pp. E5r–F3v). *The complaint of
Mary Magdaleyn* was, at times, thought to be by Lydgate himself,
erroneously, according to Walter F. Schirmer, (*John Lydgate*, Westport, Ct.
1961, p. 282); Derek Pearsall, however, is inclined to accept the ascription
(*John Lydgate*, London, 1970, p. 183). Rosemary Woolf has the somewhat
enigmatic note: " 'The lamentation of Mary Magdalen' by Lydgate, mentioned in some recent scholarly works, does not exist. [. . .] 'The Lamentation of Mary Magdalen' is a complaint of the Virgin." ('English imitations',
p. 390, n. 3).

38 Quotations are taken from 'The lamentatyon of Mary Magdaleyne' in
Thynne's edition of 1532 which is most readily available in Derek Brewer's
facsimile   reprint   of   *The   works*,   2nd   edn   (Ilkley,   1974),
pp. CCCLXIr–CCCLXVv.

39 Rosemary Woolf has pointed out the affinity of the *Complaint* with Marian
laments; see her article, 'English imitations', p. 387. For the tradition of
laments of the Virgin see her chapters on passion lyrics, particularly 'On the
compassion of the Blessed Virgin', in *The English religious lyric in the Middle
Ages* (Oxford, 1968), pp. 239–73.

40 See McCall, who notes the affinity of the Magdalen of the Complaint with
Chaucerian heroines in his 'Pseudo Origen', p. 501.

41 There may be a similarly bold appropriation of the question Pilate put to the
rabble demanding the execution of Jesus ('Quid enim mali fecit?', Mat. 27.23)
when Mary asks of her lover 'Quid mali feci tibi' (500), but this is also a
variation of the 'quid feci' formula with which Ovidian heroines reproach
their heroes.

42 'English imitations', pp. 387–8. The Ghismonda novella, incidentally, was
brought into English at about the time the *Complaint of Mary Magdaleyn*
was written. This translation will be discussed in my next chapter.

43 *The Digby plays*, ed. F.J. Furnivall, EETS ES, vol. 70 (London, 1896),
pp. 53–136.

44 For more details see Appendix A in Rosemary Woolf, *English Mystery plays*
(London, 1972), pp. 327–35.

45 *The Life and Poems of Nicholas Grimald*, ed L.R. Merrill (New Haven,
1925). A reprint of the original edition was published in the Renaissance
Latin Drama in England Series, First Series, vol. 9 (Hildesheim, 1982).

46 Ed. F.I. Carpenter, 2nd edn (Chicago, Ill., 1904).

47 *Saint Mary Magdalene in medieval literature*, p. 14.

48 Ed. H.O. Sommer, EETS ES, vol. 78 (London, 1899); B.O. Kurth places

the legend between a Pilgrimage of the soul and a biblical epic in his *Milton and Christian heroism* (Hamden, Ct., 1966), pp. 96–9.

49 The only complete copy of the first edition is in the Huntington Library; a facsimile reprint of this copy was edited by Vincent B. Leitch (Delmar, NY., 1975); there is a critical edition in an unpublished PhD thesis by John R. Gappa (St. Louis University, 1968).

50 See, for example, Louis L. Martz, *The poetry of meditation*, 2nd edn (New Haven, 1962), pp. 199–203, and Helen C. White, 'Southwell: Metaphysical and baroque', *Modern Philology* (1964), p. 160.

51 'Southwell's *St Peter's complaint* and its Italian Source', *Modern Language Review*, 19 (1924), 273–90.

52 In her study, *Tudor books of saints and martyrs* (Madison, Wisc., 1963), p. 264, Helen C. White suspected that there must be a Latin version of the *Omelia Origenis* behind Southwell's *Marie Magdalen's funeral tears*, but was puzzled by the 'In praesenti' beginning of Southwell's treatise because she only knew the 'Audivimus' version. Like most of the Southwell specialists (Nancy Pollard Brown, Christopher Devlin, Pierre Janelle, James H. McDonald), she was misled by an Italian translation of the *Omelia Origenis*, of which a manuscript is kept in the Stonyhurst library, that belongs to the 'Audivimus' group and cannot have been Southwell's source. For more details on this question see the bibliography of the German version of this study, pp. 361–3.

53 Stonyhurst MS A.v.4, 56r. Pierre Janelle discusses these drafts in comparison with their presumed Italian source in his *Robert Southwell the writer: a study in religious inspiration* (Clermont-Ferrant, 1935), pp. 184–97; he prints a transcript of the whole of the second draft on p. 188.

54 A.B. Grosart published the Latin fragments in Part V, 'Poemata latina', of his edition of *The complete poems of Robert Southwell* (Blackburn, 1872). One of these fragments is part of an elegy on a Scottish queen whom Grosart takes to be Mary Stuart (Pierre Janelle offers the more likely identification with St Margaret of Scotland). This piece is inscribed like a *Mirror for magistrates* Complaint: 'Umbra Reginae nobiles viros docet, quid sit de rebus hisce fluxis sentiendum' (p. 210, cf. Janelle, Appendix IV, 'Southwell's Latin elegies', pp. 299–302).

55 The expression is by Herbert Thurston, 'Father Southwell the Euphuist', *The Month*, 83 (1895), 235.

56 *The life of Robert Southwell* (London, 1956), p. 118.

57 Helen C. White, 'Southwell: Metaphysical and baroque', *Modern Philology*, 61 (1964), 159–68.

58 *Prosopopeia*, in *The complete works of Thomas Lodge*, ed. Edmund Gosse III, pp. 10–12. Lodge is not boasting here; see Alice Walker. 'The reading of an Elizabethan: some sources of the prose pamphlets of Thomas Lodge', *Review of English Studies*, 8 (1932), 264–81 (pp 279–81).

59 The dialogue or *colloquium* is a feature of the formal meditation; for the affinity of the Marian lament with meditative exercises see Elaine Cuvelier, *Thomas Lodge: témoin de son temps (c. 1558–1625)* (Paris, 1984), pp. 510–11.

60 See Elaine Cuvelier, *Thomas Lodge*, p. 509.

61 For doctrinal reasons behind the changes in literary presentations of the Blessed Virgin see Sandro Sticca, 'The literary genesis of the Latin Passion

play and the Planctus Mariae', in *The medieval drama*, ed. S. Sticca (Albany, N.Y., 1972), 39–68, and Rosemary Woolf, *Religious lyric*, pp. 272–3, and *The English mystery play* (London, 1972), p. 403.

62 *De obitu Valentiniani consolatio*, in *Patrologia latina*, ed Migne, 16 (1845), col. 1371. He is probably referring to John 19.15: 'Stabant autem iuxta crucem Iesu mater eius, et soror matris eius, Maria Cleophae, et Maria Magdalene.' As mentioned above the Virgin is not left alone under the Cross, the singular 'stabat' has no authority, nor has the 'dolorosa' that was added in later Passion lyrics.

63 There is a short list of imitations of 'Works possibly inspired by *Mary Magdalens Teares*' in Janelle's *Robert Southwell*, pp. 309–10; see also Herbert Thurston, 'Father Southwell the popular poet', *The Month*, 83 (1895), 383–99.

64 See Vincent B. Leitch's unpaginated introduction to the facsimile reprint of *Marie Magdalens Funeral Teares (1591) by Robert Southwell* (Delmar, N.Y., 1975).

65 The OED's first illustration of this sense is dated 1606, s.v. 'colon³'. Robert Gittings takes the word to refer to Spenser (*Shakespeare's rival: a study in three parts* (London, 1960, p. 35); this would support his allegorical reading of the poem which I will discuss in note 68, but it hardly fits in with the context. The term 'Collin' occurs in the last stanza of the Preface:

> *If you will deigne with favour to peruse*
> *Maries memoriall of her sad lament,*
> *Exciting* Collin *in his graver Muse,*
> *To tell the manner of her hearts repent:*
> *My gaine is great, my guerdon granted is,*
> *Let* Maries *plaints plead pardon for amiße.*　　　　　(A4v)

I read this as a *captatio benevolentiae*; it refers back to the first stanza of the Preface where the poet describes in terms familiar from the *Mirror for magistrates* how Mary's soul asked him to pen her Complaint (see the quotation below). Otherwise, the Preface follows the same argument as Southwell's dedication of his *Funeral tears*.

66 'Memorial introduction' to a selection of Markham's works (among them *Marie Magdalen's lamentations*, pp. 535–96) in *Miscellanies of the Fuller Worthies' Library*, (Blackburn, 1871), II, p. 487.

67 'Popular poet', p. 396. Lily B. Campbell does not name a source in her discussion of the poem in *Divine poetry*, pp. 120–1. Rosemary Woolf wonders if Markham knew the Chaucerian *Lamentation of Mary Magdaleyne* and misses out Southwell altogether in her 'English imitations', p. 388. John P. McCall also mentions Markham but not Southwell among the authors influenced by the *Omelia Origenis* ('Pseudo Origen', p. 497).

68 This stanza was added in the edition of 1604, A4v. There has been some confusion about the occasion and the addressee of the poem. Robert Gittings reads it (and its companion piece, *The tears of the beloved*), as 'secret allegories of the trial and execution of Essex, with the Earl as the Saviour', and Spenser as 'Collin' because Essex tried to befriend him on his death-bed. The role of Mary Magdalen would then suit best the Lady Frances, Sidney's widow and the wife of Essex, and Gittings hints at this possibility in a footnote (*Shakespeare's rival*, pp. 34–5 and notes 1 and 2). F.N.L. Poynter, though otherwise wary of political speculations, follows this hint (without naming Gittings) and identifies the Magdalen tentatively with the twice widowed

lady: 'Is it Mary Magdalen, bereft of her Lord, of whom he writes so feelingly, or is the pity showed by thoughts of Frances, daughter of the great Walsingham, widow of the universally admired Sidney, and now the widow of a condemned and executed "traitor"?' (*A bibliography of Markham*, p. 48). Many of these speculations evaporate, of course, in the light of the closeness with which Markham follows his model, Southwell's *Funeral tears*, of which both Gittings and Poynter were unaware. The lines 'Here where all anger lately buried was, / But none deserv'd, ah, none deserv'd alas!' (D1v), which Poynter takes out of their context (they refer to Mary Magdalen's tears) lose some of their startling aspect if set beside the parallel lines from Southwell's treatise: 'If they be teares of anger to denounce thy displeasure, they should not here haue beene shedde where all anger was buried but none deserued.' (*Funeral tears*, E1v). Nevertheless, there is an Essex connection, to which I will return below.

69 Cf. Lancelot Andrewes' 'Sermon 14 of the Resurrection: Easter 1620', *Sermons*, ed. Story, pp. 192–217.

70 See *The Poems of Robert Southwell, S.J.* ed. James H. McDonald and Nancy Pollard Brown (Oxford, 1967), pp. lxxxviii–lxxxix, for an application of this doctrine to Southwell's *Saint Peter's complaint*. The wider background is covered by Joseph D. Scallon in a chapter of his study, *The poetry of Robert Southwell, S.J.* (Salzburg, 1975), pp. 151–219.

71 *Robert Southwell the writer*, p. 59.

72 See Campbell, *Divine poetry*, pp. 52–4.

73 *The poems of Edward de Vere, seventh Earl of Oxford and Robert Devereux, second Earl of Essex*, ed. Steven W. May, *Studies in Philology*, 77, Suppl. (1980), pp. 1–132. *The Passion of a discontented mind* is no. 11 of the Essex collection, pp. 48–59 (commentary pp. 94–106). May's ascription was accepted by Edward Doughtie in an article on 'The Earl of Essex and occasions for contemplative verse', *English Literary Renaissance*, 9 (1979), 355–63.

74 For bibliographical details see *Poems by Nicholas Breton (not hitherto reprinted)*, ed. Jean Robertson, (Liverpool, 1952), pp. lv–lix.

75 These doubts were not easily dispersed; see J.B. Collins, *Christian mysticism in the Elizabethan age with its background in mystical methodology* (Baltimore, Md., 1940): 'Breton's religious affiliation is uncertain' (p. 183). Jean Robertson, who documents the debate in the Introduction to *Poems (not hitherto reprinted)*, pp. lxii–lxiii, quite rightly points out that deeply religious poetry is not a Roman Catholic privilege. An obvious example of a devotional tract crossing the lines would be the *De imitatione Christi* attributed to Thomas à Kempis which was popular with Christians of all denominations; see Helen C. White on the English adaptation of this treatise in her *Tudor books of private devotion* (Madison, Wisc., 1951), p. 28.

76 On the evidence of these parallels, J.P. Collier pondered the possibility that *The passion of a discontented mind* might be Southwell's; see the introduction to his reprint of the 1602 edition of the poem, *Illustrations of old English literature*, vol. I, no. 6, I quote from May's edition of the first printed version of 1601, a unique copy of which is kept in the Houghton Library, Harvard.

77 His metre is, however, the sixain stanza preferred in epyllia. In that he may be following the example of Southwell's *St Peter's complaint*. A plagiariser,

G. Ellis, apparently found this inadequate and reshaped 312 lines from *The Passion of a discontented mind* into rhyme royal stanzas in his poem *The lamentation of the lost sheep* (1605). See May, p. 102, and Mary Shakeshaft's article on 'Nicholas Breton's *The Passion of a discontented mind*: Some new problems', *Studies in English Literature 1500–1900*, 5 (1965), 165–74. Sixteen stanzas from Ellis's poem are printed in Edward Farr's *Select poetry, chiefly devotional, from the reign of queen Elizabeth* (Cambridge, 1845), II, pp. 408–11. The plagiarism is the more remarkable for the fact that the 30 stanzas which Ellis contributed are at least as good as those he took over from *The Passion of a discontented mind*.

78 A stanza in which the Discontented Mind invokes the Virgin Mary and the Saints in heaven as mediators (lines 31–6 in May's edition) was taken out by conscientious copyists of the poem; see May's commentary, p. 104.

79 I quote from the 1601 edition; the spelling in A.B. Grosart's reprint in *The works of Nicholas Breton* (Edinburgh, 1879), I, is not exactly diplomatic.

80 See Doughtie's article on 'The Earl of Essex', pp. 361–3.

6 Violenta and Amanda

1 *The wright's chaste wife* is attributed to Adam of Cobsham by its editor, F.J. Furnivall, EETS OS 12, 2nd edn (London, 1869). For the enigmatic *Avisa* see B.N. de Luna's edition, *The queen declined* (Oxford, 1970). Willoby's *Avisa* was answered by Peter Colse's *Penelope's complaint* (1596).

2 For details about the translations of these tales see the preface to H.G. Wright's edition, *Early English versions of the tales of Guiscardo and Ghismonda and Titus and Gisippus*, EETS OS 205 (London, 1937), which is based on Julius Zupitza's 'Die mittelenglischen Bearbeitungen der Erzählungen Boccaccios von Ghismonda und Guiscardo', *Vierteljahrsschrift für Kultur und Litteratur der Renaissance*, 1 (1886), 63–102, and cf. Joseph Raith, *Boccaccio in der englischen Literatur* (Leipzig, 1936).

3 See Wright's introduction, pp. xi–xii. For details on the Rawlinson MS C 86 cf. Raith, p. 77.

4 See Raith, p. 79.

5 *Early English versions*, pp. xxxi, xxxvi.

6 It is reproduced side by side with the Trinity College manuscript in Wright's edition of *Early English versions*, pp. 38–99.

7 Giovanni Boccaccio, *Il Decameron*, ed. Aldo Rossi (Bologna, 1977), pp. 223–4.

8 *Boccaccio in der englischen Literatur*, pp. 123; Raith follows its career in an appendix, pp. 131–4.

9 For typical traits of the novella see Erich Auerbach's interpretation of the Tale of Frate Alberto (*Decameron*, IV, 2) in his *Mimesis: Dargestellte Wirklichkeit in der abendländischen Literatur*, 4th edn (Bern, 1967), pp. 195–221 (pp. 220–1).

10 Ed. Joseph Jacobs (3 vols., London, 1890). The early reception of Italian novelle in England has been studied by Emil Koeppel, *Studien zur Geschichte der italienischen Novelle in der englischen Literatur des 16. Jahrhunderts* (Hamburg, 1890); for Bandello see René Pruvost, *Matteo Bandello and Elizabethan fiction* (Paris, 1937).

11 Bandello, *Novelle*, I, no. 42; Painter, *Palace*, ed. Jacobs, I, pp. 218–39.

12 *Heroides*, VII, 167 and III, 75–6.

13 Eleanor of Aquitaine proves a heroine of this kind in Thomas May's epic *Reign of King Henry II*; she compares herself with Medea before acting out her revenge, Book V, I4v.

14 *Palace*, ed. Jacobs, I, p. 239.

15 *Metamorphoses*, VI, 435, 459, 515, 533, etc.; cf. Orpheus, who relates the story of Myrrha and praises his country for not lying too close to Cyprus, Myrrha's home (*Metamorphoses*, X, 306–7).

16 Douglas Bush gives a number of instances where elegiac material, and in particular letters, are inserted in novelle; see his article on '*The petite pallace of Pettie his pleasure*', *Journal of English and Germanic Philology*, 27 (1928), 167–8.

17 Little is known about Achelley's personal circumstances; he was associated with Thomas Kyd and the Queen's Men; see the bibliographical note by Arthur Freeman, 'The writings of Thomas Achelley', *Library*, 25 (1970), 40–42.

18 *Geschichte der italienischen Novelle*, p. 31.

19 It is one of the commonplaces of Elizabethan ethnography that owing to the hot climate Italian women are more passionate than the English; see, for instance, Edward More's *Defence of women, and especially of English women* (1560), B1r–v.

20 'The progeny of *A Mirror for magistrates*', *Modern Philology*, 29 (1932), 403.

21 The property of the revealing mirror connects Acts III and IV of this play; see pp. 56, 59–60, 70, 72 in French's acting edition (London, 1936).

22 See F.N.L. Poynter's biographical and bibliographical article 'Gervase Markham' in *Essays and Studies*, 15 (1962), 27–39 (p. 30). Poynter describes and discusses *Paulina* in his *Bibliography of Gervase Markham 1568?–1637* (Oxford, 1962), pp. 51–2.

23 Daniel Defoe, *Roxana: The fortunate mistress*, ed. David Blewitt, Harmondsworth, 1982, p. 197.

24 See Frederick Ouvry's edition of the Complaint, (London, 1868), pp. 36–7, for these notes; the British Library copy of the original edition is cropped and some of the marginal notes are affected. Apparently an English prostitute was in need of even more companions; see Thomas Cranley's *Amanda*:

> Beside thy Pimpe, thy Pander, and thy Bawd,
> To make thee a compleate, and perfect whore,
> As necessary members to thy trade,
> To helpe thee at thy need, thou keep'st in store,
> Some well approu'd Physitian evermore.
> As his Aßistants, lest thou should'st miscarry,
> Thou hast a Surgeon, and Apothecary.   (F1v).

25 It was not until 1637 that all books had to be submitted to public censorship; see Nearing, *Historical poetry*, p. 189, n. 36. For Laud's activities as a censor see his life in the *Dictionary of National Biography*, IX, pp. 315–6. The judicial proceedings of the time are described in Bestil Johannson's *Law and lawyers in Elizabethan England* (Stockholm, 1967). On the prisons of the time see Clifford Dobb, 'London's prisons', *Shakespeare Survey*, 17 (1964), 87–100.

26 The definition is from Palgrave's French Dictionary as quoted in the Oxford

English Dictionary, s.v. 'Fleet', sb.^{2}, 2.a. For Falstaff and the Fleet see *2 Henry IV*, V, v, 91 and the note on this line in the Arden edition.

27 The first of these is mentioned in a letter of 1613 according to the OED, s.v. 'Fleet', sb.^{2}, 2.b.

28 'London's Prisons', p. 99 and n. 6.

29 *The parson's wedding* (1663), IV, ii; quoted from the OED, s.v. 'Bridewell'; cf. *The Elizabethan underworld*, ed. A.V. Judges (London, 1930), pp. lxii–lxiii.

30 Alexandre Dumas fils, *La Dame aux camélias. Le roman, le drame, 'La Traviata'*, ed. Hans-Jörg Neuschäfer and Gilbert Sigaux (Paris, 1981), p. 410.

7 Commiseration and imagination

1 'Her heyre rudely disheueled, her chaplet withered, her visage with teares stayned' etc., *An apology for actors* (rpt. New York, 1972), B1v.

2 *The rising to the crown of Richard the Third* (1593), L2r.

3 *An apology for poetry*, ed. Geoffrey Shepherd (London, 1965), p. 118.

4 *Anatomy of criticism* (1957; rpt Princeton, N.J., 1973), pp. 38–9. George R. Keiser opposes this view, with respect to Marian complaints, in his article 'The Middle English *Planctus Mariae* and the rhetoric of pathos', in *The popular literature of medieval England*, ed. Thomas J. Heffernan (Knoxville, Tenn., 1985), 167–93 (pp. 174–6).

5 The passage is quoted at greater length above, ch. 4, p. 140.

6 Aristotle's skeptic view of the suitability of tragic heroines is based on the inferior status, not the moral deficiency, of women; 'there is in fact such a thing as a good woman and such a thing as a good slave, although no doubt one of these classes is inferior and the other, as a class, is worthless' (quoted from Gerald F. Else, *Aristotle's Poetics: the argument* [Cambridge, Mass., 1957], p. 455; see also Else's commentary, pp. 457–60).

7 *Servii Grammatici qui feruntur in Vergilii carmini commentarii*, ed. Georg Thilo and Hermann Hagen, vol. I (1889; rpt Hildesheim, 1961), p. 459. Nicholas Trivet puts it even more bluntly in a commentary on Seneca's tragedies; comedy deals with 'the debauching of virgins and the love of prostitutes' (quoted from D.W. Robertson, Jr., *A preface to Chaucer*, p. 473).

8 See the Oxford English Dictionary, s.v. 'Commiseration'.

9 *An apology for poetry*, ed. Shepherd, p. 116.

10 *Omelia Origenis*, in *Bibliotheca Patrum*, ed. Combefis, V, p. 583.

11 *Marie Magdalen's funeral tears* (1591), H7v.

12 *Omelia Origenis*, ed. Combefis, p. 581. See also Ovid's Hermione, 'flere licet certe', and Ariadne, 'quid potius facerent, quam me mea lumina flerent' (*Heroides*, VIII, 61; X, 45).

13 'Die Klagen der verlassenen Heroiden in der lateinischen Dichtung', unpublished PhD thesis (University of Munich, 1958); the chapter headings are 'quo me referam' (p. 43) and 'utinam ne' (p. 85). The formula 'quo me referam' can be traced back to heroines of Greek drama, Sophocles' Antigone (*Oedipus at Colonus*, 109) and Euripides' *Medea*, 501.

14 Quoted from Robert B. Heilman, *Tragedy and melodrama* (Seattle, Wash., 1968), p. 37.

15 The French influence was spread through the circle around Mary Herbert,

the Countess of Pembroke, who had translated Garnier's *Antonius* herself in 1592; see Walter F. Schirmer, 'Shakespeares klassizistische Gegenspieler', *Anglia*, 76 (1958), 90–115, and Wolfgang Clemen's chapter on the 'dramatic elegies' of Garnier and other classicist tragedies, 'The lament in Renaissance drama', *English tragedy before Shakespeare* (London, 1961), pp. 213–15.

16 The curses do hurt in Euripides' *Medea*, 465–519; they do not in Ovid's Heroical Epistles; see *Heroides*, VII, 61–4; XII, 21–2. The women scenes in Shakespeare's *Richard III* are influenced by Seneca's *Troades*, as Harold F. Brooks has shown in detail '*Richard III*: Unhistorical amplifications. The women's scenes and Seneca', *Modern Language Review*, 75 (1980), 721–37.

17 Heinze has an appendix on epic and elegiac monologues in his 'Ovids elegische Erzählung', pp. 388–401. The distinction might have proved useful to Clark Hulse, who reads both modes into the *Metamorphoses* and the *Faerie queene* in his chapter on 'Spenser's Ovidian Epic' in *Metamorphic verse*, pp. 242–78.

18 'Poetry, history, and oratory: the Renaissance historical poem', *Studies in English Literature 1500–1900*, 9 (1969), 2.

19 For him, the suicide seems an end in itself, 'the only effective way of ending the whole wearisome and seemingly interminable processes of debate', *The rapes of Lucretia*, p. 43.

20 'Perspektivische Sicht ist menschliche Sicht', 'Bunyans *Pilgrim's progress*: Die kalvinistische Heilsgewißheit und die Form des Romans', in *Medium Aevum vivum*, Festschrift für Walter Bulst (Heidelberg, 1960), pp. 279–304 (p. 287). The article corresponds to ch. I of his *Der implizite Leser* (tr. as *The implied reader*, Baltimore, Md., 1974).

21 There had been shifts between the metrical and the modern sense in classical times already; see Georg Luck, *The Latin love elegy* (1959; 2nd edn London, 1969), pp. 25–30. Ovid's frequent use of the elegiac distich for poetry of complaint probably prepared the way for the now primary sense of mournful poetry, and the popular *Heroides* were main agents in this shift; 'the verb queror [. . .] occurs more frequently in the *Heroides* than in any other Ovidian work', writes W.S. Anderson, and he concludes that 'the basic tune of *Heroides* I–XV [i.e. all but the double letters] is complaint' ('Ovid's *Heroides*', p. 69). See also A.R. Baca, 'The themes of *querela* and *lacrimae* in Ovid's *Heroides*', *Emerita*, 39 (1971), 195–201. Ovid's *Heroides* were called 'traictés par maniere de complainte' already in the fourteenth century second redaction of the so-called *Histoire ancienne jusquà César*, a compilation of ancient history and legend which incorporates thirteen of Ovid's letters; see Léopold Constans, 'Une traduction française des *Héroides* d'Ovide au XIIIᵉ siècle', *Romania*, 43 (1914), 184.

22 See Edmond Faral, *Les Arts poétiques du XIIᵉ et du XIIIᵉ siècle* (1924; rpt. Paris, 1971), pp. 337, 346.

23 *Lateinische Literaturdenkmäler des XV. und XVI. Jahrhunderts*, ed. Karl Wotke, vol. 10 (Berlin, 1894), p. 59.

24 'Das legt die Vermutung nahe, daß die Elegie gar nicht als *Gattung*, sondern als *Grundart* (wie Lyrik, Epos, Drama) aufgefaßt wurde', *Geschichte der deutschen Elegie* (Berlin, 1941), pp. 25–6.

25 Ovid himself speaks of 'flebilis . . . Elegeia' in his *Amores*, III, ix, 3.

26 See Christine Scollen, *The birth of the elegy in France 1500–1550* (Geneva,

1967), pp. 13–37. There is no corresponding study of the early development of the elegy in England yet.

27 See the collection in Francis W. Weitzmann's article 'Notes on the Elizabethan "Elegie" ', *Publications of the Modern Language Association*, 50 (1935), 435–43; Weitzmann distinguishes eight different meanings of the term 'elegy' in Elizabethan tracts.

28 See George Puttenham's definition of the elegy as 'a pitious maner of meeter, placing a limping *Pentameter*, after a lusty *Exameter*, which made it go dolourously more then any other meeter'; *The art of English poesy*, ed. G.D. Willcock and A. Walker (1936; rpt. Cambridge, 1970), p. 49.

29 *Elegische Erzählung*, pp. 345–6. The motif was taken over by Gower and Shakespeare into their tales of Lucrece (*Confessio Amantis*, VII, 5042–4; *Lucrece*, 1716–22); Trussell transfers it to young Helen, who is hardly able to name her ravisher 'These – us'. There are numerous other instances of the technique.

30 *Poetry and metamorphosis* (Cambridge, 1983), pp. 23–47.

31 *Sermons*, ed. Story, p. 212. Cf. Hrabanus Maurus, *De vita Mariae Magdalenae*, cap. XXI (*Patrologia latina*, ed Migne, 112, 1852, col. 1472) and Anselm of Canterbury, *Oratio ad sanctam Mariam Magdalenam* (*Patrologia latina*, ed Migne, 158, 1853, col. 1013). The broken speech is, indeed, one of the symptoms of love in erotic literature from Hellenistic times; see Richard Heinze, *Virgil's epische Technik* (1915; rpt. Darmstadt, 1976), p. 130.

32 Quoted by Scollen, *Birth of the elegy*, p. 14.

33 See the chapter on the 'Letter of Dydo to Eneas' and further references in note 55 to that chapter.

34 *Mirror*, ed. Campbell, p. 442. Cf. Chaucer's Criseyde: 'Therto we wrecched wommen nothing konne, / Whan us is wo, but wepe and sitte and thinke; / Oure wrecche is this, oure owen wo to drynke.' (*Troilus and Criseyde*, II, 782–4)

35 See Jacobson's summary in his *Ovid's Heroides*, pp. 322–30, and Christoph de Nagy's chapter on 'Themes and composition of the *Heroides*; the impact of rhetoric on the *Heroides*' in his *Michael Drayton's "England's heroical epistles"* (Berne, 1968), pp. 19–25.

36 For the diffuse terminology in classical treatises see Quintilian, *Institutio oratoria*, III, 8, 12, and cf. Eberhard Oppel, 'Ovid's Heroides', unpublished PhD thesis (University of Erlangen, 1968), p. 79.

37 See Heinrich F. Plett, *Rhetorik der Affekte* (Tübingen, 1975), pp. 96–7.

38 See D.L. Clark, *John Milton at St Paul's school* (1948; rpt. Columbia, N.C., 1964), pp. 189–90.

39 Rpt. Gainesville, Fla, 1961, p. 68.

40 *Works*, ed. Hebel, I., p. 130.

41 See Scollen, *Birth of the elegy*, p. 37.

42 Cf. Richardson's Pamela, who recoils at the idea of Lucretia's fate and fights off the temptation to suicide in a lengthy *bellum intestinum* (*Pamela*, Everyman edn. I, 20; 149–52). This is the comic epic prose solution in an appropriately steadfast form.

43 'Eloisa to Abelard', 17–20; 129–70. Pope translated Ovid's 'Letter of Sappho' which contains a long description of a haunted grove.

44 'The legend of Mary, queen of Scots' (1601), lines 468–9; *The excellent history of Theseus and Ariadne* (1566), B8r.

45 The Pseudo-Origen uses it to excuse Mary's failure to recognize the risen Christ: 'Ideoque forsitan non cognoscit te, quia non est in sese, sed propter to est extra se'; *Omelia Origenis*, in *Bibliotheca Patrum*, ed. Combefis, V, p. 582.

46 'Thomas Heywood', in *Essays*, p. 181.

47 Thomas Rymer, *Tragedies of the last age* (1678), p. 75.

48 Ed. Donald F. Bond (Oxford, 1965), V, pp. 112–3.

Bibliography

Texts

Collections

Alexander, Nigel (ed.). *Elizabethan narrative verse*. The Stratford-upon-Avon Library 3. London, 1967.

Ballantyne, J. (ed.). *Certain worthy manuscript poems of great antiquity*. Edinburgh, 1812.

Benz, Richard (ed.). *Die Legenda aurea des Jacobus de Voragine*. Berlin, 1963.

Bond, Donald F. (ed.). *The Spectator*. Vol. V. Oxford, 1965.

Bryan, W.F. and Germaine Dempster (eds.). *Sources and analogues of the 'Canterbury tales'*. Chicago, 1941.

Bullen, A.H. (ed.). *Some longer Elizabethan poems*. Westminster, 1903.

Campbell, Lily B. (ed.). *The mirror for magistrates*. Cambridge, 1938.
   Parts added to 'The mirror for magistrates' by John Higgins and Thomas Blenerhasset. Cambridge, 1946.

Chalmers, Alexander (ed.). *The works of the English poets*. vol. 1. London, 1810.

Collier, J.P. (ed.). *Illustrations of Old English literature*. 1866; rpt. New York, 1966.

Combefis, F. Franciscus (ed.). *Bibliotheca Patrum concionatoria*. Vol. V. Venice, 1749.

Donno, Elizabeth Story (ed.). *Elizabethan minor epics*. London, 1963.

Dyboski, Roman (ed.). *Songs, carols, and other miscellaneous poems from the Balliol MS 354, Richard Hill's commonplace book*. EETS ES 101. London, 1908.

Ebsworth, J.W. (ed.). *The Roxburghe ballads: illustrating the last years of the Stuarts*. Vol. VI. 1886; rpt. New York, 1966.

Faral, Edmond (ed.). *Les Arts poétiques du XIIᵉ et du XIIIᵉ siècle*. 1924; rpt. Paris, 1971.

Farr, Edward (ed.). *Select poetry, chiefly devotional, of the reign of Queen Elizabeth*. Collected and edited for the Parker Soviety. 2 vols. Cambridge, 1845.

Furnivall, F.J. (ed.). *The Digby plays*. EETS ES 70. London, 1896.

Gray, Douglas (ed.). *The Oxford book of late medieval verse and prose*. Oxford, 1985.

Grosart, Alexander B. (ed.). *Miscellanies of the Fuller Worthies' Library*. Vols. II, III. [Blackburn], 1871–2.

Hammond, Eleanor P. (ed.). *English verse between Chaucer and Surrey*. Durham, N.C., 1927.

276

Judges, A.V. (ed.). *The Elizabethan underworld: a collection of Tudor and Early Stuart tracts and ballads of vagabonds*. London, 1930.

Migne, Jacques Paul *et al.* (eds.). *Patrologia latina*. Paris, 1844. ff.

Miller, Paul W. (ed.). *Seven minor epics of the English Renaissance (1596–1624)*. Gainesville, Fla., 1967.

Miller, Robert P. (ed.). *Chaucer. Sources and backgrounds*. New York, 1977.

Mozley, J.H. (ed.). 'Susanna and the Elders: three medieval poems', *Studi Medievali*, 3 (1930), 27–52.

Padelford, F.M. and A.R. Benham (eds.). 'Liedersammlungen des XVI. Jahrhunderts, besonders aus der Zeit Heinrichs VIII.: 7. The songs in MS Rawlinson C. 813', *Anglia*, 31 (1908), 309–97.

Park, T. (ed.). *The Harleian miscellany; or, A collection of scarce, curious, and entertaining pamphlets and tracts*. Vol. I. London, 1808.

Reese, M.M. (ed.). *Elizabethan verse romances*. London, 1968.

Robbins, Rossell Hope (ed.). *Historical poems of the XIVth and XVth centuries*. New York, 1959.

Saintsbury, George (ed.). *Minor poets of the Caroline period*. Vol. I. 1905; rpt. Oxford, 1968.

Shepherd, Simon (ed.). *The woman's sharp revenge: five women's pamphlets from the Renaissance*. London, 1985.

Smith, G. Gregory (ed.). *Elizabethan critical essays*. 2 vols. Oxford, 1904.

Wotke, Karl (ed.). *Lateinische Literaturdenkmäler des XV. und XVI. Jahrhunderts*. Vol. X. Berlin, 1894.

Single works and authors

A[ustin], H[enry]. *The scourge of Venus; or, The wanton lady* (1613). Ed. P.W. Miller, *Seven minor epics*, pp. 229–72.

Achelley, Thomas. *The lamentable history of Violenta and Didaco*. 1576. Rpt. The English Experience, no. 836. Amsterdam, 1977.

Adam of Cobsham. *The wright's chaste wife. A merry tale. From a MS in the library of the Archbishop of Canterbury, at Lambeth, about 1462 A.D.* Ed. Frederick J. Furnivall. EETS OS 12, 2nd edn, London, 1869.

Aeschylus. *Works*. Tr. and ed. Herbert Weit Smyth. 2 vols. Loeb Classical Library. London, 1952.

Andrewe, Thomas. *The unmasking of a feminine Machiavell*. London, 1604.

Andrewes, Lancelot. *Sermons*. Ed. G.M. Story. Oxford, 1967.

Aristotle. *Aristotle's poetics: the argument*. Ed. Gerald F. Else. Cambridge, Mass., 1957.

Augustinus, Aurelius. *The city of God against the pagans*. Ed. George E. McCracken. 7 vols. Loeb Classical Library. London, 1957.

St. Augustine's confessions. Tr. and ed. William Watts. 2 vols. Loeb Classical Library. London, 1950–1.

Aylett, Robert. *Susanna: or The arraignment of the two unjust elders*. London, 1622.

Ballard, George. *The history of Susanna*. London, 1638.

Bandello, Matteo. *Certain tragical discourses*. Tr. Geoffrey Fenton (1567), ed. R.L. Douglas. 2 vols. Tudor Translations. London, 1898.

Banester, Gilbert. 'Legenda Sismond' (*c.* 1450). Ed. H.G. Wright, *Early English versions of the tales of Guiscardo and Ghismonda*, pp. 2–37.

Barksted, William. *Mirrha, the mother of Adonis: or, Lust's prodigies* (1607). Ed. P.W. Miller, *Seven minor epics*, pp. 103–67.

Hiren: or, The fair Greek (1611). Ed. P.W. Miller, *Seven minor epics*, pp. 169–212.

That which seems best is worst. Expressed in a paraphrastical transcript of Juvenal's tenth satire. Together with the tragical narration of Virginia's death intersected. London, 1617.

Barnfield, Richard. *Cynthia. With certain sonnets and the legend of Cassandra.* Ed. A.H. Bullen, *Some longer Elizabethan poems*, pp. 187–226.

Boccaccio, Giovanni. *De casibus illustrium virorum.* A facsimile reproduction of the Paris edition of 1520. Ed. Louis Brewer Hall. Gainsville, Fla., 1962.

De claris mulieribus. Concerning famous women. Tr. and ed. Guido A. Guarino. New Brunswick, 1963.

Il decameron. Ed. Aldo Rossi. Bolgna, 1977. Tr. *The decameron* (1620). Ed. W.E. Henley. 4 vols. The Tudor Translations. London, 1909.

Fiammetta. Tr. Sophie Brentano, ed. Werner Bahner [Leipzig], n.d.

Genealogie deorum gentilium libri. Ed. Vincenzo Romano. 2 vols. Scrittori d'Italia, No. 200. Bari, 1951.

Brandon, Samuel. *The tragicomedy of the virtuous Octavia* (1598). Ed. R.B. McKerrow. Malone Society Reprint. Oxford, 1910.

Brathwait, Richard. *The golden fleece.* London, 1611.

Love's labyrinth (1615). Ed. J.W. Ebsworth, Boston, Mass., 1878.

Nature's embassy (1621). Ed. J.W. Ebsworth. Boston, Mass., 1877.

Breton, Nicholas. *Marie Magdalen's love.* London, [1595].

The works in verse and prose of Nicholas Breton. Ed. Alexander B. Grosart. 2 vols. Chertsey Worthies' Library. Edinburgh, 1879.

Poems by Nicholas Breton (not hitherto reprinted). Ed. Jean Robertson. Liverpool, 1952.

Brückner, Christine. *Wenn du geredet hättest, Desdemona.* Hamburg, 1983.

C., I. [Joseph Cresswell?]. *Saint Marie Magdalen's conversion.* [Douai?], 1603.

Cartwright, William. *The plays and poems of William Cartwright.* Ed. G.B. Evans. Madison, Wisc., 1951.

Catullus, Gaius Valerius. *Catullus.* Ed. Werner Eisenhut. Tusculum-Bücherei. Munich, 1962.

Cavendish, George. *The life and death of Cardinal Wolsey.* Ed. R.S. Sylvester. EETS OS 243. London, 1959.

Metrical visions. Ed. A.S.G. Edwards. Renaissance English Text Society 9. Columbia, N.C., 1980.

Caxton, William. *Selections from William Caxton.* Ed. N.F. Blake. Oxford, 1973.

Chaucer, Geoffrey. *The Works of Geoffrey Chaucer.* Ed. F.N. Robinson. 2nd edn, London, 1957. Revised 3rd edn, *The Riverside Chaucer*, ed. Larry D. Benson. Boston, Mass., 1987.

Churchyard, Thomas. 'Shore's wife' (1563). Ed. Lily B. Campbell, *The mirror for magistrates*, Cambridge, 1938, pp. 371–86.

A general rehearsal of wars. London, 1579.

Churchyard's challenge. London, 1593.

Chute, Anthony. *Beauty dishonoured: Written under the title of Shore's wife*

(1593). Ed. Willy Budig, 'Untersuchungen über "Jane Shore" ', unpublished PhD thesis, University of Rostock, 1908, pp. 89–111.

Colse, Peter. *Penelope's complaint: or, A mirror for wanton minions* (1596). Ed. Alexander B. Grosart, *Occasional issues*, vol 12, Manchester, 1880, pp. 159–83.

Cranley, Thomas. *Amanda; or, The reformed whore* (1635). Ed. Frederick Ouvry, London, 1889.

Daniel, Samuel. *The complete works in verse and prose of Samuel Daniel*. Ed. Alexander B. Grosart 5 vols. 1885; rpt. New York, 1963.

Dante Alighieri, *Die göttliche Komödie*. Tr. and ed. Hermann Gmelin. 6 vols. Stuttgart, 1949–57.

Deloney, Thomas. *The works of Thomas Deloney*. Ed. Francis O. Mann. Oxford, 1912.

Dickenson, John. *Speculum tragicum*. Leyden, 1605.

Miscellanea ex historiis anglicanis concinnata. Leyden, 1606.

Douglas, Gavin. *Selections from Gavin Douglas*. Ed. David F.C. Coldwell. Clarendon Medieval and Tudor Series. Oxford, 1964.

Drayton, Michael. *The works of Michael Drayton*. Ed. J. William Hebel, Kathleen Tillotson, and B.H. Newdigate. 5 vols. Oxford, 1931–41.

Dryden, John, *Of dramatic poesy and other critical essays*. Ed. George Watson. 2 vols. Everyman's Library. London, 1962.

Dumas fils, Alexandre. *La dame aux camélias. Le roman, le drame, 'La traviata'*. Ed. Hans-Jörg Neuschäfer and Gilbert Sigaux. Paris. 1981.

'An elegy on the deaths of Eleanor Cobham, John Beaufort and Duke Humphrey'. Ed. F.M. Padelford and A.R. Benham, 'Liedersammlungen', *Anglia*, 31 (1908), pp. 325–6.

Eliot, T.S. *Selected essays*. London, 1932.

The complete poems and plays. London, 1969.

Elizabeth I. *Queen Elizabeth's Englishings of Boethius, Plutarch, Horace*. Ed. Caroline Pemberton. EETS OS 113. London, 1899.

Ellis, G. *The lamentation of the lost sheep*. London, 1605. Extracts in Edward Farr's *Select poetry*, vo. II, pp. 408–11.

Essex, Earl of. 'The poems of Edward de Vere, seventh earl of Oxford, and Robert Devereux, second earl of Essex'. Ed. Steven W. May, *Studies in Philology*, 77, Suppl. (1980), 1–132.

Euripides. *Works*. Ed. Arthur S. Way. 4 vols. Loeb Classical Library. London, 1912.

Fenne, Thomas. *Fenne's Fruits*. London, 1590.

Fenton, Geoffrey. 'The disordered life of the Countesse of Celant' in *Certain tragical discourses of Bandello* (1567). Ed. R.L. Douglas. London, 1898, vol II, no. 7.

Ferrers, George. 'Dame Elianor Cobham, Duchess of Gloucester' (1578). Ed. Lily B. Campbell, *The mirror for magistrates*, pp. 432–43.

Forrest, William. *The history of Grisild the second* (1558). Ed. W.D. Macray. Roxburghe Club. London, 1875. Excerpts in R.S. Sylvester (ed.), George Cavendish, *Life of Wolsey*, pp. 259–62.

Fowler, William. *The Works of William Fowler, secretary to Queen Anne, Wife of James VI*. Ed. H.W. Meikle. Vol. I. STS NS 6. Edinburgh, 1914.

Fraunce, Abraham. *The Arcadian rhetoric*. Ed. Ethel Seaton. Oxford, 1950.

Gascoigne, George. *George Gascoigne's 'The Steele Glass' and 'The Complainte of Phylomene'*. Ed. William L. Wallace. Salzburg Studies in English Literature. Elizabethan and Renaissance Studies 24. Salzburg, 1975.

Gower, John. *The English works of John Gower*. Ed. G.C. Macaulay. 2 vols. EETS ES 81, 82. London, 1900–1.

The major Latin works of John Gower. Tr. and ed. Eric W. Stockton. Seattle, Wash., 1962.

Greene, Robert. *The life and complete works in prose and verse of Robert Greene*. Ed. Alexander B. Grosart. 15 vols. 1881–6; rpt. New York, 1964.

Grimald, Nicholas. *The life and poems of Nicholas Grimald*. Ed. L.R. Merrill. Yale Studies in English 19. New Haven, Conn., 1925.

Guillaume de Lorris and Jean de Meun. *Le roman de la rose*. Ed. Ernest Langlois. 5 vols. Paris, 1914–24.

Gyraldus, Lilius Gregorius. *De poetis nostrorum temporum*. Ed. Karl Wotke. Lateinische Literaturdenkmäler des XV. und XVI. Jahrhunderts, 10. Berlin, 1894.

Hannay, Patrick. *The Nightingale; Sheretine and Mariana* (1622). Ed. George Saintsbury, *Minor poets of the Caroline period*, I, pp. 613–74.

Henryson, Robert. *The testament of Cresseid*. Ed. Denton Fox. London, 1968.

H.T. [Thomas Heywood]. *Oenone and Paris* (1594). Ed. Joseph Quincy Adams. The Folger Shakespeare Library. Washington, D.C., 1943.

Heywood, Thomas. *Troia britanica: or, Great Britain's Troy* (1609). Rpt. Hildesheim, 1972.

An apology for actors (1612). With A refutation of the apology for actors by J.G. [John Green?]. Rpt. New York, 1972.

A woman killed with kindness. Ed. R.W. Van Fossen. Revels Plays. London, 1961.

Higgins, John. 'Elstride the concubine of Locrinus'; 'Sabrine the base child of Locrinus' (1574). Ed. Lily B. Campbell, *Parts added to the Mirror for magistrates*, Cambridge, 1946, pp. 87–109, 145–61.

Homer. *The Iliad*. Tr. and ed. A.T. Murray. 2 vols. Loeb Classical Library. London, 1946.

The Odyssey. Tr. and ed. A.T. Murray. 2 vols. Loeb Classical Library. London, 1946.

Hooker, Richard. *Of the laws of ecclesiastical polity*. 2 vols. London, 1907.

Horace. Quintus H. Flaccus. *Sämtliche Werke*. Ed. Hans Färber. Tusculum Bücherei. Munich, 1967.

Howell, Thomas. *H[owell] his devices* (1581). Ed. W. Raleigh. Oxford, 1906.

[Huchoun?]. *Susannah; or, The pistill of Susan. An alliterative poem of the XIV. century*. Ed. Alice Miskimin. New Haven, Conn., 1969.

Hudson, Thomas. *The history of Judith* (1584). Ed. James Craigie. STS, 3rd ser. 14. Edinburgh, 1941.

Jacobson, Dan. *Her Story*. London, 1987.

Justinus, M. Junianus. *Epitoma historiarum Philippicarum*. Ed. Otto Seel. Stuttgart, 1972.

Langland, William. *The vision of Piers Plowman. A complete edition of the B-text*. Ed. A.V.C. Schmidt. 2nd edn. London, 1987.

L., F. *Ovidius Naso his remedy of love*. London, 1600.

'The lament of the Duchess of Gloucester' (1441). Ed. R.H. Robbins, *Historical poems*, New York, 1959, pp. 176–80.

The lamentation of Mary Magdaleyne (*c.* 1460–80). Ed. Bertha M. Skeat. Cambridge, 1897.

'The legend of Mary, queen of Scots' (*c.* 1601). Ed. Hanna Lohmann, 'John Woodward, The life and tragedy of the royal lady Mary late queen of Scots', unpublished PhD thesis, University of Berlin, 1912.

'The letter of Dydo to Eneas'. Prt. Richard Pynson, *The book of fame*. London, [1526?], F3v–F5r.

Lever, Christopher. *A crucifix; or, A meditation upon repentance and the holy passion* (1607); *Queen Elizabeth's tears; or, Her resolute bearing the Christian crosse, inflicted on her by the persecuting hands of Stephen Gardner, Bishop of Winchester, in the bloody time of Queen Mary* (1607). Ed. A.B. Grosart. *Miscellanies of the Fuller Worthies' Library*, III, pp. 603–60, 661–734.

Livius, Titus. *Ab urbe condita. History of Rome*. Ed. B.O. Foster. Loeb Classical Library. London, 1949–62.

Lodge, Thomas. *The Complete Works of Thomas Lodge*. Ed. Edmund Gosse. 4 vols. 1883; rpt. New York, 1963.

[Lydgate, John?]. 'Complaint for my lady of Gloucester' (1428). Ed. Eleanor Hammond, 'Lydgate and the Duchess of Gloucester', *Anglia*, 27 (1904), 393–7.

Lydgate, John. *The Fall of Princes*. Ed. Henry Bergen. EETS ES 121–4. 4 vols. London, 1924–7.

The Troy book. Ed. Henry Bergen. EETS ES 97, 103, 106, 126. London, 1906–35.

M.,T. [Thomas Middleton]. *The ghost of Lucrece*. Ed. Joseph Quincy Adams. Folger Shakespeare Library. New York, 1937.

Malvezzi, Virgilio. *Romulus and Tarquin*. Tr. Henry Carey. London, 1637.

[Markham, Gervase], *Marie Magdalen's lamentations* (1601). Ed. A.B. Grosart. *Miscellanies of the Fuller Worthies' Library*, II, pp. 535–96.

Markham, Gervase. *The famous whore or noble courtesan Paulina* (1609). Ed. Frederick Ouvry. London, 1868.

Marlowe, Christopher. *The complete works of Christopher Marlowe*. Ed. Fredson Bowers. Cambridge, 1973.

May, Thomas. *The reign of King Henry the Second*. London, 1633.

More, Sir Thomas. *The complete works of St. Thomas More*. Vol. 2. Ed. Richard S. Sylvester. New Haven, Conn., 1963.

The history of King Richard III and selections from the English and Latin poems. Ed. Richard S. Sylvester. New Haven, Conn., 1976.

Murray, Sir David. *The tragical death of Sophonisba* (1611). Ed. Thomas Kinnear, *Poems: The tragical death of Sophonisba; Coelia, containing certain sonnets; A paraphrase of the CIV. psalm*, 1823, rpt. New York, 1973.

Niccols, Richard. 'England's Eliza, or, The victorious and triumphant reign of that virgin empress of sacred memory, Elizabeth, queen of England, France and Ireland' in *A mirror for magistrates*, London, 1610, pp. 771–875.

O., I. [Sir John Ogle]. *The lamentation of Troy for the death of Hector*. Ed. Elkin C. Wilson. Chicago, 1959.

Omelia Origenis. Ed. Louis Bourgain, *La Chaire française au XIIe siècle d'après les manuscrits* (Paris, 1879), pp. 373–83. Ed. Adolf Patera, *Hradecky Rukopis* (Prague, 1881), pp. 438–449.

Ovid, Publius O. Naso. *Fasti*. Ed. Sir James G. Frazer. Loeb Classical Library. London, 1951.

Publius O. Naso. *Heroides and Amores*. Ed. Grant Showerman. Loeb Classical Library. London, 1914.

Publius O. Naso. *Metamorphosen*. Ed. Hermann Breitenbach. Bibliothek der Alten Welt. 2nd edn. Zurich, 1964.

Parr, Catherine. *The lamentation of a sinner* (1547). Ed. T. Park. *Harleian miscellany*, I, pp. 286–313.

Painter, William. *The palace of pleasure*. Ed. Joseph Jacobs. 3 vols. 1890; rpt. Hildesheim, 1968.

Parker, Martin. *The nightingale warbling forth her own disaster; or, The rape of Philomela* (1632). Rpt. A. Strettell [*c.* 1820].

Peele, George. *The life and minor works of George Peele*. Ed. C.T. Prouty. 2 vols. New Haven, Conn., 1952.

Pettie, George. *A petite palace of Pettie his pleasure*. Ed. Herbert Hartman. London, 1938.

Pinero, Arthur Wing. *The second Mrs Tanqueray*. London, 1936.

Plutarch. *Plutarch's lives*. Tr. and ed. Bernadette Perrin. 11 vols. Loeb Classical Library. London, 1914–26.

Pope, Alexander. *The Poems of Alexander Pope*. Ed. John Butt. 2nd edn. London, 1968.

Procter, Thomas. *A gorgeous gallery of gallant inventions*. Ed. H.E. Rollins. Cambridge, Mass., 1926.

Puttenham, George. *The art of English poesy*. Ed. Gladys D. Wilcock and Alice Walker. 1936; rpt. Cambridge, 1970.

Reynolds, Henry. *Torquato Tasso's Aminta Englished; to this is added Ariadne's complaint*. London, 1628.

Richardson, Samuel. *Clarissa*. Ed. John Butt. 4 vols. Everyman's Library. London, 1962.

Rivers, George. *The heroinae*. London, 1639.

Robinson, Richard (of Alton). *The reward of wickedness*. London, [1574].

Robinson, Thomas. *The life and death of Mary Magdalene* (*c.* 1620). Ed. H. Oskar Sommer. EETS ES 78. London, 1899.

Roche, Robert. *Eustathia; or, The constancy of Susanna*. London, 1599.

Rowe, Nicholas. *The tragedy of Jane Shore*. Ed. Harry William Pedicord. Regents Restoration Drama Series. London, 1974.

Rymer, Thomas. *The critical works*. Ed. Curt A. Zimansky. New Haven, Conn., 1956.

Sabie, Francis. *Adam's complaint. The old world's tragedie. David and Bathsheba*. London, 1596.

Sampson, Thomas. *Fortune's fashion: Portrayed in the troubles of the Lady Elizabeth Gray*. London, 1613.

Seneca, Lucius A. *Seneca's tragedies*. Ed. Frank Justus Miller. 2 vols. London, 1953.

Servius, Maurus S. Honoratus. *Servii grammatici qui feruntur in Vergilii carmina commentarii*. Ed. Georg Thilo and Hermann Hagen. 2 vols. 1881–4; rpt. Hildesheim, 1961.

Shakespeare, William. [Plays and poems]. New Arden Shakespeare. London, 1951–82.

Shepery (or Shepreve), John. *Hyppolitus Ovidianae Phaedrae respondens*. Ed. G. Edrychus [i.e. George Etherege]. Oxford, 1586.

Sherry, Richard. *A treatise of schemes and tropes*. 1550; rpt. Gainesville, Fla, 1961.

Sidney, Sir Philip. *An apology for poetry*. Ed. Geoffrey Shepherd. Nelson's Medieval and Renaissance Library. London, 1965.

Southwell, Robert. *Marie Magdalen's funeral tears (1591)*. Rpt. Delmar, N.Y., 1975. Ed. John Richard Gappa, unpublished PhD thesis, St. Louis University, 1968.

Southwell, Robert. *The complete poems of Robert Southwell, S.J.* Ed. Alexander B. Grosart. Fuller Worthies' Library. [Blackburn], 1872.

The poems of Robert Southwell, S.J. Ed. James H. McDonald and Nancy Pollard Brown. Oxford, 1967.

The prose works of Robert Southwell. Ed. W. Joseph Walter. London, 1828.

Spenser, Edmund. *Poetical Works*. Ed. J.C. Smith and E. de Selincourt. Oxford Standard Authors. Oxford, 1912.

'The stately tragedy of Guistard and Sismond' (c. 1480). Ed. H.G. Wright, *Early English versions of the tales of Guiscardo and Ghismonda and Titus and Gisippus*, EETS OS 205, London, 1937, pp. 39–99.

Susannah: an alliterative poem of the fourteenth century. Ed. Alice Miskimin. New Haven, Conn., 1969.

Sweetnam, John. *St Mary Magdalen's pilgrimage to paradise*. [St Omer], 1617.

Sylvester, Josuah. *The divine weeks and works of Guillaume de Saluste Sieur du Bartas*. Ed. Susan Snyder. 2 vols. Oxford, 1979.

The true tragedy of King Richard the Third. Ed. W.W. Greg. Malone Society Reprint. Oxford, 1929.

Trussell, John. 'Raptus I. Helenae: The first rape of faire Helen'. Ed. M.A. Shaaber, *Shakespeare Quarterly*, 8 (1957), 407–48.

Tyndale, William. *Doctrinal treatises and introductions to different portions of the Holy Scriptures*. Ed. Henry Walter. Cambridge, 1848.

Underdowne, Thomas. *The Excellent history of Theseus and Ariadne*. London, 1566.

Virgil. Virgilius Maro. *Aeneis*. Ed. Johannes Götte. Tusculum Bücherei. 3rd edn. Munich, 1971.

Wager, Lewis. *The life and repentance of Marie Magdalene*. Ed. Frederic I. Carpenter. 2nd edn. Chicago, 1904.

Walter, William. *The amorous history of Guystarde and Sygysmonde* (1532). Ed. H.G. Wright, *Early English versions of the tales of Guiscardo and Ghismonda and Titus and Gisippus*, pp. 101–29.

Warner, William. *Albion's England* (1586–1606). 1612 edn; rpt. Hildesheim, 1971.

Whetstone, George. *The rock of regard* (1576). Rpt. J.P. Collier. [N.P.], 1870.

Willoby, Henry. *The queen declined. An interpretation of 'Willoby his Avisa' with the text of the original edition*. Ed. B.N. de Luna. Oxford, 1970.

Wither, George. *The poetry of George Wither*. Ed. Frank Sidgwick. 2 vols. London, 1902.

Wolf, Christa. *Cassandra*. Darmstadt, 1983.

Wyatt, Sir Thomas. *Collected poems*. Ed. Joost Daalder. London, 1975.
Xenakis, Françoise. *Zut, on a encore oublié Madame Freud*. Paris, 1985.

Studies

Allen, Don Cameron. 'Observations on *The rape of Lucrece*', *Shakespeare Survey*, 15 (1962), 89–98.
Allen, Walter, Jr. 'The non-existent classical epyllion', *Studies in Philology*, 55 (1958), 515–18.
Anderson, W.S. 'The *Heroides*', in *Ovid*, ed. J.W. Binns. London, 1973, pp. 49–83.
Arn, Mary-Jo. 'Three Ovidian women in Chaucer's *Troilus*: Medea, Helen, Oenone', *Chaucer Review*, 15 (1980), 1–10.
Auerbach, Erich. *Mimesis: Dargestellte Wirklichkeit in der abendländischen Literatur*. 4th edn. Bern, 1967.
Baca, Albert R. 'The themes of *querela* and *lacrimae* in Ovid's *Heroides*', *Emerita*, 39 (1971), 195–201.
Barker, Nicolas. 'Jane Shore. Part I: The real Jane Shore', *Etoniana*, 125 (1972), 383–91.
'The story of Jane Shore: a postscript to Part I', *Etoniana*, 126 (1972), 410–14.
Beer, Gillian. 'Our unnatural no-voice: the heroic epistle, Pope, and women's Gothic', *Yearbook of English Studies*, 12 (1982), 125–51.
Beißner, Friedrich. *Geschichte der deutschen Elegie*. Berlin, 1941.
Beith-Halahmi, Esther. *Angell fayre or strumpet lewd: Jane Shore as an example of erring beauty in 16th century literature*. 2 vols. Salzburg Studies in English Literature. Elizabethan and Renaissance Studies 26, 27. Salzburg, 1974.
Bennett, J.A.W. *Chaucer's 'Book of fame': an exposition of 'The house of fame'*. Oxford, 1968.
Bjork, Gary Floyd. 'The Renaissance Mirror for Fair Ladies: Samuel Daniel's *Complaint of Rosamond* and the tradition of the feminine complaint'. Unpublished PhD thesis, University of California, Irvine, 1973.
Boitani, Piero. *Chaucer and the imaginary world of fame*. Chaucer Studies 10. Cambridge, 1984.
Brinkmann, Hennig. *Geschichte der lateinischen Liebesdichtung im Mittelalter*. 1925; rpt. Darmstadt, 1979.
Brooks, Harold F. '*Richard III*: unhistorical amplifications. The women's scenes and Seneca', *Modern Language Review*, 75 (1980), 721–37.
Brower, Reuben A. *Hero and saint: Shakespeare and the Graeco-Roman heroic tradition*. Oxford, 1971.
Brown, Barbara. 'Sir Thomas More and Thomas Churchyard's "Shore's wife" ', *Yearbook of English Studies*, 2 (1972), 41–8.
Budig, Willy. 'Untersuchungen über "Jane Shore" '. Unpublished PhD thesis, University of Rostock, 1908.
Burrow, J.A. *Ricardian poetry: Chaucer, Gower, Langland and the Gawain poet*. London, 1971.
Bush, Douglas. 'Martin Parker's *Philomela*', *Modern Language Notes*, 40 (1925), 486–8.

'Classic myths in English verse (1557–1589)', *Modern Philology*, 25 (1927), 37–47.

Mythology and the Renaissance tradition in English poetry. New York, 1963.

Mythology and the Romantic tradition in English poetry. New York, 1969.

'The petite pallace of Pettie his pleasure', *Journal of English and Germanic Philology*, 27 (1928), 162–9.

Callan, Norman. 'Thyn owne book: a note on Chaucer, Gower, and Ovid', *Review of English Studies*, 22 (1942), 269–81.

Campbell, Lily B. ' "Humphrey Duke of Gloucester and Elianor Cobham his wife" in the *Mirror for magistrates*', *Huntington Library Bulletin*, 5 (1934), 119–55.

Divine poetry and drama in sixteenth-century England. Cambridge, 1959.

Clark, Donald L. *John Milton at St Paul's school.* 1948; rpt Columbia, N.C., 1964.

Clemen, Wolfgang. *English tragedy before Shakespeare: the development of dramatic speech.* Tr. T.S. Dorsch. London, 1961.

Chaucer's early poetry. Tr. C.A.M. Sym. London, 1963.

Collins, Joseph Burns. *Christian mysticism in the Elizabethan age with its background in mystical methodology.* Baltimore, Md., 1940.

Constans, Léopold. 'Une traduction française des *Héroides* d'Ovide au XIIIe siècle', *Romania*, 43 (1914), 177–98.

Cowen, Janet M. 'Chaucer's *Legend of good women*: structure and tone', *Studies in Philology*, 82 (1985), 416–36.

Craun, Edwin D. 'The *de casibus* complaint in Elizabethan England 1559–1593'. Unpublished PhD thesis, Princeton University, 1971.

Crump, Marjorie. *The epyllion from Theocritus to Ovid.* 1931; rpt. New York, 1978.

Cunningham, M.P. 'The novelty of Ovid's *Heroides*', *Classical Philology*, 44 (1949), 100–6.

Cuvelier, Eliane. *Thomas Lodge: témoin de son temps (c. 1558–1625).* Collection Études Anglaises 85. Paris, 1984.

Dean, Nancy. 'Chaucer's *Complaint*: a genre descended from the *Heroides*', *Comparative Literature*, 19 (1967), 1–27.

Delany, Sheila. *Chaucer's 'House of fame': the poetics of skeptical fideism.* Chicago, 1972.

Della Corte, Francesco. 'Perfidus hospes', in *Hommages à Marcel Renard I*, ed. Jacqueline Bibauer, *Collection Latomus*, 101 (Brussels, 1969), pp. 312–21.

Dermutz, Anna. 'Die Didosage in der englischen Literatur des Mittelalters und der Renaissance'. Unpublished PhD thesis, University of Vienna, 1957.

Devlin, Christopher. *The life of Robert Southwell, poet and martyr.* London, 1956.

Dobb, Clifford. 'London's prisons', *Shakespeare Survey*, 17 (1964), 87–100.

Dörrie, Heinrich. 'Untersuchungen zur Überlieferungsgeschichte von Ovids Epistulae Heroidum', *Nachrichten der Akademie der Wissenschaften in Göttingen aus dem Jahre 1960*, Philologisch-historische Klasse (Göttingen, 1960), pp. 113–230 and 359–423.

Der heroische Brief: Bestandsaufnahme, Geschichte, Kritik einer humanistisch-barocken Literaturgattung. Berlin, 1968.

Donaldson, Ian. *The rapes of Lucretia: a myth and its transformations*. Oxford, 1982.

Doughtie, Edward. 'The Earl of Essex and occasions for contemplative verse', *English Literary Renaissance*, 9 (1979), 355–63.

Dronke, Peter. *Poetic individuality in the Middle Ages: new departures in poetry 1000–1150*. Oxford, 1970.

'Dido's lament: from medieval Latin lyric to Chaucer', in *Kontinuität und Wandel: Lateinische Poesie von Naevius bis Baudelaire. Franco Munari zum 65. Geburtstag*, ed. Ulrich J. Stache, Wolfgang Maaz, and Fritz Wagner. Hildesheim, 1986, pp. 364–90.

Edwards, A.S.G. 'Some borrowings by Cavendish from Lydgate's *Fall of princes*', *Notes and Queries*, 216 (1971), 207–9.

'The date of George Cavendish's *Metrical visions*', *Philological Quarterly*, 53 (1974), 128–32.

Esch, Arno. 'John Gowers Erzählkunst', in *Chaucer und seine Zeit: Symposion für Walter F. Schirmer*, ed. Arno Esch. Buchreihe der Anglia 14, Tübingen, 1968, pp. 207–39.

Farnham, Willard. *The medieval heritage of Elizabethan tragedy*. Oxford, 1936.

'The progeny of *A mirror for magistrates*', *Modern Philology*, 29 (1932), 395–410.

Fisher, John H. *John Gower: moral philosopher and friend of Chaucer*. New York, 1964.

Frank, Robert Worth, Jr. *Chaucer and 'The legend of good women'*. Cambridge, Mass., 1972.

Freeman, Arthur. 'The writings of Thomas Achelley', *Library*, 25 (1970), 40–2.

French, W.F. '*A mirror for magistrates': its origin and influence*. Edinburgh, 1898.

Frye, Northrop. *Anatomy of Criticism*. 1957; rpt. Princeton, N.J., 1973.

Fünten, Wiltrud aus der. *Maria Magdalena in der Lyrik des Mittelalters*. Düsseldorf, 1966.

Fyler, John M. *Chaucer and Ovid*. New Haven, Conn., 1979.

Garth, Helen. *Saint Mary Magdalene in medieval literature*. Baltimore, Md., 1950.

Gaylord, Alan T. 'Dido at hunt, Chaucer at work', *Chaucer Review*, 17 (1983), 300–15.

Gittings, Robert. *Shakespeare's rival: a study in three parts*. London, 1960.

Guerin, Dorothy. 'Chaucer's pathos: Three variations', *Chaucer Review*, 20 (1985), 90–112.

Haas, Renate. *Die mittelenglische Totenklage: Realitätsbezug, abendländische Tradition und individuelle Gestaltung*. Frankfurt, 1980.

Hall, Louis B. 'Chaucer and the Dido-and-Aeneas story', *Medieval Studies*, 25 (1963), 148–59.

Hammond, Dorothy. 'Lydgate and Coluccio Salutati', *Modern Philology*, 25 (1927), 49–57.

Hansel, Hans. 'Die Quelle der bayrischen Magdalenenklage (Wien, Nat. Bibl. Cod. 15 225)', *Zeitschrift für Deutsche Philologie*, 22 (1937), 363–88.

Harbert, Bruce. 'Chaucer and the Latin classics', in *Geoffrey Chaucer*, ed. Derek Brewer. London, 1974, pp. 137–53.

Hardin, Richard F. 'Convention and design in Drayton's *Heroical epistles*', *Publications of the Modern Language Association*, 83 (1968), 35–41.

Harner, James L. ' "The wofull lamentation of Mistris Jane Shore": the popularity of an Elizabethan ballad', *Papers of the Bibliographical Society of America*, 71 (1977), 137–49.

Harrison, O.B. *The enduring moment: a study of the idea of praise in Renaissance literary theory and practice*. Chapel Hill, N.C., 1962.

Haugaard, William P. 'Katherine Parr: the religious convictions of a Renaissance queen', *Renaissance Quarterly*, 22 (1969), 346–59.

Heilman, Robert B. *Tragedy and melodrama*. Seattle, Wash., 1968.

Heinze, Richard. *Virgils epische Technik*. 1915; rpt. Darmstadt, 1976.

'Ovids elegische Erzählung', *Berichte und Verhandlungen der Sächsischen Akademie der Wissenschaften zu Leipzig. Philologisch-historische Klasse*, 71 (1919), 7. Heft. Rpt. in Richard Heinze, *Vom Geist des Römertums*, ed. Erich Burck. 4th edn., Darmstadt, 1972, pp. 308–403.

Heltzel, Virgil B. *Fair Rosamond: a study of the development of a literary theme*. Evanston, Ill., 1947.

Hoffman, R.L. *Ovid and the 'Canterbury tales'*. Philadelphia, Pa., 1967.

Holmes, David M. *The art of Thomas Middleton: a critical study*. Oxford, 1970.

Horvath, I.K. 'Impius Aeneas', *Acta Antiqua*, 6 (1958), 385–93.

Hross, Helmut. 'Die Klagen der verlassenen Heroiden in der lateinischen Dichtung'. Unpublished PhD thesis, University of Munich, 1958.

Hull, Susanne W. *Chaste, silent and obedient: English books for women 1475–1640*. San Marino, Ca., 1982.

Hulse, Clark. *Metamorphic verse: the Elizabethan minor epic*. Guildford, 1982.

Hunger, Herbert. *Lexikon der griechischen und römischen Mythologie*. Vienna, 1959.

Iser, Wolfgang. 'Bunyans *Pilgrim's progress*: Die kalvinistische Heilsgewißheit und die Form des Romans', in *Medium Aevum vivum*, Festschrift für Walter Bulst (Heidelberg, 1960), pp. 279–304. Rpt. as chapter 1 of W. Iser, *Der implizite Leser* (tr. *The implied reader*, Baltimore, Md., 1974).

Jacobson, Howard. *Ovid's 'Heroides'*. Princeton, N.J., 1974.

Janelle, Pierre. *Robert Southwell the writer: a study in religious inspiration*. Clermont-Ferrant, 1935.

Johannson, Bestil. *Law and lawyers in Elizabethan England*. Stockholm, 1967.

Kallendorf, Craig. 'Boccaccio's Dido and the rhetorical criticism of Virgil's *Aeneid*', *Studies in Philology*, 82 (1985), 401–15.

Keach, William. *Elizabethan erotic narratives: irony and pathos in the Ovidian poetry of Shakespeare, Marlowe, and their contemporaries*. Hassocks, 1977.

Kearney, Anthony. 'A recurrent motif in Richardson's novels', *Neophilologus*, 55 (1971), 447–50.

Keiser, George R., 'The Middle English *Planctus Mariae* and the rhetoric of pathos', in Thomas J. Heffernan (ed.), *The popular literature of medieval England*. Knoxville, Tenn., 1985, pp. 167–93.

Kiser, Lisa. *Telling classical tales: Chaucer and the 'Legend of women'*. Ithaca, N.Y., 1983.

Koeppel, Emil. *Studien zur Geschichte der italienischen Novelle in der englischen Literatur des 16. Jahrhunderts*. Hamburg, 1890.

Koonce, B.G. 'Satan the fowler', *Medieval Studies*, 21 (1959), 176–84.

Kraus, Walther. 'Die Briefpaare in Ovids Heroiden', *Wiener Studien*, 65 (1950–51), 54–77.

'Ovidius Naso', in Michael v. Albrecht and Ernst Zinn (eds.), *Ovid*. Darmstadt, 1968, pp. 67–166.

Kurth, Burton O. *Milton and Christian heroism: Biblical epic themes and forms in seventeenth-century England*. 1959; rpt. Hamden, Conn., 1966.

Kutek, Gretl. 'Ovids *Heroides* und die englischen Heroidenbriefe von der Renaissance bis Pope'. Unpublished PhD thesis, University of Vienna, 1937.

LaBranche, Anthony. 'Poetry, history and oratory: The Renaissance historical poem'. *Studies in English literature 1500–1900*, 9 (1969), 1–19.

Lewalski, Barbara K. *'David's troubles remembered*: an analogue to *Absalom and Achitophel'*, *Notes and Queries*, 209, Sept. 1964, 340–3.

Lewis, C.S. *English literature in the sixteenth century (excluding drama)*. Oxford History of English Literature, vol. III. Oxford, 1954.

The discarded image: an introduction to medieval and Renaissance literature. Cambridge, 1964.

Lord, Mary Louise. 'Dido as an example of chastity: the influence of example Literature', *Harvard Library Bulletin*, 17 (1969), 22–44, 216–32.

Luck, Georg. *The Latin love elegy*. 1959; 2nd edn, London, 1969.

McCall, John P. 'Chaucer and the Pseudo Origen *De Maria Magdalena*: a preliminary study', *Speculum*, 46 (1971), 491–509.

McDonald, James H. *The Poems and prose writings of Robert Southwell, S.J.: a bibliographical study*. Oxford, 1937.

MacKenzie, R.A.F. 'The meaning of the Susanna story', *Canadian Journal of Theology*, 3 (1957), 211–18.

Mainzer, Conrad. 'John Gower's use of the "Medieval Ovid" in the *Confessio amantis'*, *Medium Aevum*, 41 (1972), 215–29.

Mann, Wolfgang. *Lateinische Dichtung in England*. Halle, 1939.

Marschall, Wilhelm. 'Das Troja-Gemälde in Shakespeares *Lucrece'*, *Anglia*, 54 (1930), 83–96.

Martindale, Charles (ed.), *Virgil and his influence: bimillennial studies*. Bristol, 1984.

Martz, Louis L. *The poetry of meditation: a study in English religious literature of the seventeenth century*. 2nd edn. New Haven, 1962.

Mason, H.A. *Editing Wyatt*. Cambridge, 1972.

Meech, Sanford. 'Chaucer and an Italian translation of the *Heroides'*, *Publications of the Modern Language Association*, 45 (1930), 110–28.

Minnis, Alastair J. *Chaucer and pagan antiquity*. Chaucer Studies 8. Woodbridge, 1982.

Mish, Frederick C. 'The influence of Ovid on John Gower's *Vox clamantis'*. Unpublished PhD thesis, University of Minnesota, 1973.

Morgan, Gerald. 'A defense of Dorigen's complaint', *Medium Aevum*, 46 (1977), 77–9.

Nagy, Christoph N. de. *Michael Drayton's 'England's heroical epistles'*. Berne, 1968.

Nearing, Homer. *English historical poetry 1599–1641*. Philadelphia, Pa., 1945.

Nist, John. 'The art of Chaucer: *Pathedy'*, *Tennessee Studies in Literature*, 11 (1966), 1–10.

Oppel, Eberhard. 'Ovids Heroides: Studien zur inneren Form und Motivation'. Unpublished PhD thesis, University of Erlangen-Nürnberg, 1968.

Padelford, Frederick M. 'Robert Aylett', *Huntington Library Bulletin*, 10 (1936), 1–48.

'Robert Aylett: a supplement', *Huntington Library Quarterly*, 2 (1939), 471–8.

Patton, Jon F. 'Essays in the Elizabethan she-tragedies or female-complaints'. Unpublished PhD thesis, Ohio University, 1969.

Pearsall, Derek. 'Gower's narrative art', *Publications of the Modern Language Association*, 81 (1966), 475–84.

John Lydgate. London, 1970.

Plett, Heinrich F. *Rhetorik der Affekte: Englische Wirkungsästhetik im Zeitalter der Renaissance*. Studien zue englischen Philologie, N.F. 18. Tübingen, 1975.

Poynter, F.N.L. *A bibliography of Gervase Markham 1568?–1637*. Oxford, 1962.

'Gervase Markham'. *Essays and Studies*, 15 (1962), 27–39.

Pratt, Samuel M. 'Jane Shore and the Elizabethans: Some facts and speculations', *Texas Studies in Literature and Language*, 11 (1970), 1,293–306.

Praz, Mario. 'Southwell's *St Peter's complaint* and its Italian source', *Modern Language Review*, 19 (1924), 273–90.

Prescott, A.L. 'The reception of Du Bartas in England', *Studies in the Renaissance*, 15 (1968), 144–73.

Primeau, Ronald. 'Daniel and the *Mirror* tradition: dramatic irony in *The complaint of Rosamond*', *Studies in English Literature 1500–1900*, 15 (1975), 21–36.

Pruvost, René. *Matteo Bandello and Elizabethan fiction*. Paris, 1937.

Raith, Joseph. *Boccaccio in der englischen Literatur von Chaucer bis Painters 'Palace of pleasure': Ein Beitrag zue Geschichte der italienischen Novelle in England*. Leipzig, 1936.

Réau, Louis. *Iconographie de l'art Chrétien*. Vol. II, *Iconographie de la bible. I. Ancien Testament*. Paris, 1956.

Rees, Joan. *Samuel Daniel: a critical and biographical study*. Liverpool, 1964.

Renoir, Alain. 'Attitudes towards women in Lydgate's poetry', *English Studies*, 42 (1961), 1–14.

Roberts-Baytop, Adrianne. *Dido, queen of infinite literary variety: the English Renaissance borrowings and influences*. Salzburg Studies in English Literature. Elizabethan and Renaissance Studies 25. Salzburg, 1974.

Robertson, D.W. jr. *A preface to Chaucer*. Princeton, N.J., 1962.

Rohde, Erwin. *Der griechische Roman*. 1914; rpt. Darmstadt, 1974.

Rowan, D.F. 'Shore's Wife', *Studies in English Literature 1500–1900*, 6 (1966), 447–64.

Royal faces: 900 years of British Monarchy. London, 1977.

Ruggiers, Paul G. 'Notes towards a theory of tragedy in Chaucer', *Chaucer Review*, 8 (1973), 89–99.

Salter, Elizabeth. *Fourteenth-century English Poetry: Context and readings*. Oxford, 1983.

Sanderlin, George. 'Chaucer's *Legend of Dido* – a feminist exemplum', *Chaucer Review*, 20 (1986), 331–40.

Scallon, Joseph D., S.J. *The poetry of Robert Southwell, S.J.* Salzburg Studies

290   Bibliography

in English Literature. Elizabethan and Renaissance Studies 11. Salzburg, 1975.

Schirmer, Walter F. 'Shakespeares klassizistische Gegenspieler', *Anglia* 76 (1958), 90–115.

John Lydgate: a study in the culture of the fifteenth century. Tr. Ann E. Keep. Westport, Ct., 1961.

Schmitz, Götz. *'The middel weie': Stil- und Aufbauformen in John Gowers 'Confessio Amantis'*. Studien zur englischen Literatur 11. Bonn, 1974.

'Cresseid's trial: a revision. Fame and defamation in Henryson's *Testament of Cresseid*', in Dieter Mehl (ed.), *Essays and Studies*, 32 (1979), 44–56.

Die Frauenklage: Studien zur elegischen Verserzählung in der englischen Literatur des Spätmittelalters und der Renaissance. Buchreihe der Anglia 23. Tübingen, 1984.

'Gower, Chaucer, and the classics: back to the textual evidence', in *John Gower: recent readings*, ed. R. F. Yeager. Kalamazoo, Mich., 1989, 95–111.

Scollen, Christine. *The birth of the elegy in France 1500–1550*. Geneva, 1967.

Seaton, Ethel. *Sir Richard Roos: Lancastrian poet*. London, 1961.

Segal, Erich. Review of *The Dido episode and the Aeneid: Roman social and political values in the epic* by Richard C. Monti. *Times Literary Supplement*, June 11, 1982, p. 634.

Shakeshaft, Mary. 'Nicholas Breton's *The Passion of a discontented mind*: some new problems', *Studies in English Literature 1500–1900*, 5 (1965), 165–74.

Simone, R. Thomas. *Shakespeare and 'Lucrece': a study of the poem and its relation to the plays*. Salzburg Studies in English Literature. Elizabethan and Renaissance Studies 38. Salzburg, 1974.

Smalley, Beryl. *English friars and antiquity*. Oxford, 1960.

Smith, Hallett. *Elizabethan poetry: a study in conventions, meaning, and expression*. Cambridge, Mass., 1952.

Spearing, A.C. *Medieval to Renaissance in English poetry*. Cambridge, 1985.

Spriet, Pierre. *Samuel Daniel (1563–1619): Sa vie – son oeuvre*. Paris, 1968.

Staiger, Emil. *Grundbegriffe der Poetik*. Zurich, 1946.

Sticca, Sandro. 'The literary genesis of the Latin Passion play and the Planctus Mariae', in *The medieval drama*, Papers of the 3rd annual conference of the Center for Medieval and Early Renaissance Studies, State University of New York at Binghampton, ed. S. Sticca. Albany, N.Y., 1972, pp. 39–68.

Szondi, Peter. *Die Theorie des bürgerlichen Trauerspiels im 18. Jahrhundert*. Ed. Gert Mackenklott. Frankfurt, 1973.

Tatlock, John P. 'The siege of Troy in Elizabethan literature, especially in Shakespeare and Heywood', *Publications of the Modern Language Association*, 30 (1915), 673–770.

Thomson, J.A.K. *Classical influences on English poetry* London, 1951.

Thurston, Herbert. 'Father Southwell the Euphuist', *The Month*, 83 (1895), 231–45.

'Father Southwell the popular poet', *The Month*, 83 (1895), 383–99.

Tomlinson, Charles. *Poetry and metamorphosis*. Cambridge, 1983.

Vossen, Carl. 'Der Wandel des Aeneasbildes im Spiegel der englischen Literatur'. Unpublished Phd thesis, University of Bonn, 1955.

Walker, Alice. 'The reading of an Elizabethan: Some sources of the prose pamphlets of Thomas Lodge', *Review of English Studies*, 8 (1932), 264–81.

Webber, Janet M. 'The English Renaissance epyllion'. Unpublished PhD dissertation, Yale University, 1973.

Weiher, Carol. 'Chaucer's and Gower's stories of Lucretia and Virginia', *English Language Notes*, 14 (1976), 7–9.

Weitzmann, Francis W. 'Notes on the Elizabethan "Elegie" ', *Publications of the Modern Language Association*, 50 (1935), 435–43.

Wells, Robin H. *Spenser's 'Faerie queene' and the cult of Elizabeth*. London, 1983.

White, Helen C. *Tudor books of private devotion*. [Madison, Wisc.], 1951.
  Tudor books of saints and martyrs. Madison, Wisc., 1963.
  'Southwell: metaphysical and baroque', *Modern Philology*, 61 (1964), 159–68.

Williams, Clem C. 'A case of mistaken identity: still another Trojan narrative in Old French prose', *Medium Aevum*, 53 (1984), 59–72.

Windeatt, B.A. *Chaucer's dream poetry: sources and analogues*. Woodbridge, 1982.

Woolf, Rosemary. *The English religious lyric in the Middle Ages*. Oxford, 1968.
  'English imitations of the *Homelia Origenis de Maria Magdalena*', in *Chaucer and Middle English studies in honour of Rossell Hope Robbins*, ed. Beryl Rowland. London, 1974, pp. 384–91.

Zocca, Louis R. *Elizabethan narrative poetry*. New Brunswick, N.J., 1950.

Zupitza, Julius. 'Die mittelenglischen Bearbeitungen der Erzählungen Boccaccios von Ghismonda und Guiscardo', *Vierteljahrsschrift für Kultur und Litteratur der Renaissance*, 1 (1886), 63–102.

Index of heroines

Index of Authors and poems

For EU product safety concerns, contact us at Calle de José Abascal, 56–1°, 28003 Madrid, Spain or eugpsr@cambridge.org.

www.ingramcontent.com/pod-product-compliance
Ingram Content Group UK Ltd.
Pitfield, Milton Keynes, MK11 3LW, UK
UKHW042153130625
459647UK00011B/1312